BODYBUILDING

Tracing the Evolution of the Ultimate Physique

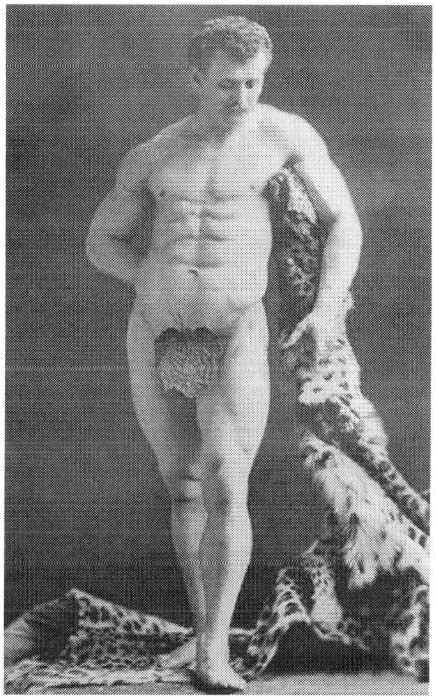

Gordon LaVelle

Romanart Books • U.S.A.

ISBN: 978-0-578-08450-3

9 8 7 6 5 4 3 2 1

Printed in the United States of America

www.bodybuilding-evolution.com

Cover photo credits: Arnold Schwarzenegger by George Butler; Jay Cutler, background image of Phil Heath, and back-cover image of Jay Cutler by Kevin Myles; Ronnie Coleman courtesy of Steve Harris; John Grimek, Steve Reeves and Eugen Sandow courtesy of Robert White; and Lee Haney courtesy of Michael Newman. Title page photo of Eugen Sandow courtesy of Robert White. Cover concept and design by Gordon LaVelle.

Contents

Introduction

On a fall evening in 1893, as part of his exhibition at the Chicago World's Fair, featured strongman performer Eugen Sandow tried something that had never been done before. Sandow stood before the audience that had assembled to see him, without props and in minimal attire, and did nothing but flex his muscles. It was a novel idea, and it worked. The crowd was mesmerized. Though his height was average and his weight was a mere 180 pounds, the phenomenal muscularity of Sandow's physique made him seem positively massive, like the ancient stone monuments his poses mimicked. He looked equally perfect. From the instant his first pose was struck, Sandow transformed himself into living sculpture. He furthermore bestowed unto the world its newest artistic medium: the human body. Most significantly, he created a new pastime: bodybuilding.

110 years later, on a fall evening in Las Vegas, Ronnie Coleman was handed the coveted Eugen Sandow trophy—an award given each year to the world's top professional bodybuilder. On that day, at a height of five-foot-eleven and in an extremely lean condition, Coleman weighed 287 pounds. The thousands of fans who had gathered to witness the latest phase of his ascendency were thrilled. Like a small handful of men who came before him, in 2003 Coleman successfully smashed through what were thought to be the limits of human muscularity.

Clearly Sandow's invention had developed into

left: Eugen Sandow. c. 1894
below: Ronnie Coleman. c. 2005

Courtesy of Steve Harris

something drastically different from his original "muscle-display performance." Over the course of the preceding 110 years, bodybuilding had become a professional occupation; a system had been created for determining which bodybuilder is best; and most critically, methods had been discovered by which men could vastly increase the size of their muscles. It was a slow, evolutionary process that guided bodybuilding from the days of Eugen Sandow to those of Ronnie Coleman, but like nearly all such processes, it was characterized by fits and starts; by lulls and flurries; and by defining moments.

The purpose of *Bodybuilding: Tracing the Evolution of the Ultimate Physique* is to describe and examine that evolution, with special attention given to three main themes: the changing physical appearance of bodybuilders; the people, events and things that influenced those changes; and bodybuilding's relationship with the general public. The topic of bodybuilding is approached here from the context of its most basic definition: it is the practice of creating a muscular build for aesthetic purposes. It's for this reason that the book begins with a brief discussion of the muscular male form in art. Bodybuilding was initially intended to be a continuation of that tradition, with marble and bronze being replaced by living tissue. Although bodybuilding would always contain an element of artistry, in time it abandoned artistic pretense and became something altogether different. The remainder of the book describes the development and transformation of this new phenomenon.

Meanwhile, no discussion of bodybuilding as a phenomenon can be considered complete without commentary on the public's perceptions of it. This is true for three reasons: the general public is the source from which new bodybuilders and their fans emerge; the public's attitudes, both real and imaginary, have affected the policies of the small group of men who came to wield power over bodybuilding; and finally, just as with any other activity, the achievements of those who have immersed themselves in bodybuilding are ultimately subject to the standards of the surrounding world.

Since bodybuilding is a topic that has been approached from a number of angles, it's important to understand what this book is not. The pages which follow contain no simple enumeration of facts. They instead supply an historical analysis that attempts to explain the dramatic transformation of bodybuilding from the time of its invention to the present day. Nor can one find here lists of contest results, a roll-call of muscle-contest greats, or a collection of their anecdotes. There have been numerous men with remarkable physiques who have nonetheless failed to influence the evolution of bodybuilding, mainly because they lived in the shadows of greater examples. Descriptions of these men and the contests they entered could fill many volumes, and this information can be found elsewhere. Bodybuilders, contests and other episodes that factored into bodybuilding's evolution are mentioned, as are non-bodybuilders who have created an impact within the world of muscle. Finally, the issue of female bodybuilding is not tackled here, since the origins and transformation of that particular pastime are complex and deserving of a separate book.

Bodybuilding: Tracing the Evolution of the Ultimate Physique isn't an *I-was-there*, tell-all personal account of a champion bodybuilder, and it isn't an exposé filled with juicy, heretofore unknown facts. It does not share the popular literary aim of "blowing the lid off" the world of muscle. The intended value of this book lies in its presentation of bodybuilding's historic and thematic timelines, so that bodybuilding's evolution—from the days of Eugen Sandow to those of Ronnie Coleman—can, if nothing else, be traced.

Before the Beginning

Bodybuilding is the practice of developing muscles for purely aesthetic purposes. It's also a lifestyle, a subculture, a form of entertainment, and the foundation upon which a large industry was created. Bodybuilding is at once enthralling, magnificent, strange, repugnant, divisive and compelling. It's also here to stay. Until the very last days of mankind's existence a tiny but fervent minority of the Earth's population will dedicate their lives to the pursuit of the ultimate physique. Some have given their lives in that quest. For something that provokes such passion, dedication, and even willingness to risk everything, it's remarkable how new it all is. For the vast majority of human history, there was no such thing as bodybuilding. That all changed on an autumn day in 1893, when an entirely unlikely series of events culminated in its creation.

It's been said that necessity is the mother of invention. It's also a fact that bodybuilding was invented. However, bodybuilding and everything that grew from it were by no means born of necessity. Had the delicate balance of inspiration, circumstance, chance and whim that resulted in its creation encountered the slightest disturbance, the practice of developing muscles for purely aesthetic purposes would have remained lost in the void, unthought-of and unawakened.

The origins of bodybuilding therefore contrast sharply with that of the competitive sports to which it's so often compared. The development of sporting competition is a near-universal phenomenon of cultures spread throughout the world, and the strong, ongoing appeal of sports reflects some basic characteristics and tendencies of human group behavior. It's arguable that humans were bound to invent and embrace sports. Bodybuilding has no such common beginnings or purpose. Its origins can be traced to a single culture; and its inception derived not from the instincts of the herd, but ultimately, from the desire of the individual to express himself.

In an essay entitled "Monday Night Hunters," the famous science educator Carl Sagan sought to explain the immense worldwide popularity of sporting events, particularly among males. He compared the excitement of watching or participating in sports to the thrill of the hunt experienced by prehistoric humans. Since our ancient ancestors stalked and killed animals as one of two primary means for obtaining food, individuals and the groups to which they belonged enhanced their chances of survival by exhibiting a passion for the hunt. There further existed the need to protect the group and its sources of food from other bands of humans. Thus we find in Homo sapiens hard-wired tendencies to band together, relish the thrill of the hunt, and on occasion, fight off other groups. For prehistoric man, his very survival depended on all three.

According to Sagan, in modern times these needs are satisfied, however unwittingly, by competitive sports. Few modern humans realize that their actions can be so strongly influenced by pure instinct, but it must be a powerful and deep-seated force that can impel hundreds of millions of men to be enthralled or even obsessed with the movement of a leather ball from one end of a grass field to another. After all, humans were designed to exist as hunter-gatherers. Modern living has done nothing to reverse this. Men therefore require an outlet. To a point, sports provide one.

Bodybuilding was created for entirely different reasons. It doesn't directly satisfy any innate, prehistoric human tendencies. There's no hard-wired impetus steering people toward it. Rather, it's a product of conscious thought, and any relationship it has to hunter-gatherer instincts that guide human actions is, at most, symbolic. Whereas the ability of a player on a football field satisfies the ancient drive to display prowess in the hunt, bodybuilding is merely a static representation of would-be prowess. Bodybuilding doesn't demonstrate ability. It symbolizes it. This is entirely appropriate, because the origins of bodybuilding can be traced to pure sym-

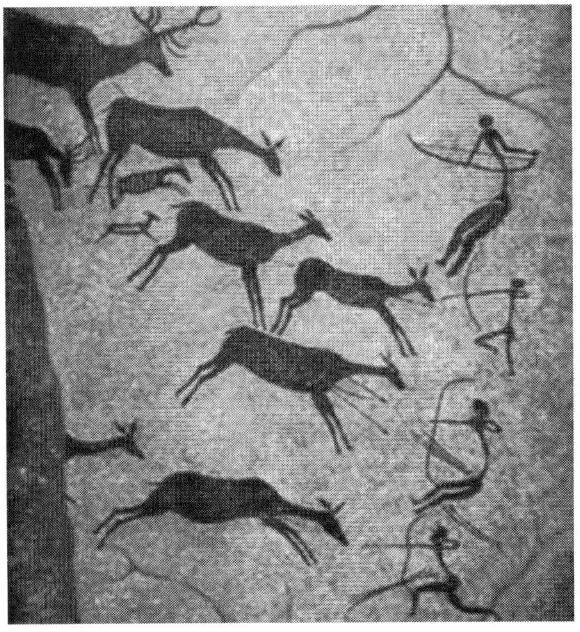

Humans hunting deer. Cave painting. c. 10,000-15,000 BCE. Lascaux (Dordogne), France.

bolism—to the simple, motionless representation of objects, otherwise known as art. It's in the artwork of the ancient Greeks that bodybuilding finds its beginnings. Thousands of years later, starting in the late 19th century, people we now call bodybuilders found inspiration in that art. However, the influence of ancient Greek sculpture certainly exceeds the simple inspiration it provided. It was in Classical Greece that the human body first came to be looked upon as a distinct aesthetic entity—and as an object worthy of idealistic depiction rather than simple documentary representation.

Of equal importance was that the Greeks considered the male form to have aesthetic value more or less equal to that of women. Finally—and relative to bodybuilding, most significantly—an ideal male physique was lean and muscular. Today these notions are often considered to be self-evident. Apparently however, they are not. Evidence of this can be found in all the other cultures of the world that did not celebrate the male physique in their art, who never thought of the human muscular system as being anything other than a useful organ, and who never invented bodybuilding.

Bodybuilding is centered on the visual appreciation of muscular physiques. For bodybuilding to have come into existence, it first needed to occur to someone that a muscular physique is an object with aesthetic value. It occurred to the Greeks, and to them alone. It just as easily could have occurred to no one.

Classical Greek civilization has long since faded into the mist of Antiquity, but its important traditions survive. Greece is, after all, considered to be the birthplace of Western culture and civilization, and indeed Western "thought." Bodybuilding itself was not invented by the Greeks. That bodybuilding owes its existence to a "desire of the individual to express himself" assigns partial responsibility for the later creation of bodybuilding to ancient Greek artisans. It was they who carved muscular bodies out of marble, or who cast them in bronze. Their ancient counterparts in Egypt, the Near East, Asia—and really, the rest of the world—didn't physically distinguish the bodies of the individuals portrayed in their art. The rigid and mainly featureless uniformity of figures in Egyptian sculptures and wall paintings are examples of this. Other cultures simply depicted their figures as clothed or without discernable musculature.

The Greeks, through their art, gave the individual physical distinction. That their art should do so is fitting, since Greek civilization was the first to place a high value on the individual—as a citizen, a member of society, or as just a human being. The importance given to the individual is in fact a major theme of Classical Greek culture, and an important reason why ancient Greece is thought to have so strongly influenced Western civilization. Prior to the Greeks, importance was given to society, the collective mass which formed its bulk, and its leaders. Except in the case of these leaders, individual human life had limited value. It's therefore little wonder that the artisans of these cultures did not labor over the finer points of human anatomy, or bother to make any important distinctions between common individuals.

Temple of Re-Herakhte for Pharaoh Ramses II.
c. 1257 BCE. Abu Simbel, Egypt.

When they weren't carving monolithic tomb structures for their Pharaohs, Egyptian artisans were kept quite busy creating treasures that would go inside them. Although they were accomplished craftsmen, the value of their work was often found more in the gold and rare stones used to render them than in the subject matter or quality of their creations. Their later counterparts across the Mediterranean didn't follow the Egyptian example. They were kept busy chiseling common marble, intending to convey personal ideas about things like the heroic might of the individual.

The importance of the individual in Greek culture in a way made it possible to communicate sentiments like these through art. To appreciate a perfectly-muscled physique is one thing, but to actually carve one out of a solid block of marble is quite another. Ancient Greeks valued all individual productive members of society, be they leaders, soldiers, scribes, architects, metalworkers, carpenters, philosophers, or sculptors. This valuation encouraged progress and excellence. Thus a tradition of exquisite sculpture arose. The master artisan was able to perfectly depict whatever object he chose. While this qualified him as an expert craftsman, he was also capable of communicating, through his craft, personal sentiments that transcended mere documentation. This made him an artist. At this period in history, the Greeks alone possessed such skill. Without it, the depiction of idealized physiques for which these artisans are remembered would never have been.

The notion that things like heroism—a character-attributable to deeds—can be suggested by a motionless stone sculpture was similarly unique to Classical Greeks. To them, a physique could be, and should be, directly representative of an individual's mind and character. Within their figures of legend these three elements were thought to form an indivisible whole. This is demonstrated in *The Odyssey,* where Homer repeatedly refers to Odysseus as "godlike." It's not mentioned whether this description should refer to his mind, character, or body; nor need it be. For a heroic figure like Odysseus, they are one and the same. In very much the same vein, in Greek sculpture we see a real attempt to describe, without words, such a connection.

Dying Warrior, from the east pediment of the Temple of Aphaia at Aegina, Greece. 5th century BCE.

Because the body was thought to be more than a mere instrument with which to carry out the whims of the mind, a Greek mythological hero was bestowed with a physique to match his intellect. Since the time of Homer, creators of romantic fiction have heavily copied this model. This is also why the classic villain became one who was wretched in both character and body. The idea was not lost on the tellers of future tales, as will be remembered by fans of William Shakespeare's *Richard III,* a play written two millennia after Homer's epics. The title character, a depraved murderer, is also a hideous hunchback. Four centuries later, the film *300* gave a similar appearance to Ephialtes, the betrayer of the valiant Spartans. Countless tales ascribe comparable attributes to their antagonists. Heroes are naturally depicted as the opposite: virile, tough, brawny and handsome. In mind, body and character they represent excellence and aspired to perfection.

If the Greeks are to be thought of as the spark that would later ignite bodybuilding, the concept of perfection itself may well be the final element that makes this true. Perhaps more than anything else, the ancient Greeks are remembered for their great philosophers—men like Socrates, Plato, Aristotle and Archimedes—and for the creation of a great tradition of philosophical thought. It was they who first gave consideration to the concept of perfection. Henceforth objects, both worldly and imagined, could be compared to this standard of faultless quality. Their artisans were in turn encouraged to create ideal forms rather than documentary portraits. The depiction of the human body was central to this movement; Greeks determined that a physique needed to exhibit certain proportions in order to be considered perfect.

In the minds of the philosophers and artists who

Discobolus. Roman marble copy after a Greek bronze original. c. 450 BCE by Myron.

made the determination, "perfect proportions" also meant more than just the ratio of physical measurements of body parts. Since a human body is an almost infinitely divisible whole, and proportion is an important criterion in the determination of physical perfection, each bodypart should in fact exhibit its own balance of proportions. In simpler terms, each muscle should exhibit a certain shape. When all parts are fitted together, the result is a perfect overall shape.

At the same time, it was never thought that perfection should apply only to an object's visual appearance. According to Aristotle, a perfect object should be complete, both in form and function, and it should be unsurpassed in quality. The object should also fulfill its purpose, whatever that may be. These criteria therefore suggest that although a muscular build can be aesthetically pleasing, it ought to perform functions beyond just being something nice to look at. Physical splendor can only symbolize a human's intended functions. The heroes of Greek epic tales possessed exteriors that directly symbolized physical might, but those figures were also the owners of intellectual and moral strength. Perfection could not be attained without equality and harmony within the three. An imbalance could cause the undoing of the individual, as happened with Achilles in *The Iliad*: a moral lapse precipitated his downfall.

Ancient Greece is regarded most prominently for its great philosophical tradition, but its association with athletics gave it nearly equal fame. Just as the Greek heroic character wasn't muscular simply because it looked good, neither was the athlete. He lifted stones to strengthen his body for physical competition, which made him strong and adept, with an exterior to match. Being an athlete also made him a privileged member of society, which entitled him to an education. The overall result was heralded as the real-world embodiment of ideal overall balance. It's therefore no coincidence that the earliest athletic contests included the recitation of Homer's epics. Those epics inspired athletes; and those athletes inspired, through their physical splendor, artists who wished to glorify the characters of Homer's tales. Many centuries hence, the art they created inspired the tiny crop of men who became the world's first bodybuilders.

Milo of Croton, 6th century BCE Greek wrestler. According to legend, Milo was the first athlete to use resistance training. 18th century depiction by Joseph-Benoît Suvée.

Although the ancient Greeks have been widely credited with providing bodybuilding with its original inspiration, that assertion is most often accompanied by a lack of answers for two important questions: why exactly did that art come into existence?; and why did no other civilizations created anything comparable? The Greeks did not one day arbitrarily decide to glorify muscularity, and their artists certainly didn't depict muscular men simply because they were nice to look at. It was through an entirely unique mixture of traditions and thought that the concept of the ideal male physique was not only hatched, but preserved for eons: ancient Greece was the first culture to place substantial value on individual life, and indeed on the individual; within that culture was created the concept of perfection, a standard to which all objects could be compared; individuals were therefore subject to a standard of perfection, and it was determined that an ideal man should exhibit a proper balance of intellect, character, and body; the concept of perfect balance also applied to each of these components separately, and it was further determined that a perfect human body should have certain physical proportions; a tradition of excellence among their artisans gave them the ability to skillfully portray this perfection; and finally, the quality of their creations was so great they were preserved for thousands of years. With all these things considered together, if any one group or culture was to precipitate the invention of bodybuilding, it was going to be the Greeks.

The entirely unique combination of circumstances that made all of the above possible demonstrates that, at a fundamental level, it was the desire of the individual to express himself that gave bodybuilding its initial impetus. This self-expression came not originally in the form of bodybuilding itself, but in the desires of the artist. The motivations of those who inspired the creation of bodybuilding are therefore entirely different from the almost involuntary attraction to sports described earlier. While the motivations of men who centuries later made themselves into modern bodybuilders likewise derive mainly from voluntary thought, bodybuilding itself is an entirely different animal. While its inspiration and origins can be found in antiquity, bodybuilding is very much a modern idea, born in the modern world and conceived of by modern humans. Man has devised countless means by which to express himself, and manipulating the appearance of his own muscular system is among the more unique and unusual. Once bodybuilding had reached its modern, 21st century state, that statement would find few doubters.

*   *   *   *   *

The importance of the ancient Greeks is beyond dispute. Bodybuilding came about because, thousands of years later, someone stood on a stage and imitated their sculptures. The seed from which bodybuilding would one day grow had been planted. Over time that seed, deeply buried, would be dormant, nearly forgotten, and almost destroyed. The next two thousand years would not see any advancement or development of the idea. Rather, that period—and the next few centuries in particular—would be characterized by a fight for the survival of Western ideas and ideals.

Ancient Greece, like any other civilization, did not have to exist; nor did anything the Greeks produced need to materialize. Yet that civilization did exist, and for hundreds of years it thrived. As is the case with any such group of people however, in order to flourish it had to survive. This was easier said than done for the ancient Greeks, who after all lived in an age of conquest. In such times, nations occupying enviable geographic regions naturally come under the glare of aggressor states. The people of the British Isles have been reminded of this, time and again, in various ages: from the arrival of the Romans in the first century CE to the invasion of the Normans in 1066; through all the hostile incursions between these dates; and in the unsuccessful attempts which followed. As late as 1940 the British were preparing to repel the armies of a conquering foe.

In the several centuries during which Greek city-states enjoyed prosperity, the geographic region they occupied was looked upon with scheming eyes. This was inevitable, since Greece is located near the center of what was once the known world. Along with its numerous satellite islands, Greece forms a peninsula of complex shape in the eastern Mediterranean, a body of water whose name literally means "middle of the Earth." Situated across open waters from Italy, Egypt, Carthage and numerous other states, it was also considered to be a gateway to the East, and to the lands of the Eastern empires. Chief among these empires was the Persian, which likewise saw Greece as the gateway to the West. Already a vast empire by the fifth century BCE, Persia occupied a substantial portion of southwestern Asia and even parts of Africa. The Persian Emperor Darius and later his son Xerxes

had clear designs on westward expansion. This could not be achieved until Greece had been overrun and subdued.

Battles fought between alliances of Greek city-states and the Persian Empire are generally thought to be among the most influential in history. Greece was, after all, the birthplace of Western Civilization. For Western Civilization to materialize and develop, Greece needed to remain Greek. If it Greece fell, it's arguable that the world may never have progressed beyond the standards of 490 BCE.

No one alive at the time had any inkling of the importance of the events that were about to unfold. The Persian Empire, bent on conquest, attacked westward into Greece. This was a problem for the Greeks in more ways than one. The peninsula's city-states not only traditionally lacked cohesion, but they were often at odds and sometimes even at war with each other. They were also now under attack from a much larger foe—one that possessed the advantages of unified composition and singularity of purpose. The situation was desperate, the prospects grim. Nevertheless, Greeks of the fifth century BCE possessed a knack for coming together when it counted. In 490 and again in 480, through the hard-fought, desperate battles of Marathon and Salamis, Greece was able to repel the Persian invaders. Greece would remain Greek, and Western thought and culture would survive. The Greek traditions of philosophy and artistic excellence would be given the opportunity to thrive.

Nevertheless, the age of conquest was far from over. In the second century BCE another neighbor would hatch and carry out plans to overrun and subdue the Greek peninsula. This time, the defenders were without sufficient cohesion or resolute posture. The tide could not be stemmed. In 168 Greece fell under the domination of a nation which

left: The Eastern Mediterranean. c. 490 BCE
above: *Reclining Roman*. c. 1st century BCE

was soon to become a great empire; one that would overshadow the Persian, one that would become the greatest of them all: Rome. This was a critical development in the struggle to keep Greek traditions alive. Instead of crushing and replacing Greek culture, Rome absorbed it. What was originally Greek therefore became Western. The eras in which Greece and Rome flourished were eventually combined to form what is now called Classical Antiquity. Like the Greeks, the Romans looked upon the male physique as an object with aesthetic value. They also adopted the Greek tradition of artisanship that made possible its accurate depiction. Finally, the supremacy and longevity of the Roman Empire insured that, sometime in the distant future, these things would be remembered. This was important, because a time would come when it would nearly all be forgotten.

The celebration of muscular male physiques would eventually fall from favor, as would the Classical tradition of deft artisanship. The demise of the former was precipitated by an abrupt change of religion by Rome's most important citizen. In 313 CE, Roman Emperor Constantine converted to Christianity. Along with his conversion came the Edict of Milan, an official decree that put an end to religious persecution. All religion would now be tolerated. Although he was later canonized for his conversion, Constantine's reasons for doing so were believed to be less than saintly. He claimed to have had a vision in which he saw a crucifix, along with the words "in this you shall conquer." Constantine read the sign literally, adopted Christianity, and thereafter waged a number of successful military campaigns. Since he continued to patronize and monumentalize a variety of gods—pagan and Christian alike—it has been thought that Constantine merely wanted to gain divine favor from all available sources. Some future Christian Roman Emperors worshipped in a similar manner, but eventually pagan gods were simply abandoned.

In time Rome officially became Christian. The great governments of Europe, for many centuries to come, followed suit. Along with this change of religion came a revision of perspective and values. The worldliness that characterized the pagan religions of the prior thousand years was entirely shunned by Christianity. According to biblical guidelines, the leading pagan deity Zeus would have been a sinner of the worst type. It was therefore necessary for artistic subject matter to change. The muscular gods and heroes of Classical mythology were no longer depicted. Eventually the tradition of carving real-life heroes from blocks of marble resumed, though the statues no longer carried a glorious musculature. No longer were they hewn with Classical expertise.

Roman Emperor Constantine.
His reign (306-337) marked the beginning of the end of Classical sculpture. Modern depiction, York Cathedral, England.

A second great event influenced the style and quality of European sculpture, forcing it into a style that lasted longer than all of Classical antiquity. In 476 AD, Rome fell. Former citizens of the great Empire lived on in darker times and under new governments. A variety of Classical traditions suffered. The creation of art became less important to a population that no longer lived under the protection of a prosperous state. Nations that took the place of the old Empire at first didn't have much interest in producing great artists or encouraging great art. Since the primary heroic figure of medieval Europe would not take shape for another few centuries, this was just as well. When that figure did emerge, a capable albeit unexpressive artisanship was available to portray it.

The great hero of medieval Europe was not the protagonist of epic poems, but the real-world defender of Christianity: the crusading knight who risked life, limb and fortune to save the Holy Land and protect his own land from the people he called infidels. Statues and crypt covers that honored the memory of these men were far removed from images of the Classical warrior. What was once fluid and dramatic became stoic and rigid. The medieval knight was portrayed as solemn and pious; he still had sword and shield, but unlike the warrior of old who wielded them in action poses, his lay by his side. His body was upright, his hands held together in prayer. The ability of the medieval artist was perfectly suited to portray such images. His were competent hands, able to execute a uniform style. While his skill did not match that of his Classical predecessors, he was nevertheless adept at rendering armor, something that now completely covered a heroic male body.

The warrior of Classical antiquity had also worn armor, though it mainly just covered his torso. Left exposed were the sinewy limbs that artists of his time found to be so magnificent. From the medieval perspective, a muscular build was little more than man's worldly exterior. It was not something to be glorified. The sole medieval artistic subject with bare skin was Christ himself, and he appeared this way only in objects depicting his execution. Such was the tradition of sculpture in the Middle Ages. In all, a thousand years passed before artists were once more granted the necessary license and ability to depict muscular male physiques.

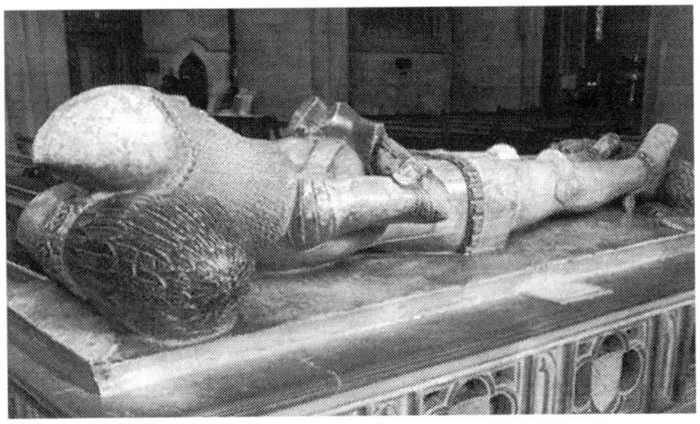

Tomb of Sir Richard Pembridge, d. 1375

The general advancement of mankind over the past 500-plus years is owed to the renaissance of thought which followed the Middle Ages. In what became known as simply The Renaissance, Classical enlightened thought was discovered, revived and championed. The Ancients themselves became figures of wonder, and they were looked to for inspiration. Significantly however, by the beginning of the Renaissance, the Roman Catholic Church had established over Europe a base of near-absolute power. The Church tolerated enlightened thinking, so long as that thinking did not conflict with its own views or attitudes. Scientists had to proceed with caution, lest they run afoul of any official religious stance. Galileo Galilei for example was handed a sentence of life imprisonment for declaring that the Earth was not the center of the Universe. He was given the option of walking away scot-free, so long as he recanted his view. He took the deal.

Although artists ran the risk of imprisonment or worse if they created anything that offended the church, this was not the reason why so many works of Renaissance art had religious themes. As the most powerful entity in 15th century Europe, the Church also had the deepest pockets. It wanted to glorify itself with great and often monumental works of art, and was willing to pay for them. The best artists of the day were therefore commissioned to create monuments of the highest order. One artist in particular was kept quite busy fulfilling important commissions. To this he owed his reputation; many of his contemporaries thought him to be the greatest artist of his era. By the reckoning of some who came later, he was the greatest of any era. Though his name at birth was Michelangelo di Lodovico Buonarroti Simoni, in time he was known simply as Michelangelo.

Michelangelo was content to portray characters of the Bible, though he also had a fascination with Classical sculpture and male musculature. His first known large marble sculpture was a rendering of the ancient Greek demigod Heracles (Hercules being his more recognizable Roman name), the strongest of all mythological figures. When Michelangelo was later commissioned to sculpt characters of the Bible, he saw no need to forsake his fascination with virile masculine images. He simply made them muscular. Since he was also keen to exalt every detail of ideal muscular form, whenever possible, he made them nude. Such was the appearance of one of his earliest commissioned pieces, the monumental statue *David.* Destined to become one of history's most famous works of art, the diminutive Biblical hero was rendered as a colossus. Hewn from a single block of marble and standing 17 feet tall, the statue took Michelangelo three years to complete. The figure displayed a level of musculature that clearly exceeded previous interpretations of David, and it set the tone, and the standard, for future renderings of the male form in general.

Michelangelo Buonarroti wasn't actually the first Renaissance artist to render muscular males in a Classical style. That distinction belongs to Antonio del Pollaiuolo, who was born 44 years before Michelangelo. In what may be del Pollaiuolo's most famous piece, his engraving *Battle of the Nudes* presented a shocking contrast to the stoic Biblical scenes that were so common to the early Renaissance. The image of naked, muscular men violently hacking each other apart, with no apparent context, seems to have been a metaphorical reaction against the artistic suffocation held over from the prior millennium. That did not however detract from the true

Antonio del Pollaiuolo. *Battle of the Nudes.*
Engraving. c. 1470

Michelangelo. *David.* 1501-04
Marble, height 18'. Academy, Florence.

importance of the piece, which derived from its inspiration.

Considering the musculature and dynamic posture of his subjects, it's clear that del Pollaiuolo had been stimulated by certain Classical art. He simply took that inspiration, infused it with passion and even rage, and unleashed it upon unsuspecting eyes. Del Pollaiuolo would have achieved greater fame for this, except that he was not a truly transcendent talent. While his depiction of muscular bodies earned the praise of contemporary artist Andrea Mantegna, whose *Battle of the Sea Gods* seized upon del Pollaiuolo's inspiration, Leonardo da Vinci was less impressed. He thought del Pollaiuolo did not depict graceful anatomical form, but that the musculature of his figures more closely resembled "sacks of nuts" or "bundles of radishes." Del Pollaiuolo nevertheless played a critical role in the revival of the muscular male form in art. However, it would take the work of a true master to get the world's attention. *David* was the true first step.

With time, Michelangelo's subjects became more muscular. His next important sculpture, a sinewy depiction of Moses, conjured images of the Greek gods Zeus and Poseidon. Later, in the piece for which is perhaps best known, even greater muscularity was given to his subjects. These figures were not hewn from solid rock with hammer and chisel, but rather with the graceful strokes of a brush. Although he did not consider himself to be a painter—in fact he's thought to have disliked the medium as a whole—Michelangelo was commissioned by Pope Julius II to create a massive fresco painting on the ceiling of the Sistine Chapel in Rome. Stated more accurately, he was ordered to. Since Julius was one of history's infamous "Warrior Popes,"—men who actively and ruthlessly used military force to secure political power for the Church—defying his requests would have been unwise.

Bowing to a Pope who would accept no refusal nevertheless resulted in another of the world's greatest, and most famous, works of art; one that cemented Michelangelo's position as one of art's all-time greats, and substantially enhanced the documented Western appreciation of ideal human physical form. Although the job was essentially forced upon him, Michelangelo lobbied for and received full artistic license. Julius originally wanted the ceiling to portray the 12 Apostles of Christ. Michelangelo meanwhile found Old Testament characters and scenes to be more interesting, varied and appealing. A convincing case for his preference was presented, and it was shortly thereafter agreed that he would depict various scenes from *Genesis.* With creative freedom secured, Michelangelo got to work. Four years later, the final stroke was made. The scaffolding upon which he worked was removed and his brushes were packed away.

The expansive ceiling of the Chapel, previously bare, was now a single masterpiece. Instead of the 12 figures of the original plan, the completed painting featured more than 300. Included were nine scenes from *Genesis*, central to which was the iconic *Creation of Adam.* In it, an unmistakably muscular God, one that in another time in the same city would have been recognized as Jupiter, soared down from the heavens to extend a life-giving hand to Adam. A muscular nude and reclining Adam awoke from his eternal slumber to receive it. When Michelangelo presented his arguments for depicting the scenes of *Genesis,* this vision may have already consumed his imagination; such was its brilliance and beauty. An examination of the remainder of the ceiling revealed that nearly all his other characters carried a similar musculature.

Clearly Michelangelo had grasped the Greek concept of overall perfection—of mind, body and character—when he conceived of his the Sistine Chapel images. If the great characters of the Judeo-Christian Bible were to be depicted, ordinary bodies would not do. An opposite sentiment could be seen in the section depicting the expulsion from Eden of Adam and Eve. The now-Earthly pair were given more ordinary bodies, as if part of God's punishment for their Original Sin was a mundane appearance.

Since Michelangelo had received from the Pope permission "to do as I liked," he intended to take full advantage. Separating each scene from Genesis were images of a sculpted stone framework, convincingly devised to appear like part of the Chapel's own architecture. Seated atop the framework's columns were 20 *ignudi*—nude and quite muscular men, in various states of modest repose. The images collectively comprise a significant portion of the overall work. Their inclusion was never really explained, and their presence in the work immediately became a topic of controversy, one that survives to this day. Without a doubt Michelangelo had boundless fascination with the male physique in its ideal form. This naturally bolstered the widely-held opinion that he was a homosexual, but to attach significance to this issue is to miss the point entirely. Those images have existed for centuries as an independent creation of one of history's great artists. Just like all his other works depicting nude males, each figure became an eternal, masterful tribute to ideal human physical form, one that would not be forgotten. The supposed sexual tastes of their inventor are irrelevant.

Moreover, the nature of Michelangelo's commission may have given him warrant to test the limits of his license; to push the envelope. Since he was essentially forced to undertake the project, it may have given him some satisfaction to divert from the intended subject and indulge himself. Michelangelo intended to create a visual epic, but he also had motive to defy his boss. The rendering of 20 nude males, without context, lends credence to

left and above: Michelangelo. *Ignudi*, detail of the Sistine Chapel Ceiling. 1508-12

Michelangelo. Cherub making an obscene gesture. Detail of the Sistine Chapel Ceiling.

this idea. It was also later noticed that one of the scores of cherubs which embellish the greater image is making an obscene gesture,[1] one quite possibly intended for Julius.

Over the years the ignudi found a few notable detractors; some found the designs to be tasteless, inappropriate or even obscene. Pope Adrian VI, whose reign began ten years after the ceiling's completion, thought it to be little more than "a stew of naked bodies" and wanted it destroyed. Since the Dutch Adrian was the sole non-Italian in a long line of Italian Popes (the next being John Paul II, who reigned 500 years later), his wish was successfully blocked. The array of Romans defending the work widely considered Adrian to be a "barbarian" of the north, and happily opposed him. Adrian's death at the end of his two-year reign was met with cheers and relief.

Nevertheless, controversy remained. Even the women of the Sistine Chapel were somewhat muscular. Most of Michelangelo's Sibyls—various women of legend who had prophesized the coming of Christ—were adorned with a musculature that would put the majority of real-world men to shame. Like the ignudi, this facet of the work was never full explained. In the end though, there was little demand for explanation. After all, this was the work of Michelangelo.

[1]The cherub has a thumb stuck through his fingers, the Italian equivalent of "giving the bird."

The Greeks were the first to find splendor in muscular male physiques; their appreciation of the male form was rediscovered and revived during the Renaissance, most notably through the creations of Michelangelo. It can be said that his art killed multiple birds with a single stone. He made his employers happy, paid unique homage to his religion, and satisfied his own urging to celebrate athletic human form. His depictions became an indelible reminder that humans can themselves be objects of aesthetic wonder.

Before long Michelangelo's standards were adopted. Numerous artists who followed portrayed the male body in what was now considered to be its ideal form. It therefore came to pass, in the post-Renaissance Western world, that when the question of what a perfectly-built male should look like was raised, there was plenty of material to reference—thanks to the Classical Greeks, the Renaissance, and artists like Michelangelo Buonarroti. Still, it had not yet occurred to anyone that man could deliberately transform *himself* into such an object. Before that notion materialized, many hundreds of years would pass.

Agesander, Athenodoros and Polydorus.
Laocoön and His Sons.
Vatican Museum, Rome. c. 25 BCE

Bodybuilding is Born

The single most important event in the history of bodybuilding was its invention. This was slow in coming. By the late 1800s, more than 23 centuries had passed since the time when muscular males were first declared to be worthy of aesthetic praise. Athletes had been using exercises that developed their musculature since long before then. Yet the final piece of the puzzle—the combining of these two ideas—had not yet materialized. Aristotle's assertion that any object ought to fulfill its purpose had therefore, thus far, held true. A lean and muscular physique, however marvelous to behold, was little more than a side effect of athletic training. It was but the practical means with which to achieve athletic greatness. No one had yet thought of making splendid musculature an end result. Finally, in the late 19th century, someone did.

It was the aspiring American entertainment financer Florenz Ziegfeld who first realized that human muscularity could be looked upon as an end rather than a means. In his earliest foray into the world of entertainment, Ziegfeld in 1893 secured rights to manage the career of a newly-arrived Prussian strongman named Eugen Sandow. For decades strongman acts had been popular attractions at Vaudeville shows. During intermissions, featured performers would thrill audiences with various feats of strength, which included things like lifting heavy objects, bending metal bars, and tearing in half multiple decks of playing cards. Sandow in particular was a big attraction. His displays of strength were impressive, but spectators showed more interest in Sandow's large and sharply-defined muscles. To Vaudeville audiences who were used to the immense though portly appearance of most strongmen, this was something entirely new and fascinating. To capitalize on his appearance, Sandow devoted part of his act to partially-clothed muscle-flexing. Onlookers were captivated. This did not escape the watchful eye of Ziegfeld.

Ziegfeld booked for his new act a spot at the upcoming World's Fair, to be held that year in Chicago. It would be his major American unveiling. In addition to his standard strength show, Ziegfeld asked Sandow to perform something he called a "muscle display performance," whereby the audience could bear full witness to his physique. The idea was that Sandow would imitate a number of Classical sculptures. In the event, Sandow walked onstage in minimal attire, with no props, and stood in front of a black background. Using a variety of different postures, he tensed his muscles. At the precise moment Sandow hit his first pose, bodybuilding was born.

Eugene Sandow. c. 1893

On a whim, by asking his client to simply stand in place and flex his muscles, Florenz Ziegfeld chanced upon what later became known as bodybuilding. He had nothing to do with the invention of bodybuilding training, nutrition, competition, or any of the things that later became associated with it. He knew nothing about any of that, nor would he have been interested in learning. As a financer of entertainment, he was only interested in giving an audience what it wanted. Ziegfeld guessed that people would want to watch a muscular man flex. He was right. The crowd loved it, and minimal-attire muscle display performances became a regular part of Sandow's act. The idea of Classical sculpture being brought to life was enthralling, captivating, exciting. People wanted to see it. A muscular build was no longer simply a means. It could also now be, in and of itself, an end. This, in the most basic sense, is the essence of bodybuilding: it is the creation and exhibition of a muscular build.

Having a great build alone does not make someone a bodybuilder. If it did, bodybuilding would already have been thousands of years old. Bodybuilding is the act of using various means to increase the size of skeletal muscles, where that increase is the desired end result. Before his first true posing exhibition, Eugen Sandow did not train to be a bodybuilder. He trained to perform feats of strength. Nevertheless, once his posing routine was underway, his muscles instantly became an end result, and his prior training therefore had a second, heretofore unknown purpose. After his routine, with more such performances planned, his training regimen was dual-purpose: strongman and bodybuilding. Thus, after thousands of years, strength training was no longer used solely for the purpose of improving athletic performance. For those who were so inclined, it now had a new, independent function, and it was all thanks to an unlikely source.

Eugen Sandow was given credit for unearthing the ancient Greek seed that flowered into bodybuilding, but it was his manager, Florenz Ziegfeld, who stumbled across it. Ziegfeld had no idea that he was the first person in history to combine, into a single concept, the millennia-old appeal of male muscularity with the effects of rigorous athletic training; he didn't know that he had turned a living human being into a representation of ideal muscularity, where previously this was accomplished only with chisel or brush; nor was he aware that from that point forward a muscular body was no longer only an object of inspiration, but one of aspiration as well; and he could not have possibly imagined what his invention would one day become. As far as he was concerned, he was just adding a gimmick to the sideshow strongman act he managed.

His promotion of Sandow gave Ziegfeld's career an initial bump, but before long he was lured away by greener pastures. In time Ziegfeld became a famous and quite successful Broadway theater promoter and financer. His contributions in that field were so significant that his life story later inspired the semi-biographical film *The Great Ziegfeld,* winner of the 1937 Academy Award for Best Picture. In the film, Eugen Sandow was played by Nat Pendleton, a man who became known as the "Hollywood Hercules."

Sandow's part in the film ended when Ziegfeld abandoned sideshow shtick and graduated to the world of song-and-dance musicals. The real-life Sandow meanwhile certainly didn't fade away once Ziegfeld departed. His fame grew. Sandow's strongman-and-muscle-display remained a highly successful touring act. Though the muscle displays were originally just one part of an elaborate show, they became the crux of his legacy. Sandow went on to enhance and embellish the concept of physique exhibition, in the process earning for himself a future, unofficial title: "Father of Bodybuilding." He lived up to the billing. Yet he easily could have

Eugen Sandow. c. 1894

lived unnoticed. The beginning of Eugen Sandow's ascent to greatness was guided largely by chance. He owed the distinction of being the world's first bodybuilder partly to Ziegfeld's muscle-display whim. The development of his physique, the thing to which he owed all his fame, came about because of an earlier, unseen, fateful event.

Born Friedrich Wilhelm Müller in 1867, at a young age he became fascinated with athletics. Unhappy with home life and keen to avoid the Prussian draft, the young Müller signed on with a traveling circus—he became an acrobat—and changed his name. Acrobatics gave the already athletic, newly-named Sandow a muscular build. As luck would have it, Sandow's circus ran out of money in Brussels, home of the famed strongman Louis Attila. The two soon met. In Sandow Attila saw potential. He took the displaced Prussian under his wing, taught him the finer points of strength-act showmanship and, most importantly, introduced him to new methods of physical training.

Before long Attila and Sandow paired up and performed a series of tandem strongman shows. Though they soon split, Sandow was now a career strongman—and he now possessed the physique that would in time win him boundless acclaim. After experiencing mild success in Europe, Sandow made his way to America, where he was discovered by Ziegfeld. By the time the two parted ways, Sandow was a major attraction, and the earliest iteration of bodybuilding had been invented.

Where chance had played a large role in his early success, determination would guide the remainder. Sandow became an active promoter of "Physical Culture"—a decades-old movement which emphasized the need for exercise and healthy eating. He was also an outspoken proponent of strength training; he opened gymnasiums, published books that outlined his training system, and started a magazine. All the while he continued to hone his physique. He was a self-described living work of art, and was photographed mimicking the postures of specific Classical and Renaissance sculptures. He claimed to have trained his body in such a way so that he might have perfect proportions—the so-called "Grecian Ideal." Although a later analysis of his exact measurements showed him to be rather unevenly and asymmetrically developed, this was not apparent to the multitude that touted his magnificence. As the turn of the 20th century neared, he was an icon, a hero, a star. Nevertheless, Sandow's most important move, the ploy that gave bodybuilding the character and identity for which it later became known, was yet to come.

Although the term "body building" had not yet been coined, the pastime of deliberate muscle-building quickly captured the imagination of a legion of young men. Since it was an offshoot from the world of athletics, its participants and fans naturally invited, and expected, that world's conventions. While team sports may very well appeal to age-old and hard-wired tendencies of human groups to band together, the lure of individual events is owed to a natural desire to compete. Thanks to a hormone called testosterone, competitiveness is an especially male characteristic. Competition also makes athletic endeavors far more exciting for participants and onlookers, and it helps to raise the standards of those events.

Vaudeville strongmen rarely stepped onstage intending to break the records of strictly-defined lifts. They instead introduced competitiveness to their strength displays by issuing challenges to their audiences. Cash sums—amounts as high as $1000 or even £1000—were promised to anyone who might match the featured strongman's feat. On occasion a rival strongman would appear, meet the challenge, expect his sum, and get disqualified on a technicality. Mayhem sometimes ensued, but such was the nature of unofficiated athletics. Regardless, the element of competition made strength displays far more interesting and exciting. It seemed only a matter of time before something similar found its way into the world of muscle displays.

The men who aspired to be like Eugen Sandow were anxious to make their new pastime directly competitive. Sandow became aware of this, and he saw opportunity. He hatched the idea of staging competitions of muscular development—physique competitions—that would reward the most perfectly built men. Unlike sporting events that measure and compare the physical ability of their participants, physique contests would be decided by appearance. It was a novel idea. The world would soon bear witness to what was essentially a masculine, athletically-themed version of a beauty contest.

Beginning in 1899, Sandow launched a series of such contests throughout Great Britain. The sole requirement for entry was that each competitor must have used the "Sandow System" of training to prepare for the event. Since his was the only muscle-building doctrine in existence, the condition was met without complaint or dissent. Sandow personally judged each event. Since it was a contest of appearance, a set of judging criteria was developed, one that has mainly remained in place through modern times. By Sandow's reckoning, an ideal physique should have impressive overall development; well-balanced proportions; good skin tone; and an appearance of overall health. Contests were spread out over a period of close to two years, and culminated in a 1901 final event called "The Great Competition" at London's prestigious Royal Albert Hall. The competition drew upwards of 15,000 spectators—it would become one of the two largest crowds ever to witness a bodybuilding contest—and lured hopefuls with a tidy £500 grand prize.

In addition to securing a renowned venue, Sandow boosted the event's legitimacy by producing a small but distinguished celebrity judging panel. Seated front and center was his first choice, the famed British athlete and sculptor Sir Charles Bennett Lawes. Had Sandow scoured the island for a decade, he scarcely could have found a more appropriate man to judge a physique contest. Lawes was himself a champion rower, runner and cyclist. He was an accomplished artist and a founding member of the Royal Society of British Sculptors. Lawes had been trained by John Henry Foley, the creator of the official sculpture of Prince Albert, for whom the Royal Albert Hall was named. It also just so happened that, at the time of Sandow's competition, Lawes was completing a colossal marble sculpture called *The Death of Dirce*—a striking work rendered in a Classical style and featuring heroically-posed muscular men. In Lawes, Sandow had a true authority on the male physique.

right: Sir Charles Bennett Lawes.
The Death of Dirce. Bronze copy of marble original.
below: Royal Albert Hall. c. 2010

Seated next to Lawes was the soon-to-be knighted Arthur Conan Doyle, the physician, activist and—most famously—author of Sherlock Holmes novels. Sandow himself assumed the role of "referee." The small panel patiently analyzed the vast array of competitors who paraded and posed before it, most of them outfitted in leopard-skin loincloths. The 1900 Birmingham Athletic Club Champion W. Arthur Long, who attended the finals as a spectator, 50 years later recalled the affair:

> I did not envy the judges and their task...Generally the judging was very boring in spite of Sandow relieving the monotony by an exhibition of weight-lifting and the whole show bore no comparison with the present attractive physical culture shows.

After an exhaustive appraisal, Lawes, Doyle and Sandow had found their winner; and at long last the evening came to an end. The event's patrons, satisfied and weary alike, filed out of the Albert and into the London night. Britain had its first physique champion, a man named William L. Murray, who collected the first-place cash, medal and trophy, made his way through the crowd—and then vanished forever from the world of Physical Culture.

Exactly 400 years and one day after Michelangelo drove the first chisel stroke into the raw block of marble that became *David*, the newest version of the ideal male form was revealed. He was chosen from among a slew of would-be champions, in London, the heart of the British Empire, the Rome of its time. Unlike the masterfully-hewn, stationary ideal embraced by the empires of ages long since past, this new standard could be found in a living, breathing human body.

The concept of the physique contest was entirely new, captivating, engrossing. Although what promised to be an elaborate spectacle was found to be "boring" by some, time and reflection would help remedy that. The majority of civilized society seemed to have little interest in the new phenomenon, but to a select group, Sandow's muscle contests were a revelation. A small legion of young men set out to make themselves worthy of such company. With this in mind, in 1904 Sandow published his third book. Called simply *Body Building,* the book furnished that generation with a new set of instructions for building muscles; and it gave all future generations a name for the thing he made so famous.

The turn of the 20th century is most prominently recalled for the inventions that arrived on or near it; these included things like the airplane, movie projector, mass-production automobile, radio, and a host of others. In an age of invention, here was yet another: bodybuilding competition. Like most new things, its formative years were characterized by innocence, of both intent and purpose. Muscle contests were created to pay tribute to the athletic male physique; and the men who entered them were intended to be viewed as simple symbolic representations of good health. In both regards early contests succeeded. They would be fondly recalled. Neither the men who competed in early shows nor the audiences who attended them were aware that a deeply-buried nerve had been touched, and that Pandora's Box had been opened. None imagined what trials a future generation would face once bodybuilding's plot had fully developed. Its earliest fans had little reason to doubt that bodybuilding would always be pure and good. After all, it was an age of optimism and innocence.

* * * * *

From the time of Sandow until World War II, the small but growing ranks of "body builders" aspired to the model of well-being and vigor advertised by the Physical Culture movement. A phenomenon of the Western world, Physical Culture was, as its name implies, a society-wide trend that emphasized a need for exercise and overall healthy living. The movement was conceived in the wake of the Industrial Revolution—an era remembered for the simple fact that it changed everything.

It was during the Industrial Revolution that the Western world phased out animal and human labor and replaced it with machines. The effects of that switch have been innumerable, but to gain a full appreciation of its magnitude one need only compare the agrarian-based landscape of the late 18th century—when the revolution began—with the state of the planet in its modern form. The Industrial Revolution catalyzed that transformation.

The revolution came about because of advances in technology in all three general categories of work: precision, ability and energy. The period witnessed the invention of a number of machines that were able to complete tasks that previously required either precise human dexterity, or were altogether impossible. At around the same time, technological strides allowed machines to tap into energy other than what was stored inside the muscles of humans or beasts of burden. Trains are obvious end-result examples of all three advances. Before the invention of railroads, people or goods could most efficiently be transported over land on single wagons, pulled by horses and guided by human drivers. A train on the other hand could much more quickly haul a vastly greater load. It was powered by a precise machine—a steam locomotive—that was able to convert energy stored in coal into a predirected forward movement. A similar effect was witnessed in the replacement of the blacksmith's hammer and anvil by the industrial forge; and in countless other instances where human or animal labor was replaced by the work of machines. Although it would take 200 years for the planet to go from the age of horse transport and wooden ships to supersonic travel and information superhighways, for people of the age, the arrival of the Industrial Revolution was not without immediate and significant effects.

Since citizens of industrializing nations were rewarded with a decreasing need to tap into their own stored potential energy in order to survive, their bodies often fell into disuse. This had unwanted consequences. Human bodies are designed to perform strenuous physical labor. A body that performs no such work will atrophy and grow soft, because there is little reason for it to do otherwise.

Detail from Michelangelo's *David*: the face that shamed the Physical Culturalists into action.

Where previous generations had been robust, virile and rugged, men of the new age were stricken with lethargy, malaise and weakness. This did not escape the notice of a segment of the afflicted urban middle classes, who called it the "disease of affluence."

It was a call to arms. The heroic sculptures of Antiquity and the Renaissance had not gone away. The soft public of the 19th century gazed up at them, only to be met by cold, stern frowns—as if the Ancients and Michelangelo knew that the world of the distant future would one day need to be shamed into action. For some the disgrace cut hard and deep; and from that wound Physical Culture was born. Whereas previously only athletes deliberately engaged in physical exercise, there was now an entire cultural movement clamoring that all men should follow suit. In time women were encouraged to exercise as well. As the Industrial Revolution gained momentum, so did Physical Culture. When bodybuilders emerged in the final decade of the 19th century, they were thought to be the movement's finest examples.

Contrary to what is sometimes believed today, bodybuilding and Physical Culture were not the same thing. Bodybuilding arose separately. However, once invented, it was quickly embraced by and assimilated into Physical Culture. Before long, bodybuilding claimed the Physical Culture name for its own, and supplied it with the now-iconic images that became the movement's trademark: photographs of men whose bodies matched those rendered by the great Classical and Renaissance artists. Their appearance in print drove home the new Physical Culture message, which was simple: the ideal physique was now attainable. All that was needed was to follow an ideal lifestyle.

It was therefore fitting that a man who possessed such a physique would become the face of the Physical Culture movement. Although he took the torch first carried by Eugene Sandow, history would remember him for far more than rippling muscles or a handsome face. When his life's work was complete, he had generated more knowledge and attracted more attention than all other members of his movement combined. A future generation bestowed upon him the title of "Father of Physical Culture," and his own made him a household name. Though that name isn't widely remembered by the at-large public of the 21st century, there was a time when the mention of health and fitness immediately brought to mind its greatest proponent: Bernarr Macfadden.

Bernarr Macfadden. c. 1894

Though his name at birth was Bernard McFadden, the future leader of the Physical Culture movement thought changing a few letters around would make him seem more masculine and virile. Born only a year after Sandow, Macfadden was a particularly weak and sickly child who nevertheless survived the abuse of an alcoholic father, the early death of both parents, the subsequent shuttling of residence from one uncaring relative to the next, and a year in an orphanage. At the age of seven an adverse reaction to a vaccination nearly killed him. The incident triggered a lifelong distrust of doctors, something that would later help set the direction of his life's work. At age 11 he was allowed to stay with a local farmer who, it turned out, was more interested in free labor than the boy's well-being. Regardless, that move was perhaps the most critical event of the young Macfadden's life. Two years of physical labor made him strong and healthy. The following two years were spent working in an office, where he experienced atrophy and a return to sickliness. Deploring the regression, Macfadden, still in his early teens, searched for a means by which to return to health and vigor. He soon began a campaign of exercise and fitness that would last a lifetime.

Macfadden read everything about strength and wellbeing he could get his hands on, all the while strengthening his own body. He became a gymnast. He excelled at wrestling. Though at only five-foot-six Macfadden wasn't a large man, ability, conditioning and strength allowed him to defeat much larger opponents. Before he reached age 20 Macfadden opened his own exercise studio, where he devised the battle cry that would one day define his life and career. Visitors to his studio were greeter with a sign informing them that "weakness is a crime!"

Bernarr Macfadden. c. 1929

The studio was just the beginning. Macfadden's passion far exceeded whipping a handful of clients into shape. He wanted to educate the masses. His plan was to inform the greater public about exercise and wellbeing by writing books on the topics. However, this was not yet to be. A lack of education had left him with poor grammar and spelling skills. At the age of 23 that changed, when Macfadden became an athletic trainer at the Marmaduke Military Academy in Saint Louis. Determined to remedy his literary shortcomings, he exchanged services for tuition. Macfadden's writing ability improved rapidly, and although he was both an instructor and student, he found time to complete his first book. Called *The Athlete's Conquest*, it was a novel about a man's quest to find a Physical Culture bride. Although the book was deplored by future generations, and although Macfadden later admitted the tale left much to be desired, all his students bought copies. Since the book was therefore a minor success, it encouraged his plans to continue writing.

While Macfadden's career was taking shape, it was not long before fate once more intervened. He attended the 1893 Chicago World's Fair and was by chance present to witness Eugene Sandow's muscle display performance. Awestruck and eager to copy Sandow, he shortly afterward began posing, in the statuesque fashion of the day, for physique photographs. Macfadden had by that point developed a lean and somewhat muscular physique, and aspiring to the Classical ideal immediately captured his imagination. Accordingly, he embraced bodybuilding, and continued to do so for the remainder of his career.

Like the Ancient Greeks however, Macfadden never thought of the creation of a muscular physique as an independent goal. Rather, he envisioned a muscular physique, along with improved health and longevity, to be important, equal products of a perfect lifestyle. Well-developed muscles just happened to be the most striking effect. When Macfadden began publishing the magazine *Physical Culture* in 1899, its covers featured photographs of muscular men.

Public fascination with muscular men presented new opportunities for a now-successful Macfadden to expand his fame and promote Physical Culture. Once more following Sandow's lead, beginning in 1902 he arranged a series of physique contests throughout the United States and Great Britain, with a final event at New York's Madison Square Garden on January 2, 1904. In a move that was a full century ahead of its time, Macfadden's physique contest was the culminating event of a Physical Culture Exhibition—a sports-and-bodybuilding festival that lasted several days. Some of the exhibition's other contests included "races for men and women, fencing championships, wrestling bouts and several fasting competitions." Although fasting has long since fallen from favor, the remaining events can all be found at modern sports-and-bodybuilding festivals. The muscle show was won by Al Treloar, a man who shortly afterward moved to southern California and helped make that region home to bodybuilding.

A repeat of the exhibition was planned for October of 1905. Posters advertising a "Mammoth Physical Culture Exhibition" and featuring photographs of the previous year's winners were distributed throughout New York City. These immediately attracted the attention of a self-appointed moral crusader named Anthony Comstock, a portly special agent of the Post Office who found any public display of bare skin to be reprehensible. To Comstock, who reportedly found the ancient and armless Venus di Milo statue to be pornographic, and who openly boasted that his crusading had driven 15 people to commit suicide, Macfadden was a smut peddler. Two days before the event, along with a half-dozen vice squad officers, Comstock raided the offices of *Physical Culture* and arrested Macfadden on obscenity charges. He was booked and released on $1000 bail, the episode made headlines, and the next day's exhibition suddenly had loads of free publicity. Eager to see the supposedly lurid display, 15,000 fans filled the venue, matching the attendance of Sandow's 1901 London show. According to estimates another 5000 were turned away.

After the event Comstock was bashed in *Physical Culture*. Macfadden personally declared: "...by branding the human body as a thing obscene he is casting an insult at the great creator." Had Michelangelo been alive, he would have applauded the sentiment. Nevertheless, Macfadden was found guilty. A sympathetic judge let him off with probation.

right: Anthony Comstock. c. 1900. Comstock once bragged that his moral crusading drove 15 people to commit suicide.
below: Madison Square Garden. c. 1905

When all was said and done, Macfadden's obscenity charge was a mere footnote to his life story. His interests went well beyond simple muscle-show promotion, and after the second big New York event he moved on to other things. His next big venture was an attempt to create a utopian Physical Culture village in New Jersey. *Physical Culture* magazine meanwhile remained a profitable enterprise. In time, it was much more. It became the cornerstone of Macfadden's eventual publishing empire. He later started or gained control of a number of publications, with topics ranging from sports to true crime to romance to variety. His was therefore a true rags-to-riches tale, surpassing that of Sandow, and creating a mold for future promoters of health, fitness and bodybuilding. He would one day inspire the greatest of them all. Yet his magazines were only part of the story.

Advertisement for Macfadden's College of Physcultopathy. c. 1925

With time, Macfadden's own literary contributions became prolific, as he eventually wrote more than 100 books. Unlike the novel that kicked off his writing career, Macfadden's subsequent books were mostly self-help, focusing on health and daily living issues. His topics were wide-ranging and often controversial, with titles like *Fasting, Hydropathy, and Exercise*; *Virile Powers of Superb Manhood*; *Health, Beauty, and Sexuality*; *How Success Is Won*; *Physical Culture for Babies*; *Manhood and Marriage*; *Truth About Tobacco*; *Foot Troubles*; *Woman's Sex Life*; *How to Reduce Weight*; and of course *Macfadden's Encyclopedia of Physical Culture*.

Macfadden gained particular notoriety as a proponent of fasting and non-medical cures for disease. In 1955 the latter proved to be his undoing, as he refused medical attention for a simple urinary tract infection. Although Macfadden once boasted that healthy living would allow him to reach age 150, complications from the infection—eight decades after his last visit with a doctor—left him dead at 87.

Bernarr Macfadden's contribution to the historical progression of bodybuilding cannot be overstated. He arranged the first American muscle contests and presented them in grand fashion before vast audiences. Even more importantly, his publications glorified muscular physiques and gave instructions to readers about how they might go about building their own. He promoted health and wellbeing, but he also popularized bodybuilding. As a promoter of muscle he picked up where Eugen Sandow left off and before long overshadowed him. In time however, that effect was reversed. Macfadden promoted a wide, almost bewildering array of ideas, and this may have undermined his legacy. Greater fame was eventually passed back to Sandow, a man with a more focused vision.

Sandow's renown and legacy are owed almost entirely to his contributions to bodybuilding. In fact he all but invented it. The 20th century saw few things attract a more devoted and fervent following—and groups like that tend to exalt their creators. As a general health and wellbeing advocate, Macfadden inspired less zeal. He came to be known as little more than one of a long line of such people. In modern times, except among enthusiasts, he is nearly forgotten. Bodybuilding meanwhile saw its torch of leadership pass to another future icon.

In an act of great irony, Bernarr Macfadden's most famous creation also happened to be one that consumed little of his time, energy or passion. In 1921 *Physical Culture* put on a "World's Most Handsome Man" contest. To be considered, an entrant simply had to mail in a photograph of himself, preferably striking a pose that showcased his physique. After sifting through a pile of such entries, Macfadden came across a photograph of a man named Angelo Siciliano. He immediately knew the contest had its winner.

Siciliano was an Italian immigrant who had come to the US at age 11. He discovered strength training at an early age, and by the time he reached full-fledged manhood his development was sufficient to land him work as a strongman on the Coney Island boardwalk. On the advice of a friend who thought he looked like a local statue of the mythical figure Atlas, Siciliano chose for himself the stage name Charles Atlas. It was catchy, and it stuck. He liked it so much he made it his legal name.

Atlas was invited to Macfadden's office for a meeting, where he was instructed to doff his shirt and strike a few poses. Macfadden wanted to make sure he had correctly chosen his winner, but he also wanted to see, in person, what he determined to be the world's greatest specimen of muscular manhood. Satisfied, he handed Atlas the contest's $1000 first-prize check and sent him on his way.

When Atlas learned of Macfadden's "World's Most Perfectly Developed Man" contest, held the following year at Madison Square Garden, he naturally made plans to compete. Unlike the mail-in format of the handsome-man contest, the new event signaled a return to the original, live style of physique competition created by Sandow. It had been 17 years since Macfadden's "obscene" display at the same location, and since Anthony Comstock was now dead, the coast was clear. The Roaring '20s were underway; and although alcohol prohibition was now law, morality crusading had, at least for the moment, fallen from fashion.

Upon receiving news of Macfadden's upcoming contest, it was as if two decades of muscular men burst forth to participate. A monstrous field of competitors—750 in all—was on hand to vie for the title. Though he was pitted against the largest group of bodybuilders ever assembled by a gigantic margin, Atlas once more reigned supreme. The accolades didn't end there. Macfadden declared Atlas' physique to be so far superior to those of other men that future contests would be a waste of time. Remaining true to his word, the World's Most Perfectly Developed Man was Macfadden's final muscle show.

Courtesy of Robert White

Angelo Siciliano, a.k.a. Charles Atlas. c. 1920

Charles Atlas was the man of the hour. Nevertheless, like winners of countless physique contests before and since, a gradual descent into obscurity loomed before him. Such may have been his fate had it not been for a simple suggestion. A Macfadden employee, Frederick Tilney, asked Atlas to partner with him to produce a mail-order muscle-building course. Atlas agreed, and the wheels of invention began turning. The two already had the world's most perfectly-developed man as their spokesman; all they needed was an original idea to pitch. They decided to sell a course outlining Atlas' system of "Dynamic Tension"—a method for building muscles without the use of weights.

According to Atlas' marketing claims, the idea originated while he was observing lions at a zoo. After all, he reasoned, lions became extremely muscular without the benefit of weights. Humans should therefore be able to as well. Discounting the fact that all big-cat species are naturally muscular, Atlas came up with the idea of pitting his own muscles against each other—of tensing them in a dynamic fashion. He went home and began uncovering the secrets of Dynamic Tension. The system was put to work, his muscles began to bulge, and in no time Charles Atlas owned the world's greatest physique. This was the tale he told, anyway.

The reality of Dynamic Tension's origin was something altogether different. The system was little more than a gimmick cooked up by Atlas, Tilney and Macfadden himself. The 64-page mail-order course, *Secrets of Muscular Power and Beauty*, bore an uncanny resemblance to Macfadden's 1906 book *Muscular Power and Beauty,* which described methods for building muscles through tension and without the use of weights. The plagiarism went virtually unnoticed, and ads for the course immediately began appearing in *Physical Culture.* Although Macfadden may have had some genuine faith in the system—after all, he did write a book on the topic two decades prior—it was falsely advertised to be the method Atlas used to build his body. Angelo Siciliano had used iron weights, just like everyone else.

The Atlas ads set an important precedent. They showed that young men, eager to build their muscles, will try almost anything to achieve that end; that those young men are inclined to believe the testimonials of accomplished bodybuilders; and, most importantly, that they are quite willing to trade money for the promise of muscles. Since muscular growth normally comes at a painfully slow rate, and it's therefore difficult to tell whether a particular product is effective, advertisements based on untrue claims became common. For example, for the remainder of bodybuilding's history, elite competitors would endorse muscle-building product lines they had, in most cases, never previously used. The film *Pumping Iron* features an example of this practice. One particular scene shows a photo shoot in which an oiled and pumped Arnold Schwarzenegger, draped with women in bikinis, holds a bendable exercise bar. The resulting ad implied that the product was at least partially responsible for the appearance of Schwarzenegger's physique. Meanwhile, except in that advertisement, Schwarzenegger never mentioned use of the device to be part of his training.

Male lion stretching. Charles Atlas claimed that observing this practice inspired him to invent the Dynamic Tension method of exercise.

In some cases, product claims were outright falsehoods. Occasionally there were repercussions. In time, even the biggest of bodybuilding's product distributors found himself facing lawsuits for promising specific, made-up results. Most others were shrewd enough to avoid specifying what should be expected from the use of a particular product.

The story behind Dynamic Tension may have been falsified, but the system was more than capable of eliciting at least a little muscle growth, especially among men who were new to resistance exercise. In an age when very few people had access to legitimate weight-training equipment, a system that required no apparatus was almost bound to succeed—and succeed it did. Ads appeared in magazines, on the back cover of countless comic books, and—several generations after it was first devised—on the internet. The Atlas course became by far the most prolific early offering of what would later be a multi-billion dollar industry: products designed to help build big muscles. Along with the magazines that became their catalogues, the muscle-product industry would one day become the very force propelling bodybuilding forward. The Atlas course, which was a fairly harmless attempt to cash in on the physique of a rising star, helped set the wheels in motion. Compared to what came later, it was small potatoes.

It time the ads would become known more for camp value than anything else. Presented in comic-strip format, the most famous version shows a 97-pound weakling getting sand kicked in his face by a bully and thereafter being insulted by his own girlfriend. He goes home, gets angry, and resolves to give the Atlas system a try. He quickly becomes muscular, returns to the beach, punches the bully, and wins back his girl. The idea was novel. Instead of merely proclaiming the effectiveness of the system, the Atlas ads directly appealed to insecurity and the primeval desire of males to assert dominance over rivals.

Bernarr Macfadden bestowed upon Charles Atlas titles that declared his beauty and perfection. Ads for Dynamic Tension meanwhile told potential buyers that large muscles are badges of manhood, tools of attraction, and when need be, effective weapons. It was an effective change of context. In time the Atlas ads became famous, cliché, kitsch, and a part of Americana; they helped bodybuilding to become, and remain, a small part of the public consciousness; and critically, they introduced the concept of bodybuilding to millions of young men. Although only a small percentage of those men would resolve to build muscle and actually follow through with it, new bodybuilders continued to trickle onto the scene.

* * * * *

Al Treloar's west coast seedling had meanwhile begun to take root. The 1930s witnessed the relocation of a number of bodybuilders and aspiring hopefuls to the small beach towns west of Los Angeles. Like many Americans who migrated to the LA basin throughout the 20th century, musclemen were initially lured by the weather. In geographical terms, much of California enjoys what is known as a Mediterranean climate, with warm, dry summers and mild winters. The Greek peninsula's position in the eastern Mediterranean naturally gave it similar weather, and it was in fact one of the reasons why its citizens were able to so deeply appreciate athletic male physiques: in warm weather, people wear fewer clothes. Such was the underlying philosophy behind bodybuilding's gravitation to southern California.

Al Treloar. c. 1904

Courtesy of Robert White

It's a move that was bound to happen. Long before tanning beds and paint-on competition color allowed anyone to look like he lived in favorable latitudes, sunny California was hard to beat. The local scenery also helped form, quite literally, the backdrop for bodybuilding's emerging image. Prototypical outdoor muscle photographs featured men flexing on the beach, a convention that has remained through modern times. When the trend was new, each shot reminded muscle fans that bodybuilding had not only established a home base, but that a built body was the key to fun in the sun. Swimsuit-clad females were sometimes posed alongside bodybuilders, further suggesting to readers that big muscles were the key to sexual attraction.

Nice weather and beautiful beaches were southern California's initial lure, but once enough top bodybuilders relocated to the area, its appeal became based more on the gathering itself. By concentrating themselves into a small area, bodybuilders greatly increased their chances of becoming known. In a time when travel was slow, photographic equipment was expensive and the internet was still several generations away, musclemen who lived off the beaten path had little hope for acclaim or notice. Moving to California would instantly change that.

California's appeal was based on more than weather and potential publicity however. In the 1930s, the average aspiring bodybuilder had access to little training information and even less equipment. He did however know that experts were congregating on the U.S. west coast. He furthermore knew that anytime experts assemble, the potential for meaningful information exchange rises. Finally, he was aware that the area had become home to a few gyms. Though by modern standards their equipment was sparse and crude, with few implements other than barbells, dumbbells, chin-up bars—and one of bodybuilding's newest and most important technological breakthroughs, the weightlifting bench—it was for the most part far superior to what could be had elsewhere. It was within these gyms that physique stars and hopefuls chalked up and got to work. The stars honed their already-admired bodies. As for the men who wished to copy them, if nothing else, they could train on the same equipment as the champions.

Santa Monica in particular was a haven for bodybuilders, and an area there known as "Muscle Beach" all but became the west coast movement's epicenter. Crowds regularly formed to watch the area's conspicuous new residents perform feats of strength or hand-balancing acts. Some were simply lured by the spectacle of handsome young men flexing their big muscles. One such man was destined for far greater things. Bodybuilding's history has seen the rise of a number of men who have been able to parlay muscle-flexing into major muscle-based enterprise. Of that group, only one—a former Muscle Beach regular named Jack LaLanne—was able to become, and remain, a household name.

As a future television exercise show host and healthy-lifestyle advocate, LaLanne's fame became so great that the Muscle Beach days became a mere footnote to his legacy. Though he easily could have become known as Bernarr Macfadden's successor, the public had in store for him a far catchier title: "Godfather of Fitness." Future generations would know him for his every-morning, oh-dark-thirty calisthenics TV show, as well as his reminders that health was the key to happiness.

LaLanne's contributions to bodybuilding were likewise important. He was first and foremost a promoter of exercise, which by itself helped draw some attention toward bodybuilding. He was also an innovator. LaLanne realized that traditional weightlifting exercises, variations of which had been practiced for more than 2400 years, had inherent limitations. He postulated that an optimal bodybuilding workout had not yet taken place, since such a workout would require the use of specialized machines that had not yet been invented. Rather than waiting for someone else to do it, LaLanne got to work inventing them. He came up with the ideas for a number of important weight-training devices, including the Smith and leg-extension machines, as well as cable-pulley devices and their pin-loaded weight selector stacks. No champion bodybuilder since the 1960s has achieved top form without using any or all of these.

Meanwhile, Harold Zinkin, a Muscle Beach regular who rubbed elbows and matched biceps with LaLanne, kept the little think-tank swirling. He became fascinated with LaLanne's ideas and had designs to expand upon them. Zinkin also fully understood that early exercise machine advocates were faced with a twofold problem: gyms typically

right: Muscle Beach, Santa Monica. c. 1950
below: Jack LaLanne. c. 1948

Courtesy of Robert White

Courtesy of Robert White

Courtesy of Robert White

Siegmund Klein Physical Culture Studio. c. 1935
At the time, this was a state-of-the-art facility.

occupied small buildings and usually didn't have much room to add equipment; and most survived on limited funds. He solved both dilemmas by inventing the Universal multi-station exercise machine—a single, free-standing device that could be used to perform more than a dozen different exercises. It was also small enough that most gyms could find space for one. It was a ground-breaking step toward the creation of modern, fully-equipped gyms.

The establishment of complete gyms—converted warehouses filled with free weights as well as the inventions of LaLanne and Zinkin—turned out to be a critical step forward for bodybuilding's growth and historical progression. In time the name of another prominent Muscle Beach regular, Joe Gold, would become more closely associated with the concept of complete weightlifting gyms than any other. Though it would be another three decades before his first Gold's Gym opened in neighboring Venice, its eventual fame would spark the rise of hardcore weightlifting gym chains. In time, most of the Western world would have access to superior weight-training equipment; and anyone with the desire to become a bodybuilder would now have the means. For bodybuilding to get big, this was important.

For the moment however, the world of muscle was still tiny. Big weightlifting gym chains would be the fruit of future generations, born from the labor of their Muscle Beach fathers. The rest of the world was meanwhile in the midst of a Great Depression. The greater US population was more concerned with feeding itself than achieving a high level of health and fitness; and with the approach of war, concerns shifted and became more grave. Bodybuilding was therefore left to its own devices.

As the 1930s wore on, the muscle culture would continue to do its own thing, oblivious to the outside world. To the men who immerse themselves in bodybuilding, this has always been part of its appeal; and never was this more true than in the '30s, when bodybuilding was still small, naïve, isolated and above all innocent.

* * * * *

Be that as it may, any age recalled for innocence requires a moment when innocence was lost. Throughout the first third of the 20th century, bodybuilding was naïve and without guilt. Muscular men who took the stage in leopard-skin loincloths, performed handstands on sunny California beaches, or fastened fig leafs to pose for statue-mimicking photographs were thought to be the greatest examples of Physical Culture—the lifestyle phenomenon that emphasized a need for exercise and healthy living. Bodybuilding made an aesthetically pleasing exterior an end result, but the key to achieving that result was always thought to be wholesome living and vigor. Eventually, that perception changed. In time it was realized that not only were there other ways with which to build a muscular body, but that these ways could sometimes be both easier and more effective. The age of innocence ended when the first seeds of that realization were planted—and when a framework was devised to reward those who cultivated it.

The notion of the Classical Ideal, sealed in cold marble for 23 centuries, in a great burst broke free and found new life in the living, breathing tissue of Physical Culturalists. Before the 20th century had passed however, a great deal would change. Physical Culture would be replaced by hardcore bodybuilding. Health and vigor would give way to muscle-for-the-sake-of-muscle. The Classical Ideal would find itself overrun, trampled back into the Earth by a mutated object of its own creation. The story of this creation is the tale of the great transformation of bodybuilding—the events that took the physiques of men like Sandow and gradually turned them into the bodies that grace the covers of modern bodybuilding magazines. Ultimately, that story tells of the demise of the culture and the emergence of the cult.

The beginnings of this creation can be traced to the efforts of two very different men, each from a very different part of the world. Remarkably, both men made their most important contributions to the great transformation of bodybuilding within the span of a single year. The first was a brilliant scientist, the owner of numerous academic awards and honorary degrees, and later, a Nobel Laureate. The second was a seventh-grade dropout with an unusual pastime and an unlikely dream. Though they led entirely separate lives and never met, their legacies remain inextricably joined; and through a series of events that neither man could have imagined, their most famous feats combined themselves into one.

The first man came from a land that's changed its name twice since his 1887 birth; the fall of the Iron Curtain finally bestowed its proper name of Croatia. Born the son of a cooper, Leopold Stephen Ruzicka discovered early in life that he had a strong liking for mathematics, physics, and especially, organic chemistry. After finishing secondary school, it was with unabated drive and unrivaled focus that Ruzicka began studies at the Karlsruhe Technical Institute in Germany. He took a double load of courses and graduated in less than two years. A mere two years after that, at the age of 22, he was awarded a PhD in Chemistry. Throughout the first half of his career Ruzicka held a variety of research,

Leopold Ruzicka. c. 1939

Courtesy of David Watson

development and teaching positions in academia as well as the private sector. His early research centered on the development of insecticides and perfumes. In the early 1930s, as a professor of organic chemistry at the Swiss Federal Institute of Technology in Zurich, the focus of his research shifted to certain types of hydrocarbons and, most notably, human sex hormones.

It was in 1935 that the primary male hormone testosterone was first identified. Ruzicka, by then one of the world's leading organic chemists, immediately focused his efforts on developing a synthetic version. He worked tirelessly on the problem, and after only a few months outlined a four-step process whereby testosterone could be synthesized from cholesterol. The speed, precision and especially the significance of Ruzicka's discovery won him a Nobel Prize in Chemistry.[1] Before long an injectable, synthetic form of the hormone was produced, and human trials began in 1937. Within a few years testosterone propionate—the very first anabolic steroid—became available as a treatment for individuals diagnosed to have insufficient testosterone levels.

Outside elite scientific circles, the discovery at first attracted only modest attention. The worldwide economic depression and gathering clouds of war easily overshadowed what was seen to be an esoteric scientific discovery. Famous inventions of the time and the years to come were things that could readily help people or, better yet, swiftly destroy them. The period witnessed the invention of things like penicillin, synthetic rubber, improved radar and television cameras, helicopters, jet aircraft, ballistic missiles and atomic weapons. In light of these advances, it's not surprising that the arrival of synthetic testosterone made few sit up and take notice. Peace and a return to prosperity changed that.

Although it would take the world of athletics more than a decade to fully appreciate the significance of the development, in time word would get out. Appreciation rapidly led to experimentation; and in the 1950s, use of synthetic testosterone by athletes for performance enhancement had begun.

[1]The 1939 prize was shared by the German scientist Adolf Butenandt, who independently synthesized testosterone only a few days after Ruzicka. Since Ruzicka completed his research first, he is naturally given credit for the discovery.

For those who simply wanted to make their muscles larger, the impact of Ruzicka's discovery was beyond measure. Apart from its own invention, the most important event in the history of bodybuilding was the discovery of anabolic steroids.

Leopold Ruzicka's synthesis of testosterone was a legitimate scientific discovery, made in good faith. Ruzicka never would have guessed it was also the great event that triggered the eventual end of innocence in bodybuilding, or that years down the road it would ignite so much controversy. His discovery was intended to benefit mankind, which it did. Nevertheless, in the very worst of cases, steroid abuse would cause suffering, sorrow, death and destruction. It was perhaps fortunate for Ruzicka that he died before his invention's dark side fully emerged and made headlines.

Ruzicka unwittingly cleared a path upon which droves of bodybuilders would one day travel, yet it was a second man who rose from obscurity to help guide them down it. While the former was completing work that would later earn him a Nobel Prize, the latter was busy ogling over images in muscle magazines. He admired the physiques, and the accomplishments, of men like Sandow and Macfadden and hatched the dream of one day becoming like them. It was a lofty goal for a scrawny teenager with limited means. Nevertheless, as a purveyor of muscle culture, that scrawny teenager would one day dwarf them both. His fame wasn't necessarily greater—to the at-large public, the names Charles Atlas and Jack LaLanne have remained far more recognizable—but the power he would one day wield over the world of bodybuilding was absolute. In that world, in modern times, Atlas and LaLanne would be nostalgia; and the kid with a dream, Joe Weider, would be king.

Weider was born in 1919 in Montreal, and grew up in a Yiddish-speaking household. Upon reaching his teenage years he more or less resembled the 97-pound weakling in the Atlas Dynamic Tension ads, and longed to do something about it. He was then visited by fate. While dropping off garbage at a local dump, the young Weider happened upon an old issue of *Strength* magazine and, with mild curiosity, cracked it open. "Instantly I was mesmerized," he later declared, as he looked at page after page of "pictures of men with muscles more powerful and impressive than ever I'd imagined." His life, at that instant, was changed forever. He was hooked on bodybuilding. Unfortunately however, gyms and weightlifting equipment were virtually unknown to depression-era Montreal. Filled with a burning desire to lift weights but with no means to do so, Weider improvised. He fashioned a barbell from scrapped railroad flywheels and an iron rod. It may have been primitive, but it was something heavy to lift. The ancient Greeks who trained with stones may have longed for such equipment.

Courtesy of Dan Hayes

Joe Weider. c. 1999

He meanwhile continued to pore over bodybuilding magazines. Weider found the physique of a man named John Grimek to be particularly fascinating. Grimek, one of the Santa Monica Muscle Beach crew and a future US National Weightlifting champion, had what was quite possibly the best physique since Sandow. Though he was never able to match Sandow's definition, Grimek was certainly the most massive man of his era. Few would dispute that he had a far better build than Charles Atlas. His fame was also characteristic of that period in bodybuilding. Apart from Bernarr Macfadden's 1922 Perfectly-Developed Man contest, there had been no major bodybuilding competitions in the US, or anywhere, since 1905. Outstanding bodybuilders therefore became known for their physiques alone, not for titles won or rivals defeated. The magazines whose pages they graced therefore represented bodybuilding in its purest form, before a preoccupation with comparison, competition and winning—and the introduction of appearance-enhancing drugs—set it on its eventual course.

Early on Weider had a little success in building muscle, though he had nothing resembling the physiques of men in *Strength* or *Physical Culture*. He would not be the next Sandow; nor would he be the next Grimek, or even the next Atlas. His contribution to bodybuilding would therefore have to be in a capacity other than neo-Greek god. Yet none of this deterred him. One way or another, the young Weider told himself, he would make his mark. What turned out to be the most important event of his life—and one of the most important events in bodybuilding history—was the simple, private moment when he resolved to become a success. "I will make the Weider name famous," he declared at age 17.

John Grimek, c. 1940

Courtesy of Robert White

For the next few years however, Joe Weider remained a little-known figure, spending his time—according to later claims—lifting weights, gaining training expertise and being hounded for advice. None of those things equated to success, much less fame, but collectively they gave him an idea: he could make his mark by disseminating information. For a large part of bodybuilding's history, the primary means for accomplishing this was through magazines.

Weider's first major step toward real notoriety therefore came in 1940 when he started writing and printing, in a one-man-shop fashion, a periodical called *Your Physique*. The seven dollars he received in initial subscriptions became the beginning of what would eventually become a $350 million publishing empire. Though the establishment of a great magazine conglomerate was in itself was a stunning achievement, it would not have been enough to satisfy Weider. He saw magazines as a means by which to achieve far greater ends.

In the universe that lay beyond the bodybuilding microcosm, it was known that any entity able to control not only the greater flow of information but also the government that it reported on stood to wield supreme power. It was therefore reasonable that the same model should also apply to the world of muscle—except that it had not yet occurred to anyone that the world of muscle was something over which power could be wielded. In those days, bodybuilding was thought of as an individual self-improvement activity, and little else. How could something like that turn into an entity that would submit to domination? At the time, no answer existed. Nevertheless, the first part of the equation—the flow of information—had already begun.

As the only true source of information in bodybuilding, magazines could be the real source of power. Anyone able to establish dominance in the realm of publishing would hold a key with which other doors of prosperity could be opened. The bodybuilding world could be told which supplements they should buy and, critically, what an ideal physique should look like. In his time, Bernarr Macfadden had such dominance, though he was too concerned with bolstering the public's health and wellbeing to concentrate on building up and exploiting bodybuilding. He could have put his energies into hocking an endless line of muscle-building supplements, though that would have gone against his personal views on nutrition. He could have organized bodybuilders into a group over which he could wield supreme authority, but as a strong proponent of organized labor, he would have found the idea distasteful. He could have established numerous contests and created a body that would govern their actions, but he had no such inclination; nor, it seemed, did anyone else. It was therefore the case that 40 years after Eugene Sandow's first physique contests were held in the UK, there was no type of governing body or federation set up to oversee bodybuilding competitions. In 1939 all of that changed, and it gave Weider another idea.

Bodybuilding Takes Shape

As the 1930s drew to a close, the concept of bodybuilding had become known to a large part of the Western World. Through magazines like *Strength*, *Physical Culture* and *Strength and Health*, not to mention the pervasive Charles Atlas ads, the notion of using exercise as a deliberate means of creating a muscular appearance was out in the open. Overall however, there were still relatively few people who actually did it. Until the popularity of weight-training exercise matched the fame of the concept, an imbalance existed, one that would take more than four decades to correct. Like their predecessors, future weight-training enthusiasts and bodybuilders would be plucked from the ranks of the general population; but before that could happen on any appreciable scale, the public would need to be supplied with the inspiration, and the wherewithal, to make the transformation a reality. In time the public would get enough of both. The popularity of weight-training exercise would indeed one day match the fame of the concept. This change was owed largely to a series of events that originated at the end of the Great Depression.

For the people of that era, the image of smiling muscular men performing and playing on sunny California beaches was an interesting distraction; and despite the economic hard times through which average people suffered, those images somehow suggested that, through it all, maybe things weren't all *that* bad. For some people, photographs of supremely-developed young men, along with the spectacle and glory of the 1936 Berlin Olympics, did no less than give new perspective to post-Industrial Revolution human existence. Those athletes and bodybuilders possessed riches of another type; a type that cannot be bought, a type that is priceless. Their images reminded anyone who was able to make the connection that humans have but one true possession: their own bodies. Not only could an impressive physique not be bought, but it was also something that could be had almost for free. All that was needed was desire, hard work, dedication, time, and especially, the right parents.

Though few people knew it at the time, the great variable in bodybuilding success has always been the genetic makeup of its participants. Both before and after appearance-enhancing drugs made their way into the world of muscle, the final word on a man's success or failure building his physique belonged to no more than a mute and disinterested combination of atoms known as deoxyribonucleic acid, or DNA. A highly complex biological molecule which was completely unknown until 1928, DNA contains the complete genetic instructions for any given organism, and determines every last one of its individual variable attributes.

DNA therefore plays a critical role in bodybuilding. Not only does it determine the shape of individual muscles, but it also establishes the number of muscle cells and, ultimately, the body's overall predisposition for muscular growth. Without the right genetic makeup—something that cannot be bought, begged, borrowed, stolen, taught, learned or in any way changed—the pursuit of bodybuilding will not yield much fruit. Certainly hard training, consistency and nutrition count for a lot, but the critical role of genetics has always made bodybuilding a luck-of-the-draw activity.

Considering the amount of muscle Eugen Sandow was able to pack on, despite relatively primitive training and with minimal equipment, he must be regarded as one of bodybuilding's genetic elite. Sandow attributed his physical proportions to a program of careful manipulation, of "sculpting" through exercise, much as Arnold Schwarzenegger did 80 years later in the film *Pumping Iron.* Those men probably knew that the actual relationship between exercise and muscle growth is far less artistic in nature, but it was in their interest to say otherwise.

The appearance of any muscle is determined, in advance, by its owner's genetic blueprint. Moreover, it is impossible to influence the shape of a muscle through exercise. It's possible in some instances to control the size of a particular muscle relative to the remainder of a physique, or even the size of *part* of a muscle[1]—but with few exceptions, these effects are subtle. Schwarzenegger likened the act of adding muscle to the technique of an artist whose medium is clay: to add muscle, you slap more on where it's needed. In practice however, building a muscular body more closely approximates pouring molten bronze into a mold: barring subtle amendment, the end result is largely predetermined.

Computer-generated image showing the molecular structure of DNA.

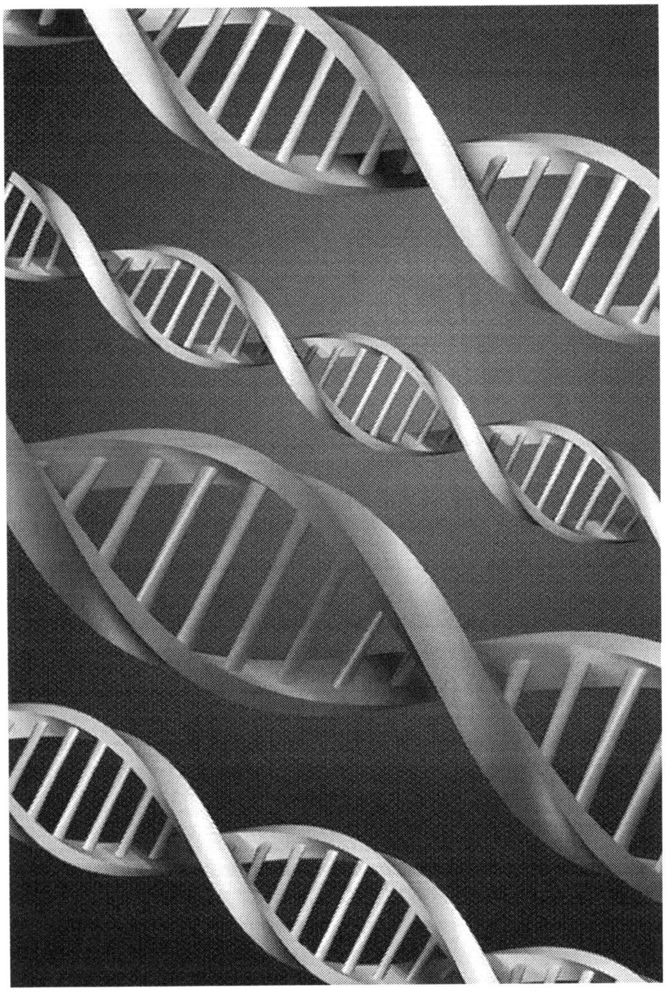

However, this mostly-unknown reality has always been a large part of bodybuilding's charm. Thanks to DNA, all men have a distinct appearance; when they build their muscles, that appearance becomes more unique. Of course muscular men look different from those with ordinary builds, but bodybuilders with equivalent muscularity also look more distinct from each other; the greater the build, the greater the dissimilarity. As bodybuilding took shape, it would become possible—and easy, actually—to identify particular champions simply by looking at their silhouettes. This gave building an added layer of character, which when combined with the personalities of the men behind the physiques, eventually helped push it closer to the long-sought-after realm of public acceptance.

* * * * *

When Sandow and Schwarzenegger boasted that their proportions were the result of careful crafting, they were simply taking more credit than they were due. The all-important role of genetic limitation was downplayed by Schwarzenegger and never even acknowledged by Sandow. According to both, superior character was the key to superior development. Theirs was therefore a simple message, one echoed by scores of champions throughout bodybuilding's history: if you want something badly enough, and you're willing to fully devote yourself to obtaining it, you cannot help but succeed. As much as any single factor, this idea helped draw men into bodybuilding. There was something about creating and owning a superbly muscular physique that enticed a small percentage of men to devote their lives to chasing that goal, even if they did not possess the biological means to reach it. This was as true in the 1930s as it is today. As such, participation in bodybuilding during that decade, though sparse, steadily inched upward.

[1] An example of this would be the pectoral muscles; the development of certain parts of it can be influenced by specific exercises.

Throughout most of the Depression and before, bodybuilding was a means of self-improvement. It was a pastime, a hobby, and for its most dedicated followers, a lifestyle. For it to grow however, it needed to be more. In the 40-odd years since bodybuilding's inception a few major physique contests had been arranged, their purpose being to determine which man had most successfully approximated the Classical Ideal. The Father of Physical Culture, Bernarr Macfadden, followed this idea to the letter. He arranged such a contest. Satisfied that Charles Atlas was a model of modern perfection and the owner of an ideal physique, Macfadden declared that all future contests would be redundant. Atlas would simply win them all, he thought. Moreover, if a competition were held in which Atlas was not present, it would be little more than a contest to pick second-best. Macfadden had no interest in such things.

The Father of Physical Culture was interested in promoting good health, not muscle-for-the-sake-of-muscle. What he and others of his time didn't realize was that good health and an impressive exterior are concepts not necessarily joined at the hip. Before bodybuilding's evolution had run its course, the two would separate from each other completely. Although that particular situation was still generations away, the psychology from which it developed was already in place. Even before potentially unhealthy aids made their way into muscle culture, the attitudes driving bodybuilding forward began to change. The bottom line was that a lot of men who got into bodybuilding weren't specifically doing it for their health. The success of Charles Atlas' marketing campaign should have made this obvious. His ads advertised muscles as a means by which to obtain power and sex, not well-being. The chord those ads struck resonated more deeply than anyone would have guessed.

Rather than supreme health, men of the 20th century's fourth decade were after big muscles. Inspired by the attention given to men in muscle magazines and on Muscle Beach, they also dreamt of getting similar praise. They yearned for their own means and venue to showcase their physiques. The time therefore appeared right to reintroduce bodybuilding contests.

Thanks to the handful of gigantic and already-legendary events staged by Sandow and Macfadden in decades past, in the 1930s the concept of muscle contests was well-known. However, until competitions were held regularly, until they were given an air of prestige and a pretext of legitimacy, bodybuilding would not be able to truly get off the ground. Bodybuilding of course did get off the ground; and like so many other things, the change that allowed this to happen was not owed to any radical restructuring, but rather to a simple philosophical shift. It therefore came to pass, right around the time of World War II, that bodybuilding witnessed the demise of one of its primary themes and the emergence of another.

The essence of both themes was brought to light through the actions of a single individual: a middle-aged weightlifting enthusiast named Bob Hoffman. Though he is not generally well-remembered in modern times, Hoffman was a figure central to one of bodybuilding's critical episodes. He owned the York Barbell Company, the only business of its type to survive the Depression. Thanks to increasing interest in weight training, York actually flourished during the period. Because of this, just about everyone who built a prize-winning physique over the next several decades did so by hoisting weights embossed with the York logo. This gave Hoffman considerable influence in the world of weightlifting.

Bob Hoffman. C. 1939

Courtesy of Robert White

He used this influence to take control of the US National Weightlifting Committee, a division of the powerful Amateur Athletic Union (AAU). Created in 1888 for the purpose of ensuring uniformity and standards in amateur athletics, the AAU also qualified American athletes for the Olympic Games.

It was within the context of Hoffman's control of AAU weightlifting that the millennia-old theme of form-versus-function came to a head. Until the last decade of the 19th century, form and function were one and the same. The appearance of human bodies more or less matched their function. Great physiques therefore belonged to those with elite physical purpose. Once bodybuilding came into being, all of that changed. Form and function could now be separately pursued.

Hoffman was a strong proponent of function. He was the most powerful figure in US weightlifting, and he intended to make it a world-beating force. In order to accomplish that, he needed to focus some of his energy on recruitment. He needed to bring new men into the sport, the more the better. Once weightlifting had a large new crop of hopefuls, the cream would naturally rise to the top, and Hoffman's AAU would have its corps of elite weightlifters.

Weightlifter statue.
York Barbell headquarters. c. 1960

Courtesy of Robert White

It was inevitable that Hoffman would dislike bodybuilding. In every bodybuilder he saw a weightlifter who was wasting his potential. He saw a man posing and flexing his muscles rather than putting them to good use. He saw self-absorption coming before national pride. If bodybuilding did not exist, Hoffman reasoned, there would be far more competitive weightlifters. As bodybuilding grew, so did his consternation. Irritating him further were the efforts of a gym owner from upstate New York named Johnny Hordines. In December of 1938 and again in June 1939, Hordines organized bodybuilding contests that were aimed at finding the best-built man in America. The winner of each carried home a trophy proclaiming him to be the owner of "America's Finest Physique." Compared to contests staged by Sandow and Macfadden, Hordines' were small-time and shoddy. They nevertheless had a significant effect on Bob Hoffman, his AAU, and the future of bodybuilding.

Hoffman correctly feared that bodybuilding was on the verge of reviving competition. If this were to happen, bodybuilding's popularity would receive a substantial boost. The monstrous contests of Sandow and Macfadden had proven this. Hoffman expected that soon even more men who should be weightlifters would be lured into what he thought were nothing more than male beauty pageants. He also had enough sense to know that they couldn't be stopped. Hoffman therefore quickly decided that if he couldn't beat them, he would join them; or more accurately, he would rule them. Fortunately for Hoffman, he was in a position to do so.

Since Hoffman knew that athletes of all sports want to compete in prestigious events endorsed by legitimate governing bodies, he decided to use the weightlifting arm of the AAU to sanction bodybuilding competitions. He didn't consider bodybuilding to be a sport, but in the spirit of furthering his own agenda—and the agenda of American weightlifting—he was willing to look past that. By 1939, the AAU was the pre-eminent governing body for American amateur sports. By making bodybuilding one of its featured events, the AAU was therefore also able to exert control over it. More specifically, Bob Hoffman was able to directly control it. Since he planned to stage contests under the prestigious AAU banner, fear became his primary weapon. If bodybuilders were to compete, they would have to do so in his contests. To do otherwise would get any competitor blackballed. All that remained was for Hoffman to begin staging contests.

He wasted little time. Less than a month after Hordines' second show, Hoffman's AAU put on its own competition, which took place immediately after the AAU Senior National Weightlifting Championships. The show would be called "America's Best Built Man." Since Hoffman had such serious concerns about the supposed problem of weightlifters defecting to bodybuilding, he came up with a solution: in order to participate in the evening's bodybuilding show, a contestant had to compete in the weightlifting contest that preceded it. Hoffman's plan therefore suggested to onlookers that muscles are okay to look at, but they must also serve a practical purpose. His own personal philosophy confirmed this, in no uncertain terms:

> For your own sake…learn to do something with your muscles.

At the event, pure weightlifters found themselves surrounded by a bevy of mainly disinterested competitors who were going through the motions, needlessly dragging out the lifting competition while waiting for the physique contest to get underway.

It was a novel attempt to keep men in competitive weightlifting, and an ultimately futile effort to keep form married to function. Considering that pure bodybuilding was by that point in the fifth decade of existence, the requirement seemed contrived and irrelevant. More importantly, the pairing of contests did not inspire bodybuilders to become weightlifters. As demonstrated by future champions Sergio Oliva and Jusup Wilcosz, the opposite was more likely to happen. The weightlifting requirement would soon be dropped and forgotten, and the AAU would begin sanctioning regular bodybuilding contests. Regardless, for now muscle shows would still be held at the end of weightlifting contests.

The establishment of regular, officially-sanctioned contests was one the most critical steps in the evolution of bodybuilding. For many men who took to iron, building a great physique was no longer the ultimate goal. From that point forward, bodybuilding, whether or not it was truly a sport, would at least be treated like one. It was an appealing concept. The clichéd thrill of victory awaited future champions, as did the agony of defeat for their rivals; and bodybuilding fans could now experience the excitement of watching their favorites go head-to-head. As big names came to light, big show-downs materialized. For all the interest generated by the giant contests of Sandow and Macfadden, those events were one-off spectacles; the ongoing physique contests of the AAU were something different.

Thus arose the second major theme in which Bob Hoffman had a pivotal role. Although the tale of bodybuilding is to a large degree told by the simple physical appearance of its leading men, the avenues by which those men emerged and gained fame ultimately became a more important part of the story: sanctioned contests, held at regular intervals, would attract far more fans; these contest would give rise to powerful governing bodies with even more powerful leaders; and critically, competition would give bodybuilders impetus to push the limits of muscularity, whatever the costs. All three elements would develop in concert over the next half-century, eventually culminating in an upheaval that produced the current state of bodybuilding. At the starting point of this transformation was Hoffman. Although he scorned bodybuilding, he saw value in controlling or at least capitalizing on it. In what became yet another of bodybuilding's great ironies, by doing so he set events in motion that would greatly elevate its fame.

At the end of his first sanctioned contest, Hoffman handed winner Roland Essmaker the immodest "Bob Hoffman" trophy; Essmaker flexed, the audience clapped, and the curtain closed. When the lights went up and the audience filed out, neither man imagined the importance of what had just transpired. Essmaker was thrilled to have won, while Hoffman was probably just happy to have gotten the show over with. Meanwhile, the world of bodybuilding was stirring. Excited that muscle competitions would now be treated like a full-fledged sport, it anxiously awaited the next AAU contest.

* * * * *

It was determined that the 1940 AAU Senior National Weightlifting Championships would be held in New York City. The location was an obvious choice, since New York would play host to

Courtesy of Robert White

Roland Essmaker. c. 1939.

the World's Fair at the same time—and it was reasonable to expect that large out-of-town crowds would account for extra ticket sales. The Best-Built Man contest would tag along and again take place after the weightlifting event. Meanwhile, bodybuilders were relieved to learn that the previous year's lifting requirement had been done away with. Weightlifters were happy as well, since there wouldn't be scores of disinterested competitors (bodybuilders) going through the motions, needlessly dragging out the lifting competition. Meanwhile, one other significant change had been made to the bodybuilding portion of the show.

The AAU is, and has always been, a sports organization. Because it sanctioned muscle contests, the AAU therefore officially recognized bodybuilding to be a sport. Yet in what may have been a partially cynical decision, the 1940 national championship contest borrowed its naming convention from female beauty pageants. The most famous such pageant was Ms. America—a contest that had been held annually since 1922 and which sought to find the most beautiful woman in the country. Although there were obvious differences between the two types of competitions, the purpose of a national bodybuilding championship was, in essence, to find her male counterpart.

To people like Bob Hoffman, bodybuilding was not much more than a male beauty contest. Those who have argued against its status as a sport have long invoked this comparison, asserting that, by definition, it is more accurately categorized as a pageant. A sport, they argue, is a measureable contest of physical skill, whereas bodybuilding is a subjective contest of physical appearance. Bodybuilding's detractors have naturally latched onto this argument, adding to it the opinion that any event that involves no more than posing the body is decidedly feminine. Hoffman may have had this in mind when he renamed the 1940 AAU national championship contest "Mr. America."

The use of "Mr." prefixes for bodybuilding titles may have been copied from beauty pageants, but this made little difference. Fans and competitors liked it, and the idea stuck. Here at long last was an award with a name that was short, memorable, catchy and instantly classic. Apart from that, *Mr. America* just seemed to fit. It sounded wholesome and manly, like a nickname bestowed upon some comic-book superhero. It was a tremendous marketing tool, and a small stroke of genius. From the moment of its inception, top bodybuilders coveted the title.

Leading that charge was John Grimek. Already a Muscle Beach fixture and magazine-cover regular, Grimek entered the first Mr. America and rolled to an easy victory. Apart from winning the overall title, Grimek walked away with all the "best body part" trophies—a collection of awards given to

John Grimek. c. 1940

Courtesy of Robert White

whichever men had the best arms, legs, chest, abdominals, and so forth. Other than picking a winner, the organizers of early contests were unsure about what exactly should transpire at muscle shows, or how the events could be made more interesting or exciting. Best body part awards seemed like a logical add-on. Unfortunately, sometimes the presentation of these awards elicited an opposite effect, like when a single competitor ended up claiming them all. At the 1940 Mr. America contest, John Grimek was that competitor. His was truly the greatest physique of the era, by a wide margin, so no one expected anything less.

Grimek was also one of the few bodybuilders with knowledge of how to strike effective poses—no doubt a perk of having posed alongside Muscle Beach experts and in front of cameras for magazine photo shoots. Since standard, "compulsory" poses had not yet been invented, most Mr. America entrants—some of whom had never seen a muscle contest—simply "winged" their presentations, making up poses on the spot. Few fared well.

The following year entrants took presentation more seriously; in fact a new set of judging criteria specified that they should. The 1941 Mr. America would be chosen by a panel of ten judges. Each competitor was to be assigned a numerical score, on a scale of 0 to 15 (with 15 being perfect), based on the following breakdown: five points for overall muscularity; five for proportion; three for posing; and two for "general appearance." The scores from all ten judges were then added together, making 150 a perfect overall score. Though this system would in time be replaced by others, its inclusion marked an important next step in the effort to give bodybuilding contests a pretext and appearance of legitimacy.

Once again, John Grimek walked away with the Mr. America title, scoring a near-perfect 146. Earning a second-place finish that was more distant than his 125-point score suggested was a man named Jules Bacon. Few were surprised by the outcome. Grimek was untouchable. Bob Hoffman was therefore faced with a situation similar to that of Bernarr Macfadden in 1922: one man threatened to dominate the top contests for years to come. Macfadden's decision to call off all future contests would not be imitated however, since there was no way the AAU was going to do the same. Bodybuilding had become too popular. Fans wanted to see muscle shows, and bodybuilders wanted to compete in them. Hoffman searched for a solution, though he may have overestimated the problem.

It was an age that did not embrace the idea of limiting victories. In 1941 Roosevelt began his third term as US President and the New York Yankees won their ninth World Series title. Yet in that same year, the AAU decided that for bodybuilding twice was too much. Out of fear that an endless string of Grimek victories would make the Mr. America contest boring and irrelevant, starting in 1942 past winners would be banned from entering. From the perspective of John Grimek, the message this decision sent was loud and clear: *you're too good to compete.* The Mr. America contest, the AAU declared, will not become the annual John Grimek show. History would therefore remember him as the only man to take home two Mr. America trophies.

Grimek had little choice but to shrug his shoulders and return to his weights. If nothing else, he was left with the satisfaction of having thoroughly trounced all rivals. Although he would remain a favorite subject of bodybuilding magazine photo spreads, it would be several years before Grimek stepped back onstage at a major bodybuilding competition. Nevertheless, those years would find him

John Grimek. c. 1940

Courtesy of Robert White

fully occupied; he was chosen to be the new senior editor of Bob Hoffman's *Strength & Health* magazine, with his off-hours spent keeping his body in top condition. Though he was perhaps the best-known bodybuilder of his era, John Grimek's legend had only yet begun to grow. His close association with Hoffman would factor into that legend.

Meanwhile, the clouds of war looming overseas finally let loose on American soil. After remaining officially neutral for more than two years, the United States marshaled its forces and sailed headlong into the torrent of destruction that soon became known as World War II. Although a significant number of bodybuilders answered the call of duty, a few notables stayed behind, including Grimek; a previous eye injured incurred while working at Bob Hoffman's York iron foundry kept the reigning Mr. America out of consideration for American military service. All told, more than ten million American men were conscripted from 1940-45. Nevertheless, for various reasons large numbers were not required to serve. There were therefore enough able bodies to fill the rosters of American and Nation League baseball teams, not to mention the Negro Leagues, the NFL, NHL and NBA.

In many cases sports teams would have to do without their stars. For example, Ted Williams, who will forever be remembered as one of baseball's all-time greats, was absent from the sport for a total of five years (including later service in the Korean War), due to his role as a naval aviator.

Bodybuilding found itself in a similar situation. Although allowing Grimek to continue his string of victories probably would have been a good idea—especially since later generations of fans found fascinating the winning streaks of future champions—there were enough quality physiques still available to put on a contest worthy of the title. The next two years saw the title pass to men who were previously runners-up to Grimek: Frank Leight in 1942, and Jules Bacon in'43. Leight's physique was somewhat reminiscent of the Charles Atlas era: he had an impressive upper body, with leg development that lagged far behind.

By all accounts the 1942 Mr. America contest should have been won by a man named Dan Lurie; however, judging "politics" almost certainly interceded. Lurie was a fantastic newcomer with excellent overall balance and complete development; in fact he was the winner of not only the Mr. America "Most Muscular Man" award, but also the majority of best-bodypart honors. Leight meanwhile had friends on the judging panel. By no means would this be the last time a bodybuilding contest's outcome was skewed by nepotism; in fact Jules Bacon's victory the very next year was said to have come at Lurie's expense. The explanation later given to Lurie was that Bacon was better-looking.

Courtesy of Robert White

left: Frank Leight. c. 1942
below: Jules Bacon. c. 1943

Courtesy of Robert White

above: Hoffman's Super Hi-Proteen. c. 1950
right: Dan Lurie. c. 1941

Courtesy of Robert White

Such were the goings-on of Bob Hoffman's AAU bodybuilding division. Hoffman had little respect for bodybuilding, so it's not surprising that he had little interest in ensuring fair judging decisions. He was far more interested in the growth of his York Barbell enterprise, and saw the Mr. America title as a reward for prominent members of his stable of competitors—bodybuilders who associated themselves with the York banner, endorsed its products, and even trained at Hoffman's gym. Lurie vocalized his dissatisfaction and before long found himself disqualified from competition. His bodybuilding-related business interests gave the AAU enough reason to take away Lurie's amateur status. The reality of the situation was that he was blackballed for opening his mouth.

Whereas Dan Lurie represented the state-of-the-art in early-1940s bodybuilding, Frank Leight's physique was a throwback to the preceding era. Many first and second-generation bodybuilders had legs that didn't look significantly different from those of ordinary athletes. Eugene Sandow was an exception to this rule; he set a standard that went unmatched until John Grimek appeared on the scene. Grimek had a lower body that was far superior to those of his competition, causing him in later times to be remembered as the world's first "modern" bodybuilder. His leg development was largely due to his background as an elite weightlifter. Although Lurie was a pure bodybuilder, his legs were well-developed, far more so than Leight.

Grimek, Lurie and virtually all bodybuilders that followed benefitted from constantly-improving training techniques and equipment. The first half of the 20th century saw a good deal of experimentation with weight training, mainly because the cause-and-effect relationship between exercise and muscular growth had not yet been fully explained. In other words, no one knew exactly why lifting weights caused muscles to grow. Without that knowledge, it was not possible to scientifically devise an ideal training regimen. Bodybuilders therefore relied on the methodology that had guided the art of alchemy for thousands of years: trial-and-error.

It was precisely that style of discovery that revealed, many hundreds of years ago, the optimal mixture of ingredients needed to produce gunpowder. Somehow, sometime around the year 1200 and probably somewhere in China, someone combined sulfur, charcoal and potassium nitrate, and set fire to it. The result was a loud bang and a bright flash of light. After the initial shock wore off, the accidental inventor got to work duplicating the feat—first once, then again, then over and over. Sometimes the explosions were bigger than others, and sometimes the ingredients just burned up quickly. Before long, simple experimentation revealed that a precise ratio of ingredients—10% sulfur, 15% charcoal and 75% potassium nitrate—consistently produced the most powerful blasts. It wasn't until the late 18th century than man knew exactly *why* gunpowder exploded, but this information hadn't been required by those intent on optimizing its effectiveness.

A similar situation existed in the field of bodybuilding. No one knew what biological processes took place between the time a weight was lifted and muscle grew—but everyone knew that one event led to the other. There was, however, one critical difference between the formulation of gunpowder and the development of an ideal weight-training methodology: muscular growth often takes place at a rate similar to the movement of glaciers. Whereas the ratio of ingredients in gunpowder could be mixed and tested, over and over, with instantaneous measureable results, a single bodybuilding training experiment could go on for weeks or even months before any appreciable results showed themselves.

Moreover, since the human body is an extremely complex biological organism, it is exceedingly difficult to control all the variables in any experiment on it—especially an experiment that lasts several months, in conditions that are nowhere near laboratory-like. There further existed the problem of finding a methodology that could work for everyone. Often the men who were approached to try new strategies or techniques were genetically superior and much more likely to benefit from any type of resistance training.

There were certainly experiments that yielded good results; their ideas were latched onto and worked into training routines. Because some results were so good, the methods that produced them were declared to be optimal—something that was not necessarily true. Strong differences of opinion about training emerged, heated arguments ensued, and the world of bodybuilding saw a significant source of infighting take shape. Many more would come. Meanwhile, the polarization of opinion over training was used to the advantage of magazines, personal trainers and even some gyms—all of whom advertised the superiority of their own systems. The general confusion that confronted bodybuilding newcomers was also used to the advantage of dietary supplement companies, who naturally declared their products to be the correct path to success.

For bodybuilding training, there existed a tendency to simply go with whatever worked. Nevertheless, one thing seemed certain: to build big muscles, it was important to lift heavy weights. John Grimek's lower body development drove home this point. Grimek came from a background of traditional weightlifting, where the objective was to lift the greatest amount of weight possible. Two of competitive weightlifting's three events[1]—the clean-and-jerk and snatch—required extraordinary leg strength. Apart from the competition lifts themselves, Grimek supplemented his training with movements specifically designed to increase leg strength. Foremost among these was the barbell squat, which even in modern times is considered to be the best overall lower-body strength-building exercise. Since strength and size rise hand-in-hand, it was no coincidence that Grimek had a foundation of good lower-body development. His combination of overall size and proportion, along with his style of training, helped to usher in a new era. Frank Leight, whose lower body was completely outclassed by Grimek, represented the end of another. From the mid-1940s onward, as competitors with good leg development hit stages and won titles, men like Leight began to be passed over.

The 1943 Mr. America title was won by Grimek's last runner up, Jules Bacon—a man with above-average lower-body development. Steve Stanko won the title in '44 with similar proportions. Like Grimek, Stanko built his foundation by training for competitive weightlifting. With his win a trend had officially begun.

Bodybuilders of the early 20th century had, by and large, not lived up to the standards set by Michelangelo or the Ancients. The 430-year-old ceiling of the Sistine Chapel featured male figures with leg development that easily surpassed Charles Atlas or Frank Leight. In an age of barbells and bodybuilding magazines this was inexcusable. Once John Grimek rose to prominence, things changed. Bodybuilders now had a better idea of what an ideal physique should look like and how one might be obtained. The 1945 Mr. America winner, a previously unknown bodybuilder named Clarence Ross, embodied this new knowledge. Ross, who became

[1]The third event was the overhead press, a lift that was later dropped from competition.

known to friends and fans alike as "Clancy" was one of the millions of Americans who didn't wait to be drafted after the Japanese attack on Pearl Harbor. He joined the US Army Air Force on Halloween in 1942 and was eventually stationed at the Las Vegas Army Airfield in Nevada. His non-duty hours were spent lifting weights.

His fellow servicemen watched in awe as Ross, still in his early 20s, forged one of the most remarkable physiques of his era. Upon learning that the 1945 Mr. America contest was going to be held in Los Angeles, he attacked the weights with even greater focus and vigor. A simple look in the mirror told Ross that he was better than Leight, Bacon or Stanko. Really, he was better than anyone, save perhaps Grimek himself. L.A. was but a single day's drive from Nevada. A confident Ross secured leave, packed a bag, and headed west.

The Mr. America judges and audience were as impressed as had been the slender airmen who had gathered to watch the young phenom train at the desert airbase. Ross won easily. Bodybuilding instantly gained a bright new star, and just as quickly John Grimek gained a legitimate rival. The two men had more-or-less equivalent size, though two primary factors distinguished them. Ross was about two inches taller, which gave him a slightly lankier appearance. Grimek packed the same amount of muscle on a smaller frame. Time and the emergence of numerous elite competitors would demonstrate that Grimek's height—a shade above five-foot-eight—was ideal for bodybuilding. Yet all was not in his favor. Ross had better definition.

Although a competitor's height could never be altered, there was no such fixed limitation on the clarity of his musculature. Though this fact was not yet widely appreciated, it was definition—the thin skin that allowed each muscle to be clearly visible—that truly set bodybuilders apart from other well-developed men. By the time Eugen Sandow shocked the world with the muscularity of his body, there were already a handful of larger strongmen on the scene. At least a few of them had bigger muscles than Sandow, yet none caused a stir remotely close to that of the transplanted Prussian. This had everything to do with Sandow's definition. The depth of the "cuts" separating his muscles made them look much bigger than those of typical strongmen, and the absence of fat around his waist gave him the greatest possible "V" taper. It also gave him the all-important favorable waist-to-limb ratio. A small waist with big limbs never fails to impress.

Sandow weighed no more than 180 pounds, but his definition made him look much bigger. Because most knew him only from carefully-posed photographs or dramatically-lit stage performances—both of which made his cuts look deeper and sharper—

right: Clancy Ross. c. 1947
below: Steve Stanko. c. 1944

Courtesy of Robert White

Courtesy of Robert White

any weight or measure given him seemed irrelevant. He appeared tall as the *David* statue and looked heavy as a lion. Sandow trained hard and ate a reasonable diet; he also had a genetic makeup that inclined him toward both muscularity and low body fat levels. The result was so sensational that an entirely new cultural phenomenon—one that over time involved millions of people and generated billions of dollars—was founded upon it.

At first things progressed slowly. Sandow's combination of size and definition may have been the cornerstone of bodybuilding, but decades went by before that combination was matched—and before physique competitors learned to fully exploit the variable nature of their own body fat levels. Following in the footsteps of Sandow, the first several generations of bodybuilders owed their definition to little more than genetics, training and overall good eating habits. None followed anything resembling a modern precontest diet; nor did any come close to the ultra-lean, contest-day look of modern bodybuilders.

In an age when an average member of the general population was far leaner than his modern-day counterpart, bodybuilders were likewise inclined toward a more defined year-round appearance. Before the advent of microwave ovens, convenience stores, fast food, huge portions, endless high-calorie snack foods, the proliferation of high-fructose corn syrup and large-scale food processing plants, the general population had little choice but to either follow a relatively healthy diet, or to just plain eat less, or both. Men who took the plunge into bodybuilding were therefore likely to be relatively lean from the get-go.

It could therefore be said that although the methods of early bodybuilders were by today's standards naïve, their results were entirely honest. The onstage appearance of bodybuilders of the 1950s and before differed little from how they looked the remainder of the year; and early bodybuilding presented a what-you-see-is-what-you-get product. Back then, there was no "offseason." This would contrast sharply with the modern era, in which bodybuilders on contest day often look nothing like their between-contest selves.

However honest the appearance of early bodybuilders may have been, none were lucky enough to possess a natural body fat level as low as Sandow's. John Grimek certainly wasn't; nor was Clancy Ross, though he was luckier than Grimek. The man who perhaps came closest was Armand Tanny, another member of the Santa Monica Muscle Beach crew. Like Ross, he served his country during WWII, though Tanny chose the Coast Guard. He largely disappeared from the bodybuilding scene during those years, returning in the late 1940s to capture a couple major titles. Like a few of the era's more defined musclemen, he had a slightly lanky appearance. Grimek was still the most massive of the current crop.

As the post-war era got underway and bodybuilders returned to civilian life and dedicated training, many more joined the scene. The culture was guided by figures who had set enduring standards—and who had, in a sense, carved themselves into stone. Not only did Eugen Sandow and John Grimek look like monuments hewn by the greatest hands of Antiquity or the Renaissance, but fans of bodybuilding looked upon them with reverence worthy of that comparison. Under the guidance of such images did bodybuilding move forward. Before long however, a new standard was set, and a fresh monument was presented to the world of bodybuilding. It came in the form of a young man destined to become its favorite son and most cherished example. First however, winds of change of another sort had begun to blow.

Armand Tanny. c. 1950

Courtesy of Robert White

When John Grimek won the Mr. America title, news of his victory was not broadcast for the world to hear; nor did newspapers find his triumph to be worthy of headlines. Jules Bacon and Frank Leight experienced a similar lack of publicity after their big wins. When Bernarr Macfadden's 1905 physique contest packed Madison Square Garden with 15,000 fans, newspapers covering the event focused almost entirely on Macfadden's war with moral crusader Anthony Comstock. In light of the event's supposedly obscene nature and Macfadden's recent arrest, its ability to draw a large crowd made the conflict that much more interesting—and newsworthy. Of far less significance was the fact that a huge number of fans had come to witness not a display of depravity and debasement but a physique contest. As far as newspapers were concerned, the name of the winner was worthy of little more than a footnote.

Great bodybuilders became famous, but that fame was mainly restricted to the small, insular world of bodybuilding. The vehicle they rode to this limited stardom was not mainstream press coverage, but muscle magazines. Virtually all fans bought them, and through their pages muscle stars became known. Photographs of top bodybuilders have always been the magazines' chief selling point. They gave fans simple images at which to marvel. Up-and-comers were meanwhile given inspiration.

From the moment Joe Weider opened his very first bodybuilding magazine, he was a fan. Shortly thereafter he became an up-and-comer. He didn't, however, remain one for long. By comparing himself to men like John Grimek and Jules Bacon, Weider astutely concluded that his physique would not be the means by which his vow to become famous would be fulfilled. Men like Grimek and Bacon—and really, countless others—were simply far better than him. Thus, rather than banging his head against a wall trying to become a celebrated muscleman, Weider modified his goal. He would make a splash in bodybuilding all right, but not by flexing his muscles. He would become famous by showcasing the bodies of others.

Bodybuilding was growing, and so were opportunities to profit from it. Though his brother Ben volunteered for the Canadian Army, Joe managed to avoid military service in World War II, concentrating instead on building his muscle business. First came his magazines. After its original, tenuous launch, by the end of the war Weider's *Your Physique* had grown and matured.

Shortly after the war and his brother's return to civilian life, the two teamed up to launch another magazine, this one called *Muscle Power*. Both were used to promote Weider's next venture, bodybuilding-related merchandise. The first step came during the war, when he partnered with Dan Lurie to launch a barbell company. The two later had a bad falling out, with Lurie alleging that Weider stabbed him in the back, but the venture's significance lay in the fact that Weider now had an up-and-running merchandizing arm. In time he would sell a variety of workout equipment and dietary supplements.

In five short years, Joe Weider had established a legitimate place in the world of bodybuilding magazines and training equipment. He might have happily concentrated on developing those ventures, and nothing more, had Bob Hoffman not shown such contempt for bodybuilding and arrogance in governing it. Hoffman's insistence on holding bodybuilding shows after weightlifting events, his apparent ability to pre-decide an event's outcome, and his power and willingness to blackball competitors didn't exactly win him the love of the at-large bodybuilding community. Hoffman didn't seem to care.

As far as Hoffman was concerned, the AAU was the 800-pound Gorilla of the bodybuilding world. No one dared challenge it. Since the AAU had taken bodybuilding under its wing and given it new life by sanctioning not only an annual national championship but local contests as well, all the while giving it an official "sport" label, anyone wanting to make a legitimate name for himself had to compete in its events. Doing otherwise would invite immediate blackballing. Likewise those intent on promoting contests all but needed to secure AAU sanction.

Bob Hoffman's actions and the way he wielded power were based on a combination of his own personal attitudes toward bodybuilding, and the AAU's weight as a governing body. In the world of American amateur sports, that weight was mighty. The federation had earned for itself, over several decades, respect and legitimacy. No American amateur sports federations came close to rivaling it. When Hoffman added bodybuilding contests to his weightlifting division, the remainder of the organization assumed those contests were run like any other sporting event. They apparently did not comprehend how entirely subjective its judging criteria was, or how this made it so easy to manipulate outcomes. Nor did they fully grasp that the man who oversaw its biggest competition had a vested interest in its outcome.

The AAU's policy was that it should never profit from contest proceeds—that any and all profits should be put back into the organization. Within his capacity as director of the bodybuilding division of the AAU, Bob Hoffman should have had no interest in exactly which men won its contests. His job was to ensure that competitions were carried out according to official AAU rules. However, since Hoffman had bodybuilding-related business interests outside the AAU, this complicated matters considerably. He owned the York Barbell Company. Though he disdained bodybuilders, he was happy to take their money. There was no better way to attract their attention and eventually their dollars than to have a growing stable of Mr. America winners, in his camp, endorsing his products. Because of this, men associated with York kept winning and men like Dan Lurie kept being told they were second-best. The question of whether York-endorsed bodybuilders actually deserved to win would not have interested Bob Hoffman. Fairness in bodybuilding contests was unimportant. Profits came before principles. Future bodybuilding leaders would learn this lesson well.

Before long another lesson was brought to light, one learned hard throughout history by men of power in countless fields of interest: Bob Hoffman took full advantage of his power, but he made the fatal error of overestimating its scope. The basis of his problem was that even though he considered bodybuilding to be a non-sport, he expected its participants to behave as if the opposite were true. Amateur athletes did not dare compete outside the AAU. Hoffman assumed the same would be true of those who competed in muscle contests.

Bodybuilding, however, was a very different animal; and regular, structured bodybuilding contests were a very new phenomenon. The men who competed in them wanted to display their physiques, best their rivals, bring home trophies and earn great titles. If an organization other than the AAU came along that could give them those things, especially if that organization specialized in and showed respect for bodybuilding, competitors would be willing to leave the AAU. Fans would follow. Bob Hoffman's threats of banishment would wither on the vine.

Joe Weider and his brother Ben were at least hoping this was the case when they announced, in late 1947, the formation of their new International Federation of Bodybuilders. Much like the AAU, the IFBB was going to be a governing body that sanctioned contests. The main differences were that the IFBB would govern bodybuilding only (there would be no weightlifting events or any other sports); there could now be a professional division; there would be no restriction on their ability to make profits[1]; and—critically—Bob Hoffman would be cut out of the picture.

Like Weider's magazines, the IFBB started small. Regardless, the Weider brothers' tireless efforts ensured its eventual growth. Hard work and cunning counted for much, but the IFBB had two other factors in its favor. Even in its formative years, Bob Hoffman recognized the threat the upstart federation posed to his domination of bodybuilding. He therefore used his York muscle magazines as a platform to lash out at the IFBB and the Weiders. Aspersions were cast, but with them came free publicity for the people he meant to discredit. Before long much of the bodybuilding community had at least heard of the IFBB.

The second factor was owed ultimately to how bodybuilding was perceived by the outside world. With few exceptions, no one other than its participants and fans considered bodybuilding to be a sport. This being the case, there were no bodybuilding events in the Olympics. The AAU was the avenue through which athletes had to qualify for the Olympics, ensuring their devotion to that organization, but to bodybuilders this was irrelevant. The absence of an Olympic lure naturally gave the AAU's grip on bodybuilding far less might. The Weiders understood and made note of this. The absence was used to their advantage, but within their minds a latent seed had been planted: they might one day have to address the same problem.

For the time being however, the Weiders had their hands full. Their self-appointed task was to manage and grow a business that consisted of magazines, merchandizing, and now, a competitive governing body. No one at the time realized it, maybe not even Joe Weider himself, but the critical pieces of a future empire were now in place. In time that empire would not only foster the growth of bodybuilding, but its leader would rightfully claim responsibility for bringing bodybuilding to its modern-day form.

[1]The IFBB later became a non-profit organization.

Although the International Federation of Bodybuilders had a grandiose name, at first it could do no better than stage local contests in Montreal and upstate New York. That would eventually change, and the organization would one day truly live up to its name, but for the moment the AAU was still the big kid on the block. Likewise, at least for the time being, the Mr. America title was bodybuilding's premier event. Its 1946 winner, Alan Stephan, embodied the spirit of the title like no man before.

Born Alan Steponitis, the Greek heritage evident in his name—combined with his finely-developed physique—was reason to think that perhaps one of his ancient ancestors had been the inspiration for a heroic sculpture. At the same time, Stephan's looks were "all-American": tall, with blonde hair, blue eyes, square jaw, a winning smile and overall good looks. He possessed a superior build: his six-foot frame gave his development a sleek, shapely look; topped with sharp definition and featuring a small waist, excellent back development and good overall balance, Stephan certainly looked like a Mr. America. His shortened name seemed to fit better too, since it had a less "ethnic" and more Anglo-Saxon ring to it. In the United States throughout much of the 20th century, this was desirable. Accordingly, the magazines ate him up. He soon appeared on the cover of more than 20.

Alan Stephan. c. 1946

Courtesy of Robert White

Sadly however, and like many top bodybuilders of his time, Alan Stephan would later be largely forgotten. Though the names of early champions would forever be held dear by fans with a special interest in its early eras, within the greater bodybuilding community most such men faded from memory. The timing of Stephan's reign may therefore appear doubly compromised, since it became so thoroughly eclipsed by that of his successor.

As sensational as the first generation of Mr. America victors may have been, the passage of time diluted their impact. The gradual rise in bodybuilding's popularity brought with it an expanding pool of men from which even greater physiques emerged; and thus, one by one, stars like Alan Stephan faded behind the ever-brightening light cast upon their heirs. Nevertheless, there have been a few notable exceptions to this rule: men with physiques that conformed to the standards of their eras, but who were—and continue to be—remembered with fondness and acclaim. A few of these men actually became genuinely famous. This was rare. Achieving legend status in bodybuilding and fame in the outside world required qualities that went beyond bicep measurements and body fat percentages.

A great physique could, by itself, only make a man so famous. After all, the eyes of the public were untrained. Before them, any top-notch bodybuilder would appear magnificent. He would grab their attention. The problem was holding onto it. That required something extra. This is an important reason why bodybuilding competition never achieved any sort of mainstream appeal: big muscles are visually striking, but most people can only look at them for so long before becoming bored.

The man who won the 1947 Mr. America contest had that something extra, and then some. From the moment he was handed the trophy, Steve Reeves became an icon of bodybuilding. By the time he retired, two decades later, he was world-famous. Reeves remains the most highly-revered figure of his era, his fame towering above all those who came before him—and above all those who took to iron in the age before Leopold Ruzicka's greatest scientific stride found its way into bodybuilding. Greats like

Courtesy of Robert White

Steve Reeves. c. 1947

Grimek, Ross, Lurie and Bacon, and even Sandow himself may have been the giants upon whose shoulders Reeves stood, but none have rivaled his eventual fame.

Reeves was born in Montana and lived there until he was ten, when his father was killed in an accident. His family shortly thereafter relocated to the San Francisco Bay Area. Before long the young Reeves discovered bodybuilding and began training at the now-legendary gym of Ed Yarick in Oakland. Small and spartan like most gyms of the time, Yarick's was, nevertheless, more than adequately equipped. It was also at one time home to a surprising number of top bodybuilders. In addition to Reeves, Clancy Ross and future Mr. America winners Jack Delinger and Roy Hilligenn also trained at Yarick's. Such was the model for successful gyms, especially in decades past: top bodybuilders gravitated to establishments that provided good equipment, camaraderie, and instructtion. York and Santa Monica were bodybuilding's opposite-coast epicenters. California now also had a second muscle factory. More were to follow, including the greatest of them all.

For the time being however, Oakland began to churn out top physiques. Proffering advice to his slew of champions was Yarick himself, a 6-foot-4, 250-pound behemoth who had won a few titles in his day. As an emerging trainer of champions, he knew he was onto something when a high school kid named Steve Reeves started lifting at his place. The teenage Reeves progressed quickly, and by the time he graduated high school in 1944 he was already in possession of a physique that would likely have won any local bodybuilding contest.

How Reeves would fare in competition would not quickly be known however, since able-bodied young men were still needed by the military. The 18-year-old Reeves enlisted in the Army, was assigned to the 25th Division, and before a year had passed was in the fight for Balete Pass in the Philippines. A bout with malaria soon forced him the front lines. By the time he fully recovered atom bombs had fallen on Japan and the war had ended. A stint with the island's occupying force followed, and by September of 1946 Reeves was release from service. The campaign to build his body resumed.

After several months of consistent stateside training, Reeves produced a physique that, by all accounts, could win the Mr. America title. He set his sights on that goal. The winners who came before him had their own, trademark strengths: Grimek with his mass; Bacon with his definition; and Stephan with his balance and all-American looks. Beginning with those men and continuing for the next 50 years, as the ranks of competitors grew and the development of champions reached new levels, each would become known for his own unique and characterizing features. Steve Reeves' strength was, quite simply, perfection. Reeves was

Yarick's Gym, c. 1947

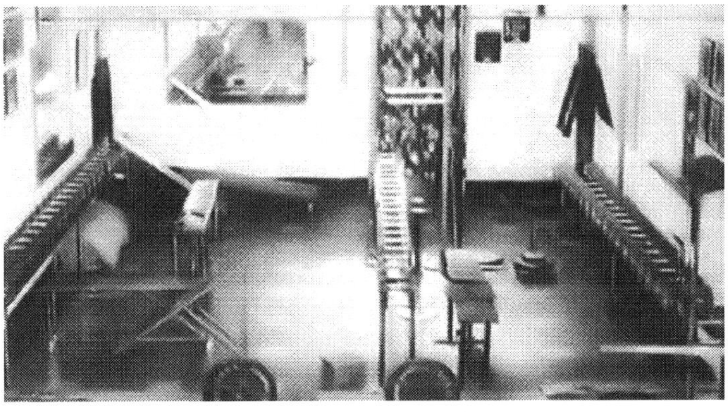

Steve Reeves. c. 1945. Official U.S. Army photo

close to perfect, anyway, or as close as anything yet seen in bodybuilding. Though he didn't have the size of Grimek, he was more sharply defined and certainly more shapely. This was what truly distinguished Reeves from his competitors. The lines of his musculature flowed together in almost artistic harmony. He was entirely pleasing to behold. Though Reeves was tall for a bodybuilder at six-foot-one, he didn't appear lanky or awkward. He was quite the opposite.

Eugen Sandow had once contrived to boast that the ideal, Classical proportions of his physique were made possible only by his thoughtful, skillful chiseling. Had that actually been true, then the materialization of Steve Reeves would have forced the world to rethink the aesthetic standards of the Ancients. Sandow was magnificent, but in the eyes of some, Reeves was a work of art—as if one of Michelangelo's Sistine Chapel Ignudi had been brought to life to walk amongst mortals. Yet Reeves was more muscular—and certainly more handsome—than any figure conceived for that ceiling. The world had been gazing up at that fresco for more than 430 years, at figures that were in some cases more muscular and shapely than even mid-20th century bodybuilders. The Ignudi were rendered as self-indulgent add-ons by an indentured artist who was gasping to express himself, and through them, the world came to know what Michelangelo felt an ideal male physique should look like. It was quite a vision. It was also, for his time, perhaps a little unrealistic. Those figures were objects of fantasy, male forms exaggerated to suit their creator's tastes. They also, and rather anachronistically, looked like the products of modern, dedicated weight training. The Ignudi had therefore set an unwitting standard—as if Michelangelo was challenging mankind to produce living men who rivaled his visions. Finally, in the personage of Steve Reeves, that challenge had been met.

The judges and audience of the 1947 Mr. America contest fully appreciated the striking new specimen standing before them. Reeves was declared winner. A flood of publicity followed, with his image appearing on the cover of no less than seven magazines before the year was out. Despite all the press and accolades however, Reeves was now just another man with a great physique who, by virtue of his Mr. America victory, was ineligible to compete at a high level in the AAU. This made for an unhappy arrangement. Fans naturally disliked the idea that great physiques were showcased at the Mr. America contest and then shelved. They clamored for more contests and greater titles. Before long they were obliged.

There had already been a few unsanctioned "Most Muscular Man in America" contests, a few having been won by Dan Lurie. A challenge by Lurie had even prompted York favorite John Grimek to enter the show in 1946. Those events existed in the shadow of the sanctioned and established Mr. America contests however, and are therefore today mainly forgotten. They also illustrated a simple truth: to achieve lasting notoriety, bodybuilding contests required a strong governing body and a catchy name. The fledgling IFBB, which had recently begun holding competitions, would learn this lesson well.

Other contest organizers already knew these things. Such was the case with a brand-new federation called the National Amateur Bodybuilding Association. Whereas the IFBB started small and ramped up, the NABBA burst onto the competition scene in grand fashion. The new federation was in fact initially created to fulfill a single, all-or-nothing purpose: in London, at the same time as that city's 1948 World's Fair, it would stage a first-ever world championship bodybuilding contest. Considering the success that physique displays and contests enjoyed when staged in or near previous World's Fair events, and taking into account that the competition would be put on by an important-sounding new organization, its success was virtually assured. All it needed was a title.

It was decided that the competition would be called "Mr. Universe." Selecting something like "NABBA World Championships" would have been perhaps more appropriate, probably more accurate and certainly less cartoonish, but none of that mattered—not when mister-prefixed contests had been so successful. Also, like Mr. America, *Mr. Universe* had a nice ring to it, certainly nicer than the other obvious choice, Mr. World. The latter would nevertheless also be stamped across numerous trophy nameplates as time wore on and competition spread. For now though, there was no greater title on planet Earth than Mr. Universe.

Fans were eager to see which man truly had the best physique on the planet, and one look at the first Mr. Universe lineup card guaranteed they wouldn't walk away disappointed. John Grimek and Steve Reeves, the first and most recent Mr. America winners—the two greatest bodybuilders of the era—both made the trip from the United States to vie for the title.

In the event, entrants were divided into four height classes, with Reeves and Grimek easily winning the tall and medium categories respectively. When class winners were placed side-by-side however, the judges found themselves faced with a quandary—one that would be revisited on countless occasions, in myriad contests, from that point until the dawn of the new millennium. It was a dilemma that would eventually determine the shape and character of bodybuilding itself. Here the judges were faced with two great yet entirely distinct body types. Grimek was massive, stocky, powerful-looking and impressive. Reeves, though not as big, was muscular, shapely, handsome and pleasing. The inaugural Mr. Universe contest was therefore a battle not only between those two physiques, but what each represented. It was beast versus beauty. The judges couldn't bring themselves to deny either, and the contest was determined to be a draw. This, however, would not do. The purpose of competition is to pick a winner. This being the case, befuddled judges needed to quickly figure out some way of breaking the tie. The problem was that early bodybuilding judging systems made no such provisions. Bodybuilding, after all, is a subjective contest of physical appearance. There was certainly a lot of flexing and posing, but unlike competitive sports there was no overtime, extra innings or shootouts.

Legend has it that one of the judges, none other than AAU bodybuilding chief Bob Hoffman, came up with an idea: the Mr. Universe trophy would be given to whichever man could give a better display of gymnastics. As his employer, sponsor and friend, Hoffman was well aware of Grimek's ability to execute gymnastic moves. Reeves on the other hand was not prepared. He graciously accepted defeat, and offered praise for the already near-legendary Grimek—who, in addition to all his other accomplishments, had now captured the world's greatest title.

Hoffman meanwhile was doubly, smugly satisfied: Not only had one of his York men won, but his "learn to do something with your muscles" mantra was reinforced. He was able to successfully sneak a contest of physical skill into a bodybuilding competition. Though this is a now-famous episode, whether the contest was actually decided in that manner has been disputed. Whatever the case, Grimek walked away the victor.

The significance of 1948 NABBA Mr. Universe contest was sevenfold: it was the first offering of a new federation; it enhanced the legend of John Grimek; it gave Steve Reeves greater fame; it started the trend of world-championship bodybuilding contests; it exposed, through its supposedly tied result, a weakness in judging conventions; it reminded fans that favoritism could influence outcomes; and it was the first major confrontation of beauty versus beast.

Reeves was undeterred. An unaffiliated Mr. World contest had been scheduled for the following week in Cannes, France. Reeves hopped the Channel, found himself among a field of competitors that had no John Grimek, and easily triumphed. The two would cross paths again the following year, at the new Mr. USA contest. Once more Grimek came out on top. This time the decision was made easier by precedent; if two competitors were closely matched and it was difficult for judges to choose a winner between them, they could always defer to past results. Precedent would continue to affect contest outcomes all the way through to modern times.

Reeves gave the Mr. Universe title a final go in 1950, and just like the '49 Mr. World event, the absence of Grimek assured his victory. It wasn't necessarily easy going however, because a sensational British newcomer named Reg Park had also entered the show. The 22-year-old Park had a powerful, thickly-developed physique like Grimek but was nearly a half-foot taller; he was also shapelier and more sharply-defined. In the end though it was Reeves' complete package and awe-inspiring lines—he had by then earned for himself the nickname "Mr. Everything"—that carried him to victory. Having now ascended bodybuilding's highest peak, he set his sights on greater challenges.

The potential star-power of Steve Reeves was simply too great to be contained by the tiny world of bodybuilding, and he knew it. Reeves had a head-turning, traffic-stopping physique. He also had movie-star good looks. He therefore hung up his posing suit and joined the Screen Actors Guild. Though his acting career started slowly, before the end of the decade he found his niche and path to stardom. Sword-and-sandal movies became popular in the late 1950s, and like all movies, it was important that the right people be cast for lead roles. As best they could, producers sought men who at least approximately resembled Greek and Roman heroic sculptures.

The mythological figure Hercules was in particular deserving of silver-screen portrayal, although casting for the role presented the obvious problem of finding someone who looked the part. After all, Hercules was the world's strongest man. A believable portrayal required not only bulging muscles but height. In Reeves, Italian director Pietro Francisci found an easy answer. Though in only two of his 18 films would Steve Reeves portray Hercules, it was his defining role. To action-movie aficionados of the late '50s, Reeves *was* Hercules. His voice was dubbed into Italian and then re-dubbed for English-language release, but that mattered little. For his efforts he became the most highly-paid actor in Europe.

Steve Reeves. c. 1949

Courtesy of Robert White

It was in a way fitting that the most modern artistic medium, film, should pay homage to Classical heroes—the same heroes who were glorified by the ancient medium of sculpture—by using men who were collectively inspired by those figures. It would have been even more fitting had the movies actually been good, which they weren't, but a tribute to the Ancients had been made nonetheless. More importantly, muscle had once more found its way into the mainstream. Like Charles Atlas before him, Steve Reeves put bodybuilding into the public eye. Yet there was one major difference: whereas Atlas only advertised the path to muscularity, Reeves was a living, breathing result.

* * * * *

The next phase of bodybuilding was characterized by the rise of new governing bodies, and along with them, new national and world-championship level contests. The period also witnessed the invention of professional competitions—contests that offered small cash prizes in addition to trophies and titles. Against this backdrop the next generation of bodybuilders would emerge: men who would form a bridge between bodybuilding's early years and its period of consolidation; between those who copied the poses of ancient sculptures, their modesty at times enforced only by simple fig leafs, and their next-generation counterparts, men distinguished by great strides in muscular mass and the standard poses that showcased them.

One of the most important figures of the period was 1955 NABBA Mr. Universe Mickey Hargitay. A Hungarian guerilla fighter during WWII, Hargitay moved to the United States after the war and worked as a plumber and carpenter. He also performed in an acrobatic act with his wife. His transition to bodybuilding began the moment he first saw a photograph of Steve Reeves. Hargitay picked up weights, progressed quickly, and before long won bodybuilding's most coveted title. His contribution to bodybuilding mainly came after that. He joined he joined Mae West's New York muscle-man revue and there met Hollywood starlet Jayne

Mansfield. A romance quickly ensued.

Mansfield wanted Hargitay to star in movies alongside her. Thanks to her status as a major Hollywood actress and immense pull with studio executives, this happened quickly. In 1957 Hargitay appeared in *Will Success Spoil Rock Hunter?* alongside Mansfield and Tony Randall. Another film followed that year, and in 1958 Hargitay, now divorced from his wife, married Mansfield. He starred in another 12 films over the following decade and 18 more overall. Though never a big star, through movies he was nevertheless able to notch higher the public's consciousness of bodybuilding. His marriage to the ill-fated Mansfield took it higher still. When Arnold Schwarzenegger portrayed Hargitay in the 1980 made-for-TV movie *The Jayne Mansfield Story*, his legacy was assured.

Mickey Hargitay's competitive bodybuilding legacy would nevertheless fall under the shadow of his peers. Foremost among this group was Reg Park. It was appropriate that the departure of John Grimek and Steve Reeves—in 1949 and '50 respectively—should leave Park in its wake, because he seemed so much to be a combination of the two. Park had Reeves' height but Grimek's thickness; likewise his shape was better than Grimek but not quite on par with Reeves. Once he had reached top form, in Park bodybuilding witnessed its first truly herculean physique; in a side-by-side comparison, he would have dwarfed Sandow. Feats of strength reinforced his image as a Hercules reincarnate, while helping—rather ironically—to separate bodybuilding even further from the sport of weightlifting.

Traditional, Olympic weightlifting movements—the clean-and-jerk and snatch—had over the years become less and less appealing to pure bodybuilders, who naturally inclined themselves toward exercises that more directly worked target muscles. Although the clean-and-jerk utilizes just about every skeletal muscle in the human body, its successful execution does not work any single muscle or muscle group as thoroughly as a specifically-designed bodybuilding exercise. The lift requires synergy—a special combination of both strength and skill—but it's far from ideal for bodybuilding. The physiques of a few Olympic weightlifting greats, for example legendary Soviet world champion Vasiliy Alekseyev, testify to this.

Gradually the shortcomings of Olympic lifting were realized, and bench presses, barbell rows, myriad cable exercises, and scores of other movements replaced it. American weightlifting's biggest advocate, Bob Hoffman, would see his relevance eventually dissolve; and with that, Olympic lifting movements would vanish completely from bodybuilding workouts. There were simply better ways to create a muscular appearance. In bodybuilding, appearance was the name of the game.

left: Reg Park. c. 1950
below: Vasiliy Alekseyev. c. 1972

Courtesy of Robert White

Getty Images

Reg Park didn't use old-style lifts or Olympic weightlifting movements. He favored more modern exercises like the bench press, and was by various accounts the first bodybuilder to lift 500 pounds in the movement. Feats like that enhanced both his image and physique, and the example he set was seized upon by generations to come: using modern exercises and heavy weights, he set a new standard for muscular mass. In 1951 Park took another shot at the Mr. Universe title. This time he would not be denied. Trophy in hand, he ascended the platform's top tier, flexed, smiled, waved and posed for a few pictures. Satisfied, he returned to his transplanted home of South Africa and disappeared from the world of competitive bodybuilding. He would be back, but not before several years had passed.

In modern times Reg Park is seen as not only an all-time great, but also as a transitional figure. His muscular mass and proportions famously bridged the gap between bodybuilding's two most disparate eras. Unbeknownst to bodybuilders of the early 1950s, the final decade of bodybuilding's first major period was upon them. A wave of scientific progress, one that would end the current era and usher in the next, had been steadily building. Once the wave broke upon American shores, bodybuilding would be changed forever.

Meanwhile, the IFBB, the young federation destined to ride that wave to fame, acclaim and infamy, was picking up steam. Its next order of business was to compete in the most direct way possible with the AAU. In 1949 it created its own national championship and—just like the AAU—called it "Mr. America." Alan Stephan entered and won, thus becoming the only man to win the title in both federations. Because he competed in the rogue IFBB, whose contests were all categorized by Bob Hoffman as being "professional," Stephan was banned from all future AAU contests. The ban was meaningless however, since his 1946 victory at the AAU Mr. America essentially created the same effect. The IFBB didn't hold the Mr. America contest the following year, staging instead a similar contest called "Best Developed Athlete in America." Reg Park won it as a prelude to his Mr. Universe triumph. The IFBB Mr. America contest would in fact be absent until 1959, as the Weiders opted to promote other titles instead.

More and more, bodybuilding was becoming its own, freestanding entity. The century-old "Physical Culture" label, still often used in the 1950s to describe bodybuilding, was falling into disuse. More importantly, it was losing meaning and relevance. The term was invented during the industrial revolution to describe efforts to steer an increasingly sedentary population toward deliberate exercise and healthy living. Just before the turn of the 20th century, Physical Culture absorbed bodybuilding, touted it and put it on display. Physical Culture made bodybuilding its face.

As the years passed, bodybuilding became more specialized. Its focus became more narrow. It began to separate itself from the pretense of ideal, healthy living. Physical Culture was a somewhat vague term anyway; it was based on broad concepts; its meaning was subject to interpretation; it required explanation; and ultimately, it meant different thing to different people. "Body building" on the other hand was self-explanatory and specific. Its purpose was building the body—period. The symbolism of the change was significant. In the most concise manner possible, the simple replacement of the old term Physical Culture by a new one, bodybuilding, told the tale of how the world of muscle changed during the 20th century.

The world of muscle was ready to accept this change. This should have been anticipated. After all, the writing was on the wall—or, more accurately, it was in the pages of magazines and comic books. The already decades-old and successful Charles Atlas ads embodied the spirit of the transformation. Those ads didn't advertise healthy living. They appealed to the longing of males to assert dominance. This has always been an important factor driving the popularity of bodybuilding onward and upward. Men often perceive physical stature by itself to be a category of male competition. A bodybuilding contest is simply a literal and direct representation of that competition. In fairness, there have always been men who get into bodybuilding for purely aesthetic reasons, who view contests merely as a means for showcasing their physiques. Yet regardless of what was driving individuals to build and display large muscles, the healthy-living emphasis of Physical Culture was gradually becoming peripheral to what was becoming "hardcore" bodybuilding.

* * * * *

The rise of new federations dedicated only to bodybuilding more than chafed Bob Hoffman. In true last-stand fashion, the AAU attempted once more to steer bodybuilders away from muscle-for-the-sake-of-muscle. The greatest weapon in Hoffman's arsenal was the still-popular Mr. America contest, which in 1957 implemented new rules designed to draw emphasis away from pure muscle and toward the well-rounded iron athlete. According to the rules, a muscular physique was still critically important; however, an ideal competitor should have should have athletic ability and a nice general appearance. "Athletic ability" was determined by a competitor's performance in the three Olympic lifts, something which obviously favored men with a background in competitive weightlifting.

The general-appearance factor meanwhile became the focal point of future consternation and protest. Because the criterion was so subjective and loosely-defined, it appeared that much room had been left for judges to exercise favoritism; and it's hard to argue that appearances did not deceive. The requirement gave event officials leeway to reward or exclude whomever the AAU wanted. Favoritism in the first few decades of the organization's Mr. America contest extended to York favorites and, apparently, to men of the right race. To a generation that had just witnessed the abolishment of "colored" units in the United States military, and that had recently seen the first black man in a Major League Baseball game, it was little wonder that all prior bodybuilding greats had been white.

Bob Hoffman was called a racist. This was not without warrant. Although his magazines featured black bodybuilders, his contests were obviously not ready to reward them; and Hoffman's own words belied his true world view. He went on record calling Joe Weider a "kike" (something for which he shortly thereafter apologized), and he was accused of uttering far more harsh epithets off-record. Yet, as they say, the proof was in the pudding: it was the placement of black bodybuilders in AAU shows that drew the greatest and longest-lasting ire. Although blacks would come close to dominating bodybuilding in later eras,[1] the Mr. America title was not awarded to a black competitor until 1970, when Chris Dickerson finally broke through.

Jackie Robinson. He broke the Major League Baseball "color barrier" in 1947. The AAU's Mr. America color barrier was broken 23 years later.

Getty Images

Back in 1957 however, Hoffman thought, or hoped, his rule changes could stem the tide of pure bodybuilding. The changes reflected his personal philosophy and attitudes about muscle contests and their competitors: apart from a muscular build and athletic prowess, a Mr. America winner should also have strong morals, an education, an ability to speak publicly, and a friendly and congenial demeanor. With such criteria, the Mr. America now more than ever resembled a beauty pageant. The contest also seemed more contrived, and more removed, from what competitors and fans really wanted: an updated version of the very thing that propelled Sandow to great fame. That thing was the spectacle of muscular men, flexing and posing. As future bodybuilding leaders would find out, not much else was needed or wanted. The new AAU criteria, in the end, amounted to little more than a failed attempt to obstruct something that now couldn't be stopped. Bodybuilding—pure, muscle-for-sake-of-muscle bodybuilding—was here to stay. It was also ready to grow.

It was to be expected that new federations which did nothing but stage pure bodybuilding contests would begin to draw competitors away from the AAU. Apart from the simpler and more desirable competition format of the new federations, bodybuilders weren't forced to become proficient in Olympic lifts. This was just as well. Those movements were obsolete and irrelevant. In appearance and practice weightlifting looked as though it was about to lose whatever influence it once wielded over bodybuilding. However, before long and in a way that no one expected, that situation would change dramatically.

[1]Black competitors won 16 of 22 Mr. Olympia titles from 1984-2005.

Leopold Ruzicka, a man scarcely known to the microcosm of beachside musclemen and squabbling muscle-contest promoters, was nevertheless about to become one of that world's most important historical figures. His 1935 synthesis of testosterone was recognized by the scientific community as something from which a number of practical applications could derive; and to that end, a flood of research was conducted. The research first showed that testosterone therapy amplified certain male traits. It had been known for ages that males exhibit an ability to increase muscular size that far exceeds that of females. Testosterone was strongly suspected to have anabolic (muscle-building) qualities, and it was therefore expected that testosterone injections would produce an increase in the lean body mass of test subjects. Research confirmed the suspicion.

Scientists then realized that chemical manipulation of the testosterone molecule could produce slightly different compounds—testosterone analogues, otherwise known as anabolic steroids—that generated effects which were different from simple testosterone. For example, it was noticed that there was a variance in the ratio of anabolic to androgenic (sex-related) effects when various testosterone analogues were compared. Androgenic effects included things like increased libido, body hair growth and subcutaneous water retention, to name a few. The pharmaceutical firms Searle and Ciba invested heavily in testosterone-derivative research, and by 1954 had reportedly produced thousands of such chemicals. Before long a number of brand-name anabolic steroids had been produced, in both oral and injectable forms.

1954 was also the year that anabolic steroids came crashing into the world of competitive sports. At that year's World Weightlifting Championships in Vienna, the Soviet team completely dominated the event. This naturally piqued the interest of American team physician John Ziegler, who discovered the Soviets' secret: they had been receiving injections of a testosterone derivative. After the event Ziegler returned to the United States, armed not only with that revelation, but with a resolve to close the gap between American weightlifters and the Soviet juggernaut that had just trounced them. Before long the team he advised was on board. They blew past their fellow countrymen and offered a legitimate challenge to Soviet supremacy.

Anabolic steroids, when combined with hard training, good nutrition and adequate recovery, allowed the muscles of these weightlifters to become much stronger than normal. Their muscles were stronger because they were bigger. It was therefore only a matter of time before bodybuilders, some of whom were still also weightlifters, became privy to this information. Bodybuilders eventually would have discovered anabolic steroids on their own; regardless, competitive weightlifting can be credited for introducing the two. To some, it was a marriage made in heaven; to others, hell was a better name. Nevertheless, and independent of all perception, bodybuilding was about to change forever.

The Golden Age

According to its most basic definition, bodybuilding is the act of deliberately increasing the size of one's muscles for aesthetic purposes. The term also refers to competitions where people who pursue this activity are visually compared to one another. Importantly however, bodybuilding is a term used to describe the culture that bases its identity on both things. Since bodybuilding is a culture (or perhaps more accurately, a *subculture*[1]), cultural measures and conventions can be, and have been, applied to it. One such convention is the practice of dividing its historical timeline into distinct eras or ages. This practice has been strongly warranted in bodybuilding's case, since the world of muscle has undergone a number of significant changes from the moment of its inception through to modern times. The gaps between these changes form its eras.

Some of these eras are simply named for the decades in which their primary events transpired, the 1980s being one of the more prominent examples. Others got their names from the era's position in the greater timeline of bodybuilding. For example, the first few decades of the 20th century are often referred to simply as "the early years," while the final decades and beyond have collectively earned an equally simple and informal title: the modern era.

In the history of bodybuilding, one era stands above all others; not only is it the most distinguishable of various periods, but it is perhaps also the most fondly remembered. Within its years were witnessed the emergence of men whose physiques set enduring standards; the establishment of contests that became the launching-points of their rise to prominence; the creation of bona fide bodybuilding celebrities; the ascent of bodybuilding as a whole to greater levels of fame; and behind it all, the end-game struggle for control of the industry that meant to capitalize on that fame. The men who became its principle figures didn't know it at the time, but they were living in the Golden Age of Bodybuilding.

In any culture, the term "golden age" is bestowed retroactively on years that are perceived to be its high point—the period when the culture's achievements and advancements reach their greatest level. If the timeline of those achievements could be plotted on a graph, the golden age might appear as the top of a bell curve. At the same time, bodybuilding's own version of a golden age, the period that began sometime around the mid-1960s and lasted until the end of the following decade, did not produce the most muscular physiques ever witnessed. In fact the bodybuilders of that era were generally smaller and less muscular than their latter-day counterparts. They were, nevertheless, extraordinarily developed—and in the minds of some, ideally so.

On the surface, it's tempting to say that the great physiques of the '60s and '70s by themselves distinguished the era and made it golden; or that when compared to previous eras, the sheer number of these men, all rising to prominence within a relatively short period of time, gave it its enduring overall character. Perhaps of equal importance however were the personalities behind the physiques.

It was in the '60s that bodybuilding finally, and firmly, planted its banner on the west coast of the United States, not far from storied Muscle Beach. The group that rallied beneath it would be remembered by future generations as being at once collectively elite and exclusive, yet charming and sincere. From this assemblage prominent individuals arose and distinguished themselves. Critically, all of this came to light in the images of a now-famous film that not only documented the group but marked the high point of the era. The 1977 release of *Pumping Iron* not only assured the era's golden status; it gave the world its first up-close look into the world of bodybuilding. Its impact was nearly beyond measure, although the growth of bodybuilding in the decade-plus after its release testified to its value.

[1]A subculture is a culture-within-a-culture.

Before all of this could happen however, the world of muscle needed to embark upon its next great evolutionary step.

It was upon the shoulders of its current crop of giants that bodybuilding advanced into its Golden Age. It had been several years since Steve Reeves graduated to the world of acting, but his 1958 trademark role in *Hercules* put him on the silver screen, front and center, as its lead. The film was no *Ben Hur*, but its target audience didn't care. Here was a real-life bodybuilder, one of the greatest ever, wowing audiences with a physique worthy of the role. Unlike previous men who portrayed the demigod, Reeves' on-screen feats of strength looked plausible.

The man who would eventually succeed Reeves as the silver-screen Hercules, Reg Park, returned to competition the same year and won the NABBA Professional Mr. Universe contest. In 1960 the title went to Paul Wynter, a black competitor from the West Indies. Unlike the AAU prior to 1970, the NABBA was willing to hand top awards to non-white competitors. The IFBB, which more or less had similar policies of equality, quickly made plans to hold its own amateur version of the contest. In 1959, the first year of its existence, Eddie Sylvestre was declared winner. In 1960 the title was captured by Chuck Sipes, another of the greats who rose to prominence just prior to the Golden Age and achieved greater fame within it.

After Reeves and Park, the most important and influential bodybuilder of the period between WWII and the mid-'60s was Bill Pearl. In the single year of 1953, Pearl won the Mr. California, AAU Mr. America, and NABBA amateur Mr. Universe titles. He won the tall class of the '56 NABBA Professional Mr. Universe, and after a five-year competitive absence, captured the overall title in '61. Unlike competitors of later eras, Pearl didn't owe his fame to any lengthy string of victories. Reeves and Grimek were proof that trophy-hoarding added little to a bodybuilder's legacy, and Pearl was no different. He stepped onstage enough to make his mark, the imprint of which did no less than usher in a new era.

Paul Wynter. c. 1961

Courtesy of Robert White

Courtesy of Michael Newman

Bill Pearl. c. 1962

At his peak, Bill Pearl had a physique much like that of John Grimek, only bigger, thicker, and with limbs that were unequaled. He did no less than set new standards in arm and leg development. In modern terms, his muscles were full and round, and his thighs presented one of the earliest examples of impressive outer sweep. Yet it was his arms that generated the most attention. Although it's common to think of upper-arm size as being dependent upon the biceps, it's actually the triceps that account for the large majority of that region's mass. The upper arms of Bill Pearl drove this lesson home, thanks largely to his trademark, exceedingly well-developed triceps.

Pearl's overall proportions compared favorably with Reg Park, though the latter's graduation to other pursuits made comparisons like this moot.

Courtesy of Robert White

Reg Park. c. 1958

Park was tall and handsome; following Steve Reeves' example in the most literal sense, he retired from competition to pursue a career in acting and landed several lead roles in Hercules movies. Park came out of competitive retirement twice, in 1965 and 1970, and although he was in championship-caliber shape, he was looked upon more as a pillar of legend than as a member of the new wave of bodybuilding stars. It thus came to pass that Park and Pearl—along with giants of the recent past, Grimek and Reeves—helped to inspire the great competitors who soon followed.

That group of newcomers went on to form the nucleus of bodybuilding's Golden Age. The high point of muscle culture was approaching. Accordingly—or, depending upon whom is asked, ironically—this was also the era that witnessed the widespread adoption of anabolic steroids by bodybuilders. From the mid-1960s moving forward, virtually all world-class competitors took them. To do otherwise was to be passed by. Steroids therefore became a necessary component of success. Understandably however, the exact date of their introduction to bodybuilding and the identities of their first users remain unclear.

There has always been a veil of secrecy surrounding use of appearance-enhancing drugs, for a variety of reasons. For at least the first two decades after their appearance in bodybuilding, steroids were often considered to be the greatest weapon of the "cheater"—they were magic pills that did away with the need for hard work. Savvy fans knew better. To those who understood bodybuilding's realities, steroids were the gateway to the next, otherwise unattainable level of muscular development. This was the fundamental purpose of appearance-enhancing drugs, but it was also the key to understanding one of bodybuilding's greater realities—that the connection between bodybuilding and ideal health was becoming increasingly coincidental. The emergence of regular, structured bodybuilding contests, and especially the rise of bodybuilding-only federations like the IFBB, deepened the divide between health and appearance. The practice of creating a muscular build came to be about more than the mere end result. Bodybuilding was now about *winning*.

The chance to be the next Mr. America or Mr. Universe, like the men glorified on the covers of muscle magazines, beckoned like the Sirens of ancient legend. With their eyes fixed on titles and trophies, competitors wanted to be bigger, more muscular, more defined. If a magic pill came along that could help them realize this goal, most would bite. At the same time however, no bodybuilder wanted attention diverted from the hard work he put in forging his physique. An admission of drug use would make many doubt there ever was any such hard work. He would be branded a cheater, someone looking for an easy path to big muscles and victory. He could expect no understanding.

Nor could he expect empathy. Many people consider drug use to be a symptom of depravity, of moral degeneration—regardless of the type of drug or the reason for taking it (drugs prescribed for legitimate medical purposes notwithstanding). In the case of bodybuilding, there has always been an element of the culture that sincerely championed the need for good overall health and wellbeing. Bernarr Macfadden all but fathered this movement, and those who adhered to it in the final third of the 20th century often took personal exception to what they considered to be the polluting influence of steroids. As far as that group was concerned, drugs were destroying bodybuilding—and their users were agents of destruction.

It will never be known who the first bodybuilder to take steroids was, although Bill Pearl is sometimes thought be one the earliest notable competitors to receive chemical help. Circumstantial evidence supports this view: at a peak competition weight of 242 pounds at a height of five-foot-ten, Pearl's physique was more massive than anything that had come before it. He also grew substantially between his 1952 Mr. America win and the 1960s. Although his muscular definition was never up to the level of modern-day, world-championship-caliber competitors, his height-to-weight ratio—not to mention the measurements of certain body-parts—was roughly on par with future, steroid-enriched champions. Pearl also admitted taking the anabolic steroid Nilevar in early editions of his book *Getting Stronger*, after learning of the existence of steroids from Nautilus exercise machine inventor Arthur Jones.

In modern times Pearl has vehemently denied ever using anabolic steroids, calling the practice "sheer madness." Although in the 1960s there were no laws against steroid use, and there was little reason to believe that they were capable of producing negative long-term effects, he claimed to have known better anyway, and to have staunchly resisted their use. The ardor of Pearl's denial, issued decades after his competitive run had ended, seemed a faint echo of the impassioned testimonies of modern baseball stars caught with their hands in the cookie jar.

Bill Pearl wasn't on any Congressional hot seat when he made his claim about never using steroids. He may have simply been out to preserve his legacy, or his reputation as an author. Pearl had produced an encyclopedic work called *Keys to the Inner Universe*, a book which aimed to catalogue the myriad bodybuilding exercises that had come into existence by the end of the 1960s. An admission of drug use on his part—which may or may not have happened, depending upon which of his statements is true—could arguably skew the publication's relevance. Regardless, with or without drugs, Bill Pearl built a physique with barrier-smashing size.

The trail of steroid use in bodybuilding was blazed by *someone*; that much is true. It's therefore no surprise that the light of speculation has periodically been cast on the man who most noticeably bridged the gap between the eras before and after steroids were introduced, Reg Park. In a modern interview with bodybuilding.com, Roger Walker (a top Australian competitor of the 1960s and '70s) implied that Park owed his level of development to the help of chemicals. According to Walker, in the early 1950s Park gained 50 pounds of muscle within a six-month period—an accomplishment that greatly exceeded anything that could be accomplished naturally (without drugs). This was a problematic claim however, for a few reasons. Not only was there no evidence of steroid use among bodybuilders or athletes until a couple of years after Park's alleged growth spurt, but Park reportedly increased his bodyweight by only a single pound from the time of his 1951 Mr. Universe victory until his win at the professional version of that event seven years later. Moreover, except in extremely rare cases of muscle memory (the ability of a muscle to quickly return to a previous state of size or skill), no one has ever come close to gaining that much muscle in a six month period. It should however be noted that Park was able to capture the 1965 and 1970 NABBA Pro Mr. Universe titles with a physique that compared favorably with admitted users.

Pearl and Park never failed a steroid test, although neither ever took one; nor would their innocence or guilt matter, if either had been conclusively proven. No single competitor was responsible for the proliferation of steroids in bodybuilding. In all likelihood, the very first bodybuilder to take them, whoever he was, never achieved anything approaching notoriety or lasting fame. The identity of the very first user is of little consequence. Bodybuilders were destined to discover and use anabolic steroids, and no prodding or famous examples were needed. What mattered was that within a few years of their emergence, appearance-enhancing drugs became a necessity for anyone with serious designs on winning major bodybuilding titles.

* * * * *

As the 1960s got underway, bodybuilding's expanding fan base and competitor pool warranted the creation of more contests, and with them, new titles. Those contests became the platform upon which the next wave of great bodybuilders—men who would form the heart and soul of the Golden Age—rose to prominence. Near the vanguard of this movement was bodybuilding's first well-known black competitor, a young man named Harold Poole. Born in 1943, Poole began serious weight training at the age of 12. His progress was Astonishing. In 1960, before he had reached his 17th birthday, he competed in the AAU Mr. America contest placed 18th out of a field of 25. The next year he climbed to fourth. In 1962, at the age of 18, he came in second, though he won the "Most Muscular" trophy. The following year an improved physique got him the same result; Poole lost out to a man named Vern Weaver but was once more declared to be the most muscular man onstage. By all appearances, the Mr. America Most Muscular award had often been given as a consolation prize to superior competitors who didn't full satisfy the AAU's general appearance requirement. Its winners were rarely consoled. Based on some past judgments, and on a few which were yet to be rendered, the term "general appearance" could have been replaced with "white" without loss of meaning. The AAU's color barrier was still firmly in place, and in 1963 it appeared that it might be forever. After his second runner-up finish, Poole came to the conclusion that no matter how good he looked, he was bound to finish behind a white competitor. Exasperated, he switched allegiance to the IFBB.

The Weiders knew better than to cling to any doomed white-winners-only policy, especially considering the growing number and quality of bodybuilding's up-and-coming black competitors. They also knew that in an increasingly civil-rights minded hemisphere, where blacks now had a presence in every professional sport (except hockey, though not because of any official policy), excluding blacks from victory was a lost cause. In these early days, they were also willing to put their money where their mouths were. Harold Poole won the IFBB Mr. America title on his first try.

Rising to prominence around the same time as Poole was Larry Scott, a competitor destined to become Poole's rival and nemesis. In appearance Scott also happened to be Poole's antithesis—a blond-haired, blue-eyed Adonis—something that could have only helped his eventual ascent to muscle-contest domination. There was much more to Scott than mere All-American good looks, however. He had complete, even development, with full muscle bellies, better-than-average definition, and particularly large biceps.

Although they're among the smaller of the human body's skeletal muscles, biceps have historically been the most celebrated. A man with large biceps commands attention, inspires wonder and provokes envy. He makes heads turn—and he makes bodybuilding audiences sit up and take notice. At his competitive apex, Larry Scott probably had the world's largest biceps. They secured his fame and became his trademark. A popular bicep exercise—the "Scott curl"—was even named after him. The rest of his physique was scarcely far behind. Within a couple years he possessed a combination of mass and quality that was rivaled by few. Scott's only detriment was a slightly below-average stature: he was five-foot-seven. Reeves and Park, the greatest stars of recent years, were a half foot taller. As future events would demonstrate however, it didn't matter.

Larry Scott, like many men before and since, owed his lifelong commitment to bodybuilding to a chance encounter with a muscle magazine. At age 16 he stumbled across one such publication, was awestruck by a photo of a bodybuilder named George Pain, and shortly thereafter began lifting weights. A few years later Scott captured the Mr.

Courtesy of Robert White

left: Larry Scott. c. 1960
below: Harold Poole, c. 1968

Courtesy of Michael Newman

Idaho title. He relocated to the Los Angeles area to enroll in electronics school and shortly thereafter began receiving instruction from the famed trainer and gym owner Vince Gironda. Scott's physique improved significantly, and he was able to secure top honors at the 1960 AAU Mr. California contest. He was approached afterward by Joe Weider, who persuaded him to forgo the AAU Mr. America contest and enter instead the IFBB competition with the same name. Scott agreed, and in 1962 he competed in and won the contest. By doing so, Scott had won a much sought-after title; and the IFBB gained credibility by producing a top-notch winner.

Although Joe Weider originally entered the contest-promotion business with reluctance, it didn't take long for him to realize the venture's potential. Heading a bodybuilding federation entailed structuring operations and arranging contests, but it also opened the doors of profit. Muscle contests and the bodybuilders who entered them could be excellent advertisements for products and magazines. Bob Hoffman made this lesson quite clear when bodybuilders who endorsed and promoted his York Barbell Company consistently placed well in or won his AAU Mr. America contest. There was no reason why IFBB competitors could not one day show similar loyalty to Weider. Granted, at least early on Weider had no intention of exercising favoritism when choosing his winners. Those days were yet to come. For the time being he had a dragon to slay.

As the mid-1960s got underway, Bob Hoffman's problem was not only that he made a lot of critical errors, but that Joe Weider supplied a lot of solutions. Hoffman looked down on bodybuilding while Weider praised it; Hoffman made bodybuilding second-fiddle to weightlifting while Weider rhetoric placed muscle contests above all sports; Hoffman demanded that bodybuilders take up weightlifting while Weider thought the requirement was useless and stupid; Hoffman's contest decisions appeared racially prejudiced while Weider's were not. Even in the days when Hoffman was a much bigger fish than Weider, the writing was on the wall. Unlike Hoffman, Weider actually liked bodybuilding. This may have been the most important factor of all. He knew what bodybuilders and fans wanted. His rise to domination would require only time, a great deal of dedication and hard work, and a few good ideas. In 1965 he had one of his best ideas ever.

The landscape of competitive bodybuilding had undergone a significant transformation since the late 1930s. Almost as soon as the concept of the competitive bodybuilding organization came into being, the AAU Mr. America became the world's premier muscle contest. Within a decade of its inception, rival Mr. America competitions cropped up, as did multiple versions of the new Mr. World and Mr. Universe contests. In such an environment, any single title was bound to lose some meaning, simply because there were men walking around with the same title, won in the same year. The only thing separating the awards were the initials of sanctioning federation stamped across their baseplates. Except to the most dedicated fans, the situation was becoming confusing. Complicating matters was that there was no longer any dominant governing body with the ability to declare authority in the matter.

During the 1940s the AAU dominated the world of bodybuilding competition. Its scope and influence had built-in limitations however, due to the greater purpose of the AAU. Since 1888, the AAU has been an organization dedicated to the promotion and development of American amateur sports. It could not hold international competitions of any sort, and it certainly could not stage professional events. Hoffman's bodybuilding division was but a small part of the AAU. No exceptions would be made on his behalf. His Mr. America would be considered the definitive version of that contest throughout the 1950s and beyond, but the creation and popularity of international and professional contests by other federations would naturally chip away at Hoffman's dominance.

The time was ripe for a non-AAU entity to step up and into a position of authority. Weider seemed the most likely candidate to accomplish such a move. His magazines were adding readers, his contests were gaining credibility and his products were attracting buyers. He had a competitive share of the markets for each, but he hadn't yet taken any kind of clear lead. For that to happen, he needed an edge; something to set him apart from the other publishers, promoters and peddlers. He found that edge when he came up with the idea of creating a new IFBB contest, one whose winner would be looked upon as uncontested world champion. Weider envisioned this contest becoming dominant and definitive, like the AAU Mr. America had been in the 1940s—only much more so. It would also distinguish itself from the old AAU show in four important ways: the IFBB contest would be international; its entrants would be professional; it would strive to render fair judgments; and there could be repeat winners. The bodybuilding world was bound to laud these changes, but it would still have to be convinced that this new event was indeed a contest above all others. For this the wheels of the Weider propaganda machine were oiled and at the ready.

The only thing left was to give the contest a name. A perfunctory title like "IFBB Professional World Championship" wasn't going to cut it. Something catchy was needed. On top of that, the successful "mister" naming convention for bodybuilding contests was still very much in place in 1965, and would be for some time to come. It was therefore certain that the contest name would begin with "Mr."—but Mr. *what*? According to Weider, as he was mulling the issue over a cold beer, the name suddenly came to him. The beer he was drinking was Olympia. On the spot he announced that the new contest would be called "Mr. Olympia."

It seemed a fitting name. It wasn't just catchy; the name also conjured images of both majesty and divinity. Mount Olympus was, after all, the home of the ancient Greek Gods. The new title furthermore paid tribute, however faint, to the civilization that worshipped those deities—the same civilization that had planted, a very long time ago, seeds from which bodybuilding would eventually grow. The name Olympia is also close in meaning to Olympic, which is the very pinnacle of sporting competition.

Plus, in a world where "Mr. Universe" was taken seriously as a world championship title, a corny-sounding name like *Mr. Olympia* could do no worse. It was just crazy enough to work.

The drink that gave the world's greatest muscle contest its name. Olympia Beer, 'Stubby' bottle. c. 1965

Although Olympia Beer got its name not from the home of the Ancient Immortals but from the town of Olympia, Washington, this really didn't matter. What mattered was that the soon-to-be greatest muscle contest the world has ever known now had a name. It also had a bright young champion itching to compete in it. Joe Weider's professional courtship of Larry Scott had quickly turned into friendship, and before long the two began to strategize about Scott's competitive future. If it lived up to its concept, the Mr. Olympia contest would be a fitting next step. The competition thus partially owed its invention to Weider's opinion that no existing event would do justice to Scott's greatness. Scott was even present to witness Weider's Olympia beer epiphany. As a devout, teetotalling Mormon, he was somewhat taken aback by the notion that the new bodybuilding world championship was named after a beer, but Weider mollified him.

The Mr. Olympia was conceived to be the absolute pinnacle of bodybuilding. Only open to holders of top titles—for example Mr. America, World or Universe—its winner would be considered the world's most perfectly-developed male specimen. The rule allowing past winners to enter the Mr. Olympia also insured its legitimacy. Weider knew better than to prevent competitors from winning more than once. By 1965, the repeat-winner concept had already been proven quite successful by the world of sports. The New York Yankees had by then won the World Series 20 times. Because of this people loved them, or loved to hate them. Either way, the Yankees' huge collection of titles didn't turn people off to the World Series, and certainly not to baseball itself. Nor did Joe Louis' successful defense of 25 titles cause people to lose interest in him or in boxing. Repeatedly winning the world's top title in any sport had become the stuff of legends. Since bodybuilders and their fans widely considered bodybuilding to be a sport, there was good reason to believe the concept would work well there too.

Weider further hoped that the contest would inspire bodybuilders to continually improve. Competitions that allowed only single victories didn't give champions reason to make themselves more muscular and defined. After winning the Mr. America and the Mr. Universe for example, a bodybuilder had nowhere left to compete, and no reason to make his physique more impressive. Reflecting on the decision to allow multiple winners, Weider later declared "I wanted to push muscular development to the limits." The desire would later remind him that he should be careful what he wishes for, but for the moment he appeared to be on the right track. Nevertheless, there was still some uncertainty. Whether Weider's visions would realize themselves couldn't be known until the contest was actually staged. The Brooklyn Academy of Music was selected as the venue for the event, and September 18, 1965 was determined to be its date. As would become customary, the Mr. Olympia was held on the same stage and on the same night as the IFBB Mr. America and Mr. Universe shows. The Olympia would be the headlining event. Holding it at the end of a show that featured two established titles ensured that a large crowd would be on hand to witness the competition—and the crowning of the first-ever Mr. Olympia.

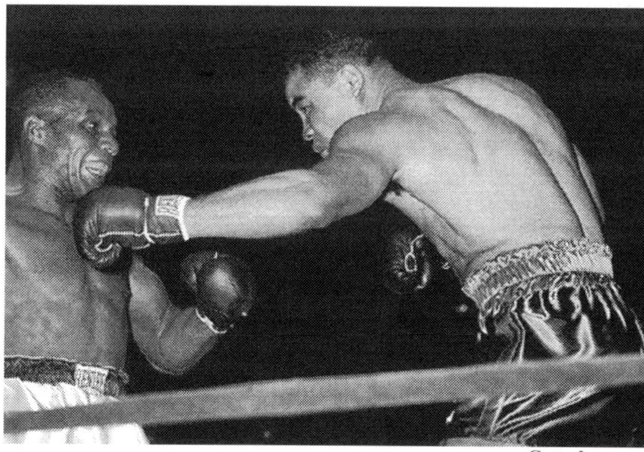
Getty Images

Joe Louis (*right*). By 1952, he had successfully defended his boxing titles 25 times. 13 years later, the IFBB did away with its one-win-only policy.

At the event, fans were treated to what may have been the most impressive collection of physiques the world had yet seen. Winning the Mr. America was 23-year-old Dave Draper—a tall blonde competitor with good looks, broad shoulders, a tremendous back and impressive overall upper-body development. Although he was born and raised in New Jersey, Draper looked as though he had just stepped off a southern California beach, set his surfboard down and hopped onstage. He instantly became a fan favorite. Hollywood loved his looks as well, and Draper had already embarked upon a minor career in television and film.

Capturing the Mr. Universe title was Earl Maynard, winner of the 1964 NABBA version of the contest. Like a number of men before and since, Maynard was soon lured away from competition by better opportunities. He embarked upon a successful career in film—as an actor, director and producer—and had already begun a prosperous run as a professional wrestler. Combined with the physiotherapy degree he earned in the late 1950s, Maynard has to be one of the most accomplished men to ever win a major bodybuilding title. After collecting his IFBB Mr. Universe trophy and posing for pictures, he exited the stage, set down his new hardware, did an about-face, and marched straight back onstage—this time as part of the Mr. Olympia lineup.

It was a good thing he did. Only two other men had shown up to compete in the inaugural installment of what was billed to be the greatest muscle contest ever held. Fortunately for the Weiders, the audience, and the future of the Mr. Olympia competition itself, the two entrants were arguably the world's greatest active competitors: Harold Poole and Larry Scott. In the end it was Scott who triumphed. Poole and Maynard were second an third, respectively. Scott was presented with an elaborate crown but no cash prize. Joe Weider later claimed that expenses for the contest ran so high that the $1000 first-place award he planned to surprise the winner with had to be withheld.

Dave Draper. c. 1968

Courtesy of Michael Newman

Courtesy of Michael Newman

Earl Maynard. c. 1965

The contest ended sometime around midnight. According to both Weider and Scott, once the audience filed out of the auditorium and onto the street it turned into an excited mob, cheering and chanting "We want Scott! We want Scott!" Weider and Scott lingered inside for fear of being overwhelmed by rowdy fans. By 2:00 the crowd had not dispersed, so with the help of a police escort the two made their way out the back and into a waiting car. They sped away into the night and without further incident.

To those familiar only with modern, 21st-century bodybuilding, Weider and Scott's tale of near-riot and quick exit might seem hopelessly exaggerated, as if the story was drummed up after watching *A Hard Day's Night*—the hit Beatles movie from the previous year. Here a bodybuilder was getting the same treatment as a rock and roll star, which if true would indeed be stranger than fiction. Bodybuilding contests sometimes attract a great amount of interest, but they don't incite passion—not the type of passion exhibited by the crowds of Weider and Scott's recollection, anyway.

Then again, this was 1965. The Olympia was hyped, and Larry Scott more than lived up to it. Though his height was below-average, inch-for-inch and pound-for-pound Scott was more massive than Park, Grimek or any of bodybuilding's major figures up to that point. The audience of the first

Mr. Olympia contest had never seen anything quite like it. If a mob was ever going to create a disturbance in the name of a muscle-contest hero, it would have been then and there.

Incredible claims of near-riots aside, the first Mr. Olympia more than lived up to its billing. The contest promised to identify and reward the best-built man on the planet, and it delivered on that guarantee. A different outcome might have doomed the event; had a second-rate bodybuilder walked away with top honors, the contest might never have established credibility. As the event drew near, Larry Scott's assurance that he would enter alleviated all worries. His presence made the event a sure winner, and in the end Joe Weider and the IFBB delivered a quality product. More importantly, bodybuilding now had a legitimate world-championship title. With each passing year the Mr. Olympia contest's prestige grew. The contest's winners became the standard of excellence, and each came to represent a distinct phase in the progression of bodybuilding. From 1965 onward, the evolution of bodybuilding could be most directly traced by examining the results of the Mr. Olympia contest.

* * * * *

To the world of muscle, the importance of 1965 didn't end with the unveiling of bigger and more muscular physiques, or with the creation of the premier event for showcasing them. That year also saw the beginnings of what would become bodybuilding's permanent epicenter. In 1965 Joe Gold opened the original, now-legendary Gold's Gym in Venice, a few miles south of the old Santa Monica Muscle Beach location. World-class bodybuilders, up-and-comers, hopefuls and wannabes now had an official headquarters. Of all such muscle hubs—including York, Yarick's, Vince's, Johnson's in Chicago, and of course Muscle Beach—the original Gold's would become the most influential. Within its walls, and within the first decade of its existence, the bar of excellence in bodybuilding was raised to such a level that it remained largely fixed until the final decade of the 20th century. The gym's significance would be made known to the world in *Pumping Iron,* the 1977 film that used the establishment as one of its primary shooting locations. Until then, it was just another new southern California gym—albeit one at which an ever-increasing number of Mr. Olympia competitors would one day train.

Since the 1965 Mr. Olympia contest was such a success, the bodybuilding world looked to the 1966 version with a good deal of anticipation. Taking advantage of its multiple-entry rule, Larry Scott resolved to build upon his fame as the first-ever Mr. Olympia by also becoming the event's first two-time winner. Once more the Brooklyn Academy of Music was chosen as the event's venue, and like the previous year, an orchestra was on hand to provide theme music for the onstage flexing and posing.

Again the Mr. America and Mr. Universe contests would precede the Olympia, but for 1966 a fourth contest was added: Mr. World. Although for all intents and purposes the contest was a redundancy of Mr. Universe—both were amateur "world championship" titles—the addition was a wise move, especially since the Mr. Olympia contest had already demonstrated a need for more qualified entrants. The other important change was that the majority of judging for all four events would now take place earlier in the day, in a phase referred to as "prejudging." In theory, prejudging allows judges to carefully and fairly rate and place competitors, without distraction. The idea was determined to be successful, and preliminary judging sessions became a fundamental part of all major bodybuilding contests from that point forward.

Winning the 1966 Mr. America was Chet Yorton. A top-notch competitor, Yorton had just won the '66 NABBA Mr. Universe in London, where he defeated a sensational young Austrian named Arnold Schwarzenegger. Rather than attempting to knock Larry Scott off his Olympia throne, Yorton gave the Mr. America title a run instead, where his

Arnold Schwarzenegger and Chet Yorton.
1966 Mr. Universe contest.

Courtesy of Michael Newman

chances of victory were far greater. His strategy panned out. It wasn't all easy sailing however, because another good young competitor, this time an American named Frank Zane, threatened to upend his strategy. In the end Zane came in second; like Schwarzenegger however, the world had not seen the last of him.

The Mr. World was won by Sergio Oliva, a former member of the Cuban national weightlifting team who had defected to the United States in 1962. Oliva displayed world-class size and remarkably full muscle bellies. His definition wasn't quite on par with that of other world-title holders and his presentation was bad, but his physique was far too good to be denied. Like Maynard the year before, he entered the Mr. Olympia contest the same night as his amateur title victory. First however, the Mr. Universe contest went through its paces, with Dave Draper taking home top honors.

With Oliva's last-minute entry, the Mr. Olympia had increased its field of competitors from three to four. Like the previous year, quality made up for a lack of quantity. Oliva's size was easily on par with the other competitors—Scott, Harold Poole and Chuck Sipes—but a lack of refinement proved to be his undoing. He nevertheless appeared to possess immense potential. Oliva came in fourth, with Sipes in third. Scott and Poole were left standing. By all accounts Poole had improved greatly since the '65 Olympia, so a repeat Scott victory was by no means a foregone conclusion. Some in attendance, including Poole, believed that the reigning Mr. Olympia was now second-best. An additional round of comparison poses was asked for by the event's judges, who were apparently having a difficult time determining the outcome. After a brief intermission, Scott was declared victorious.

Considering the overall history of physique competition up to 1966, it would have been reasonable to wonder if Scott's second victory was owed to the color of his skin. However, the IFBB was not the AAU. While Bob Hoffman's federation—after 27 years of staging contests—had still not allowed a black Mr. America, Weider's was awarding top titles to black competitors regularly. Barring hard evidence, any claim that the IFBB had by 1966 rendered racist decisions is speculation. This didn't mean that other factors were not in play. Throughout its history the IFBB has conspicuously shied away from dethroning a reigning Mr. Olympia. It would not do so in 1966, and this may have set the precedent. Regardless, a strong case was made for Scott's victory. His physique was completely different from Poole's, and in any type of competition with entirely subjective criteria, there's bound to be disagreement. As bodybuilding matured and the quality and size of competitive fields grew, this problem would be amplified.

The world of bodybuilding was happy with its two-time world champion. It was also surprised to hear Scott, immediately after he was handed the $1000 first-place prize, announce that he was retiring from physique competition. Scott told the audience he wanted to give other competitors a chance to win the event, though he later cited a conflict between his religious beliefs and the temptations that came with being a bodybuilding star as the true reasons. In his memoirs, Joe Weider speculated that Scott left competition so he wouldn't have to face future editions of Sergio Oliva.

Whatever Scott's actual motivations for hanging it up may have been, his fellow competitors were no doubt relieved, for there would be no reigning champion to unseat at the 1967 Mr. Olympia contest. Strangely however, out of dozens of qualified men, there were still only four bodybuilders on hand to vie for the title. The list of competitors was the same as 1966, except that Larry Scott had been replaced by Dave Draper.

There was also a change in the rules of presentation for the evening show. 1967 was the first year that competitors were allowed to pose to their own selections of recorded music. For several years to come, virtually all of these were bombastic classical pieces. Selections from biblically-themed

Sergio Oliva. c. 1968

Courtesy of Michael Newman

movie soundtracks like *Exodus* became favorites. In an era that still clung to the Victorian-age connection between bodybuilding and Classical sculpture, dramatic orchestral music seemed most fitting. Over time, the erosion of that connection, along with changes in music, posing styles, and the physical appearance of bodybuilders themselves turned muscle shows into something entirely different. Individual posing music was a fundamental part of that change, and it all started in 1967.

In the event Draper finished fourth, with Poole coming in third. Poole's slip in the placings was due more to the improvements made by the two men who placed above him than anything else. Sipes and especially Oliva had become more muscular and defined since the previous Olympia, so it was easy for judges to award them the top spots. In the end though, Sipes' mass and lines couldn't match those of Oliva. As part of his coverage of for *Muscle Builder*, staff writer Dick Tyler summed up the spectacle:

> The words to describe Oliva haven't been invented yet. I may never again see such a display of muscle as long as I live. His musculature was an assault upon believability.

Oliva had been sensational in 1966, but only a year later he was otherworldly. The overall thickness of his physique was now unrivaled. His arms, with their impossibly long muscle bellies, were particularly amazing. His waist was tiny, his back was wide, his thighs and calves huge. Oliva's overall package was furthermore topped off with much-improved definition. A single pose—his trademark hands-over-head arm shot—showed all of these things at once, in spades. It was the exclamation point of his dominance. No other poses were even needed. Larry Scott had caused a furor when his re-scaled physique was revealed at the '65 Olympia, but it was nothing like this. Not since Grimek—or perhaps even Sandow himself—had any one man of muscle so thoroughly distanced itself from all others. Scott's early retirement was beginning to look like a wise move. The reaction of the bodybuilding world to Oliva bordered on shock. His peers were impressed as well, so much in fact that the first opportunity to challenge the new champion found no takers. Oliva won the 1968 Mr. Olympia contest unopposed.

Not only did the IFBB have its have its second two-time Mr. Olympia winner in its first four years, but it also proved that it was willing to award its greatest title to a black competitor. Most importantly, the Olympia contest was fulfilling its mission: in each installment, the contest produced a winner that was arguably the best in the world. It really was a legitimate world championship, something that bolstered the IFBB's standing tremendously. With each passing year that would become more true. The IFBB also now had a champion that looked as though he could collect Olympia titles at leisure. Simply put, there just didn't seem to be anyone capable of beating Sergio Oliva.

* * * * *

For a bodybuilding federation to appear legitimate, for it to be taken seriously, it needed to attract high-quality bodybuilders. For much of the 1940s Bob Hoffman didn't have to work very hard at this, for two reasons: the AAU was already a large and well-respected sports organization; and it was the only real organization staging bodybuilding contests. Smaller federations like the IFBB meanwhile had to make real efforts, from the get-go, to get competitors whose physical appearance lived up to the titles it awarded. Joe Weider understood the value of attracting such men. It was, after all, his successful courtship of Larry Scott that made the Mr. Olympia contest a true world championship.

Nevertheless, as the 1960s were drawing to a close, the IFBB was by no means the monopolizing force that it would one day become. The AAU and NABBA still had considerable clout. Weider was therefore keen to lure competitors, whether they were established champions like Larry Scott and Harold Poole, or young unknowns who showed promise. Accordingly, the exploits of the 19-year-old Austrian who narrowly lost to Chet Yorton at the 1966 NABBA Mr. Universe contest did not escape his notice.

Arnold Schwarzenegger, despite having a name that gave American bodybuilding fans pause, was nevertheless also giving them cause to learn how to pronounce it. In 1967 he took another shot at the NABBA Mr. Universe contest and won handily. The constantly improving Schwarzenegger next claimed victory at the '68 NABBA Pro Universe, meaning that at 21 years of age he now stood atop the highest tier of European bodybuilding. A search for greater challenges drew his gaze westward. In order to reach his competitive potential, whatever that may be, he knew that traveling to the United States—or ideally, moving there—was a necessity.

The wait wouldn't be long. A trip across the Atlantic was already in the works.

According to Joe Weider, Bob Hoffman easily could have had first dibs on the Austrian phenom. Schwarzenegger, who made known his desire to compete in the US, had been warned by NABBA officials about aligning with Weider. In an age when rival federation heads regularly accused each other of shadiness, underhandedness, back-stabbing and depravity, the young Schwarzenegger may have thought it best to steer clear of the IFBB chief. Although the door was therefore wide open for Hoffman to add Schwarzenegger to the still-relevant York stable of musclemen, the AAU boss "had no use for a full-time bodybuilder."[1]

Weider stepped in. He invited Schwarzenegger to compete in the '68 IFBB Mr. Universe contest and offered to cover all expenses. Any misgivings the young Austrian may have harbored were vanquished. The journey of a lifetime—the chance to win fame in America—had just dropped in his lap. He arrived at the Miami venue where the event was staged, beaming with confidence, ready for victory. Things could not have been going better for Schwarzenegger—that is, until the contest got underway. At six-foot-two and 240 pounds, with stunning bicep and chest development, Schwarzenegger was easily the largest competitor in the event. He lacked much refinement however and came in second to a smaller but more polished Frank Zane.

Schwarzenegger appeared to have blown his one big chance to be a star in America, and, according to Weider, was crushed by the defeat. Weider saw things differently. Schwarzenegger didn't deserve to win the 1968 IFBB Mr. Universe, but it wasn't because of any inherent limitations. He was simply not in the kind of shape needed to compete at that level, in that day and age. But he was by no means through. Schwarzenegger had potential, lots of it.

In bodybuilding, nothing is more important than potential. When it's combined with astute planning, determined execution and unshakeable resolve, the result is a championship-level physique. When those factors are applied to a body with limited or poor potential, the result is an also-ran.

Schwarzenegger had potential, and Weider knew it. The two spent several days together following the contest; and although Schwarzenegger's English was poor and their friendship was new, Weider was also able to get more than an inkling of the young Austrian's resolve. Here was a man dead-set on achieving glory; a man who would stop at nothing before that end was met. By 1968, Joe Weider knew bodybuilding. He knew that Schwarzenegger had the drive to be a world-beater, and that fulfilling his all-important potential would require little more than changing his approach. It's therefore no surprise that Weider moved Schwarzenegger to southern California and put him on the company payroll.

In his new locale, Schwarzenegger rubbed elbows with bodybuilding's top stars and received instruction from its top trainers. Upon entering Vince's Gym for the first time, the outspoken and often rude Gironda told Schwarzenegger he looked fat. Since Schwarzenegger had rare talent for turning disparagement into motivation, it was probably the best thing he could have heard. Criticism of his lower-body development likewise became fuel for his fire. Yet Schwarzenegger didn't move halfway around the world just to be insulted. He soaked up the advice of experts like a sponge. His training sessions were relentless. His already-rapid improvement accelerated.

Frank Zane. c. 1976

Courtesy of Michael Newman

[1]Taking a final jab at his long-deceased former rival, Weider in his autobiography criticized Hoffman's decision to pass on Schwarzenegger by declaring "what a genius."

A pair of subpar legs notwithstanding, the young Austrian had come to the US with a solid foundation of muscle, built by years of heaving heavy barbells. Starting in late 1968, the majority of his focus shifted to refining his physique. For this he was in the right place. There was a reason why weightlifting machines had been invented, and why even by 1965 they occupied the greater part of a good bodybuilding gym's floor space: an ideal physique cannot be built with barbells and dumbbells alone. Gold's Venice had one of the world's best collection of these machines, and it was there that Schwarzenegger trained in preparation for the busiest competitive year of his career, 1969.

He returned to Europe for two events, the new IFBB Mr. Europe and the NABBA Pro Mr. Universe. Even though Schwarzenegger was now on the Weider payroll, he competed in and won the NABBA event two more times. Weider certainly wasn't going to blackball him for it, and really, from the IFBB chief's perspective, it may have been a good thing: it demonstrated than an IFBB amateur Mr. Universe runner-up could roll right through an NABBA Pro Universe lineup. It left little doubt about which federation was better. With the Mr. Europe and Mr. Universe titles under his belt, Schwarzenegger once more set foot on American soil, where Sergio Oliva was waiting for him.

Much like the confrontation between Harold Poole and Larry Scott, the inevitable Oliva-versus-Schwarzenegger showdown promised to be a study in opposites. One was black and one was white. Schwarzenegger was about five inches taller and 20 pounds heavier than his rival. Both men had staggering arm development; Schwarzenegger had the greatest biceps peak of all time but triceps that were merely good; Oliva had the world's greatest triceps but biceps that were without much peak. Although Schwarzenegger's legs were already much improved, they were not up to the level of Oliva.

Arnold Schwarzenegger. c. 1970

Courtesy of Michael Newman

There were similarities as well. Both men had world-class chest development; both had exceptional backs, though Oliva's flared more dramatically in lat-spread poses. Schwarzenegger had been receiving a great deal of help with his presentation, and was now rather capable. Oliva's presentation skills were passable.

The 1969 Mr. Olympia contest was again held in New York. Joe Weider's investment in Arnold Schwarzenegger was already paying dividends, since his young star's impending showdown with Sergio Oliva naturally generated a good deal of interest. Unlike the previous year, this would be a real competition. In a way, the specter of Oliva's unchallenged victory added to the drama: in 1968, the world's top bodybuilders had apparently been too intimidated to stand next to the reigning Mr. Olympia. But there now emerged a man, almost out of nowhere, who not only wanted to seize the King's crown, but who actually looked capable of doing so.

Fans who hadn't seen Schwarzenegger since his stateside debut were awed by his improvement. There was far more separation and polish. His legs were also now much closer to matching his upper body. All Schwarzenegger's poses were remarkable. Upon their unveiling, his front-double-bicep and side chest poses were though to be among the greatest ever witnessed. The audience roared with approval.

Unfortunately for Schwarzenegger, Oliva expected the young Austrian to be a legitimate threat; and he knew that a successful title defense would require not only matching his previous best condition, but surpassing it. Before the event he announced to *Muscle Builder* reporter Rick Wayne: "You gonna see somethin' but you ain't gonna believe it." What Wayne and the rest of the Olympia audience saw, whether they believed it or not, was Sergio Oliva in top, jaw-dropping form. He was bigger than ever, with good definition and a miniscule waist. Never before had they seen a man so muscular. As it turned out, he would need every bit of that muscularity to triumph. Schwarzenegger's muscularity wasn't far behind, and his significantly larger frame made him look just plain bigger. It was one of the closest contests the world of bodybuilding had yet seen. In the end the judges gave the nod to Oliva.

Shortly after the spoils of victory were lavished upon Oliva—$1000 and a silver tray—he told Wayne that he was hanging it up. He planned to return to Chicago and concentrate on managing his gym business. After winning the world's greatest title in front of a riotous crowd, and after hearing fans loudly chanting his name, it seemed a strange declaration. Those fans would be bound to wonder if Oliva, the same man who only a year prior had intimidated the entire IFBB, had now himself been driven into hiding by Schwarzenegger. The following morning, upon realizing this, Oliva recanted. He would be onstage at the 1970 Mr. Olympia contest, defending his title. Schwarzenegger, hungrier and more determined than ever, would be there to meet him.

* * * * *

Some of the same fans who attended the 1969 Mr. Olympia contest in New York were on hand, a few months later, to watch the famed ball drop in Times Square on New Year's Eve. In appearance that scene differed little from years which came before or after: as the seconds counted down to midnight, the ball began its slow decent; once it hit bottom, the crowd cheered, music was played, kisses were exchanged, and the grand, riotous party continued. Within the precise system that humans contrived to mark the passage of time, midnight on New Year's Eve amounts to nothing more than a resetting of the annual clock. To humans however, being the emotional creatures that we are, it's far more meaningful moment. A new year represents a fresh start—and a renewal of hope, aspirations, and ambitions. The New Year's celebration also represents closure. As the year 1970 was rung in, much had been closed. Not only was the year 1969 in the books, but the entire decade of the '60s was gone as well.

It had been one of the most important periods in American history. A vast cultural transformation took place, incited on the most fundamental level by the very government under which American society existed. Two underlying factors—a lack of civil equality among its citizens and the rise of the military-industrial complex—precipitated the events which characterized the transformation. A counterculture movement took shape, and civil unrest, disobedience and protest became the means by which it communicated its purpose. The movement's surface identity was created as a simple reaction against the recent past; the clean-cut, antiseptic, McCarthyist 1950s gave way to the free-loving, long-haired, anti-establishment '60s. Conformity gave way to psychedelia. Yet the greater movement was by no means a mere fad. Although hippies, love-ins and communal living would soon vanish from the public eye, by the time the '60s came to an end the United States was a different place. American and Western culture had been changed forever.

Amidst the backdrop of a pop-culture explosion, bodybuilding was able, like it always had been, to occasionally pop its head up and get noticed. The appeal of muscle certainly hadn't gone away; and as the decade progressed, bodybuilding became more popular than ever. The expansion of visual media helped to make this possible. The Hercules movies of Steve Reeves and Reg Park could still be seen at drive-ins on Saturday nights; millions of viewers saw Dave Draper appear on *The Beverley Hillbillies*; bodybuilding magazines and muscle-building products were selling like never before; and for true fans of muscle, there was now a large competitive federation with real structure and a legitimate world-championship title.

Like a big part of society, bodybuilders dropped the high-and-tight haircut look of the '50s in favor of longer, shaggier hair. Their new base of operations, Gold's Gym—not to mention the newly-relocated Muscle Beach—was in Venice, a town famous for its high-flying freak flag. Bodybuilders of the '80s and early '90s were stupefied by the hairstyles and clothes they saw in *Pumping Iron*, but they helped the film achieve cult status nonetheless. It wasn't until retro-'70s-inspired fashion came back that the fashion sense displayed in the movie once more made sense.

Hair and clothing styles have come and gone in bodybuilding, but ultimately, it's always been about the muscle. In 1970, there was a whole lot of it to go around. There were quite a few more bodybuilders walking the Earth than in 1960, but more importantly, individually they were quite a bit bigger. While greater society had just changed forever, bodybuilding underwent its own dramatic and permanent transformation. Concerning how this all transpired, much has been said elsewhere; but suffice to say that the scientific revolution was changing bodybuilding to a degree similar to how the Industrial Revolution changed transportation. But that was by no means the end of the story.

During the 1960s more changed in bodybuilding than just the widespread adoption of steroids. By the end of the decade bodybuilders had a far greater understanding of nutrition, and they were able to make their musculature more defined, especially at contest time. Gone were the days when a bodybuilder could step on stage on any given day and do well or win. Standards had risen too high for that. There was now such a thing as a precontest phase of training—a period of several weeks or even a few months leading up to a contest, when a bodybuilder's focus shifted from building muscle to shedding bodyfat. More than a few top bodybuilders who rose to prominence during the Golden Age were initially ignorant of the steadily increasing importance of muscular definition; and not until they suffered the rude shock of defeat did they change their ways. Two such men—Sergio Oliva and Arnold Schwarzenegger—were now the world's greatest bodybuilders. Both spent the year preparing for a rematch of 1969.

Oliva came to represent the other great change in bodybuilding. Federations, judges, fans and competitors were forced to accept the reality that black bodybuilders are sometimes better than white ones, and deserve to be rewarded as such. With the arrival of Oliva, there was just no getting around that fact. Considering his dominance in 1967 and '68, denying him the Mr. Olympia title would have been outrageous. By the late 1960s, times had changed just enough to make a black champion acceptable. A world that was okay with Muhammad Ali crushing opponents in the ring would simply have to accept the black Cuban defector Sergio Oliva as bodybuilding's greatest champion.

Despite all this, the AAU stuck to its doomed guns all the way through the '60s, finally awarding its Mr. America title to a black competitor, Chris Dickerson, in 1970. The first year of the new decade seems to have been a rather feisty one for the AAU. It was also in 1970 that the federation broke its 82-year tradition—and defied its very reason for existence—by staging the Professional Mr. World contest. Afterward the AAU resumed its role as an amateur-only sports and bodybuilding federation. In modern times the event is thought to be little more than bodybuilding trivia, although it did produce one significant effect: in the contest, Arnold Schwarzenegger defeated Sergio Oliva. The myth of Oliva's invincibility having been shattered, fans who had been licking their chops at the prospect of a bigger and better Mr. Olympia showdown became even more excited.

The Olympia was held yet again in New York and was preceded by the Mr. America and Mr. World contests. The America was won by popular former lineman for New York Jets football team, Mike Katz. Things had been going well for Katz in the NFL until a leg injury ended his career. He attributed much of his gridiron effectiveness to the fact that he lifted weights, something that only two other members of the team did during his late-'60s tenure. Coaches initially had strong misgivings about his "muscle-bound" stature, as this was believed to limit athletic ability, but he proved them wrong. Katz therefore helped to blaze the trail of resistance training in competitive sports. Weight training is now considered an elemental component of physical conditioning in not only the NFL, but virtually all major-league sports. In modern times even golfers lift weights.

The Mr. World contest was won by Dave Draper. As the owner of one the era's greatest physiques, Draper was by 1970 an icon of bodybuilding and a minor celebrity. He was however no match for Oliva or Schwarzenegger, and he knew it. Instead of taking another useless crack at the Olympia, he instead opted to compete in a show that he had a chance to win. He chose wisely, and the Mr. World trophy was his. A total lack of hope didn't stop a man named Reg Lewis from entering the Mr. Olympia however, and for the duration of the Oliva/Schwarzenegger battle, he was onstage too, flexing away.

An IFBB Mr. America from 1963, Lewis' presence offered fans a chance to see a live comparison of eras—what bodybuilding once was, and what, in 1970, it had become. Lewis could not compare with the other two men, but as circumstantial evidence would suggest, nor did it seem he wanted to. Once promoters began staging "natural" (drug-tested) contests in the early 1980s, Lewis immediately started competing in them. On his second try he won the masters category of the Natural Bodybuilding Association's Mr. America contest (open to competitors 40 years and older).

Lewis was politely received by the Olympia audience, but their applause was nothing like the frenzied cheers that erupted once Oliva and Schwarzenegger started trading poses. Like the previous year, the contest appeared close. In the end however, the scales appeared to tip in Schwarzenegger's favor. He was noticeably improved, and his muscular definition was in particular superior to the previous year. Oliva, while still magnificent, was about on par with his 1969 form. Schwarzenegger's improvement proved the difference, and the trophy went to him. Oliva may have wished he stuck to his pledge of retirement.

In bodybuilding competition, close decisions beget controversy. Some felt Oliva deserved to keep the title. Regardless, there was no changing the fact that Schwarzenegger was now Mr. Olympia—or that the IFBB and Joe Weider also now had a dominant, huge, handsome and charismatic new champion to exalt. Although that federation had proven on several occasions that it was willing to award top titles to black competitors, it was also ready to once more have a white champion. In a bottom-line-driven industry, it seemed to be a good business move.

Joe Weider ran contests, published magazines and sold products, all for profit. In the world of business, his competitive edge derived ultimately from the marketability of the competitors who flexed under the Weider banner, in his contests, on his magazine covers, and in his ads. From a pure business standpoint, Weider knew that Schwarzenegger was hands-down a superior marketing tool, and he didn't mind saying so to his associates. In a now-famous quote, he explained: "I put Sergio on the cover, I sell X magazines. I put Arnold on the cover, I sell 3X." [1]

This certainly doesn't mean that the 1970 Olympia had been fixed. The IFBB had the opportunity to pick Schwarzenegger over Oliva in 1969 and had refrained, choosing instead to give the title to the more deserving competitor. In 1970 the Olympia judges declared that Schwarzenegger now had the superior physique, and a good case could be made for the decision. The majority of fans appeared to be satisfied by the outcome, and they wanted to see more of their new champion. Arnold Schwarzenegger had by 1970 tapped into only part of his potential, and everyone seemed to know it. He was also now completely loyal to Weider.

[1]Irving Muchnick, from his 1991 SPY magazine article "Pimping Iron."

With the world's greatest bodybuilder now firmly in his camp, Weider decided the time was right to put the screws to his competition. From 1971 moving forward, bodybuilders who entered contests sanctioned by other federations would be suspended by the IFBB. This rule immediately affected two of bodybuilding's biggest names. Although he had supposedly been warned of the new regulation, Sergio Oliva entered and won the 1971 NABBA Pro Mr. Universe in London. His plan was to compete in that show before hopping the Channel and taking on Schwarzenegger at the Olympia in its new location, Paris. Things went according to plan until he arrived at the Olympia venue and was told he would not be allowed to compete. Exasperated, Oliva begged for the opportunity to go onstage as an exhibition poser. He was given permission only after he signed an official letter of apology. His routine brought the house down.

The second competitor to suffer disqualification should have known better. A Sardinian named Francisco Columbu, a close friend of Schwarzenegger, was disqualified from the Mr. Universe competition for having previously entered an unspecified professional contest. The rationale was made known to the Paris audience by no less than the President of the IFBB, Ben Weider. He explained that strict rules regarding the amateur status of competitors would have to be adhered to if bodybuilding was going to secure a place at the 1976 Montreal Olympic Games. While many fans had no idea such plans were in the works, Weider imparted the good news that "favorable progress" had been made in the effort. Meanwhile Columbu, who was soon known to bodybuilding fans as simply "Franco," was allowed to put on a posing exhibition. Though he was technically not in the contest, by the end of the display the audience realized that they had just witnessed one of the world's three greatest physiques—and certainly the greatest under 200 pounds.

Shortly after Schwarzenegger was relocated to southern California, he beseeched his patron to do likewise for his buddy Franco, whom the Austrian declared to be the world's best bodybuilder after himself. Eager to keep his brightest star happy, Weider complied, only to be disappointed by Columbu's stature: he was nearly a foot shorter than Schwarzenegger. Columbu could therefore never be the world's premier specimen of muscle, though this was thought to have been part of the reason why

Courtesy of Michael Newman

Franco Columbu. c. 1971

he and Schwarzenegger became such good friends: despite Columbu's statements to the contrary, there was never really any question of who possessed the superior physique.

Beyond all that, the "short-man" category of bodybuilding needed a dominant figure too. By financing Columbu and pairing him with his old friend under the Weider banner, the IFBB chief's grip on the bodybuilding world tightened. Columbu would just have to learn that the IFBB's rules, at least for the moment, would be bent for no man. Lesson learned, Columbu returned to IFBB competition the following year. Schwarzenegger meanwhile won the 1971 Mr. Olympia contest unopposed.

Overall the first international Mr. Olympia contest turned out to be disappointing. Fans who turned out expecting to see another clash of bodybuilding's titans were treated instead to a pair of guest-posing routines and a contest outcome that produced zero suspense. The awards presentation of the Mr. Universe contest meanwhile nearly touched off a riot.

A new, experimental scoring system awarded the medium class title of the Mr. Universe contest to Ahmet Enulu of Turkey over British favorite Albert Beckles. Apparently the judges were mystified by the placing as well, and on the spot Ben Weider called an emergency meeting of the panel. After much commotion, Weider returned to the podium and announced that the outcome had been changed. For a federation that was looking to garner a nod from the International Olympic Committee, the scene didn't inspire a great deal of confidence. Weider may have prayed no IOC officials were in attendance.

After the event, no one was more disappointed than Sergio Oliva, who had been defeated before he even entered the pump-up room. His spirit hadn't been beaten however, and he resolved to return in 1972, bigger and better than ever. With the intention of helping him achieve that end, Oliva was contacted by the eccentric Nautilus exercise machine inventor and muscle-growth theorist Arthur Jones. Never one to mince words or appear humble, Jones emphatically proclaimed his own methods of resistance training to be far superior to conventional techniques. Eager to get a real edge, Oliva gave Jones a shot. He was glad he did. As the contest drew near, Oliva was larger and more defined than ever.

In a bit of a surprise move, the IFBB decided to hold the 1972 Mr. Olympia contest in Essen, Germany. After beginning its run as the world's premier bodybuilding contest by being held in New York for five straight years, for the second year in a row the contest was held in Europe. As a native of neighboring Austria, Schwarzenegger felt nearly at home in Germany, and he arrived at the venue confident the Mr. Olympia title would remain in his hands. An equally confident Oliva greeted him, as did three other top-quality bodybuilders. Though it was held in the event's most remote venue to date, the Essen Olympia nevertheless produced what was by then the contest's greatest lineup. In addition to Schwarzenegger and Oliva, Columbu, Frank Zane and the 1970 Mr. Europe winner Serge Nubret were on hand to vie for the title.

Arthur Jones. c. 1972

Courtesy of Robert White

As good as the other three may have been, the top spot was certain to go to either Schwarzenegger or Oliva. Since he was the reigning champion and Weider's favorite, it was expected that Schwarzenegger would triumph. Once Oliva revealed his new and improved physique however, serious doubts were raised. As good as Oliva may have been when he was champion, he was now significantly better. His limbs were gigantic and his waist was small. The muscles of his torso were thicker than anything that had yet been witnessed. Topping it all off was an improved level of definition. Arthur Jones' boasts had not been hollow. As a brilliant inventor and man of adventure who was famous for his abrasive and boorish personality, nor were they ever. To the chagrin of some, the world of bodybuilding had not heard the last of him.

Making things interesting was the fact that Schwarzenegger was improved as well. At least partially offsetting the contender's strengths were Schwarzenegger's advantages of height, markedly better biceps development and marginally better overall muscular separation. Nevertheless, the reigning champion simply did not look as muscular as Oliva. It appeared as if the title could once more change hands. According to many who witnessed the contest, it should have. Considering what the still-young Schwarzenegger era had already meant to the IFBB and Joe Weider however, the title just wasn't going to be handed back that easily.

The contest was with a doubt close, but according to those whose opinions mattered—IFBB judges—Schwarzenegger was better. The reigning champion prevailed. The decision was controversial, but bodybuilding competition is, after all, judged subjectively. If differences of opinion did not exist there would be no need for judges, or even for contests. New professional Franco Columbu betrayed his potential and came in fifth. Zane was fourth and Nubret finished third. Oliva, supremely confident before the contest and profoundly exasperated after, promptly quit the IFBB.

Based solely on the outcome of its contests for the first 30 years of its existence, it's difficult to escape the conclusion that the AAU enforced racist judging criteria. The IFBB was able to take advantage of this flaw, and before long part of its success was owed to its policy of racial equality. That did not mean however that the IFBB never exercised favoritism when rendering decisions. That very well may have happened at the 1972 Mr. Olympia contest. Some bodybuilding fans certainly think so. Of those who watched the event or who later saw pictures or film of the same, a large and vocal portion felt that Oliva got shafted.

* * * * *

Sergio Oliva may have been through with the IFBB but he definitely wasn't done competing. The former Mr. Olympia immediately began entering world-championship level contests of rival federations; and since Oliva was arguably the world's greatest bodybuilder, he rolled to easy victory in each. His wins came at long-forgotten events such as the WBBG[1] Mr. International, Mr. Galaxy and Mr. Olympus events, as well as the WABBA[2] World Championship and Pro World Cup contests. He learned well the taste of hollow victory. The contests generally took place in front of smaller audiences, they were without the press or prestige of the Weider events, and Oliva's fellow competitors were a cut below their IFBB counterparts. There was certainly no Arnold Schwarzenegger to contend with, or anyone close for that matter. None of Oliva's post-IFBB contests turned into epic battles of muscular display, as was the case with all his Schwarzenegger encounters.

Epic showdowns generate big interest. Oliva's defection was unfortunate for the IFBB, because that organization's annual, grand battle between the world's two greatest physiques had just dissolved. Nevertheless, the IFBB and Weider would be fine without that showdown, and fine without Oliva. The federation and its leader were now big and well-established, far bigger than any one competitor. It was due to his own decision to excuse himself from this company that Sergio Oliva, despite a string of post-IFBB victories, mostly vanished from the world of bodybuilding. After all, Weider and the IFBB were one and the same; Weider magazines were not going to cover—and therefore give free advertising to—the events of rival federations. They certainly weren't going to give mention to an organization like the WBBG, which apart from being run by Weider arch-enemy Dan Lurie, now had a champion, in the personage of Sergio Oliva, who was arguably better than anyone in the IFBB.

Oliva would continue to get some coverage in other magazines, although these were becoming increasingly overshadowed by Weider's *Muscle Builder*. The mediocre overall quality of shows like

[1]World Body Building Guild
[2]World Amateur Body Building Association

Mr. Galaxy and Mr. Olympus also made them less interesting to the bodybuilding press, and few magazines were on hand to cover them. Most of the bodybuilding world did not know, for example, that the 1975 Mr. Olympus contest was a two-man showdown between Oliva and Ralph Kroger—a competitor who had recently placed fifth in the AAU Mr. America contest. Buildup for the event wasn't quite the same as when Schwarzenegger was the opponent.

Nevertheless, it takes two to tango. When Sergio Oliva quit the IFBB he took with him a great deal of the Mr. Olympia contest's excitement. Gone was the promise of epic battles like those of '69, '70 and '72. Interest in the event would now have to be generated by Schwarzenegger's growing star-power, along with the strides in quality that he and other top IFBB professionals were making. Men like Columbu, Zane and Nubret kept enough pressure on the reigning champion for the bar to be continually notched higher. The physiques of competitors were becoming larger and more sharply-defined each year, and by the time the 1980s arrived bodybuilding had an almost entirely new look.

In the absence of epic mano-a-mano showdowns, an ever-rising level of overall quality topped off by a dominant champion would keep fans happy. Since

Serge Nubret. c. 1975

Courtesy of Michael Newman

The Brooklyn Academy of Music.

the very first bodybuilding contest, and indeed the first Sandow exhibition, the lure has always been the simple spectacle of muscular men flexing. Close contests were merely icing on the cake—and big new rivalries were bound to eventually take shape anyway. Since the popularity of bodybuilding was continually growing, it would only be a matter of time before new blood would emerge: men who could legitimately threaten anyone's hold on the title. Until then, Columbu, Zane, Nubret and a number of others promised to keep things interesting enough.

In 1973, Columbu and Nubret were once more on hand to compete in the Mr. Olympia, which was moved back to the Brooklyn Academy of Music in New York. Since the event had returned to the US, the Mr. America was once again the warm-up event. To explain Oliva's absence to a disappointed fan base, in his after-action report for *Muscle Builder* Joe Weider opted to cast stones: "Oliva chickens-out" was the opening line. In the event, his nonappearance was compensated for by the startling improvement made by the remaining three men. All seemed slightly more muscular, with more polish and certainly more definition.

Schwarzenegger once more triumphed, and the perennial champion now had four Olympia wins under his belt. This was significant. Although the Olympia was still relatively young, it was universally recognized as the world's greatest bodybuilding competition, even by the growing ranks of Weider's sworn enemies. With his fourth victory, Schwarzenegger now had more wins than anyone, which by itself made him arguably the greatest bodybuilder who ever lived. He had pledged to friends a few years earlier that he would be able to extend his win streak as long as he liked. After the '73 Olympia, he had few doubters. It looked as if he could keep collecting trophies indefinitely.

* * * * *

After he retired from competition and began kicking in the doors to real fame, Schwarzenegger became known less for his physique and more for the personality that lay within. This shift in how he was perceived was gradual, as was his climb to the very pinnacle of renown. He became and stayed world-famous, but most of those who learned his name nearly forgot that he had ever stripped down, oiled up, stepped under bright lights and flexed his muscles. Some people never knew he did these things. That group would have therefore never understood the impact he had on bodybuilding, or why, in his heyday, he was so dominant.

When viewed purely as a physique competitor, there were a lot of things that made Arnold Schwarzenegger truly great. He had the biggest biceps and chest of any bodybuilder to date. His shoulders were broad, the taper on his back was pronounced, and his waist—especially when viewed from the side—was small. A deep ribcage made it look even more so. His lower body was more than adequate for the day and age, and once he had reached his peak, the separation in his thighs was world-class. At that stage his overall muscular definition was excellent as well.

Schwarzenegger's style of presentation was exceeding effective. It was characterized by perfectly-executed poses and fluid movement. He had also mastered the quick transition, a posing technique in which the movement from one pose to another is executed as rapidly as possible. This allowed him to squeeze in more poses over any given period of time than conventional transitions allow, and in situations where competitors are asked to pose freely next to each other, the quick movements drew attention to him. To increase its impact, he employed the technique sparingly. It was used for leading into poses like the twisting three-quarter back double biceps, or his trademark dual-straight arm side chest display—poses that made Schwarzenegger appear particularly dominant, and especially, large and imposing.

Courtesy of Michael Newman

Arnold Schwarzenegger. c. 1974

Schwarzenegger's dominance was owed partly to his immense silhouette. Although height has nothing to do with muscularity per se, all things being equal, a taller competitor looks bigger than his rivals. He also carries more muscle. By the time of his fourth victory, no competitor could touch Schwarzenegger in this regard. Oliva was almost a half-foot shorter. Columbu was shorter still. Serge Nubret was nearly as tall as Schwarzenegger, but his physique was more sleek than herculean. It therefore caused a great stir when the 1973 Mr. America contest was won by a competitor with the potential to beat Schwarzenegger at his own game.

In order to compete in the Mr. America, this sensational new man of muscle who went by the name of Lou Ferrigno didn't have to travel far. Ferrigno was a native of Brooklyn, and in 1973 both lived and trained there. He was only 21 years old when he captured the Mr. America title, thanks to a physique that reminded fans of a young Arnold Schwarzenegger. Ferrigno was in fact more like Schwarzenegger than not; he possessed an immense, herculean physique, with massive biceps and chest. Ferrigno, like Schwarzenegger before him, also appeared to have much untapped potential. Wide-eyed spectators, conditioned to believe that height was a critical ingredient of excellence, wondered whether he had even *more* potential than Schwarzenegger, for the simple reason that Ferrigno was six-foot-five—a full three inches taller than the champion. The victory Ferrigno claimed later that year at the Mr. Universe contest in Geneva added to their excitement.

It therefore came as no surprise that the 1974 Mr. Olympia contest was hyped to be, in the words of Joe Weider, a Battle of Titans; and just like that, Weider had solved the dilemma caused by the departure of Sergio Oliva. Here was Oliva's replacement: a six-foot-five, 260-pound, American-born Hercules with unmatched measurements and a racial background that wouldn't factor into the judging. Whereas the Schwarzenegger/Oliva showdowns presented judges and fans with an apples-to-oranges comparison of physiques, Schwarzenegger and Ferrigno fell from the same tree. Their ancestors came from neighboring countries, not opposite hemispheres. There were no fundamental genetic differences between them. Instead of apples and oranges, the bodybuilding world prepared itself for a test of fresh versus seasoned.

Ferrigno improved rapidly. He won the 1974 IFBB Mr. International title, and as a tune-up for the Olympia, the young star once more entered the Mr. Universe. Held in Italy that year, Ferrigno defeated 64 other competitors to claim the title. With each successive victory, the threat he posed to Schwarzenegger's dominance grew. Fan interest in the upcoming Mr. Olympia contest was raised further by Ferrigno's hometown-hero status: yet again, the Olympia would be staged in New York. This time however, a famous venue in the city's premier borough would play host.

* * * * *

With Arnold Schwarzenegger as its centerpiece, the Weider's IFBB was now without question bodybuilding's premier governing body, and it was continually gathering momentum. Its Mr. Olympia contest was now easily the most important event on the bodybuilding calendar. Bob Hoffman and his AAU were meanwhile gradually sinking into obscurity. With each passing year, the two were pushed further to the sidelines by the growing market share of the IFBB—the organization Joe Weider reluctantly started as a means to avoid AAU bullying. When all was finally said and done, it was easy to draw the conclusion that Hoffman messed with the wrong guy.

In 1974 Weider was in the driver's seat. He had the world's greatest contest and, save for Sergio Oliva, the loyalty of the best bodybuilders. The 10th installment of that contest was about to get underway. A grand venue called for. The 113-year-old Brooklyn Academy of Music was a first-rate auditorium, though not a lot of non-New Yorkers were aware of that. Since bodybuilding now had a fan base that extended to six continents, securing a venue with greater name recognition would be ideal. It also seemed that the Academy's 2,200 seats would not nearly be enough for the anticipated crowd. It was therefore decided that the Mr. Olympia contest would pack up and head over the East River.

For the first time since the AAU Mr. America heyday, a bodybuilding contests was visited upon Manhattan's prestigious Madison Square Garden. However, the main auditorium with its 15,000 seats would not be used. Demand for tickets in no way warranted such a venue, nor had bodybuilding attracted that type of interest since Bernarr Macfadden's "World's Most Perfectly Developed Man" contests of 1905 and 1923 were held at the Garden. The 5,500 Felt Forum was chosen instead.

The men who competed in the 1974 Mr. Olympia arrived in a condition appropriate to the stage and contest. Not only were there more competitors than ever, but collectively they were bigger and more defined than anything yet witnessed. Unlike previous years, the prejudging was itself a large event, with *Muscle Builder* later reporting that 2,000 pe-

Lou Ferrigno. c. 1974

Courtesy of Michael Newman

ople showed up for it. Except for the addition of Ferrigno, the same men vied for the title as in 1973. However, the newcomer's stature prompted Weider to divide the field into two separate classes, one each for men above and below 200 pounds.

As was customary for physique contests, lighter competitors took the stage first. The two-man contest between Zane and Columbu was a study in opposites, perhaps even more so than the earlier comparisons of Schwarzenegger and Oliva. Zane was relatively tall, with a light frame, flowing lines and excellent overall shape. Columbu meanwhile was short, squat, and almost stubby in appearance. However, he had an incredibly thick torso, with a monstrously wide back and the world's thickest and most deeply-striated pectorals. His limb development, though not on par with that of his torso, was nevertheless above average. Thus was witnessed the latest iteration of bodybuilding's oft-recurring theme of beauty versus beast. In this instance beast carried the day, simply because Columbu was far too muscular to be denied. Few complained; and with Columbu's victory, the IFBB had its first Under-200-Pound Mr. Olympia.

Next came the heavies. One problem with public-viewing prejudging is that it sometimes kills the suspense of big matchups; when the reigning champion and the hometown-hero challenger marched onstage for the afternoon judging portion of the 1974 Olympia, it quickly became apparent that the event wouldn't live up to its billing. Ferrigno had previously overwhelmed his opposition with a physique that was enormous but needed refinement, much like Schwarzenegger had in 1969. Ferrigno had no illusions about the effect this formula would have against the current champion however. Schwarzenegger had significantly sharpened his appearance since '69, and now sported world-class muscular definition. Ferrigno attempted to follow suit, but like so many competitors bent on significantly reducing their fat stores, he ended up overdoing it.

Ferrigno improved his definition but sacrificed some muscular size. Schwarzenegger, who showed up in absolute top form, looked to be the clear winner. The night show brought no surprises, and he was handed the first-place trophy. Ferrigno followed, and Nubret finished third. The judges also had no trouble choosing Schwarzenegger over Columbu for the overall title; and with that, the Austrian's fifth Mr. Olympia win was in the books. His thoughts turned to retirement.

Schwarzenegger had soundly defeated the last legitimate threat to his supremacy. The world of bodybuilding had been conquered. He had ascended and remained perched atop its greatest heights, and the lay of the land was his alone to survey. That view only made more clear the fact that far greater heights loomed in the distance. He reached the same, easy conclusion as two other men that once stood upon that perch, Steve Reeves and Reg Park: in spite of the rich history, the contests, the great champions, the glory of victory, the magazines and the warring factions, bodybuilding is small.

Strictly defined, bodybuilding is an end, not a means; but for those after real fame, the opposite is true. Schwarzenegger saw this clearly. He therefore decided to follow the example of Reeves and Park, and become an actor—with one amendment. He did not just want to become a movie star; he wanted to become the biggest star of them all.

In a move that had become practically standard for bodybuilders who wished to become actors, in 1970 Schwarzenegger landed a role portraying Hercules. *Hercules in New York* was both the title and plot summary of the movie. Although his voice was dubbed, he was required to use the name "Arnold Strong," and the production later earned the distinction of being one of the worst movies ever made, Schwarzenegger's film career had nevertheless begun. There it languished for five years, with little to show but a few bit parts in television and movies. Schwarzenegger was off to a slow and almost hopeless start, but he was also undaunted. By 1975 he was ready and eager to make a run, in earnest, at film stardom.

Conquering the world of bodybuilding had not abated his ambitions. It encouraged him; it added fuel to his fire. A desire for new challenges and greater fame consumed him. It's therefore ironic that Schwarzenegger's first real shot at mainstream celebrity required that he stay in bodybuilding.

Reg Park as Hercules. 1963

In 1972, in an attempt to spice up its content, *Sports Illustrated* entertained the idea of featuring articles with "unconventional subject matter." The concept was given a green light, and the magazine's editorial staff decided that bodybuilding should be one of its topics. Writer Charles Gaines was commissioned by the magazine to travel to western Massachusetts, where he would investigate and report on something called the "Mr. East Coast" contest. He brought along photographer George Butler, a personal friend, to document the event. While both men had some familiarity with bodybuilding, what they witnessed that evening was something unexpectedly weird and wonderful. They were fascinated by the spectacle of muscular men flexing their muscles before a spirited crowd of cheering fans. After the contest, Gaines and Butler immediately began putting together their story. Each also now knew a little more about bodybuilding: that it was strange and enthralling; at its core was a group of men who dedicated their lives to the pursuit of muscle; and it had a small legion of devoted fans. Their report was submitted and the article was a success.

Gaines and Butler were happy but not satisfied. The two felt as if they found a secret door, cracked it open and found that an exciting, fascinating alternate universe lay beyond. Too curious to simply walk away, the pair looked for an opportunity to enter that world—where they expected to find many more strange and interesting things. Reasoning that a fair portion of the public would be bound to share their captivation, an exploration was planned. The easiest and most direct way to tell the tale of bodybuilding was to write a book on the topic.

Gaines and Butler were able to convince Doubleday Publishing to not only publish it, but to finance the necessary fact-seeking mission. The two traveled the country, interviewing and photographing bodybuilding's biggest stars: Schwarzenegger, Ferrigno, Mike Katz, Ed Corney, and a number of others. Upon completion, the manuscript was dropped off at Doubleday's New York headquarters.

Doubleday hated it and demanded repayment. "No one will ever read this book," Butler was told, "and no one will ever be interested in Arnold Schwarzenegger." Considering Doubleday's offices were a short cab ride from the site of Bernarr Macfadden's giant physique contests of days past, the statement spoke to the power of ignorance. It was a heavy blow nonetheless. The situation was meanwhile far from hopeless. Gaines and Butler were after all in the publishing Mecca that is New York City. All they needed to do was find a publisher with even a faint understanding of bodybuilding's appeal. As fate would have it, Simon & Shuster fit that bill.

Pumping Iron: The Art and Sport of Bodybuilding was released in 1974 and became an immediate success. Through that book, the world was given its first-ever introduction to the world of bodybuilding, written from the standpoint of the detached observer. Throughout the prior 80 years bodybuilding had remained at the periphery of public consciousness, periodically surfacing in the form of strongman exhibitions, Charles Atlas ads, Steve Reeves movies or magazine covers. Although these things teased the public with images of bodybuilders, they also deepened the mystery of who these people were, where they came from, and how they got that way. *Pumping Iron* was different. It showed that public exactly what bodybuilding was and who bodybuilders were. The public ate it up. *Pumping Iron* found its way onto the New York Times' best-seller list.

Despite this success Gaines and Butler were once more happy but not satisfied. They had introduced bodybuilding to the world, but as in case of the *Sports Illustrated* article, print media didn't capture the essence of the subject matter. By their reckoning, only a film could do that. At the same time, it wasn't just bodybuilding per se that so strongly warranted the transition from book to film; that leap was owed in large part to the man who would become its star.

Arnold Schwarzenegger had not only built the world's greatest physique since coming to the United States in 1968; he also remarkably improved his English skills; and perhaps most importantly, he developed a magnetic, engaging, larger-than-life personality. Through their book, Gaines and Butler had amply demonstrated an understanding of what the public would find interesting. They knew that with the bodybuilding underworld as his backdrop, Schwarzenegger would carry their film. It was bound to be a success. They just needed to drum up funding and convince Schwarzenegger to go along with it.

When Gaines and Butler began raising money for the film, the wretched public image of bodybuilding weighed heavily against their efforts. In a modern interview with the *Iron Age* website, Butler characterized that image: "The prevailing view was that it was purely homosexual, that bodybuilders were totally uncoordinated, and that when they grew older that their muscles would turn to fat and that they had no intelligence whatsoever. Charles Gaines said that it was like trying to promote midget wrestling." Butler didn't give up. He independently approached no less than 3,000 investors before finally being able to secure an amount he though would cover costs: $400,000.

As for Schwarzenegger, no amount of coy posturing about retirement could conceal the fact that his participation was a sure thing. He wanted to get into movies. The book *Pumping Iron* was a bestseller. The film that would wear the same name could be a godsend, a huge push to a career that had gotten out of the blocks slowly and dreadfully. It's true that the film was going to be a documentary, which would be a clear deviation from Schwarzenegger's ambition to be a dramatic actor, but this turned out to be the best possible scenario for the bodybuilding champion who wished to make it big in the movies.

In *Pumping Iron*, Schwarzenegger would merely have to be himself. By the estimation of Gaines and Butler, that would be enough to make him a star. The route of his predecessors, who had slashed their way to Italian sword-and-sandals glory, could be bypassed entirely. This would be something altogether different, something that promised to directly satisfy the public's curiosity about bodybuilding and the men who did it. In *Pumping Iron*, cameras would capture Schwarzenegger in his element, in his world—something a Hercules flick would never do.

Gaines and Butler once more got to work. Their strategy was to follow for 12 weeks three of the men who would compete in the 1975 Mr. Olympia contest: Schwarzenegger, Lou Ferrigno and Franco Columbu; and one who would compete in the accompanying Mr. Universe contest: Mike Katz. Filming took place at the stomping grounds of the film's characters: Katz in Connecticut, Ferrigno in New York, Schwarzenegger and Columbu in California. The film's events culminated at the Mr. Olympia contest in Pretoria, South Africa—the most far-flung location in the event's history. Travel expenses put a big dent in the film's budget but the South African setting enriched its subject matter, something that would hopefully pay off at a later date.

Once shooting was complete Gaines and Butler faced the daunting task of editing 100 hours of footage down to 85 minutes. They also ran into money problems, as the production had run seriously over budget. Since it couldn't be finished without additional funds, a ploy was devised that not only aimed to raise money, but to increase awareness of the upcoming film. Since New York is arguably the cultural capital of North America, Butler came up with the novel idea of exploiting the element of artistry in bodybuilding. In 1976 he convinced the Whitney Museum of American Art to stage an exhibition called "Articulate Muscle: The Male Body in Art," which would feature live posing by three of *Pumping Iron*'s top bodybuilders: Schwarzenegger, Ed Corney and Frank Zane.[1] Accompanying the display of muscle would be a high-brow discussion of the male form in art by six prominent members of the New York art community—artists, critics, and art historians.

Standing atop a rotating platform, one by one the three men assumed the form of living sculpture. It was a carefully-selected trio; Schwarzenegger was the film's star, while Corney and Zane were masters of artistic posing with physiques to match. The art community, most of whom had never seen real-live bodybuilders, turned out in droves. A heavy January snowstorm that threatened to shut down the city kept no one away.

[1]Although Zane would become an all-time great, his total screen time in *Pumping Iron* did not exceed a few seconds.

Whitney Museum of American Art.
New York City. c. 2005

Sports Illustrated's Katharine Lowry was on hand to cover the event. Though the evening was intended to be a celebration of muscle, she declared it had been ruined by "academic flabbiness," with "unforgivably dull" banter from the panel and "much-too-brief" posing displays. Lowry further wrote that patrons "left feeling as if they'd just been to a compulsory night-school class." The comments were interesting, considering they were printed by the same magazine that got the entire *Pumping Iron* ball rolling four years earlier. Nevertheless, Lowry's opinions were entirely without consequence. It was a one-time-only event, and its mission was accomplished. Along with additional funding from existing investors, enough money had been made to finance the remainder of the film.

Butler, Gaines and their production team got back to work. A little less than a year after the Whitney event, on January 18, 1977, *Pumping Iron* was released. Butler and Gaines now had to their credit a solid documentary, and for Butler in particular it was a promising beginning to a career in film direction. For most of the film's audience, it was an entertaining and interesting look at the cultural phenomenon of bodybuilding. For the subculture of bodybuilding itself however, *Pumping Iron* was something entirely different. Although it would take more than a decade for the film's gravity to be fully realized, its eventual impact on the world of muscle was nearly beyond measure.

The release of *Pumping Iron* was one of the most important events in the history of bodybuilding. Though its purpose was pure and simple documentation, the film inadvertently became a supremely effective advertisement for muscle culture and competition. The film brought people out to see contests, and especially, it brought them into gyms. It was an 85-minute recruiting tool that successfully turned a small legion of men into competitive bodybuilders. The massive increase in the number of people entering contests starting in the early 1980s testifies to its contribution. The period that elapsed between the release of *Pumping Iron* and the beginning of the '80s just happened to be the same amount of time that average bodybuilders require to progress from their first workout to their first contest. Simply put, a number of people saw the movie, joined a gym, became devoted bodybuilders, and a few years later, oiled up and stepped onstage. It's a rare film that can have such a dramatic impact on the lives of its viewers.

For those so affected, mostly young men, the film

Gold's Gym, Venice. c. 1975
The primary shooting location for *Pumping Iron*

struck a nerve. It gave them a sense that, until they became accomplished bodybuilders themselves, they were missing out. An untold number resolved to emulate its stars. As for the hard work required, the 1976 film *Rocky* had already put on display for that generation the romance of toil—the appealing image of the solitary figure battling it out with himself, testing the limits of his own physical constitution. Bodybuilding did one better. There were rewards other than the satisfaction of having overcome physical obstacles. A bodybuilder turned his body into a living, breathing badge of honor, an awe-inspiring sight, one worthy of parade. Anybody with a tough mind and a gym membership could do it. At least these were the thoughts that went through the minds of young men for whom their first screening of *Pumping Iron* was a life-changing experience.

A number of new gyms and health clubs sprang up to accommodate and hopefully profit from the newfound appeal of bodybuilding. The Gold's Gym brand in particular had been given a gigantic shot in the arm, since that establishment was one of the primary filming locations of the movie. Before long there were dozens, and then scores, of Gold's Gyms throughout the United States. 30 years after the release of *Pumping Iron*, Gold's was a long-established licensing corporation with more than 600 franchises in 30 countries.

Pumping Iron did not single-handedly create these effects. Nor did any single entity. However, it gave bodybuilding a gigantic push. The film's other primary effect, in time and on its own, would push bodybuilding even further. *Pumping Iron* effectively launched the film career of Arnold Schwarzenegger. His magnetism and charisma were undeniable, and these elements were conveyed quite effectively in his scenes. Schwarzenegger also didn't come across as if he were on a mission of self-propping. He didn't mind appearing underhanded, calculating or selfish. Future employers wouldn't care if he was. Hollywood wants stars, not nice guys. Audiences wanted more of Schwarzenegger, and studio heads were prepared to oblige.

Arnold Schwarzenegger went on to be a big star, something that George Butler fully expected, even back in 1973. Schwarzenegger's blockbuster action movies were a showcase of muscle, and each one increased the magnitude of *Pumping Iron's* importance. Although those movies were not fundamentally different from the Hercules flicks of Steve Reeves, the question of how either man became so muscular was no longer a mystery. *Pumping Iron* had cleared all that up. It put on film the demands and methods of creating a world-class physique—or at least gave an extended sneak-peek as to how this was accomplished.

Young men saw movies like *Conan the Barbarian, Commando* and *Predator,* un-dropped their jaws, and bought memberships at local gyms. Every film Schwarzenegger made, every time he appeared in public, and even every time his name was mentioned—these were all advertisements for bodybuilding. He became a fascinating study in determination, success and influence. Any attempt to establish why he became so big—or how he spurred the growth of bodybuilding—has to place a great deal of importance on *Pumping Iron*.

That wasn't all. In yet another instance of happenstance guiding the evolution of muscle culture and competition, any explanation of how Schwarzenegger and bodybuilding got so big must also place a great deal of importance on the *Sports Illustrated* decision to run articles about unusual subject matter. If not for that whim, the talented and passionate duo of Gaines and Butler might never have even given a thought to covering bodybuilding. As fate would have it, they did cover bodybuilding, and they did make *Pumping Iron*.

Partly because of that film, the next generation would do no less than rethink bodybuilding's timeline. The Golden Age of Bodybuilding was previously considered to be the era of Grimek, Reeves, Yorton and Park. For the majority of muscle culture, this would be no more. Though it has no firm beginning or end dates, the Golden Age is now widely considered to have begun sometime in the early 1960s, with its peak being the mid-'70s. The scenes captured in *Pumping Iron*, those fond remembrances of how things once were, formed that peak—and the film's content was the very thing that made the age Golden.

Although the important events of *Pumping Iron* were faithfully documented, a few inconsequential facts were either changed or deleted in order to create a storyline. The audience was given the impression that the champion Schwarzenegger had not yet stood onstage next to the monstrous Ferrigno. The tension of their impending head-to-head matchup was the plot around which the rest of the film revolved. In reality, Schwarzenegger had already faced Ferrigno at the '74 Olympia, and had seen him off in convincing fashion. Unless Ferrigno was to improve significantly, the '75 outcome would be no different.

Outtakes from *Pumping Iron* include a conversation between Schwarzenegger and Joe Weider, in which Weider advises his champion that Ferrigno now posed a real threat to take the title. According to Weider (who had recently seen Ferrigno), the challenger looked "very massive." Although this may have been a ploy on the part of Weider to spice up the conversation and overall scenario, Schwarzenegger nevertheless responded with worried contem-

Ed Corney. c. 1975

Courtesy of Michael Newman

plation. This interaction accorded well with the film's original storyline, which was that the massive and mysterious newcomer could very well knock the King off his throne. Because of how the contest turned out, the scene was cut.

The story told in the movie was instead tailored to reflect reality. It was a tale of the confident champion soundly defeating the wet-behind-the-ears newcomer. Although Ferrigno wasn't technically a newcomer, he was decisively beaten in Pretoria. His attempt to gain additional mass cost him precious definition. By 1975, muscular detail that was anything less than sharp would not do. He fell to third place. Serge Nubret was once again in the mix, and was perhaps the most defined man in the contest. He swapped his previous year's position with Ferrigno and came in second.

Franco Columbu, bigger, thicker and more defined than ever, once more captured the lightweight title, easily defeating Ed Corney, Albert Beckles and Frank Zane. He posed off against Schwarzenegger for the overall title, but the contest could really only have one outcome. Olympia emcee Reg Park, when announcing the winner, delivered the words that succinctly summarized the Austrian's place in the history of bodybuilding: "The one and only; the greatest; Arnold Schwarzenegger." With that, Schwarzenegger took the podium, thanked the judges and fans, and declared his retirement.

Thus came to an end the competitive career of Arnold Schwarzenegger; and with his departure, the Golden Age of Bodybuilding entered a phase of epilogue. Bodybuilding's greatest champion, the dominant figure of his era, was gone. His Mr. Olympia throne lay vacant. The remainder of the era would be characterized by a fight for the title by men whom Schwarzenegger had defeated. There were a number of great competitors during this period, but no dominant champion. Another decade would pass before one emerged. In spite of this, fans didn't lose interest. The departure of a virtually unbeatable champion also meant a farewell to foregone conclusions. No one knew who the next Mr. Olympia would be. Eager fans therefore looked ahead to the next installment of the contest, and with it, the crowning of a new champion.

* * * * *

1976 was supposed to have been a banner year for the IFBB, though not because of anything that might happen at the Mr. Olympia contest. Five years earlier much noise had been made about the IFBB's need to run a tight ship, since a bid to get bodybuilding into the'76 Montreal Olympics was in the works. To that end, the federation put in place strict new rules regarding the amateur status of competitors. Fans might have recalled that Franco Columbu was disqualified from the 1971 Mr. Universe because he entered a professional contest of a rogue federation. Now, on the eve of the '76 Olympia, Columbu was the leading candidate to take the title; and as for the Montreal Games, they came and went without a bodybuilder in sight and without a peep from the IFBB or the Weiders. The '76 Olympics brought fame to athletes like Nadia Comanici, Vasily Alexeyev and Bruce Jenner; but there was no such glory in store for amateur bodybuilders like Robby Robinson, Roger Walker or Mike Mentzer. The International Olympic Committee had listened to Ben Weider's sales pitch, thanked him for his time, and told him no.

The Weiders refused to give up on their Olympic dream, and after another decade had passed they gave the idea another, bigger push. That effort would eventually trigger a bizarre and tumultuous series of events, but for the time being they had contests to put on. The 1976 Mr. Universe was held in Montreal. Although the IFBB had not been invited to the Montreal Olympics, apparently it figured it would be able to make some sort of impression on the IOC with the professionalism and size of its proceedings. This was not to be however, since the Olympics had been over for a few months by the time the contest got underway. As for the '76 Olympia, their choice of location represented a marked philosophical departure from contests of the recent past. Whereas

Opening ceremonies, 1976 Olympics, Montreal. The IFBB bid to secure a spot for bodybuilding at the Games was unsuccessful.

the first six years of the decade saw the event staged in New York, Europe and the African subcontinent, this time around the less-famous American Midwestern city of Columbus, Ohio would play host.

A few years prior, Arnold Schwarzenegger formed a friendship with Jim Lorimer, a Columbus resident who promoted events in the area. The two decided that Columbus, with its somewhat central location, adequate venues and inexpensive lodging, would make an ideal city to stage the greatest muscle show on Earth. Lorimer had expertise but limited pull, something that was easily offset by Schwarzenegger's now-great influence and rising star-power. The Columbus idea was proposed to Weider, he gave it the green light, and the Lorimer/Schwarzenegger promotional duo got to work.

Fan speculation swirled around the prospect of a Ferrigno victory. He had essentially beaten himself in '75, displaying a level of muscular definition that wasn't on par with his over-200-pound class rivals. Were he to correct that situation, winning the Olympia was a distinct possibility. Remarkably, Ferrigno was still only 24 years old. He appeared to have vast untapped potential, and fans knew it. They also knew that subpar conditioning was a very correctable fault. Such speculation was all for naught however, since Ferrigno was conspicuously absent from the '76 lineup. He later admitted that Schwarzenegger had been a hero figure to him—"I wanted to be like Arnold" was his remark—and it's possible that the Austrian's retirement prompted Ferrigno to consider other uses for his muscles. There was little doubt that greater opportunities lay elsewhere.

Even with endorsement and personal appearance fees factored in, no one had yet come close to making a decent living from bodybuilding alone. The winner's check at the Mr. Olympia contest was still a paltry $1000. Ferrigno was smart enough to realize that he could suffer through decades of hard training and strict dieting before he ever got the opportunity to cash one. The level of competition was rising every year, and although Ferrigno was something very special, the same could be said for a number of his peers. The eye-popping muscularity of Columbu, despite his short and blocky composition, was enough to discourage any entrant.

By the time Columbu retired, Ferrigno had moved on. In spite of a hearing impairment that severely limited whatever dramatic range he might possess, Ferrigno decided to give acting a shot. Within a year, a casting call went out for a television adaptation of *The Incredible Hulk* comic book. In a situation that could not have been more appropriate, Ferrigno was chosen to portray the tale's green monster. Not only was he physically perfectly suited for the role, but playing The Hulk also allowed him to become a famous actor—even a household name—without having to utter consonants other than *r*.

In a manner that was more Boris Karloff than Steve Reeves, Ferrigno carved out his own on-screen entertainment niche. Yet the manner of his fame mattered little. Ferrigno had reached the pinnacle of muscle stardom. History has demonstrated that the ultimate prize in bodybuilding isn't any Mr. America, Universe or Olympia title. It's a star on the Hollywood Walk of Fame.[1]

Franco Columbu therefore became the clear favorite to take the 1976 Mr. Olympia title. Once the contest got underway however, his superiority came into question, thanks to the improved condition of Frank Zane. Since 1970, the only man other than Schwarzenegger to defeat Columbu was Zane, when he did so at the '72 Olympia. By '76

[1]Thus far Arnold Schwarzenegger and Jack LaLanne are the only bodybuilders with stars on the Walk.

Lou Ferrigno as the Incredible Hulk. c. 1978

Getty Images

Columbu had returned the favor twice, but Zane was now more complete and certainly more polished. After all, polish was his strength. Although Columbu possessed a small array of mind-boggling bodyparts, the manner in which those parts fit together was never a point of praise. Zane was the opposite. He possessed an array of bodyparts which by themselves were far less impressive, but the way those parts fit together inspired awe. He was a bodybuilder in the tradition of Steve Reeves. Columbu meanwhile broke all existing molds; and once more, this was the factor that carried him to victory—albeit by a single point—in the under-200-pound category.

The heavyweight division had only two entrants, the '75 Mr. Universe rivals Mike Katz and Ken Waller. *Pumping Iron* had not yet been released, so fans had not yet started booing Waller for playing the role of Katz's villainous nemesis. Although Katz had serious shortcomings as a bodybuilder, he was a fan favorite. Apart from being a somewhat famous ex-NFL player, he was also bodybuilding's version of the likeable, perennial underdog. None of that was enough to reverse the misfortunes of the'75 Universe however, and once more Waller came out on top. He therefore replaced Schwarzenegger as Columbu's adversary for the overall title. Waller was no Schwarzenegger however, and the contest was no match. Columbu won.

For the first time in the Mr. Olympia contest's history, the physique of the winner was widely considered to be inferior to that of the previous champion. Yet this mattered little. Even after taking into account the fantastic display put on by Frank Zane, there really were no active IFBB competitors who seemed capable of beating Columbu. He was king of the hill, and looked like he might be for some time to come. The time could have been right for a Sergio Oliva return, but he had already committed to enter the 1977 Professional World Championships of Serge Nubret's newly-created World Amateur Bodybuilding Association. Oliva probably wouldn't have come back anyway. He was sorely disappointed by what he considered to be the Weiders' policies of favoritism, and his departure over that issue likely burned his IFBB bridge anyway. As for Nubret, his bridge without question burned. Because of his WABBA venture, the Weiders expelled Nubret from the IFBB for life.

* * * * *

In January 1977, *Pumping Iron* hit the theaters; and with it, a light was cast upon the previously shadowy world of competitive bodybuilding. From that point forward, more attention was expected for all levels of bodybuilding. Those expectations were met. Bodybuilding instantly had more fans. The ranks of bodybuilders slowly began to swell. Muscle contests gained publicity.

Something that wasn't expected was the way *Pumping Iron* helped boost publicity for the newly-created "World's Strongest Man" contest. Originally developed in 1977 for the CBS television network by a company called Langstar, the contest's title left little doubt about its intent: it would pit the world's top strength athletes against each other in an effort to determine who on Earth could lift the most. As part of a calculated strategy, the contest didn't make use of traditional weightlifting movements like the clean-and-jerk or the snatch. After all, the world already knew who the world's strongest Olympic lifter was. It had just witnessed the Soviet weightlifter Vasiliy Alexeyev dominate those events at the 1976 Olympics. Beyond that, the American public found Olympic-style weightlifting to be rigid and boring.

Powerlifting, with its bench press, deadlift and squat, was even worse. The general population has never understood the excitement of watching a barbell travel in a short, linear path. Nor could that public easily relate to the apparatus used for any type of competitive lifting, or certainly the weight heaved. Only a small percentage of people who lift weights seriously can appreciate the gravity of a 500-pound clean-and-jerk or a 900-pound squat.

It's a different story when everyday items become lifting apparatus. For example, most people can appreciate how hard it is to push a car up even a slight

Franco Columbu bending iron rod. c. 1976

Courtesy of Michael Newman

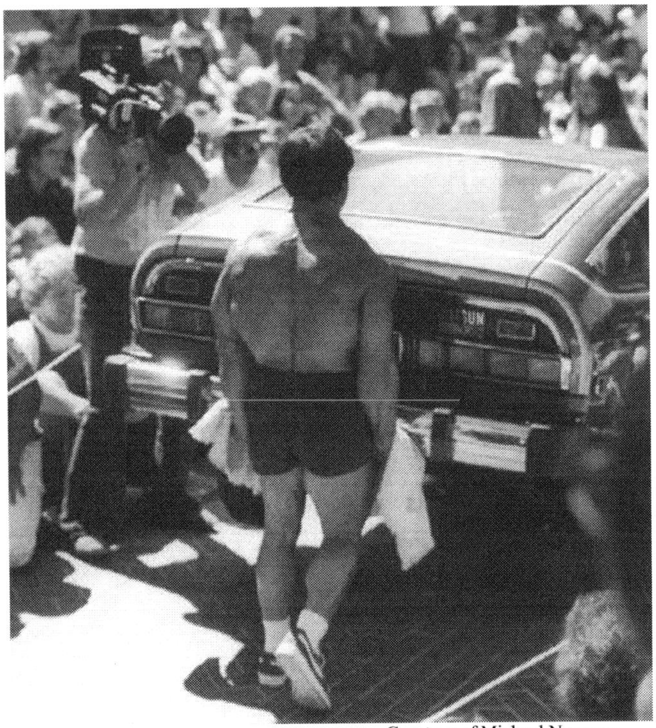

Courtesy of Michael Newman

Franco Columbu lifting a car. c. 1976

incline, or how difficult it can be to move a refrigerator up a single step. It was therefore a brilliant stroke when Langstar and its chief coordinator David Webster made plans to have strongmen not only lift things like the back ends of cars, but in the case of objects like refrigerators, pick them up and race with them. The good ideas didn't stop there. Langstar and CBS pulled off a coup when it got two of *Pumping Iron's* biggest stars, Lou Ferrigno and Franco Columbu, to compete in the event. Without that pair, the biggest name in the show would have been Bruce Wilhelm—a man whose greatest exploit had been placing second in the snatch event as a super-heavyweight at the Montreal Olympics.

Columbu in particular was an obvious recruiting target. His silver-screen boast of being the strongest bodybuilder who ever lived made it seem as though he would jump at any chance to back up that claim with action. He happily signed the contract to compete. It was therefore a moment of both irony and infamy when, near the end of the competition, Columbu came crashing to earth with a refrigerator on his back. The fall severely and hideously dislocated his lower leg. Columbu's tendons and ligaments tore away under the weight of the massive appliance, and with them, decades of weight training were undone. The injury was so horrendous that Columbu's doctors told him he might very well never walk again.

For someone who made a living and based his identity on physical prowess, it should have been a devastating blow—except that Columbu never believed it. Although his doctors' judgment was based on what could be expected from a typical patient, those doctors would soon learn what the bodybuilding community already knew: how atypical the Sardinian bodybuilder really was.

That being said, there was zero chance of Columbu recovering in time for the 1977 Mr. Olympia contest. It was therefore guaranteed that for the first time in the event's history, a third champion would be crowned in three years. A decade earlier, something like this would have threatened the legitimacy of the title. But now, after the legendary reigns of Oliva and Schwarzenegger; after the failure of rival organizations to keep pace with the IFBB; after a substantial increase in the number of that federation's professional competitors; and after *Pumping Iron* had sealed the grandeur of the Olympia forever into celluloid—the forced departure of Columbu only heightened the upcoming event's intrigue.

That being said, Frank Zane was quietly poised to steal the show. Although he had previously come out on the losing end of beauty-versus-beast contests against Columbu, the latter was a breed apart. The lineup opposing Zane featured beasts of a more earthly variety, and he had a solid history of defeating those. There was however one man with the potential to upset Zane's date with destiny. Robby Robinson, an amateur competitor who received some

Robby Robinson. c. 1977

Courtesy of Michael Newman

screen time but no introduction or dialogue in *Pumping Iron*—despite having one of the most impressive builds in the film—had joined the IFBB professional ranks by defeating a field of 50 men at the 1976 Mr. Universe competition. By late 1977 he had improved even further; and at his first Mr. Olympia contest he was already a legitimate threat to take the title. He was that good.

Robinson had full muscle bellies, deep separation, tremendous back and arm development, a tiny waist, large thighs, and a good overall level of definition. As an unabashed product of his era, he topped it all off with a thick Fu Manchu mustache and a voluminous afro. When viewed in silhouette, there was no mistaking Robbie Robinson. In contests, it looked like there might be no beating him either. With his emergence, Zane had his hands full.

Since the 1976 Columbus Olympia had been such a success, Lorimer and Schwarzenegger decided to repeat the formula in '77. There was also now little uncertainty about the effect of *Pumping Iron* on ticket sales: The 4,000-seat Veterans' Memorial Auditorium sold out six weeks before the event. Bodybuilding was enjoying a general revival of enthusiasm. As for the '77 Olympia in particular, the guaranteed crowning of a new champion boosted the crowd's excitement. Once the competition was underway the excitement rose further still.

Although Robinson had previously competed at a bodyweight of less than 200 pounds, for the '77 Olympia he wisely came into the contest above that mark. With the recent departure of notable giants, the prospect of competing in the over-200 pound class was no longer daunting; in fact the category's competitors had been surpassed in quality by those of the lightweight division. There was no Arnold Schwarzenegger, Lou Ferrigno or Serge Nubret with which to contend. Robinson instead faced off against Dennis Tinerino, Roger Walker and Ken Waller.

Although it seemed clear that Robinson would defeat that trio, a curious amendment to the contest's proceedings rendered class divisions to be, for the most part, irrelevant. During the evening portion of normally-structured bodybuilding contests, after the members of a specific class all complete their individual posing routines, those men once more assemble together onstage. After a brief pose-off, placings are announced. The next class repeats this procedure. In the contest's final phase, the first-place contestants of each class are called back onstage, so that the judges may determine who among them is best. The contest ends with the announcement of the overall winner.

In 1977, standard procedure was done away with. Instead, competitors were assigned two placings: one to reflect the competitor's standing within his own weight class, and the other to reflect his standing relative to the entire field of competitors. In an even more odd break from tradition, at the end of the contest, after all the individual posing routines had been completed, the top three competitors from each class were called out to pose-off together. The final strange twist came when the name of the overall winner was announced before any of the other placings.

In light of this unusual new convention, it didn't matter that Robby Robinson was over 200 pounds. Nor did it matter that Frank Zane, who was under 200 pounds, looked as though he had beaten fellow class members Albert Beckles, Boyer Coe, Ed Corney and Bill Grant. All those men would be assigned an overall rank, regardless of how they placed within their class. Nevertheless, since the Olympia throne was deemed to have so many worthy claimants, and since the identity of the winner might have been so unsure, the ploy almost made sense. Theoretically, any of the top six—Zane, Robinson, Corney, Tinerino, Coe or Waller—could have won that night.

In reality there was far less uncertainty. The title went to Zane. In a lineup devoid of behemoths like Schwarzenegger, and with no specimens of stunning muscularity like Columbu, judges opted not to endorse a second-rate replacement for either. They instead followed a completely different path, rewarding the sleek, shapely and statuesque lightweight. Though they may not have known it at the time, those judges were also ushering in a new era, one that seemed perfectly suited for the times.

There could not have been a more appropriate champion for the late 1970s than Frank Zane. In the world of popular culture, those years are remembered for a lot of things: disco; outrageous polyester fashion; bell-bottoms; hair that was shaggy on men and feathered on women; the cocaine surge; and the movies *Saturday Night Fever* and *Star Wars*. As much as any of those things however, the late '70s are remembered for their rail-thin celebrity sex symbols. The most famous female model was named Twiggy; and it's arguable that the closest thing to an action hero the era produced was Luke Skywalker, played by the fit but slightly-built Mark Hamill. In that environment, it wasn't difficult for shaggy-haired, polyester-wearing bodybuilding fans to embrace the most slightly-built of all the Mr. Olympias, a man who rolled the muscular mass clock back to the late 1950s.

Beyond that, Zane was handsome. He looked as if he easily could have landed roles as an extra for a number of the era's movies or TV shows. (Zane ventured into television once during the era, when had a small part in a 1981 episode of *Hart to Hart*.) That's not to say that Zane was deemed man of the hour because he was good-looking and his physique was an appropriate match for the current tastes of the outside world. Zane won bodybuilding's highest award because he was considered to be a living work of art. He had an overall muscular shape reminiscent of Classical monuments, Michelangelo's Ignudi, and even Steve Reeves.

It almost seemed as if Zane dared to limit his size; as if he deliberately held back growth, so as not to disturb his perfect balance. Eugen Sandow boasted that he employed such a strategy, but Zane would never have uttered such nonsense. He simply took his physique to its genetic limit, put it on display, and reaped the rewards. A legion of much larger men came onto the scene after his reign, but all of them together have not blocked Zane from memory, nor will they. He is admired more each year. Once bodybuilding had reached its eventual state, Frank Zane became not only an icon of antithesis, but a reminder of how things once were. He cast a fitting final light over the Golden Age dusk.

Frank Zane. c. 1979

Courtesy of Michael Newman

Although Frank Zane was widely praised by the bodybuilding community for his "symmetry," that assessment wasn't quite accurate. In the case of a human physique, symmetry refers to the degree of balance between the left and right halves. In instances of perfect symmetry, those halves are an exact reflection of each other. No living human has this, including Frank Zane. His left and right halves had a slightly different shape, and the lines of his abdominals were slightly diagonal rather than perfectly horizontal. Nevertheless, a large part of Zane's brilliance as a competitor was accurate self-assessment. He knew his strengths and exploited them. He also knew his weaknesses and was able to disguise them. He posed in a manner such that both these things were accomplished simultaneously. Without this ability, he might not have been acknowledged as the world's best bodybuilder.

It was therefore no surprise that Zane again won in 1978. Although significantly larger men once again surrounded him, Zane rose above the pack. Robinson repeated as runner-up. The pair were pushed harder this time however, since not only did the Olympia field swell to a record 13 competitors, but its overall quality was likewise at an all-time high. It was a glimpse of things to come. Gone were the days of two-man weight classes. From that year forward, all Mr. Olympia lineups would have both depth and breadth.

In 1978, that depth and breadth came in the form of new heavyweights Roy Callendar (second) and Kal Szalak (third), and lightweights Danny Padilla (third), Tony Emmott (fifth) and Mohamed Makkawy (sixth). Callendar would continue to threaten the title for years to come; and Makkawy, despite standing a mere five-foot-two, would rise to a position of even greater prominence. Meanwhile, casualties were inevitable. Ed Corney fell two places from '77 and Albert Beckles four.

The Lorimer/Schwarzenegger duo had once more hosted the Olympia in Columbus in 1978, and in '79, for a fourth and final time, the same would be true. The list of entrants also grew again, this time to 15. Notable newcomers included Tom Platz, winner of the '78 IFBB World Amateur Championships and owner of the world's largest quadriceps. Joining him was Mike Mentzer, the first and only man in history to record a perfect score of 300 in the Mr. Universe contest. In 1978, the IFBB still used a variation of the old AAU scoring system, in which a competitor was assigned a grade on a scale of 1 to 20 for each of the judging rounds. When all judges' scores were added together from the three rounds, the highest possible score was 300. The current system instead ranks entrants relative to other competitors.

Mentzer owed his perfect score to remarkable head-to-toe thickness and a particularly impressive his upper body. Though his hips were slightly wide, this was offset by exceptional back and arm development. Mentzer's overall shape was passable—not in a league with Zane, but far better than that of Columbu. At five-foot-nine and 225 pounds he may have been inch-for-inch the largest man of his age, and quite possibly the largest bodybuilder ever to that point.

Except for his thicker midsection and hips, it's tempting to recall Mentzer as a white version of Sergio Oliva. Mentzer however had somewhat angular lines, which contrasted starkly to Oliva's dramatic, sweeping curves. Apart from his three Olympia titles, it's for this reason that Oliva has enjoyed more enduring fame. Nevertheless, hypothetical comparisons avail little. In 1979 Oliva lurked in exile. As for Mentzer, it went without saying that he was a serious threat to win the heavyweight class and possibly the overall Mr. Olympia title.

At the event, the first prediction immediately proved true. Dennis Tinerino, Roger Walker and Roy Callendar were good, but Mentzer rolled right through them; and again, Mentzer was awarded a perfect score. Zane likewise laid waste to his competition, albeit to slightly lower marks. Boyer Coe came in second. Robby Robinson, taking cover from the approaching Mentzer storm, had for '79 ducked below the contest's 200-pound dividing line. In the end the move proved ill advised, and Robinson fell to third. Since the Olympia had returned to the normal structure of class winners facing off against each other, the audience got what it came to see: a Zane-versus-Mentzer showdown.

Mike Mentzer, c. 1979

Courtesy of Michael Newman

The rules of the 20-point system stipulated that once the class winners assembled onstage for the final pose-off, scores from previous judging rounds were rendered irrelevant. The overall winner would be determined, after the class winners' pose-off, by polling the judges. Mentzer's perfect score was now a point of trivia. He traded poses with Zane, and without question out-muscled him. In the eyes of some, Mentzer was unquestionably the victor. Nevertheless, in a contest that had come to place importance on factors other than the size, shape, proportion, condition and presentation of the men on stage, out-muscling an opponent might very well not be enough. Mentzer did not fall completely short in this regard; in fact, in one important way history was on his side. In bodybuilding contests, beast had most often defeated beauty.

Franco Columbu's 1976 refrigerator catastrophe had cleared the way for a pair of Frank Zane victories. No one with Columbu's level of muscularity had competed for the Olympia title since then. Now however, a much taller man, with similar mass but better proportions and lines—bodybuilding's new great beast—stood firmly in the path of a third Zane victory. Yet Zane was able to match Mentzer's advantage of historical precedent with one of his own: only once in the Mr. Olympia contest's 14-year history had a crown been pried from the head of a reigning champion. That rare event was the handiwork of the rarest of champions, Arnold Schwarzenegger, when he unseated Sergio Oliva at the beginning of the decade. Now, at the decade's end, Schwarzenegger waited offstage, ready to congratulate that year's winner. Next to him was the Sandow Trophy—a bronze statue of Eugen Sandow that since 1977 has been presented to Mr. Olympia contests' winners.

Sandow would have been pleased to learn his likeness was being used to reward the world's best-built man. He likewise would have found satisfying the notion that his own invention, the physique contest, had endured, prospered, and created new fame for a few of its participants. The following decades would see one of these competitors—the man waiting to interview the winner of that year's trophy—increase his fame far beyond what was pre-

Giant replica of Sandow trophy.
IFBB Headquarters, Bucharest, Romania

viously thought imaginable. Before any of that could happen however, the final Mr. Olympia title of the 1970s had to be awarded.

The contest's judges decided that although the newcomer Mike Mentzer had put on an amazing muscular display performance, it would not be enough to topple the neo-Greek God incumbent. Zane was again champion. The Veterans' Memorial Auditorium erupted in cheers. Some fans left unhappy with the decision, but they understood its rationale. Zane did not just own a more graceful silhouette. He had a more polished appearance with a demeanor to match. *Pumping Iron* had taught audiences the value of that combination.

Afterward, in a scene familiar to all bodybuilding fans, the champion stood by himself onstage. He struck poses he had already hit a dozen times in front of an audience that was thrilled to watch. A fitful rhythm of cheers and flashbulbs formed the evening's coda. Later, after the final interview had been given and the last congratulations had been made, after the last fan had left the building, the Veterans' Memorial Auditorium's staff went about their post-event routine. They dismantled the posing tier and packed away the velvet ropes and judges' tables. Higher-ups tallied the evening's proceeds. Sometime after midnight, the auditorium's lights were turned off and its doors were locked. For the moment, there was darkness and silence; and with that, the sun had set on the Golden Age of Bodybuilding.

* * * * *

While the 1979 Mr. Olympia may very well have been the final contest of bodybuilding's Golden Age, it should be said that there is no universal agreement about the beginning or end dates of that period. There can be no doubt however that the period came and went. By definition, a golden age is the historical high point of a culture; but since it is a high point, it must therefore also be followed by a period of decline. Because the Golden Age of Bodybuilding is thought to have ended sometime in the late 1970s, an obvious question is raised: what about bodybuilding went into decline after that point?

Interest in bodybuilding certainly did not wane starting in 1980, nor did its pool of competitors dry up. The industries that profited from bodybuilding sure didn't tank. In fact the opposite is true, on all three counts. Contest ticket sales and competitor entry fees continued to steadily increase, and profits from magazine, supplement and equipment sales soared. So where was the decline? The answer lies in the fact that golden-age status for any culture or pastime is rarely bestowed solely by looking at trends in ledgers. It was for intangible, emotional reasons that the era is remembered more fondly than all others.

The Golden Age of Baseball, for example, is widely considered to have taken place sometime between 1920 and 1960, but not because it was during that period that more people attended games or player salaries were highest. The age was considered golden not only because of the quality of individual players, but because of the mystique that surrounded them. The age was golden because of what we know about it, and perhaps of equal importance, what we don't. Baseball in 1940 wasn't documented like it is today. Virtually all footage from the era was shot in black-and-white film. There were no modern, clever camera angles taking in the action, and in fact the few games that were filmed were often shot with a single camera from one of the stadium's press boxes. Nevertheless, poor documentation by itself makes nothing golden. It does however place a veil of mystery over the subject matter; and when that subject matter is something great, it fills the viewer with wonder and leaves him wanting more. That veil helps to turn former players into legends.

The documentation of the Golden Age of Bodybuilding came primarily in the form of black-and-white still photography. The favored indoor technique of stark black backgrounds and dramatic lighting gave the era's prominent figures a surreal appearance—something that cannot help but lend mystique. Contest movie footage was meanwhile almost universally poor, especially up until the mid-1970s. It was an era when high-quality motion picture equipment and film were expensive; and since the home video market wouldn't materialize until the late 1970s, there was little reason to take decent movies of contests. It was therefore the case that bodybuilding, an activity that generated limited funds, couldn't afford to properly document itself.

That all changed with the release of *Pumping Iron*, a professional documentary produced by outsiders and filmed in high-quality color. Its subject matter, the 1975 Mr. Universe and Olympia contests, became the only two properly-documented events of the era—yet another reason why the film became and has remained so popular. It was the film's action, the crystal-clear, moving images of the era's greatest bodybuilders, and of course their stories, that helped fans fall in love with the age. *Pumping Iron* made regular appearances on television for several years, but when the film was released on home video—and much later, on DVD, the adoration grew. Participation in bodybuilding also grew because of the film, and this became one of the factors that contributed to end of the age.

Pumping Iron conveyed the notion that bodybuilding was a small and exclusive clique; and among its chief competitors there existed a sense of camaraderie, a we're-all-in-this-together spirit, as if elite bodybuilding was an informal social club and Gold's Venice was its clubhouse. Numerous photographs from the era show any one of a number of top competitors posing in the middle of the gym, flanked by admiring, encouraging pals, many of whom were his onstage rivals. Those images are unforgettable, but it was that individuals within those shots who were most responsible for giving the era its character. The quality of their physiques was outstanding, but so was their individuality.

Perhaps more than any other factor, the age was remembered fondly because of one individual in particular. Without the emergence, rise and dominance of Arnold Schwarzenegger, the era probably never would have been called Golden. *Pumping Iron* would never have been made. Bodybuilding would have followed a much different course; and the Golden Age would still be thought of as the era of Grimek and Reeves. The departure of Schwarzenegger therefore left a giant hole, one that effectively ended an era, or at least triggered its eventual close.

If it was for intangible, emotional reasons that the period 1960-1979 became golden, it must be for similar reasons that the era that followed marked a decline. Nevertheless, this "decline" was in reality nothing more than a shift in the overall character of bodybuilding, one that would become more pronounced as time marched onward. That shift all began with the retirement of a hero and the release of a movie. Bodybuilding would eventually take on an appearance that was quite a bit different than that of the Golden Age—different enough to make fans of the future embrace its images and lament its passing.

The 1980s

Bodybuilding's Golden Age will forever be perceived through the looking-glass of romance. Its mystique has grown with the passage of time. Yet no amount of Golden Age romance or mystique has blurred the character of the decade that followed; nor can it skew the affection with which those years are recalled. A generation later, when the evolution of the ultimate physique had reached its climax, those years, the 1980s, were thought to form one of bodybuilding's greatest decades, if not the greatest. The period was certainly among its most important. It was during the 1980s that bodybuilding not only grew explosively, but in many ways peaked.

A general fitness boom was underway, and the culture of muscle-building found itself well within the radius of impact. Bernarr Macfadden would have been pleased. Since during at least part of the 1980s high-level competitive bodybuilding was still considered to be a practice congruent with general health, a new "bodybuilding lifestyle" image was enthusiastically sold to the public; and if muscle magazine sales are any indication, a good portion of the public bought into it. Ultimately however, bodybuilding's connection to physical fitness was only part of the reason why it grew so dramatically. The factor that truly thrust bodybuilding into prosperity was something more simple: the public was prepared to embrace it. As the 1980s got underway, there prevailed a pure and simple fascination with muscle.

This new acceptance of muscularity didn't come about all by itself; rather, it was a symptom of a greater cultural shift, and a general change in attitude, from the recent past. After all, in modern Western culture it's often the case that the character of any given decade is, in a sense, a reaction against the one that came before. The most obvious example of this phenomenon is found in the 1960s. The wholesome, straight-laced, family-oriented veneer of the prior decade gave way to the equal and opposite reactions of individualism, nonconformity, protest and free-love.

The 1980s of course turned out to be quite a bit different from the '60s, but the attitudes of the '80s nevertheless formed a reaction against what had come before. Contrasts could be seen in every layer of society, beginning with the very highest levels of government. The liberal presidency of Jimmy Carter, thought by many to be sluggish and ineffective, was replaced by a new, flag-waving and gun-toting brand of politics, with Ronald Reagan leading the charge. The American public's weariness that came from political and economic stagnation was replaced by the optimism of resurgence. Reagan refreshed the American public by reminding it that the United States had historically been a nation of strength and action, and he hoped to spur it on with assurances that it could become mightier than ever: economically, politically, and especially, militarily. Threats from abroad were sold a public which, for the most part, favored a new buildup of American military might. The allure of might in fact became an important theme of the decade. Brute strength was looked upon with equal fascination, and in some cases, admiration.

Meanwhile, changes in attitude that took hold once the '80s were underway were reflected in more than political movements and personalities. It was in the arena of popular culture that the reaction against the previous decade was most deliberate and certainly most visible. Much like the '60s, pop culture attitudes of the '80s followed a simple rule: everything should be the opposite of whatever came before. The simple particulars of fashion—pant leg, lapel and tie widths, and color choices in clothing—contrasted sharply from one decade to the next. The bluesy, bloated, and often melancholic guitar-based rock performed by shaggy musicians gave way to upbeat pop tunes played on synthesizers by hair-sprayed teen idols. There was also a visible and quite vocal movement to eradicate disco, the 1970s' signature pop culture phenomenon. This reaction in particular suggested that the transition into the '80s was more than a mere cultural makeover. The music and fashions of the latter often aimed simply to obliterate all traces of the former.

The film industry underwent a significant transformation as well. If the virtues of strength and action found favor in the world of American politics, Hollywood was not slow to exploit these sentiments. Arnold Schwarzenegger's early-'80s graduation to action-movie hero was therefore perfectly timed. His ascent to true stardom arrived in 1982, when he played the lead in *Conan the Barbarian*—a major studio production with a big budget, veteran actors and a good storyline. *Conan*, a box-office success, bore no resemblance whatsoever to *Hercules in New York*—or to the Steve Reeves Hercules films, for that matter. A sequel with a big budget but an awful plot followed, but this was completely overshadowed by what came next.

In 1984 Schwarzenegger was cast to play the villainous killer robot in *The Terminator*. A huge hit, the film defined the acting career of the man who was now known to Western audiences as simply *Arnold*. A slew of action movies followed. Schwarzenegger's characters were delightfully unapologetic caricatures of Hollywood shoot-'em-up heroes. He played over-the-top brutes you were glad to have on your side, men who killed first and asked questions later. Audiences ate it up. Most of the movies were big hits. Considering the character of the '80s, films like Schwarzenegger's hit the spot.

Schwarzenegger's muscles—the visual manifestation of his on-screen attitudes—were on display for a public that was ready to see them. In an era when might-makes-right became an attractive political stance and a popular theme for Hollywood movies, objects of strength and power were naturally held in esteem. The spike in interest in muscularity was a natural effect of this thinking, and looking back, it should have been easily predictable. At the most easily understandable level, muscles symbolize power. Charles Atlas ads had been driving this point home for half a century. Schwarzenegger's action movies were but one of a number of muscle-based media unleashed upon the public throughout the decade. Professional wrestling enjoyed a massive resurgence. Compared to previous decades, the average behemoth to don tights and step through the ropes was also more muscular, sometimes much more so. The television show *American Gladiators* witnessed similar displays of muscularity, though without the contrived violence and cartoonish plot lines. And finally, sales of bodybuilding magazines skyrocketed. All these forms of entertainment put over-the-top muscularity on display, and all of it was well-received.

Arnold Schwarzenegger as the title character from *Conan the Barbarian* (1982).

Getty images

By the mid-1980s, the rail-thin chic of the '70s had an entire beach of sand kicked in its face. The big-muscle aesthetic had taken hold. The whole fitness industry was transformed. Jogging was out and weightlifting was in. Suddenly a lot of people wanted to be muscular, even if they had no interest in muscle contests. As for those who were interested in competition, bodybuilding itself saw massive growth. Amateur contests multiplied, attracted large numbers of competitors, and drew hundreds or occasionally thousands of spectators. After all, bodybuilding had been preparing, however unwittingly, for the '80s. *Pumping Iron* inspired a new generation of dedicated physique competitors. Once the decade was underway, the block-busting films of its biggest star roused even more.

It was against this backdrop that the world of competitive bodybuilding came into its heyday. In terms of the sheer number of competitors and the size of audiences that regularly congregated at bodybuilding contests of all levels, nothing could touch the '80s. Meanwhile, at the highest levels of competition, the Mr. Olympia contests in particular, a new phase would take hold, one remembered with fondness in some ways equal to the Golden Age. One of bodybuilding's greatest eras, the 1980s, was getting underway. It was therefore a matter of no small irony that the decade began with one of bodybuilding's more infamous episodes.

David Iliff

Sydney Opera House

To kick off the new decade, for the first time since 1975 the Mr. Olympia contest was held abroad. It was determined that Australia would host the event, with the iconic Sydney Opera House as the chosen venue. The IFBB would now be able to boast that by the 16th year of its existence its greatest contest had visited four continents. Of the 15 competitors registered to compete, Mike Mentzer and three-time winner Frank Zane once more figured to be in the middle of the action. Their showdown at the '79 Olympia provided fans with bodybuilding's latest study in opposites; and the minor controversy ignited by the triumph of the light but shapely Zane over the massive and imposing Mentzer thickened the plot.

However, any lingering concerns about misjudgment at the most recent American Olympia were washed away by the storm that was about to make land in Australia. Mentzer and Zane were central to the action as expected, although their influence over the contest's outcome was quite different from anything that had been anticipated. Repercussions were far-reaching. By the time the storm had run its course, a mutinous howl had risen up from within bodybuilding's fan base, the entire competitive balance of the IFBB's upper echelon had been turned asunder, and faith in judging practices lay dashed upon rocks. What made the calamity most remarkable was it all revolved around a single man, one who stood at the eye of the storm, an unexpected 16th competitor.

For the first time in five years, Arnold Schwarzenegger would not help promote the Olympia. A heavy schedule of on-location filming in Spain for the upcoming *Conan* film had consumed his time, and this naturally precluded all other ventures. Since Schwarzenegger was out of the picture, the lure of once more holding the Olympia in Columbus—the hometown of his promotion partner Jim Lorimer—diminished sharply. Other cities beckoned. There was a whole world outside of Ohio, and there had been bodybuilding fans on six continents for some time now. The International Federation of Bodybuilders needed to once more live up to its name.

Holding the Olympia in Australia therefore made sense. Relative to Columbus, Sydney is quite literally on the other side of the world. It's the sixth-largest city in the southern hemisphere and the largest in an English-speaking country. It's a first-world metropolis with a first-rate venue. Apart from that, by 1980 bodybuilding had gained a significant following in Australia. Local fans could be counted on to fill seats. Fans from other countries who could tolerate the airfare costs and flight times would without doubt show up as well.

The number of competitors registered to compete, 15, was the same as the prior year, though the lineup's composition had a few notable changes. Absentees included Robby Robinson and Albert Beckles; meanwhile, taking his first crack at the Olympia was a Lebanese national named Samir Bannout, the first Middle Eastern bodybuilder to vie for the world's greatest title. He had qualified for professional status the prior year by winning, in a literal sense, an amateur version of the Olympia: the IFBB "Best in the World" contest. A '79 World Amateur Championships victory followed,[1] and the next year he was on board a plane headed Down Under. The remainder of the contest's lineup was mostly unchanged from the year before.

A CBS television crew was on hand to document the event for later broadcast. Big-three network coverage was not only a coup for the Weiders, the IFBB and bodybuilding in general, but it amply testified to the rising popularity of muscle contests. Also in Sydney was Schwarzenegger, with a second film crew in tow. Principal filming for *Conan* had ended a couple of months earlier, and it was presumed that the former champion was at the Olympia to provide commentary. It was therefore a rather large surprise when it was made known that Schwarzenegger was at the contest not as a TV personality, but as a competitor.

This created immediate controversy. Official IFBB rules state that competitors must file entry forms at least one month in advance of an event. Schwarzenegger had not done so; otherwise his return would have been common knowledge. He instead declared his intentions the day before the contest. This should have made him ineligible. IFBB President Ben Weider, who was always on hand to oversee the Olympia, took the issue under advisement. He quickly declared that the entry-deadline rule would not apply to the six-time champion.

Charges of favoritism had become as common at bodybuilding contests as lat-spread poses, but for the first time in the history of the IFBB an official federation rule had been bent for the benefit of a single competitor. During the AAU heyday something like this might have figured, but coming from the IFBB—the organization that was once known for its level playing field—it was a sobering revelation. To more than a few of the 1980 Mr. Olympia contest's competitors, it was like a bucket of cold water in the face. Their grumblings didn't go unnoticed.

From there the storm intensified. While the deadline ruling caused complaints and brooding amongst the field of competitors, another last-minute change of rules nearly triggered a fistfight. The episode stemmed from a vigorous campaign that had been waged by Boyer Coe to eliminate weight classes from the Olympia. Beginning earlier in the year, Coe, with the support of a number of other competitors, voiced his desire see the contest return to the single-class format that had been used during the period 1965-73. His reasons were simple. With each passing year, the under-200 pound category had grown, both in the number and quality of its participants. The over-200 pound class was meanwhile always numerically smaller. Especially after the departure of Oliva, Schwarzenegger, Ferrigno and Nubret, the heavyweight class had also been qualitatively inferior to the lighter group. The '76 Olympia—with its one-two finishes of Columbu-Zane in the lightweight class and Waller-Katz in the heavies—was perhaps the most glaring example of this discrepancy in quality.

During the contest's final comparison phase, the two-class system gave an advantage to the heavyweight winner. He need beat only a single, smaller competitor to secure the overall title. If there was only one class, that same individual would have to defeat five men of all sizes. (Until the ranking system of judging was introduced, any one of the six competitors in the final comparison could be selected as overall winner.)

Coe's campaign had gained too much support to be ignored by the IFBB. Keen to avoid further controversy, the federation this time struck a politically correct posture when it allowed the event's competitors to resolve the issue themselves. A vote was therefore taken at the Olympia competitor's meeting. The tally was 15-to-1 in favor of eliminating weight classes. Predictably, Schwarzenegger cast the derelict vote. Coe declared that in the spirit of fairness, Schwarzenegger should be given the opportunity to voice his rationale. According to various reports, Schwarzenegger, who was not prepared for this, instead began hurling insults. He asked Coe "Why don't you quit acting

[1]It's common in bodybuilding for a federation to hold different contests that essentially offer the same title. The NPC National and USA Championships, traditionally held four months apart, are the most visible modern examples.

like a boy and act like a man?" At this Mentzer, who had also been the target of Schwarzenegger's jabs, became incensed, rose to his feet and approached the former champion. Schwarzenegger remained seated while Mentzer loomed over him. Bill Pearl, who was present as a judge,[1] stepped between the men, effectively defusing the situation.

The meeting broke with the issue decided: there would be only one class. Schwarzenegger had failed in his bid to prevent this from happening, but his primary objective—side-stepping the entrance requirement—had been achieved easily. He was officially back in the Mr. Olympia lineup. There were also cards stacked in his favor. Schwarzenegger was a good friend of the Olympia's promoter, Bill Graham. More importantly, he was friends with a number of the judges, including Reg Park, with whom he had formed a close personal bond. Yet perhaps above all else, Schwarzenegger had the eminent distinction of being bodybuilding's favorite son; he was the star of *Pumping Iron*, the leading personality of what would soon be known as the Golden Age, and a big reason why muscle culture was beginning to boom. It could be argued that by 1980, bodybuilding *owed* him.

Fellow competitors feared that Schwarzenegger would be given a lifetime achievement award in the form of a seventh Mr. Olympia title, regardless of whether he truly deserved victory. For those men, and for a substantial segment of fans, the dark clouds of 1972—Schwarzenegger's final and most controversial victory over Sergio Oliva—had not faded from memory. Together they prepared for what could be a replay.

* * * * *

Arnold Schwarzenegger was now officially out of retirement and back in contention for the Mr. Olympia title; that much was known. What was not yet known was how he looked; and more importantly, how he would measure up against the current crop of competitors. Meanwhile, although Schwarzenegger's name had been absent from precontest advertisements and it didn't appear on the official contest program, rumors of a surprise comeback swirled amongst the now-full auditorium of fans.

[1]Pearl voluntarily relinquished his position as judge because he had worked closely with Olympia competitor Chris Dickerson.

The heated competitors' meeting had delayed the start of prejudging for more than an hour. When the 1980 Mr. Olympia field finally took the stage, the comeback rumors proved true. There indeed was six-time champion Arnold Schwarzenegger, flanked by bodybuilding's current crop of top competitors. The character of the event therefore shifted from *Zane vs. Mentzer Part II* to *The Return of the King.* At six-foot-two, Schwarzenegger was significantly taller than most of his competition and therefore stood out in the lineup. Although he exhibited a good degree of muscular separation, it was clear that he was not in top form. He certainly didn't have the same mass he put on display during his reign, especially during the years 1973-74. This thickened the plot.

An all-time-best Schwarzenegger would be a lock to again take the title, regardless of whom he might face; but how would a partially deflated former champion fare? Fortunately for him, Frank Zane had a similar problem. He stepped onstage in his now-trademark excellent condition, but with diminished size. Word out of Zane's camp was that he had suffered an unspecified but severe injury at home. Although the mishap was unrelated to training, the lengthy hospitalization it required was not; Zane had apparently missed too many workouts, and when it came time to pay the piper, about ten pounds of muscular mass was the price. Muscle, let alone ten pounds of it, was something Zane could ill afford to part with. Regardless, there he stood, noticeably smaller than the previous year. It looked as though he might very well slip from the top spot, regardless how Schwarzenegger placed.

It was a different story with Mike Mentzer. He arrived in Sydney prepared—and almost expecting—to win. Both big and defined, Mentzer was in his all-time best condition. He seemed the man most likely to give Schwarzenegger trouble. Meanwhile, five other men—Chris Dickerson, Boyer Coe, Roy Callendar, Roger Walker and Dennis Tinerino—likewise took the stage in top form. As an Australian national, Walker was naturally a crowd favorite, though few considered him a legitimate threat to take the title.

All eyes were on Schwarzenegger. *Pumping Iron* had brought him fame, but it also supplied to dedicated bodybuilding fans indelible images of the 1975 Olympia, and of the champion near the top of his game. When fans thought of Schwarzenegger, they thought of the unbeatable victor from that movie. What they got in Sydney was something else.

George Butler

Comparisons, 1980 Mr. Olympia contest, viewed from the rear. From left to right: Roger Walker, Arnold Schwarzenegger, and Boyer Coe. In the foreground: Roy Callendar.

What fans got in Sydney was a very beatable-looking competitor, maybe a little past his prime, surrounded by physiques that were, at the very least, comparable. It was only moments into prejudging when Schwarzenegger's decision to compete was brought into question. Here was the greatest champion the world of bodybuilding had ever known, appearing once more a half-decade after his retirement. He was for unknown reasons banking his entire legacy on a physique that wasn't worthy of his fame. What, it was wondered, was he thinking?

It wasn't that Schwarzenegger wasn't good. He was. However, he clearly wasn't up to the level he had brought to the Mr. Olympia contest when he dominated the event in 1973-75. In 1980, he was merely another good competitor. Had an unknown brought the same physique, he likely would have fought for third or fourth place. However, this was no mere unknown competitor, no newcomer. This was Arnold Schwarzenegger. If ever a competitor could receive points not for how he looked but for who he was, it was him. According to the accounts of a large number of people in attendance, that's just what happened.

Outcomes lay bare the integrity of judging practices. Judges didn't mind that Schwarzenegger's physique had regressed considerably since his last outing—something that normally guarantees a slip in the placings, especially when close competitors have improved. They didn't care that his previously supreme confidence had regressed to an equal degree. They tolerated his refusal to strike mandatory poses properly, and they were okay with his interjection of free-posing into strict comparison rounds. None of that mattered. As each name was called during the announcements of final placings, this became more and more evident.

At a modern Mr. Olympia contest, awards are presented to the event's six finalists immediately after the conclusion of the final comparison round. In succession, each placement is announced, starting with sixth and finishing with first. The 1980 Olympia deviated from that procedure. In Sydney, after the final comparison round ended all competitors filed offstage and there awaited the announcement of placings. With each, the chosen competitor came back onstage individually to receive his award. Considering what went on backstage before the contest and what was about to transpire, this was a reasonable course of action.

In sixth was Roger Walker. An obligatory chorus of boos rose up from the partisan crowd, but this placement was more or less in line with what was reasonably expected. Had the event not been in Australia, there's a good chance Walker wouldn't have finished in the top six. The hometown hero was therefore rewarded with a spot in the finals. In the spirit of delivering an entertaining product, this would become the IFBB Professional Division judging model for contests that featured good-quality local competitors.

In fifth place was Mike Mentzer. This was the evening's first big surprise. Those who had witnessed Mentzer's backstage tiff with Schwarzenegger wondered if it had influenced his placing. Clearly something was amiss. Mentzer was one of the favorites to take the title, yet here he was, finishing fifth. Even louder boos echoed through the Opera House. One place ahead of Mentzer was the man whose side he had taken in the Schwarzenegger run-in, Boyer Coe. Since either man looked as if he could have taken the title that night, the announcement of Coe's placement was met with like consternation.

The next big surprise was the announcement of Frank Zane for third place. Although it was thus far evident that Schwarzenegger would not be punished for allowing his appearance to slip, Zane would be extended no such courtesy. He regressed only marginally, but this didn't stop judges' pencils from slashing without mercy. In the contest's 16-year history, he became only the second Mr. Olympia to be forced from his throne, and the first to fall more than one place. Ten years earlier reigning Mr. Olympia Sergio Oliva suffered defeat at the hands of Schwarzenegger, the same man who had in 1980 made an unexpected, unlikely and unexplained comeback. After dethroning another champion, Schwarzenegger now waited to hear how he would place: first or second.

By this point an otherwise befuddled audience had few illusions about how this story would end. Chris Dickerson, whom a number of fellow competitors felt was the best man on stage that fateful evening, was announced as runner-up.

Photographer Robert Nailon recalled standing next to Schwarzenegger when Dickerson was declared to be second. "I can't believe it. I can't believe it" he heard the now seven-time Mr. Olympia say. Schwarzenegger was clearly being coy. He knew he was going to win. Had he doubted the outcome, he never would have entered. He had too much to lose and too little to gain.

A large faction of the audience may have had trouble believing it, but since that group had but one opportunity to collectively voice an opinion, they let loose. The chorus of boos that erupted as Schwarzenegger came out to accept his Sandow earned a place in bodybuilding lore. The Sydney Opera House—the famed hall which over the years had played host to performances of Verdi, Wagner, Tchaikovsky and Mozart—never knew such noise.

The judgment was not universally despised. A large part of the crowd cheered. Their reasons varied; they were either Arnold fans, they were swept up by the King's unannounced, dramatic return, or they simply felt that Schwarzenegger deserved to win. Some in attendance could claim they cheered for all these reasons. Nevertheless, an equal number booed long and hard. Schwarzenegger's acceptance speech was cut short by the crescendo of angry howls. Displeased fans who had come to see a fair-and-square contest of muscle were certain they had just witnessed a travesty of historic proportions.

Meanwhile the IFBB, the same organization that has never once admitted that the wrong man may have won, in any of its contests, nevertheless had at least theoretically plausible grounds for handing Schwarzenegger the victory. He wasn't outclassed in the definition department, and his overall mass was more or less competitive with the rest of the field. Perhaps the most obvious exception to the latter point was Mike Mentzer, who at five inches shorter shared Schwarzenegger's weight of 225 pounds.

The event's biggest perceived injustice lay in the judges' decision to reward a regressed competitor over improved men of roughly equal quality. Before and since, with rare exception, the opposite has been true. In bodybuilding, regression equals failure.

Chris Dickerson, c. 1981

Courtesy of Michael Newman

Courtesy of Michael Newman

Aftermath: as promoter Paul Graham (center) looks on, Arnold Schwarzenegger addresses the 1980 Mr. Olympia audience.

Frank Zane suffered this fate at the Sydney Olympia, which made the reward of Schwarzenegger seem an even more glaring injustice.

Headlining the list of displeased spectators was the CBS television crew who had lugged equipment 7500 miles to record the event. The contest was in fact never aired. According to Sherman Egan, the man who headed the crew, even untrained eyes could see that Schwarzenegger should not have won. CBS later found out that Schwarzenegger had personal or financial ties to several judges. It refused to broadcast the contest on the grounds that a competition with an obviously fixed outcome cannot be represented as a legitimate sporting event.

For the large number of new fans who had no real knowledge of the '72 Schwarzenegger-Oliva controversy, the Sydney Olympia became their introduction to the realities of bodybuilding competition. Contests are judged according to purely subjective criteria, and they're run by organizations with the power to pick and choose winners. Factors other than pure physical appearance can and have played an important role in the outcome of numerous competitions, especially at bodybuilding's highest levels. This has been true as long as bodybuilding federations have been in existence. Nevertheless, fans pay to watch. As long as their money fills federation coffers, federations will run contests how they see fit.

In the event's aftermath, the issue which caused the greatest degree of exasperation was Schwarzenegger's eligibility waiver. According to the rules that everyone else had to follow, he simply should not have been allowed to compete. Had Schwarzenegger submitted his application on time, a number of competitors would have dropped out—not necessarily out of fear of losing a fair contest to the six-time champion, but because they knew that fairness would only nominally enter into the equation. Boyer Coe claimed to have known this would be the case; that if Schwarzenegger showed up in passable condition, he was a lock to win a seventh title. "I would have stayed home," he said. "I wouldn't have gone ten thousand miles and stayed two weeks down there in Australia."[1]

Schwarzenegger knew he would win the show. However, he also wanted to be certain that no competitors would drop out on his account. The only way he could do this was by crashing the contest at the last minute, something he also knew would be allowed. After all, there was no way the IFBB was going to stop him from competing. That federation's rules were never carved into stone. They were written on common paper, which can be crumpled up and thrown in the trash. In Sydney in 1980 that's exactly what happened, and it was no less than IFBB president Ben Weider's hands that did the deed. He later washed them, as well he might, because it seemed he could do little else. A comeback of bodybuilding's greatest-ever champion could not be blocked. It would generate far too much fan interest. It would sell lots of the elder Weider's magazines and boost sales of Weider's Schwarzenegger-endorsed products. Given those circumstances, the younger Weider couldn't say no.

Yet as great as things may have looked to the Weiders when they rolled out the red carpet for Schwarzenegger's return, the outcome changed all that. The controversy was big enough that they couldn't pretend it didn't exist. Although the nature of the controversy placed responsibility squarely on the shoulders of the organization behind the event—the Weiders' own IFBB—*Muscle & Fitness* ran articles that aimed to expose its roots. In one such piece an Olympia judge, Jacques Blommaert, admitted to making the following statement about Schwarzenegger before prejudging: "People who don't know how he used to look are impressed. But

[1]Bodybuilding.com interview with David Robson.

he just doesn't have it. He shouldn't enter the contest. It will be a mistake."[1]

In another *Muscle & Fitness* article, Schwarzenegger was asked about his motive for entering the show and his rationale for showing up at the eleventh hour. Schwarzenegger's first reason seemed obvious. Competing in the Olympia was a publicity stunt for the upcoming release of *Conan the Barbarian*. Schwarzenegger was forced to whip himself into shape quickly for the role, and once filming ended, he was in fairly good condition. Close friend Franco Columbu noticed this. He suggested that Schwarzenegger put his condition to use by preparing for the upcoming Olympia, which at the time was about two months away. This created the right circumstance for a return, though it told but a small part of the tale.

Schwarzenegger's real reasons for competing in Sydney revolved around a recently-damaged ego. In his mind, Frank Zane and Mike Mentzer had cast uncalled-for stones. The most visible hit came in the form of a televised interview he conducted with Zane in 1979, immediately after his third Olympia victory. When Schwarzenegger asked him how it felt to win his third Sandow trophy, Zane replied "almost as good as when I beat you." Zane was referring to his victory over Schwarzenegger at the 1968 Mr. Universe contest. Rumors at the time held that the otherwise humble Zane had been testing acting waters, and he was following the advice of someone who told him to act cocky on camera. Regardless of what his motivations may have been, Schwarzenegger felt humiliated by the quip—which may be a rare glimpse into the fragile inner-workings of a man who built his entire image upon a bulletproof façade. Schwarzenegger privately vowed that given the opportunity he would teach Zane a lesson.

The six-time champion meanwhile had an even greater score to settle with Mentzer. The latter had developed and used a system of weight training based on the theories of Nautilus exercise machine inventor Arthur Jones. Mentzer's program, which he called "Heavy Duty," was founded on the idea that a single high-intensity set for each exercise is sufficient for stimulating optimum muscular growth. He contrasted the method against conventional schemes, which he called "volume training," that advocate the use of 20 or more sets per body part.

Mentzer declared that such training is illogical, wasteful and harmful, and used Schwarzenegger's workouts as examples of flawed thinking. To this Schwarzenegger took offense. The former champion was determined to prove that his methods were superior, and he came to the conclusion that defeating Mentzer fair and square in a bodybuilding contest would provide indisputable proof.

Mentzer and Zane were both certain to compete in Sydney. If Schwarzenegger were to enter and win, he could kill two birds with one stone. He could put both "in their place." In the process, he would also collect his seventh Mr. Olympia title, drum up a little extra publicity for the *Conan* movie, and impress new debutante girlfriend Maria Shriver—bringing the total number of killed birds to five. He cast that famous stone, brought down all five birds, and later gloated to Rick Wayne (in the same *Muscle & Fitness* interview). Schwarzenegger was especially proud of winning a seventh Mr. Olympia title. "Seven times," he said. "Nobody will ever come close to that."

* * * * *

The outcome of the 1980 Mr. Olympia contest has remained a topic of debate to this day. One of the episode's critical effects was that it inspired Schwarzenegger's sidekick, 1976 Mr. Olympia Franco Columbu, to make a comeback of his own. Columbu had finally recovered from the trauma of his 1977 strongman accident, and deemed himself fit for a return. He resumed heavy training and planned to take the stage at the 1981 Olympia, which, after the Sydney aberration, was returning to its home base of Columbus.

Since Schwarzenegger's win had set an important precedent, and because he and Jim Lorimer were once more tabbed to promote the event, an ideal stage had therefore been set for a Columbu return and victory. This was certainly how Frank Zane and Boyer Coe saw things anyway. Both men learned of Columbu's plan to return, and both felt certain a toned-down replay of Sydney was in the making. Accordingly, the '81 Olympia application deadline came and went without a peep from either. Their silent boycott surprised few.

Sydney's other important effect did manage to raise a few eyebrows. Mike Mentzer, declaring that the '80 Olympia "was definitely fixed," quit bodybuilding competition forever. Though Mentzer never claimed that he should have won the show, he was convinced that Schwarzenegger should not have either. Whatever faith Mentzer had in the sys-

[1]Feb. 1981 *Muscle & Fitness*

tem was lost. He was furthermore astute enough to realize that the world of high-level competitive bodybuilding provides but two choices for those who feel betrayed: put up with it or quit. Based on what happened in Sydney, Mentzer realized his future could hold many more such outcomes. He therefore chose the second option and hung it up for good.

A minor exodus had materialized. Four of the top five finishers from 1980—Schwarzenegger, Zane, Coe and Mentzer—would be absent from Olympia lineup in '81. If not for the return of Columbu, the contest would have appeared wide-open, with the previous year's runner-up Chris Dickerson being the favorite to win. Dickerson had no thoughts of boycott; nor did the other seven bodybuilders from the Sydney Olympia who committed to compete in Columbus—Roger Walker, Roy Callendar, Danny Padilla, Tom Platz, Samir Bannout, Ken Waller and Dennis Tinerino. None of their placings had been affected by Schwarzenegger's finish, they didn't feel personally jilted by the event's judging, and most importantly, they were anxious to take advantage of the vacuum that had formed at the top.

At least a few of those men years later made public their opinion that the Sydney Olympia was fixed, but at the time they knew better than to publicly cry foul or boycott when they personally hadn't been victimized. There was no bodybuilders' union to shelter behind. In bodybuilding, the greatest champions were treated exceptionally well, which insured their loyalty to the IFBB and the Weiders. All others were expendable. In accord with this script, the red carpet was rolled out for Franco Columbu.

Like Schwarzenegger the year before, if Columbu showed up in a condition that was somewhat close to that of his glory days, the title would be his. That being said, a few things were turning out to be clearly different than the year before. There were no heated exchanges in the competitors' meeting and no disagreement over how to structure the contest. There was also no network television crew on hand to document the event. When CBS purchased the rights to film and air the 1980 Mr. Olympia contest, it had obtained exclusive permission to do so in '81 as well. After what the network perceived to be a blatant case of contest-fixing in Sydney, Columbus was written off. CBS lost all interest in bodybuilding.

Fans were meanwhile upset about absence of several top competitors. According to Rick Wayne, in a chapter called "The greatest booing contest of all time" from his book *Muscle Wars*, Ben Weider's introductory speech at the evening show was loudly heckled by fans who demanded to know why Mentzer, Zane, Beckles and Coe were not present. Schwarzenegger was booed when announced as copromoter. Since he had become a temporary symbol of contest-fixing, a loud contingent of fans let him have it.

From the standpoint of pure physique judging, the 1981 Olympia was similar to '80. Once prejudging got underway, it was clear that former champion was not in top form. His physique was good, but it undoubtedly was not at the level that last carried him to victory. This was especially true of his lower body. Moreover he was surrounded by a closely-matched field that had for the most part improved over the past year.

Columbu's brilliant career in bodybuilding was owed to stunning muscularity. His torso in particular was one for the ages. His pectorals were massive, and the striations that ran across it produced the deepest grooves yet witnessed on a human chest. It therefore speaks volumes that it wasn't his chest, but his back, that became Columbu's signature bodypart. No one could match him in that department. Deeply-chiseled abdominals completed the most dominant trunk of bodybuilding' Golden Age. The images of *Pumping Iron* forever made him an indelible component of that period.

Franco Columbu. 1981

Courtesy of Michael Newman

As great as those years may have been, a new era was underway—and this didn't change the fact that Columbu's physique still had the same old flaws. The '76 Olympia champion was impressive but blocky; his torso often appeared too short; his lines were angular; and his limbs lagged behind the rest of his physique. For as deep as the striations on Columbu's chest ran, it was in his legs that he gave it all back. His lower body looked hard but often appeared totally devoid of separation. On top of that, in 1981 the primary effect of his strongman injury was plain to see: his left leg was noticeably smaller than his right.

Columbu owned an uneven build to begin with, and now he was off his game and flanked by competitors who didn't share those faults. This became startlingly evident when he stood next to Danny Padilla. Both men were about the same height, so comparisons were straightforward. Where Columbu was stocky and angular, Padilla was shapely, with graceful lines; and where Columbu's thighs were without sweep or separation, Padilla's were world-class. Padilla's arms were also significantly better—larger, more shapely, and better-defined—and his back was nearly on par with that of the former champion. In a pure comparison of physiques, according to IFBB judging guidelines, Padilla possessed the superior build.

A similar case could be made for either Chris Dickerson, Tom Platz or Roy Callendar; all three looked more than capable of turning Columbu's comeback into an exercise in poor judgment. Like Padilla, Dickerson's calling card had always been good shape and balance. Tom Platz meanwhile competed more directly with Columbu, as both were specimens of stunning muscularity. That being said, Platz's trademark, a freakishly large lower body, naturally contrasted sharply against the sub-par legs of Columbu. Otherwise their physiques were somewhat evenly matched. Rounding out what some were expecting to be the top four was Callendar, a man with excellent size and balance. His lack of flaws made Columbu's even more glaring.

Tom Platz. c. 1981

Courtesy of Michael Newman

Beyond all direct comparisons however was an issue confounding Columbu alone: he had an unsightly growth on his right pectoral muscle that appeared to be a textbook case of Gynecomastia.[1] Yet it didn't matter. Just like with Schwarzenegger the year before, Olympia judges proved themselves willing to look past all Columbu's flaws. They were prepared to declare him to be the world's best-built man. This time the outcome surprised few.

Despite the evidently preordained outcome of the 1981 Mr. Olympia contest, and perhaps also because of it, a hearty chorus of boos tested the Veterans' Memorial Auditorium's acoustic integrity. Like the Sydney Opera House, the building held firm. The integrity of IFBB judging practices meanwhile teetered upon a shattered foundation. A complete collapse was averted only by a loud attempt by Columbu supporters to drown out the angry taunts with cheers. It worked, but only for a moment. Angry fans carried a more impassioned message and won the contest. As for the thing they had just witnessed onstage, it also was a contest, apparently judged by criteria that couldn't all be found in the official IFBB rulebook.

Of the eight competitors who entered both the '80 and '81 Olympias, Chris Dickerson was—at least theoretically—punished most. Dickerson was again runner-up, making it the second straight Mr. Olympia title he could have won had judging conventions been properly enforced. Tom Platz meanwhile shot all the way up to third place. The '81 Olympia turned to be a launching point for Platz, as he went on to become a popular competitor and an icon of '80s bodybuilding. His perceived mistreatment in Columbus became the rallying-cry of his fan base for years to come. Roy Callendar finished fourth, and Danny Padilla came in fifth. Under more normal circumstances Padilla's finish

[1]See p. 171 for further information.

would have been perplexing. However, the Schwarzenegger comeback had taught fans a lesson about the power of nepotism and its effect on contest results. It was sarcastically wondered whether Padilla's scores had accidentally been switched with Columbu's. Rounding out the top six was German newcomer and former Olympic lifter Jusup Wilcosz.

Thus did the 1981 Mr. Olympia contest come to its inglorious end. Seasoned competitors and savvy fans had correctly predicted the outcome. That group remembered that the Mr. Olympia contest had been created for the purpose of identifying the world's best-built man; and they also were aware that a special effort had been made to portray the Olympia as bodybuilding's premier sporting event. Now however, they could see that with the successful comeback adventures of both Schwarzenegger and Columbu, the Olympia had turned into something that was more like a rock concert: if you knew who was on the bill, you pretty much knew what was going to happen.

* * * * *

Although the perceived injustices of the 1980 and '81 Mr. Olympia contests would not ever be forgotten, those episodes did nothing to slow the growth of competitive bodybuilding. The results of those two competitions were generally thought to be little more than anomalies affecting only the most elite of competitors; and of that group, only Mike Mentzer walked away for good. Amateur contests have never been immune to suspect judging decisions, but a large majority of competitors never fall victim to them. When a title is won, it's most often won fairly. Amateurs therefore happily continued filling out the competitive ranks of a variety of physique organizations throughout the world.

It was this rapidly growing base of amateur competitors that fed the IFBB professional division its yearly crop of new stars. To this end, a restructuring was in the works. Starting in 1982, a new organization, the National Physique Committee, would take over the administration and sanctioning of American amateur physique contests. The IFBB Mr. America title was a thing of the past. The AAU, which owned sole rights to use that name, during the 1970s insisted that all other federations cease and desist. This demand suited the IFBB just fine, since that organization decided to do away with all "mister" titles anyway. Mr. Olympia would be sole exception.

During the 1970s, the IFBB made its first concerted push to get bodybuilding into the Olympics. Part of that effort mandated that the federation undertake a campaign of restructuring. Under the direction of new IFBB vice president Oscar State, a number of important changes were made: a federation constitution was created, as was a code of ethics; and judging and technical rules guidelines were made official. State was a long-time sports administrator, Secretary-General of the International Weightlifting Federation, and had organized the weightlifting portion of the 1948 London Olympic Games. His advice was therefore heeded when he told the IFBB to do away with the mister naming convention. Such names made contests seem like more like beauty pageants than sporting events, he declared. For bodybuilding to be accepted by the International Olympic Committee as a sport, it would at least have to be made to look like one. To State, the Weiders and the IFBB, changing contest titles was a simple fix with a potentially large upside.

Following this directive the new NPC gave sanction to a large number of amateur contests, none of which had the old mister prefix. For example, what was once the Mr. California contest was now the California State Bodybuilding Championships. That, however, didn't stop the old naming convention from remaining a part of bodybuilding vernacular. For example, the Florida State Bodybuilding Championships is often still casually referred to as "Mr. Florida," the Los Angeles Bodybuilding Championships is called "Mr. L.A.," and so on. Even though more than a full generation had passed since the changes were made, bodybuilders and their fans continue to show a liking for "mister" titles.

One name that did disappear from casual use was Mr. America. At one time the world's greatest physique competition, the IFBB version of the contest eventually became the NPC National Bodybuilding Championships. Often called simply "The Nationals," the contest's weight-class winners qualify to compete in IFBB amateur world championship contests. The most important of these events was the aptly-named IFBB Amateur World Championships—or what had previously been called Mr. Universe. A weight-class victory there came with an invitation to turn professional. Other countries had similar amateur federations which qualified bodybuilders for the Amateur World Championships.

To relieve the ever-tightening logjam of top-quality American amateur competitors seeking professional status, the NPC National Championships became a pro-qualifying event all by itself. It was a good start, but the crowded amateur ranks were deserving of further relief. A second American national championship contest was therefore created. Called the USA Bodybuilding Championships, it qualified American competitors to compete in amateur world championship events. Starting in 1987 the USA overall champion was invited to join the IFBB professional division as well.

Such were the avenues through which the next wave of professional bodybuilders would arrive. At the time of Schwarzenegger's seventh Olympia victory, some hadn't yet entered a local contest. By decade's end, they would have almost completely replaced the current field. Bodybuilding would soon have a new character, a new look, and a very new presence. With each passing year bodybuilding would become bigger than ever.

* * * * *

The first step toward the establishment of bodybuilding's new identity was that the Mr. Olympia contest should once more make sense of itself. It needed to again become a legitimate competition. In the spirit of resurrecting its image, the IFBB made arrangements to stage the contest in London. Sydney had actually been the first international Olympia contest in a period that would feature many of them; and now, in 1982, London was the next. Ideally the Olympia would alternate between American and international locations: one year it would be held in the US, the next it would be held abroad. There were a few deviations from this scheme, but for more than a decade the model remained largely intact.

Save for Canada, which most Americans would hesitate to call "international," the United Kingdom was about the easiest non-US place to hold the event. It was but a single transatlantic flight from a number of American cities and a short hop from almost anywhere in Europe; and there was no language barrier to contend with for the large majority of competitors, staff and fans. On top of that, there were lots of British muscle-contest fans, as there had been since the time such things were first staged. The UK was in fact the first nation to hold bodybuilding competitions. Now, 81 years after Eugen Sandow's Great Competition had packed Royal Albert Hall, a London audience once more assembled to witness the crowning of the world's best-built man. A Mr. Olympia contest with sense and order was therefore called for. Fortunately for fans in attendance and bodybuilding in general, that's what was in store. Sense and order did in fact return. In 1982, there were no unannounced comebacks, no heated exchanges, no charges of contest-fixing. There was simply an array of great physiques, assembled and ready for action.

The '82 Olympia saw the return of Frank Zane and Boyer Coe. With enough dust having settled since the Sydney controversy, both men decided the time was ripe to re-emerge. Joining them was another man who steered clear of the '81 Olympia, former NABBA Mr. Universe Casey Viator. Mike Mentzer would not ever don posing briefs again, but his spirit was to some degree carried forth by Viator. Both men owned rugged, massive physiques, and both were students of Arthur Jones. Viator had famously been the subject of Jones' "Colorado Experiment"—a 28-day procedure conducted at the University of Colorado that attempted to prove the effectiveness of high-intensity training. After finishing 14th in Sydney, Viator was at his all-time best in '82 and seemed certain to finish much higher. Also on the bill were Tom Platz, Samir Bannout and Albert Beckles—the only professional from the 1970s with the good fortune of having missed the previous two Olympias.

For the first time since 1979, no one knew for certain who would win. In the end, amends were made to Chris Dickerson, the dignified and uncomplaining chief victim of the Schwarzenegger-

Albert Beckles. c. 1984

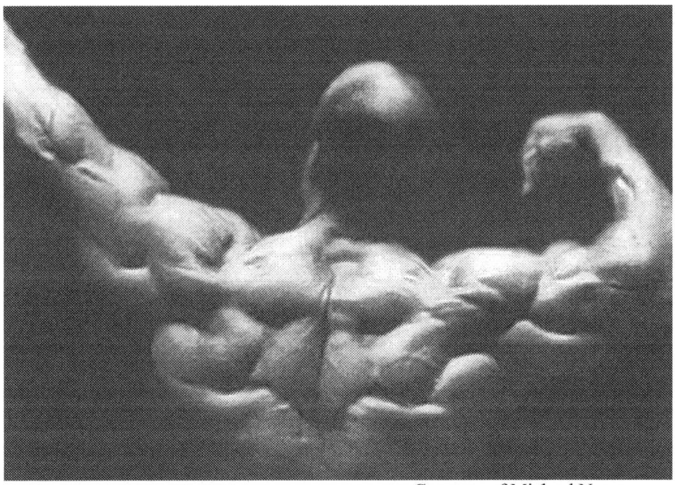

Courtesy of Michael Newman

Columbu comebacks. In what was announced beforehand to be his final contest, he did indeed capture the Sandow. Whether or not it was Dickerson's intent, his announcement of retirement sent a message to judges: they had but one last chance to bestow upon him the prize he was already denied twice. Although it was never made clear if this was a deliberate attempt to pry at the conscious of each judge, the outcome of previous contests needn't have factored into the final decision. There was after all a good and simple reason why Dickerson finished above all other competitors save for Schwarzenegger and Columbu over the previous two years: he brought to the stage a state-of-the-art physique.

Standing only five-foot-six, Dickerson certainly wasn't a large man like Schwarzenegger. Nor did he have striking mass like Columbu. Dickerson's strengths were balanced muscularity, sharp definition, and exceptional development in his back and lower body. He had better-than-average shape, especially when viewed from the back. When viewed from the front however, his shape didn't quite compare to that of his chief rival, Frank Zane. It was likely for this reason that Zane showed visible disappointment upon hearing his name announced for second place. Nevertheless, being the class act that he is, Zane quickly composed himself.

The world of bodybuilding had just witnessed a close match between a unique pair. Not only did Zane and Dickerson have the best two physiques of 1982, but both were highly intelligent, well-spoken and educated men. Zane taught math and chemistry and had by 1982 published the second of an eventual nine books. Dickerson studied music and was an accomplished opera singer. Both later assumed roles as television commentators for the Olympia.

A gracious Casey Viator came in third. Tom Platz, who had recently torn his left bicep, fell to sixth. The evening's biggest surprise may have been the improvement of Samir Bannout. Having placed 15th in 1980 and ninth the following year, in '82 Bannout jumped all the way to fourth. He now owned one of the era's best physiques, due to his combination of balance, sharp separation and very good mass, particularly through his back and arms. Although he didn't have classic lines when viewed standing from the front, thanks mainly to a vertically abbreviated and slightly wide midsection, he looked striking in nearly all other poses.

As 1982 came to an end, Bannout began to look more and more like a serious threat to win the next year's Olympia. Larger men would be on hand to vie for the title, but none were expected to match Bannout's balance of size and quality. There was no Arnold Schwarzenegger waiting to blitz the contest at the last moment, and at least for the moment, no Sergio Oliva either. Since Chris Dickerson had retired, only Frank Zane and Casey Viator stood in the way of a Bannout victory. Viator would have trouble comparing lower bodies with the improved Bannout. As for Zane, his saving grace would have to be, as it always had been, his classic shape. In all other categories Bannout was superior.

All these things considered, it figured that Samir Bannout would triumph at the 1983 Mr. Olympia contest, held that year in Munich. By doing so, Bannout became the seventh man to win the title in the 19th year of the show's existence. He defeated what was by 1983 one of the richest fields in recent memory, perhaps one of the greatest ever. It also had a unique composition. Bannout's chief competition came not in the form of a behemoth, as is often the case when a medium-sized competitor triumphs in an open field; he was instead chased by the IFBB's smallest professional. Mohamed Makkawy had by 1983 made great strides of his own, and he now brought to the stage a stunning combination of shape, mass and separation. Except for a subpar back, inch-for-inch his physique was

Mohammed Makkawy. c. 1983

Courtesy of Michael Newman

unequalled. However, at a mere five-foot-two[1] and a weight that was reported to be only 160 pounds—only four pounds heavier than the lightweight limit of the new NPC classification system—Makkawy was just a little too small to be handed the title. Nevertheless, he would be back and even better.

In third was newcomer Lee Haney. A native of Georgia, Haney had received an invitation to turn professional after defeating a monstrous field of 79 other men at the 1982 NPC National Championships. The Olympia had reached a state where a bronze-medal debut was significant; but to have secured this award by defeating Frank Zane and a small host of veterans was particularly noteworthy. The placement therefore fit well, because Haney was deserving of special praise. He owned a monstrous torso, with a massive chest and shoulders. However, it was his Haney's back—his signature bodypart—that sent audiences and judges into a tizzy. It was both incredibly wide and thick; maybe the widest and thickest yet witnessed on a human. It was comparable to that of Franco Columbu, although the nearly six-foot-tall Haney was regarded to be the more impressive specimen. Had the two ever faced off, Haney would have towered over Columbu. He also still had a lot of room for improvement. In 1983 his limbs were not up to the level of the rest of his physique, and this gave him a lanky appearance. The problem looked like it could be fixed, and his competition rightly feared what might happen if it were.

A disappointed Frank Zane took home the fourth-place medal, surveyed his predicament, and soon thereafter called it quits. He last won the contest four years earlier; and with each passing year his light but shapely physique was surrounded by more bodies with more muscle. The owner of one such body was Britain's Bertil Fox, whose fifth-place finish earned the loudest boos of the evening. Fox had what was perhaps the most muscular upper body yet seen; it was on par with that of Sergio Oliva, but with much deeper separation and sharper lines. Fox however was somewhat shorter than Oliva, narrower through the shoulders, and without Oliva's sweeping thighs. For this judges gave him no quarter.

This didn't stop Fox from becoming the hardcore crowd's hero. A segment of fans wanted to see muscle, the more the better, aesthetics be damned. Throughout his upper body Fox had more muscle than anyone. His most-muscular "crab" pose took bodybuilding to a new level; and when he finished behind Zane, a man who never hit a crab shot, a howl of dismay shook the roof.

* * * * *

The departure of Frank Zane didn't quite mark the end of an era. The era to which he belonged had already passed; and although his physique and his placings were still good, he had assumed the role of lingering relic. Yet his exit wasn't the story of the contest. What was more important was that another successful Mr. Olympia contest had come and gone. For a second straight year, the event's proceedings were mainly guided by sense and order. Though memories of '80 and '81 would not fade quickly, or ever, faith in the process was mainly brought back to life. Top bodybuilders would continue to vie for the title; and, ultimately, this would keep fans coming back for more. Although in bodybuilding large emphasis would forever be placed on contest results, fans would continue lining up to see the world's most spectacular physiques, regardless of what those results were. Perceived injustices would be tolerated. Dedicated bodybuilding fans after all had no choice. As the year 1984 got underway, the IFBB was the only real game in town.

Bertil Fox. c. 1983

Courtesy of Michael Newman

[1]Makkawy is often cited as being five-foot-four or taller. It's common for shorter bodybuilders to inflate their reported height.

Joe Weider's vision was gradually becoming a reality. Bodybuilding had grown considerably since he first threw his hat into the publishing ring 44 years earlier; and now, though much room was left for growth, that growth was his to foster—for he alone was master of the game. If George Orwell had followed bodybuilding in the 1980s, he would have been interested by what he saw. Although the colorful world of muscle bore little resemblance to the bleak dystopian future Orwell described in *1984*, there was one striking similarity: the omnipresent face of Big Brother. With his bushy mustache, Weider even fit the description of the story's undefeatable, villainous overlord. In a remarkable coincidence, by 1984 Weider's image was everywhere.

Weider was the guiding force behind the IFBB. By 1984 all other professional organizations paled in comparison. He put on the biggest contests and commanded the loyalty of the best bodybuilders. Just as importantly, Weider's publishing arm owned a dominating share of the magazine market. This was critical. Before the rise of the internet, magazines were the only real source of information about bodybuilding. Weider therefore controlled not only bodybuilding's governing body but also the most important outlets that reported on it. In the relatively small and insular world of bodybuilding, he wielded supreme power.

Of course non-Weider magazines existed, but these had a smaller market share and were run for the most part by men who, apart from Dan Lurie, were keen to not rock any boats. Meanwhile, there were no true independent news sources keeping tabs on Weider, his contests, or bodybuilding in general. Mainstream news outlets have historically favored running stories about the cultural phenomenon that is bodybuilding, but they have never shown the least interest in reporting on it as a legitimate sporting event. They certainly gave no notice to its power structure. Had the opposite been true, a proper governing body would likely have materialized. The public would not have stood for a monopolized system and fixed contests. Weider's power would have been checked. As things stood however, it wasn't. The reason was simple. Nobody cared. No part of the outside world cared that bodybuilding's governing body and its news outlets were under the control of the same force. Only a small part of the world was aware these things even existed. Bodybuilding was indeed small and insular, and its value was ultimately owed to a ferociously dedicated group of men who quite willingly submitted to its power structure. This being the case, Weider could do as he liked; almost, anyway. He was busted on multiple occasions for attaching false advertising claims to his products, and for this he paid. Yet these occasions did nothing to chip away at his perch or his organizations' prestige. As for the remainder of his products—and these were many—profits were abundant. Weider's magazines served as catalogues for his products, and this became one of the most important reasons they were printed. Another purpose was recruitment.

Weider knew better than anyone that there was no more effective tool for luring young men into bodybuilding than muscle magazines. He himself became immersed in the world of muscle because of an accidental discovery of one such publication, as did Larry Scott and untold others. Nevertheless, Weider, Scott and those like them found the appeal of owning a muscular build to be self-evident. Those men were all but bound to discover and embrace bodybuilding. Yet Weider was interested in reaching the remainder of the male population—those individuals for whom a muscular build was not the end-all be-all of human existence. He could show them the light. To achieve this end, Weider needed only to consult the ghost of Charles Atlas.

It was Angelo Siciliano—more famously known as Charles Atlas—who spelled out for the world in unapologetically blatant and crude terms the association of muscles, power and sex. Atlas' single-page comic book ads recounted the odyssey of a 97-pound weakling who got sand kicked in his face, suffered female rejection, resolved to act, grew muscles, physically overpowered his enemy, and won the girl. The ads declared in no uncertain terms that large muscles were the key to power, sex and manhood.

Detail of Charles Atlas' "Hey Skinny" comic book advertisement. Fan reproduction. c. 2005

The pre-eminent Weider publication *Muscle & Fitness* conveyed a similar message in an equally blatant style. The tactic was simple: the covers of most issues of *Muscle & Fitness* from 1983 onward show a bodybuilder making physical contact with an attractive female next to the word "sex." The word always appears as part of a headline, some examples being: "Muscle Gets Sexy"; "Sex & Flex"; "The Power of Testosterone: Its Effect on Sex and Success"; "Stronger is Sexier"; "Strong Body: The New Sexuality"; "Rugged & Fit: The New Sexuality"; "Trim, Strong, Sexy You!"; "High Sexuality: Looking Good, Feeling Great"; "America's Sexiest Bodybuilders!"; "Why Bodybuilders Are Sexy"; "Dangerous Sex"; and scores of others. Sometimes the word "sensual" is used instead of sex. Except in rare instances, the headlines do not correspond to specific articles within the magazine. For example, on the cover of the December 1986 issue of *Muscle & Fitness* the largest headline reads "Redesign Your Body!" and then lists bullet points, including "Sexual Renewal." Yet there is no reference within the magazine to any such topic.

The male on a typical cover is plainly meant to represent the effects of bodybuilding. A muscular build is therefore intended to be viewed as a means for attaining sex, hopefully with a woman who resembles the one on the cover. The only element of the Atlas formula missing from *Muscle & Fitness* covers is violence. Considering the muscular size of the men on the covers—nearly all of them are professional bodybuilders—the message that bodybuilding is a means by which to obtain power is adequately conveyed. The men are huge. No direct demonstration of their martial capabilities is necessary.

Since 1983 *Muscle & Fitness* has run a number of covers which show only males. However, the magazine has done this only if the model is either Arnold Schwarzenegger or Lou Ferrigno, for a simple reason: apart from being icons of bodybuilding, both men are legitimate celebrities. There have been a few exceptions to this celebrity rule; the February 1985 and September 2000 covers respectively feature only Lee Haney and Lee Labrada.

On all *Muscle & Fitness* covers without a female, the word "sex" is conspicuously absent. This is a clear indicator of the second purpose served by having females on the covers of muscle magazines: there has always been at least some degree of public association of bodybuilding with homosexuality. Magazine covers from the early 1960s and before lent themselves heavily to this connection. A typical cover would show a shaved and oiled muscular male, often wearing nothing but a faux-fig leaf, frequently reclining in a pseudo-suggestive position.

Weider himself published gay-oriented "beefcake" magazines in the '60s, but he knew that reaching the general population would require, as much as possible, distancing his current product from that imagery. Weider-brand bodybuilding from 1980 moving forward would be advertised to be a manly, heterosexual activity. There was no better way to do this than by mandating that a female should not only accompany the bodybuilder pictured on the cover, but she should be pressing her body against his. The change of the magazine's title from *Muscle Builder* to *Muscle & Fitness* helped cement the new image. Alliteration jokes later made the rounds; *Muscle Builder* featured "Men and Boys" while *Muscle & Fitness* showed "Males and Females." Be that as it may, that magazine's market share was no laughing matter. Sales skyrocketed.

* * * * *

Throughout 1984, *Muscle & Fitness* advertised the return of the Mr. Olympia contest to the United States. After a ten-year absence, the greatest muscle show on Earth would also return to what had been bodybuilding's greatest stateside venue: New York's Madison Square Garden. The Felt Forum would stage the actual event. Most of the previous year's top competitors had committed to compete. Foremost among these was Samir Bannout, who was also the first reigning champion since 1980 to defend his title. Although Frank Zane had hung up his posing suit for good, he was present in his new role of television broadcast commentator. The articulate and knowledgeable Zane was an obvious choice for this assignment, and he carried it out admirably.

As was typical for early-'80s major network broadcasts, the contest's evening show was filmed, edited down to a half-hour (including commercial time), and televised later. It was correctly decided that a full two-hour evening show with 15 complete posing routines would be far too long and tedious to retain the interest of the public. If a full-length contest were broadcast, few casual viewers would be expected to stay tuned long enough to find out who actually won. For real bodybuilding fans it was a different story. That group would love to see a full-length televised Olympia, and they were intensely interested in the outcome.

As the New York Olympia neared, precontest speculation swirled, just as it always had. In 1984 there was much to speculate, since a fresh set of unknown variables had been introduced to the mix. No less than 12 men who hadn't entered the 1983 Olympia were registered to compete; and of those, half had the potential to secure a place in the top six. Of that group, half again were at least theoretically capable of winning the whole show; and of that minority, one seemed to have the greatest chance.

Emerging from the abyss was none other than The Myth himself, Sergio Oliva, registered and ready for the first time since 1972 to vie for the Mr. Olympia title. He fully intended to reclaim the crown he had already worn, a generation earlier, on three occasions. In what seemed like the distant past of the late 1960s, Oliva reigned supreme. He had no doubt been encouraged by the comeback adventures of Arnold Schwarzenegger and Franco Columbu, and after a long absence declared that the time was ripe for a comeback of his own.

Oliva's situation was of course quite a bit different from those two men. Schwarzenegger and Columbu were Weider favorites while Oliva was an outcast. Oliva quit the IFBB out of frustration in 1972 when he was beaten by what he perceived to be an inferior Schwarzenegger, and thereafter competed in rogue federations, including bitter Weider rival Dan Lurie's WBBG. It seemed unlikely the IFBB would bend over backward for Oliva the way it had for Schwarzenegger and Columbu. It probably wouldn't bend at all. Nevertheless, the only man since 1966 to suffer upon him defeat, Schwarzenegger, was long gone. Surely, Oliva felt, he was better than current champion Samir Bannout. If he could somehow return to his '72 form but with a modern level of definition, Oliva would indeed pose a serious threat. Until the outcome was known, he had the crowd's roar of approval to remind him his return was appreciated.

Also making a comeback from retirement, albeit after an absence of a single year, was Chris Dickerson. He could likely expect the same scorecard leeway as Oliva. Boyer Coe returned to the Olympia in '84 as well, as did Robbie Robinson. Since the pair weren't getting any younger—both were 38 years old—and they belonged to a generation that was quickly being replaced, it was unclear how they might fare.

The last prominent figure to be added to the Olympia roster was 24-year-old newcomer Bob Paris. As part of his television commentary, Zane referred to Paris as a modern-day Steve Reeves—a statement that spoke volumes about the stunning, graceful shape of Paris' physique. He was worthy of the compliment. Paris was of course a product of modern bodybuilding culture and was therefore significantly larger than Reeves, but this gave the comparison no less merit. Both men had exceptionally pleasing lines and equally striking good looks;

right: Bob Paris. c. 1988
below: Samir Bannout. 1983

Courtesy of Michael Newman

Courtesy of Michael Newman

and both men had the advantage of height. Paris stood an even six feet tall; and at 220-plus pounds he was also—and somewhat ironically—one of the contest's bigger entrants. The question was therefore raised whether his mass and definition would be enough to propel him above the contest's behemoths.

As things turned out, Paris was good enough to best a number of other big men, including three-time champion Oliva. The Olympia's latest big-name comeback had therefore, and without ceremony, fallen flat. Oliva's thighs were noticeably smaller than what he brought to the stage in '72, and his definition, particularly throughout his lower body, was not competitive with most of the field. Nevertheless, Oliva was certainly no worse than Franco Columbu when he successfully came back earlier in the decade. If Oliva had the powers-that-be in his corner like Schwarzenegger and Columbu, precedence strongly suggested that the '84 Sandow would have been his. Yet he had no such connections. Years spent as an outcast won him no favors. It thus came to pass that Sergio Oliva, The Myth, the man who had once completely dominated the world of bodybuilding, was given the treatment of an ordinary competitor. He was awarded the contest's eighth-place medal.

Paris, who had even greater problems with lower-body definition, placed seventh. Amazing shape can only atone for so many faults, and the harsh reality was that Paris' lower body simply didn't belong on a modern Olympia stage. This knocked him out of real contention. He would however be back and much improved.

All things considered, the final placings of Bob Paris and Sergio Oliva were not big surprises. Their awards did however precede the evening's biggest eyebrow-raiser: defending champion Samir Bannout fell to sixth. Bannout was perhaps only slightly off the full and razor-sharp condition he brought to the stage in Munich, but this misstep was enough for judges to nearly expel him from the final comparison group. In the event's entire history, never has a reigning Mr. Olympia been so soundly defeated.

Placing just ahead of Bannout was the improved pair of Albert Beckles and Roy Callendar, who finished fourth and fifth respectively. In third was yet another greatly-improved competitor, the former German weightlifter Jusup Wilcosz. That left Mohammed Makkawy and Lee Haney. Makkawy owned a physique that was close to perfect, but he gave up a full nine inches of height and 80 pounds of muscle to the newly filled-out Haney. Direct comparisons moreover told the tale of the contest. Once Haney and Makkawy faced the curtain, Makkawy's subpar back paled next to Haney's monstrous lats, erectors, traps and rhomboids. Few doubted the outcome. Lee Haney was the newest Mr. Olympia.

* * * * *

Whereas the final few years of the 1970s formed a period of epilogue, the first few years of the 1980s together created an age of prelude. Together the years 1976-83 formed an era of transition, a bridge between the Mr. Olympia contest's first great dynasty, the reign of Arnold Schwarzenegger, and what looked like might be the next, that of Haney. Although Lee Haney had only just captured his first Mr. Olympia title, with his revised proportions he looked unstoppable. It seemed he could go on collecting Sandow trophies as long as he liked. Not since 1975 did bodybuilding have such a champion. Haney himself the next year spoke of how truly great physiques define bodybuilding's eras. As for the current era, Haney said "thankfully, I *am* that physique." Not only was this no empty boast, but it would have been overly modest to say otherwise. Starting late in 1983 and continuing through the following year, Haney evened out his physique. His lagging limbs were brought up. Though Haney's arms and legs were never able to match the development of his jaw-dropping torso, they improved enough to make his physique the greatest of his era. As the second half of the 1980s got under-

Lee Haney. c. 1985

Courtesy of Michael Newman

way, that physique began to create a dynasty of its own.

The old AAU Mr. America rule that prevented past winners from re-entering the contest got it all wrong. Bodybuilding loves dynasties. Fans love to watch dominating champions ride long win streaks. During its most prominent streaks the Mr. Olympia contest more or less became a fight for second place, but this in no way subtracted from the event's appeal. Bodybuilding grew in popularity during reigns of domination. Great champions not only helped characterize the eras in which they reigned; they also gave those eras a face and an identity. Sandow; Grimek; Reeves; Park; Scott; Oliva; Schwarzenegger—each became the specimen for which his era was most clearly recalled. With each passing year that connection has strengthened.

It was determined that 1985's Sandow trophy would be presented in Brussels, Belgium—the same city in which Louis Attila first trained Eugene Sandow 99 years earlier. There was, however, no pause for reflection. Other than that Sandow's image was used for bodybuilding's greatest award, all connections to the past had dissolved. Bodybuilding had assumed a form quite distinct from Victorian Vaudeville.

A Haney repeat was widely expected. When he presented a physique that inspired greater awe than the year before, his victory became a forgone conclusion. The recently-implemented IFBB scoring system which ranked competitors as opposed to assigning them grades told the tale. The lowest score wins; and next to the name Lee Haney there was a slew of ones. Haney cruised to victory; and with his triumph, for the first time since 1979 the IFBB was able to hand a Sandow to the same man on consecutive occasions. An all-time best-condition Albert Beckles finished second.

Although a simple look at scorecards told the tale of the 1985 Olympia, two other stories generated interest. The first centered on the event's 14th-place finisher, a second-tier professional named John Brown. After wallowing in the AAU doldrums for the larger part of the prior ten years, Brown finally advanced to and won both the WABBA and NABBA amateur Mr. Universe titles. By the time of the '85 Olympia he had only been competing in IFBB events for a little over a year, and as a consequence, few fans knew who John Brown even was. Those who did weren't expecting much from his Olympia debut. It was therefore a rather large surprise when, after the contest let out, Brown was perhaps the most talked-about competitor. Fans weren't excited about his physique. Though it was good, he had just stood next to the world's best. He deserved to be in the bottom ten. Those on hand to witness the event were instead enthralled by his posing routine.

Louis Attila. Late 19th-century photograph. 99 years after taking Eugen Sandow under his wing in Brussels, the world's greatest bodybuilding contest came to his city.

Physique presentation had been gradually evolving from the time bodybuilders first synchronized their poses to music in the 1960s. For at least the first decade of choreographed presentation, competitors almost exclusively posed to bombastic orchestral pieces. The drama-oozing theme music from the movie *Exodus* could be heard several times at any given bodybuilding contest during the 1970s. The grandeur of the score was thought to be appropriate accompaniment for the living sculpture displayed onstage. This was but one of many selections which were used to achieve a similar effect. Toward the end of the decade this thinking began to change. Aspiring to be living sculpture was neat but confining. For audiences, two straight hours of it was often boring.

Although dramatic classical music remained popular among competitors well into the '80s, different styles began to be used. Foremost among these was hard rock. Nevertheless, posing itself changed little. Styles were highly interchangeable. An identical series of poses could be used for routines featuring Prokofiev or Pink Floyd, for Straus or Stevie Wonder. When John Brown took the stage at the 1985 Mr. Olympia contest, all that changed.

Brown began his routine with conventional posing, as part of a calculated attempt to all but lull his audience into complacency. His music then changed. Individual poses were no longer punctuated by standard transitions, but rather by break-dancing moves. Soon he was dancing more than posing. The Brussels crowd howled, cheered and clapped to the music's beat. They had never seen anything like it and were happy to contribute. Brown was onstage for a total of more than ten minutes. The routine had little effect on his placement, but it eventually had a large impact on the character of bodybuilding competition. Through his routine, Brown added an entirely new dimension to physique presentation. He showed that it need not always be stoic, rigid and aloof; that a posing routine was a blank canvass rather than a color-inside-the-lines exercise. For better or worse, this message resonated and gained traction. There followed many imitators. Within two decades, bodybuilding presentation would be something completely different from what was witnessed before 1985.

Another reason bodybuilding presentation—not to mention physique standards—would later change completely had much to do with the '85 Olympia's other big story. A 22-year-old rookie named Rich Gaspari grabbed the event's bronze medal. Gaspari had turned professional after winning the light-heavyweight class of the '84 NPC National Championships, and followed the victory with a runner-up finish to Beckles at the '85 Night of Champions contest in New York.

On paper Gaspari was impressive, though perhaps not outstanding: at five-foot-eight he weighed in the neighborhood of 210 pounds. Though he had decent individual lines, they configured into a build that was slightly blocky, with an undesirably thick mid-section. Gaspari's arm and leg measurements were respectable but not particularly striking. All these things considered, it should have been unrealistic to expect him to secure a finalists' spot, much less a place in the top three. Yet Gaspari's fame and value as a competitor never derived from graceful lines or shocking proportions. He was nothing like Bob Paris or Sergio Oliva. He didn't need to be. Gaspari was a specimen of incredible, rock-hard muscularity.

When IFBB officials came up with competition judging criteria many years earlier, they never even considered that anyone like Rich Gaspari would one day materialize. Before he came onto the scene, competitors were assigned a score based on the size, definition, shape and symmetry of their physiques. Gaspari, almost by himself, introduced a fifth criterion: hardness. It was the seemingly bulletproof hardness covering his physique that made him a truly remarkable and important bodybuilder.

Starting in the 1960s, high-level competitors gradually began reducing their bodyfat levels. As the tissue covering their bodies became thinner and thinner, the muscles which lay underneath began to appear harder and harder. The chemicals bodybuilders started using during the period exacerbated these effects: they helped burn fat, and they gave muscles an unnaturally hard appearance. By the mid-1980s, anyone qualified to compete as an IFBB professional exhibited a significant level of hardness.

Gaspari simply took it to the next level. The hardness of his fellow competitors was nothing like that exhibited by the young rookie. Yet he was no mere anomaly, no mere curiosity. Gaspari's physique set a new standard, one against which all competitors of his era were compared. In the process, he changed bodybuilding forever. Being big, defined, shapely and symmetrical was no longer enough—

Rich Gaspari. c. 1985

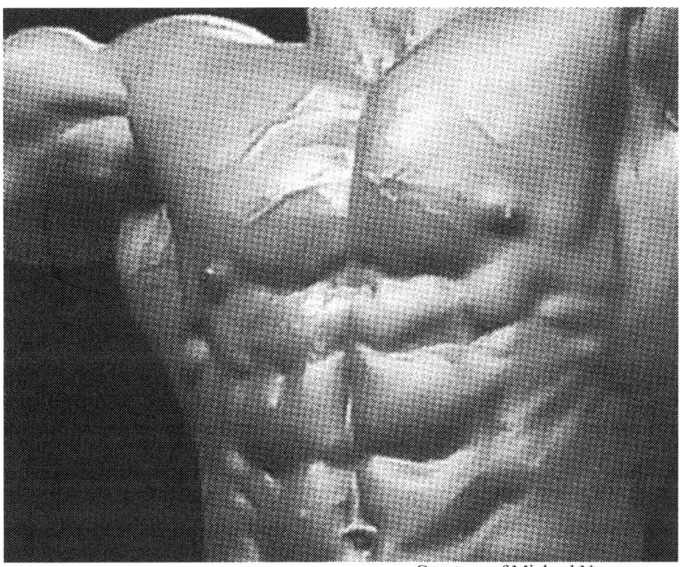

Courtesy of Michael Newman

not when competitors with similar qualities looked as though they had been cast in bronze. Early on Gaspari let it be known that he wanted to set a new standard in bodybuilding. He succeeded.

Gaspari also owned the distinction, dubious or otherwise, of being the first competitor to make a point of flexing his gluteus muscles. He had reason to show them off. Gaspari's glutes had striations and separation on par with the rest of physique; and, with the possible exception of Tom Platz, they were unlike anything yet seen. Striated glutes became the new badge of ultimate definition. After Gaspari made his mark, it became the case that unless a competitor had definition and hardness in this area, he wasn't truly in top shape. The newer and smaller posing suits that came into vogue in the mid-1980s made a good portion of the muscle visible, and this made the striated-glutes trend possible.

Although in a later era the practice of overt glute display would create problems for contest judging and bodybuilding in general, for the moment it was merely a slightly racy addendum to the evolving standards of competition. Bodybuilding increasingly embraced men who possessed striking muscularity, and the emergence of Rich Gaspari was a big reason why this is so.

The rookie soon became a favorite of many fans, especially those from his geographical region. Gaspari hailed from New Jersey. The United States east coast had attracted a significant number of men into bodybuilding, and it was natural that Gaspari should become a hero to many of them. Judges found him nearly irresistible as well. It was therefore no surprise when, in 1986, Gaspari moved into the runner-up position at the Mr. Olympia contest. As part of a campaign to reduce the thickness of his waist, he cut down on heavy abdominal work. To a small degree this worked, and Gaspari was rewarded. The remainder of his physique meanwhile lived up to the hardness standard he unveiled in Brussels.

Although Lee Haney couldn't match Gaspari's hardness, his physique was simply too massive and separated to be overcome. His victory at the Olympia, held for the sixth and final time in Columbus, effectively turned his small string of wins into a legitimate reign. Haney was now a fixture atop the Olympia throne. The two-year-old conjecture that he would collect a large number of Sandow trophies was becoming simple fact. During his reign, Haney dominated bodybuilding more thoroughly than even Schwarzenegger during his.

1986 may have been the year of Haney's best-ever condition. He was even more massive than the year before, with equivalent definition. With Gaspari firmly in second, the '86 Olympia therefore became a battle for third place—one fought by a slew of competitors who helped define the era. Winning the battle was Mike Christian, a competitor who turned professional the same time as Gaspari and who shadowed him in IFBB contest placings. Until after the '87 Olympia, wherever Gaspari finished, Christian was never more than two spots behind. At six-foot-one, Christian was one of the IFBB's tallest competitors. He possessed overall good mass and a particularly monstrous upper body. His lower-body size was perhaps suited better for the previous decade however, and because of this he was never a real threat to win the Olympia. As things stood, he was a threat to win any contest that didn't feature Haney or Gaspari.

In fourth was Golden-Age holdover Albert Beckles. Up until 1986 Beckles had steadily improved with age, defying those who waited for his years to catch up with him. His all-time peak came at the '85 Olympia, but it now seemed as though he had crested the hill. He had regressed slightly since the previous year, and this allowed Gaspari and Christian to get by him. Over the next few years Beckles' downward momentum would turn into a plummet.

Mike Christian. c. 1986

Courtesy of Michael Newman

Finishing behind Beckles was Berry DeMey, a Dutch national who was quickly proving himself to be everything that Bob Paris was not. Since both men were about six feet tall, comparisons were straightforward. Paris' strength was the awe-inspiring shape of his upper body, particularly when viewed from the front and sides. From the standpoint of pure aesthetics, he was nearly untouchable in certain poses. Much to DeMey's credit, his lines were nearly as good. It was in the remainder of his physique that he distanced himself from Paris. DeMey had a wider and more muscular back and, critically, narrower hips. The pair were equally matched in lower-body size, but DeMey had much sharper definition. DeMey first competed in the Olympia in 1985 and placed sixth, three spots ahead of an improved Paris.

Bertil Fox was seventh. Considering the steady stream of top-quality bodybuilders that had been filling the IFBB's competitive pool, Fox no longer stood out as he once had. With the emergence of Lee Haney, he also no longer owned the most striking crab pose in bodybuilding. In eighth was '85 NPC Nationals heavyweight champion Ron Love. Placing ninth was John Terilli, an Australian national who, before turning professional, had been present as a spectator at the 1980 Olympia. Witnessing firsthand what appeared to be a fixed contest hadn't quite destroyed Terilli's faith in the system as a whole, and he rose to become a steady top competitor. He had good shape, full muscle bellies, excellent definition, and a slender midsection.

John Terilli. c. 1989

Courtesy of Michael Newman

Once bodybuilding had reached its evolutionary apex a generation later, small waists—all but taken for granted during the '80s—became a rarity. The era of men like DeMey, Paris and Terilli therefore later became known for this attribute, and it's partially for this reason that these men are now considered to be paradigms of '80s bodybuilding. It's because of physiques like theirs that the second half of that decade is sometimes thought to be bodybuilding's aesthetic high-water mark.

The list of men of with small waists did not exclude Lee Haney, whose fairly trim midsection made the remainder of his physique appear that much more massive. This was one of many reasons why he once more stood well above the heap. Yet the '86 Olympia wasn't merely another Haney win. His third victory was also the fifth straight Mr. Olympia contest in which the outcome did not cause widespread concern. The apparently fixed outcomes of 1980 and '81 now seemed more distant. The idea that bodybuilding could be a legitimate sport would therefore once again be tolerated by the television networks which aimed to cash in on its appeal. There would be no more instances where a network would refuse to televise a contest because of its outcome.

The time was ripe for television and bodybuilding to make amends. Cable TV was rapidly overtaking the old airwave method of transmission, which proved to be a boon for bodybuilding. Whereas before there had often been less than a dozen airwave broadcast stations—depending upon one's market—there were now 40, 50 and sometimes many more cable channels. With more than quadruple the time slots to fill with programming, and with program directors searching for marketable content, room was occasionally made available for muscle contests. Most of these executives knew little about bodybuilding and nothing about the '80 and '81 Mr. Olympia contests, nor would they have cared. They had schedules to fill and their bosses' bottom lines to consider. It therefore became the case that a few times a year a big event like the Olympia would make an off-hour appearance on cable TV. Unlike major network broadcasts however, cable presented the evening show in its entirety. The contests were never televised live, but fans never expected them to be. They were ready and willing to wait.

Although the IFBB professional division considered itself to be the major league of a legitimate sport, when compared to any of the world's major-league sports there existed a vast chasm of revenue. Muscle contests generated paltry dollars compared to the NFL, the NHL, or even the WSA.[1] Its fan base therefore held little sway. Fans would have loved to see the Mr. Olympia contest broadcast live on cable TV, but they had been conditioned to not expect such things. The collective power of fans did increase somewhat during the 1980s, thanks to things like the successful off-hour broadcasts of that contest, but it wasn't enough to move TV executives.

Bodybuilding fans would have to be content with non-live broadcasts. As it turned out they were. Any bodybuilding on TV was appreciated. Meanwhile, the collective power of bodybuilding's fan base was given a marginal boost by its general increase in popularity. As the final years of the '80s got underway, this popularity was largely owed to bodybuilding's emerging crop of stars.

A number of these stars were sold to the public with vigor. The cream of the crop made it onto the cover of *Muscle & Fitness* magazine. Except for winning a Mr. Olympia title or starring in an action movie, appearing on the cover of that publication represented the pinnacle of success in bodybuilding. Anyone who made the grade would have his image seen by several million people, from the magazine's three-million-plus monthly readers to the untold numbers who noticed it in supermarket checkout stands. No other bodybuilding magazine has matched this exposure. For the select few bodybuilders who made it onto these covers, it was a badge of stardom.

There was much calculation in determining who was worthy of this privilege. *Muscle & Fitness* was out to promote a specific image; to do so, it needed to display men and women with a certain "look." The covers had undeniable sexual overtones, but they also expressed a simple message: bodybuilding is not only an activity of beautiful people, but it can itself be a gateway to beauty. Special individuals were needed to get this message across. On a typical cover, an attractive and fit female with slight but visible muscles appeared as an accessory to an Adonis-caliber male specimen. He was chosen for the career-making shot because of his fantastic build, but more importantly, because of his good looks.

Bob Paris became one of several *Muscle & Fitness* favorites. Although he and Bertil Fox enjoyed roughly equivalent success in IFBB contests, the number of *Muscle & Fitness* cover shots for each spoke volumes about the image the magazine meant to convey: Paris appeared six times; Fox, zero. Lee Haney, the greatest physique of his era, made the cover twice. Rich Gaspari, who never came close to beating him, tripled that number.

Unlike the AAU of the '50s and '60s, official IFBB rules had no divisive "general appearance" criterion. The IFBB declared that the best bodybuilders should win its contests; and factors not specifically listed in the rules should not enter into judging decisions. For the most part—perhaps excluding the '72, '80 and '81 Olympias—this proved true. The AAU Mr. America contest existed for 30 years before a black competitor won the title, while the IFBB Mr. Olympia title was around for only two before crowning Sergio Oliva. That being said, IFBB publications—especially the best-selling *Muscle & Fitness*—gave far more front-cover press to competitors who were deemed to have a favorable general appearance.

1987 saw the emergence of two such men—competitors who became icons of the era, and later, all-time greats. One eventually made the cover of *Muscle & Fitness* six times; the other, two. The first was Lee Labrada, middleweight champion of the '86 IFBB World Amateur Championships. His '87 Olympia appearance became one of the most successful debuts of the post-Schwarzenegger era. The second was Shawn Ray, overall winner of the

Shawn Ray. c. 1999

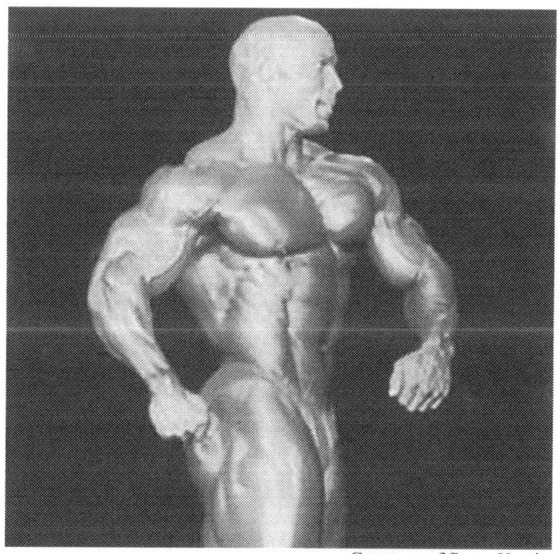

Courtesy of Steve Harris

[1] Western Soccer Alliance

'87 NPC National Championships. Both men had excellent balance and size; both had impeccable presentation skills; both were handsome; and both had fantastic, for-the-ages shape. Both were also below average in height, and this may have been the only thing stopping them from rising, in tandem, to the very top of bodybuilding's competitive ladder.

Ray would have to wait until 1988 for his hat to land in the Mr. Olympia ring. As for Labrada, in '87 he simply picked up where Mohamed Makkawy had left off. Makkawy had amazing shape and size but was too short to threaten the Olympia title. Had he achieved peak form in '82 rather than two years later he might easily have won it all. By '84, the emergence of Lee Haney had quashed any such hope. Three years later the Olympia stage had Labrada, a taller and more complete competitor who nonetheless owned similar classic lines. In one fell swoop Labrada bypassed Mike Christian, Berry DeMey, Albert Beckles and a dozen more of the IFBB's best. He came in third, behind only Haney and Gaspari. It was a placing foreseen by few but lauded by many. With shape and balance as his calling card, Labrada now held aloft a torch previously carried by Reeves, Zane, Makkawy and Paris.

Gaspari meanwhile was far too muscular, hard and thick to be overtaken by Labrada. Their finish was reminiscent of the previous generation's Columbu-versus-Zane matchups. Above them both towered Lee Haney, much as Schwarzenegger had done during his time. It was Haney's fourth Olympia title, and it seemed more true than ever that no one—up-and-coming or otherwise—seemed capable of beating him. Christian finished fourth and DeMey wound up in sixth.

Finishing a surprising fifth was another resurrected Golden Age icon, Robbie Robinson. Although Robinson was in his 15th consecutive year of active competition, a slew of lower placings in the mid-'80s caused him to largely drop out of sight. Magazines of the era had too many young stars to cover to give Robinson the time of day. As a consequence, fans thought he had retired. Nevertheless, at 41 years of age he showed up in all-time best condition and was rewarded. The final years of the decade would mark the peak of his career. Meanwhile, the slope had finally become slippery for Robinson's Pumping Iron cohort Albert Beckles. In what would be his last-ever appearance in an Olympia top ten, he finished seventh. His free-fall began the following year.

* * * * *

As part of the IFBB's mission to bring the Olympia to a variety of US and international locations, in 1987 the contest had been held in Gothenburg, Sweden. For 1988, something entirely different was planned. For the 24th installment of the contest, Los Angeles was selected to be the host city. Since the LA metropolitan area had long-since become the world's center of bodybuilding activity, fans wondered why the region hadn't played host sooner. For a number of competitors—many of whom lived nearby and trained at the new Gold's Gym in Venice—the location couldn't have been more convenient.

In 1981, the storied Gold's Gym on Pacific Avenue in Venice closed its doors for good. The building which served as the primary shooting location for *Pumping Iron*, the same building which echoed for 16 years the clanging weights of the Golden Age's greatest competitors, was no more. The original Gold's in 1965 was a leading-edge weight-training establishment. It was better equipped for bodybuilding workouts than anything in existence. This was its original draw, the thing that attracted the greats in the first place. Before long it was the greats themselves who became the draw. Top bodybuilders came to the Venice Gold's to associate with men like themselves. They became friends, trained together, and exchanged information and pointers. Together they formed an exclusive clique.

By the time the 1980 New Year was rung in, times had changed. The Golden age had ended. The Pacific Avenue Gold's was both aging and inundated. It was dated. The fitness boom rapidly in-

Gold's Gym, Venice. c. 1967

Gold's Gym, Venice. c. 2007

creased demand for gym memberships, and because of this, big new exercise facilities were beginning to open throughout the United States. As the years passed this growth accelerated. Gold's got in on the act and began opening more gyms. It would eventually license its name to more than 650. Nevertheless, as the 80s got underway its flagship gym in Venice was in danger of falling behind.

Bodybuilding was also growing bigger and more slick. If Gold's was to remain relevant, it needed to provide a facility to match. Its new owner, former IFBB professional Pete Grymkowki, knew this. He arranged for Gold's to move from its decades-old structure to a modern building on Hampton Drive—one that would house the newer and better equipment that had been created since 1965. The new building was also bigger. It would more aptly accommodate the growing list of Gold's members.

The original gym's serviceable weights and racks were loaded onto trucks for the three-block journey north. Before long the Hampton gym was ready; and the second edition of the accurately self-described "Mecca of Bodybuilding" was open for business. The original Gold's became a distant memory, another part of the Golden Age that was gone forever and could never be experienced by those who came later. Its disappearance added to the mystique and romance of the age. As the decade progressed, the number of top bodybuilders who had never even seen the inside of the original Gold's grew. Meanwhile, more professionals than ever regularly trained at the new facility. One man who later became a regular also happened to be the first competitor to look like he might threaten Lee Haney's grip on the Mr. Olympia crown.

Gary Strydom was a South African national who relocated to the US in 1980. In 1984, in only his second contest, Strydom won the overall NPC USA Championships. In '86, after securing US citizenship, he entered and won the NPC Nationals. Strydom kicked off his IFBB professional career with a decisive win at the '87 Night of Champions. As the owner of a massive physique characterized by impressive shoulders, pectorals and thighs, Strydom was also good-looking, fair-haired and blue-eyed. At six-foot-one he was also tall. Some dared to believe he was the second coming of Arnold Schwarzenegger—except that this new version had much better leg development.

A showdown with Haney was anticipated. Strydom had foregone the Olympia in '87, but in '88 he fully committed himself to the cause. The outcome was not easy to predict, since Strydom had thus far brought to the stage two distinct looks. He won the Nationals at an extremely lean and hard 228 pounds, while at the Night of Champions he was significantly bigger and more full, and at least 25 pounds heavier. His musculature was certainly defined at the heavier weight, though it was without the lighter Strydom's razor-sharp striations. It was not known if either of these two bodies would show up in Los Angeles, or if Strydom would be able to combine the best attributes of both physiques into a single entity. Beating Haney would almost certainly require the latter.

Gary Strydom. c. 1992

Courtesy of Michael Newman

Strydom's condition was by no means the contest's only unknown variable. Shawn Ray, who had years earlier declared that it was his destiny to win the Mr. Olympia, was now ready to make his first attempt at fulfilling that claim. Both men belonged to the most impressive rookie class the Olympia had yet seen, maybe the most extraordinary ever. The group of first-timers included Phil Hill,'87 NPC National Heavyweight Champion; Mike Quinn,'87 NPC USA Overall Champion; Mohamed Benaziza, '87 IFBB Lightweight World Champion; Brian Buchanan, '84 NABBA Mr. Universe; Luis Freitas, '87 IFBB Heavyweight World Champion; and Ralf Moeller, '86 IFBB Heavyweight World Champion. These eight competitors could have by themselves filled out the lineup of a world-class contest. As things stood however, they merely occupied eight of the contest's 20 spots.

The final unknown variables in 1988 were Bob Paris, who after brief hiatus had returned to Olympia contention, and Samir Bannout, who was making a comeback after a four-year absence. Bannout had quit the IFBB after his '84 sixth-place Olympia finish, and in '85 pledged allegiance to the rouge WABBA. He won that federation's Professional World Championships but was unsuccessful in collecting the promised $25,000 first-place prize money. According to the *Musclemag* coverage of the event, part of the sum was imparted to him in the form of a tanning bed. The article further stated that Bannout became enraged and chased after the promoter. Now, three years later, the Olympia was visiting Bannout's transplanted home of Los Angeles. Although the IFBB put on much tougher contests, its checks didn't bounce and it paid what it promised. It was not known how Bannout would fare. As a former Olympia champion, he had a lifetime invitation to compete and had thus foregone any warm-up events.

Paris' situation was different. He had needed to re-qualify. He showcased a significantly improved physique seven months earlier at the '88 Night of Champions and finished third, which not only made him eligible to compete in the Olympia, but it also made him a legitimate threat to crack the top six. Meanwhile, the contest's known variables—Haney, Gaspari, Labrada and DeMey—were on hand and prepared to once more vie for the title. Along with the group of newcomers, it was the greatest group of competitors yet assembled. This was appropriate, since they were all about to be put on display at the center of the bodybuilding universe, at the peak of bodybuilding's popularity. Maximum publicity was guaranteed. However, this didn't stop the IFBB from milking things further.

An official weigh-in was held. This was a curious move, since there was only a single class with no weight restrictions. Moreover, for physique contest judging, bodyweight is not taken into consideration, nor has it ever been part of physique evaluation criteria. Weighing competitors was an irrelevant gesture. That being said, most everyone liked the idea. For those who don't sit on a judging panel, bodyweight adds a finite, objective measure to a type of competition that is otherwise devoid of them. In print or otherwise, virtually all discussions of bodybuilding competitions make reference to the weight of competitors. The IFBB knew this quite well when they planned the weigh-in. They knew fans would show interest; and now, for the first time since weight classes last appeared nine years earlier, spectators got to see exactly how much everyone weighed. It also gave onlookers a preview of how each competitor looked.

Such was the state of affairs as fans began streaming into the Universal Amphitheater for prejudging. In the event, judges cut to the chase. Strydom and Haney were placed side-by-side for direct comparisons. The contest appeared close through the first few poses, but once the comparison group was asked to turn toward the rear of the stage, speculation over who owned the better physique quickly ended. Next to Haney, whose back development was the greatest yet seen, Strydom looked totally outclassed. It was after all the lighter and leaner

Lee Labrada. c. 1988

Courtesy of Michael Newman

Strydom who had shown up in Los Angeles. At 229 pounds he was sharper than Haney's 244, but he was also two inches taller than the reigning champion. Although Strydom had the best definition of the entire field, gone was much of the previous year's size increase; and his back, always an area of weakness, was especially affected. It seemed that the 15 pounds he gave up to Haney all came from that area.

Strydom's evening show presentation didn't help any of this. Compared to Haney's professional, finely-choreographed and climactic posing routine, Strydom's appeared amateurish and poorly-conceived. Their use of the same posing music made the disparity even more evident. It was hoped that the Haney-Strydom showdown would be a modern version of the Schwarzenegger-Oliva battles. It was nothing of the sort. Exactly four poses into their first comparison, the showdown turned into a schooling. Strydom was awarded fifth place.

Lee Labrada dropped one spot from his previous finish to fourth, though not because of any regression on his part. It was instead the dramatic reinvention of Berry DeMey that displaced him. Like Strydom, DeMey had shown up in an extremely lean condition. Unlike Strydom however, DeMey was balanced and complete. Though the thickness and width of his back did not match Haney—no one's did—the level of detail he brought to the stage inspired awe. DeMey's lower back had striations that were quite unlike anything yet seen. His upper arms were not as large as in previous outings however, and this may have been the one factor that prevented him from knocking Gaspari out of what had become his perennial runner-up spot. Gaspari was bigger and harder than ever, but it didn't matter; not when he stood staring upward at the figure of Lee Haney.

Of the 1988 Mr. Olympia rookie class, Gary Strydom fared best. Just behind him was Mike Quinn, whose thick and deeply-separated torso secured for him the final spot among the group of six finalists. Brian Buchanan, the British bodybuilder known for his freakishly small waist and huge arms, finished seventh. Some thought he should have been first. Mohamed Benaziza ended up in 11th place; and Phil Hill was 12th. The format in 1988 called for all 20 competitors to assemble onstage after the evening's free-posing round so that the top 10 could be called forward. When the awards entourage bypassed Hill, fans began calling his name and booing. A large part of the Universal Amphitheater audience soon joined in. Though he possessed a monstrous physique that reminded fans of Bertil Fox—only with more rounded lines and far more massive thighs—Hill had amazed onlookers with a graceful and artistic posing routine. Fans loved the juxtaposition of beauty and beast within a single performance, and their displeasure over Hill's placing was made abundantly clear.

Meanwhile, hometown prodigy Shawn Ray's graceful and artistic presentation had fallen flat. He had now used the same posing routine in a number of contests, and although it was expertly choreographed and executed, it was also old and tired. His condition didn't help this. The razor-sharp lines his put on display at the '87 Nationals were absent. Ray was reported to be in absolute top condition at posing exhibitions as far as six weeks in advance of the Olympia, and this may have contributed to his decline.

Once bodybuilders began bringing modern levels of muscular definition to bodybuilding stages in the mid-'70s, it quickly became evident that those levels can only be maintained for short periods—from mere days to a few weeks—before physical and mental burnout sets in. It was widely thought this may have been the predicament faced by Ray. Whatever the case, the Mr. Olympia contest had now advanced to a point where it was totally unforgiving. The smallest flaw or conditioning error could send a competitor plummeting in the placings. Such was the case with Shawn Ray. He owned what was perhaps the most perfectly-constructed

Phil Hill. c. 1988

Courtesy of Michael Newman

physique the world of bodybuilding had yet seen, yet a relatively mild conditioning mistake let a number of men with inferior DNA slip by him. He finished 13th but was far from done.

Samir Bannout ended up in eighth place and a greatly improved Bob Paris was 10th. The continued slide of both men in Olympia placings was owed to the ever-rising size and quality of event's field rather than any specific shortcomings. Such was not the case with Albert Beckles and Robbie Robinson, who finished 15th and 17th respectively. Both men simply seemed too far past their prime to contend.

Finishing last was the event's largest competitor—and to that point, the largest bodybuilder ever—six-foot-eight, 288-pound German behemoth Ralf Moeller. Though he was undeniably impressive, Moeller was simply too tall and lanky to be competitive at bodybuilding's highest level. There were however greener pastures laying before him, one of which came in the form of moderate Hollywood movie stardom. Though Moeller may have been more curiosity than contender at the '88 Olympia, the fame he gained outside the world of muscle became greater than any of the 19 men who finished ahead of him. The small role he played in a single movie—2001's Best Picture *Gladiator*—ensured this.

Although bodybuilding as a form of exercise had enjoyed a massive increase in popularity during the decade, and although the world of competitive bodybuilding and its associated subculture also grew significantly, that world was still relatively small and insular. When the minor fame of last-place Olympian Ralf Moeller eclipsed the notoriety of multiple champion Lee Haney this point was driven home. Only bodybuilding fans have reason to know who Samir Bannout or Shawn Ray are. The same could be said for Berry DeMey, Mike Quinn, Roy Callendar or any of the great legions of men who at one time or another stripped down, oiled up and flexed their muscles. To the rest of the world, barring some other claim to fame, these people were, and are, invisible.

Sergio Oliva had one such claim. His name briefly became known to the public, though not because of anything he accomplished under the bright lights of bodybuilding contests. Mainstream media outlets mentioned him because he was the victim of well-publicized shooting. When not moonlighting as a world-champion bodybuilder, Oliva was a Chicago police officer; and by 1986 he was a ten-year veteran of the force. 1986 also happened to be the year his turbulent marriage to Arleen Garrett came to a head. An argument between the two ended when Garrett seized Oliva's .38-caliber service revolver and shot him five times. Oliva survived,[1] and local news outlets reported the story. The primary significance of the crime was that its victim was a Chicago cop. In news reports, references were made to Oliva's bodybuilding career, and Chicago-area residents learned that a former world champion had been patrolling their streets. Few of them would have known this had Oliva not been shot.

* * * * *

Oliva's former chief rival had meanwhile experienced something quite the opposite. Arnold Schwarzenegger became bodybuilding's one true bona fide celebrity, the man who kept its beacon burning brightly. Schwarzenegger wasn't a direct purveyor of physical culture like Eugen Sandow, Bernarr Macfadden or Jack LaLanne. He let other people devote themselves to the promotion of exercise, healthy eating and bodybuilding. Schwarzenegger instead pursued a career as an entertainer. More specifically, he put his muscles on display in action movies. By the end of 1988 he had a solid string of hits, including *Predator*, *Commando*, *Raw Deal*, *Red Heat*, *The Running Man* and his first comedy, *Twins*. Along with the general fitness boom, the image of Schwarzenegger's muscular body, which seemed to be everywhere, was enough to keep the public's interest in weight training expanding. Although bodybuilding competition and culture were relatively small and insular and its champions who weren't named Schwarzenegger were largely unknown to the general public, he helped those two things grow as well, perhaps more than any other single factor.

And grow bodybuilding did. On the eve of the decade's final year, the world of muscle was bigger than ever. The distribution of bodybuilding's biggest magazine, *Muscle & Fitness*, amply testified to this expansion: the January 1989 issue boasted 5,200,000 monthly readers, an increase of more than 100% in just three years. Other magazines enjoyed a similar bump in popularity. Schwarzenegger decided to directly cash in on this growth when in 1989 he began promoting a new contest—the Arnold Schwarzenegger Classic—that aimed to

[1]Although Oliva fully recovered and returned to work, the incident ended his bodybuilding career.

rival the Olympia as bodybuilding's premier event. By 1988 the total prize money for the Olympia was $150,000, with $70,000 going to the winner. The "Arnold Classic," as it became known, offered similar prizes. The existence of two contests offering these types of prizes would have been unfathomable ten years earlier; in 1989 however it was but another indicator of bodybuilding's new popularity.

A brisk pace of expansion was an important part of what made '80s bodybuilding unique, but any real attempt to define the era has to look beyond anything that can be plotted on a graph. The world of muscle had created for itself a new and unmistakable complexion, one that matched the character of the decade as a whole. Bodybuilding in the 1980s, like much of the decade's pop culture, had turned into something that was slick, deliberately packaged and big. While physiques of the era had a distinct appearance, the men who built them adopted an even more particular style. Whereas gyms of the '70s were populated by men who wore shaggy hair, old sweats and sometimes no shoes, new-era devotees had carefully styled hair, spandex tights and Reeboks. They watched Schwarzenegger's movies and attempted his trademark accent at the slightest provocation. They revered bodybuilding magazines and rooted for their favorites. They followed the contests. They also showed special interest when a big new event appeared on the 1989 IFBB calendar.

With March came the first Schwarzenegger Classic contest. For the event, Schwarzenegger followed his tried-and-true formula of pairing up with longtime promoting partner Jim Lorimer in Columbus. A number of top competitors signed on, though Lee Haney was not among them. Despite the lure of a handsome payoff, Haney kept to the reigning Mr. Olympia tradition—in place since the days of Larry Scott—of forgoing all other events.[1] Since he stood to tie Schwarzenegger's record of six consecutive Olympia titles later that year, Haney decided to avoid anything that might hurt his chances. Achieving peak condition twice in a single year can sometimes be enough to do this. It therefore surprised few when three-time Olympia runner-up Rich Gaspari claimed the first place award.

[1]During his reign, Haney did compete in one other contest: the 1987 German Grand Prix, which immediately followed the Olympia.

Second place on the other hand was a big surprise. Robbie Robinson had quickly risen from the ashes of his '88 Olympia disaster and secured the runner-up spot. Gary Strydom was third. That trio was followed by Samir Bannout, Bob Paris, Bertil Fox, and Albert Beckles.

Schwarzenegger had aimed to create a contest that rivaled the Olympia. After-action analyses of its first installment concluded that he came close to fulfilling that goal. An awe-inspiring lineup had come loaded for bear. A great champion had triumphed. However, an abstention by the era's most dominant competitor had put the event in perspective. The Schwarzenegger Classic was won by the world's second-best bodybuilder. The contest had glitz, glamour and prize money, but it had no history. The Mr. Olympia contest on the other hand had the richest history of any bodybuilding title. This was important. *Pumping Iron* documented Schwarzenegger winning his sixth Olympia; to competitors of the future, winning the same title had value beyond measure.

The 1995 television broadcast of the Schwarzenegger Classic hoped to lure unsuspecting fans into believing the contest had much more history, that it was more than just another non-Olympia event. A brief segment outlining the event's background showed, for just a few seconds, grainy, black-and-white footage of Rich Gaspari striking a series of onstage poses. The narrator referred to him as the event's first champion, and at the bottom of the screen was a year: "1969." It was implied that by '95 the show was in its 27th year, not its seventh. Real fans knew this was nonsense. They knew that Gaspari was only five years old by March of that year, and that Schwarzenegger had yet to even compete in an Olympia. It would have been rather incredible for a five-year-old to win a major bodybuilding title, and rather pretentious for a new and untested competitor with poor English skills to launch a "classic" professional contest under his own name. The principle of plausible deniability dictated that the narrator should never actually say the year, which he didn't, and that the network might be seen as having made a simple typo with the year—listing 1969 instead of 1989.

Nevertheless, the purposely-grainy black-and-white footage gave away the ruse. It was a cheap ploy, a type of stunt that would have been immediately exposed had it been tried with a major-league sport. But this was bodybuilding; when convenient, anything goes. For those who detected it, the ruse backfired. It was an unwitting admission of the Schwarzenegger Classic's true status. The contest was a first-rate event, but it would then and forever play second fiddle to Mr. Olympia.

Dedicated bodybuilding fans always knew this. The Schwarzenegger Classic was something new and neat, but it could not compete with history, especially when a rare milestone was about to be reached. The inaugural event predictably generated less interest than Lee Haney's upcoming attempt to tie Schwarzenegger's record for consecutive Olympia victories. Fans didn't care that the attempt would meet success or failure in the Adriatic Coast vacation town of Rimini, Italy—a place that was to the large majority of them a far-flung location. Before long those fans would learn the contest's outcome, and in a month or so magazines would treat them to pictures.

For 1989, the Olympia lineup was mainly unchanged, with two notable exceptions. The first was that Mike Christian had returned. Despite the fact that he was a Los Angeles-area resident and had won the 1988 IFBB U.S. and World Professional Championship events, Christian strangely skipped that year's LA Olympia. The second important addition was Vince Taylor, winner of the '89 Night of Champions. Taylor had earned for himself professional status by winning the overall title at the '88 NPC Nationals. The 33-year-old rookie had taken up weight training at a relatively late age, but in bodybuilding such starts are often without penalty. Taylor's rapid ascent was owed to his large,

Vince Taylor. c. 2001

Courtesy of Steve Harris

well-proportioned, deeply-separated and shapely physique. Like Lee Labrada and a number of other champions over the years, no single bodypart on him stood out; he was great nowhere but good everywhere. Most importantly, Taylor's lines fit together exceptionally well—and for this he was rewarded.

Relative to Taylor, Mike Christian had a slightly harder and more massive upper body. His lower body lagged however, and Taylor's balance forced him down into a sixth-place finish. A greatly improved Mohamed Benaziza was fifth, thanks to his ownership of the contest's most thickly-muscled physique. Only his short stature—he was five-foot-three—prevented him threatening to crack the top three. In fourth place was Rich Gaspari. He was unable to precisely duplicate the condition he had brought to bodybuilding stages over the previous four-plus years and therefore fell from his previously secure runner-up position.

Gaspari was known for having passable lines and superior torso thickness, but it was conditioning that earned him fame. In 1989 the myth of his infallibility was shattered, and he now teetered over a chasm of his own creation. Gaspari had single-handedly changed conditioning standards in bodybuilding. Year after year he brought to the world's top contests unmatched hardness. A wide gulf had therefore formed between him and his fellow competitors, who were now scrambling to catch up. Berry DeMey made his best attempt to bridge the gap in '88, nearly succeeded, and shot up to third place as a result. More successful attempts by other competitors followed, and soon Gaspari had company. In time a number of men would display hardness close to that of the trend's originator. This bode ill for Gaspari, who was almost always outclassed in size, proportion and shape. As his side of the chasm became crowded, Gaspari was gradually forced closer to its edge. His drop from second to fourth at the '89 Olympia was the first step.

Other factors came into play as well. In modern professional bodybuilding there has existed among judging panels a spirit of letting someone else have his time under the spotlight. If a particular competitor has been near the top for several years, he will sometimes get nudged aside in favor of other, newer professionals of similar quality. Although this practice has on occasion produced heartbreak and even anger among those who get displaced, it keeps things fresh and interesting for judges and fans. It's

Courtesy of David Moore

Mohammed Benaziza. c. 1990

good for business, and after all, that's what it's all about. As for the displaced competitors, they learn the hard lesson that bodybuilding competition can be a ruthless endeavor.

That being said, rarely has the practice of periodically assigning lower placings to previous favorites affected the reigning champion. The IFBB, through its judging panels, has repeatedly proven that it favors Olympia dynasties. Barring unusual circumstances, a reigning champion is always the odds-on favorite to win. Although Haney was for the first time in his reign truly pushed hard by his competition—he was trailing in points after the first two rounds—few expected his bid to tie Schwarzenegger's consecutive-win record to fail. Nor were many surprised when Vince Taylor finished third. He was new, in great condition, and he appeared to possess everything Rich Gaspari lacked. Taylor's was a spectacular debut, one of the most impressive of the modern era—but there was no way he was going to finish ahead of the reigning champion.

That left Labrada and Haney. The scene was reminiscent of 1984, the year of Haney's first victory, when he and Mohammed Makkawy were the last two men standing. A similar outcome was expected. Though he was taller and more evenly-developed than Makkawy, Labrada was still a small man in what was historically a big man's contest. He finished second.

Although the event was closely-contested, Lee Haney had once more come out on top; and with that victory, the end of bodybuilding's biggest decade was at hand. Its story had been written. Haney's sixth Mr. Olympia victory was a final exclamation point on a ten-year span that had been full of them. The world of muscle was now more than just big. It was unified, curiously tidy, and somehow, almost relevant. In ten years much had changed. In later times the bodybuilding world would recall the decade of the 1980s with a special fondness, not only for the events that took place within it, but because of those which came later. No one realized it at the time, but everything was about to be turned upside down.

The Rise and Fall of the World Bodybuilding Federation

"The IFBB will not put up with steroid use."
-Joe Weider, *Muscle & Fitness* Magazine
February 1986

By the second half of 1980s, Joe Weider was the undisputed king of bodybuilding. He claimed full responsibility for the muscle-world's ascent from the dark days of the Great Depression, and anyone who had been paying attention knew this was no mere empty boast. Weider ran the biggest contests and published the biggest magazines; he sold large amounts of muscle-related merchandise; he presented unto the world the personage of Arnold Schwarzenegger. All these things helped to fuel bodybuilding's growth, which during the first half of the 1980s had been spectacular. Interest in bodybuilding increased so greatly that it led some to wonder where the true limits of its popularity lay—or if such limits even existed. Joe Weider had for a long time been certain that they didn't. He now saw before him a vast expanse of unconquered territory, and great legions of unconscripted fans. Weider had already helped lead bodybuilding to a level of popularity few thought possible. If it was to go further, or even *all the way*, he had every intention of taking it there too. This had long been his dream. As would soon be revealed, the dream was not his alone.

When muscle contests were in their infancy, such dreams were unthinkable. Nevertheless, as the 20th century progressed, bodybuilding gradually gained popularity; and with each passing year more people became full-fledged bodybuilders. Numerous others joined bodybuilding's fan base. Eventually it occurred to men like Weider that muscle contests had the potential to break out from the realm of exclusive gatherings and into the sphere of public acceptance. As early as 1950 he openly hoped for this, and for much more. In the July 1950 edition of *Your Physique* Magazine, Weider predicted that bodybuilding would not only be looked upon by the at-large public as a sport, but that "it will one day be recognized as the king of all sports." Considering that in 1950 bodybuilding was still quite small, it was a rather audacious claim. Nevertheless, Weider's prophesy foretold far greater things. He believed muscle contests were destined to be recognized as things of transcendental value. From the same article:

> Bodybuilding will one day become one of the greatest forces in existence, and…it may be hailed as the activity that actually saved civilization from itself.

These incredible visions of the future aside, by the mid-1980s Weider had no illusions about his relative share of the greater sports market. Compared to things like golf, hockey, tennis, boxing or basketball, the dollars generated by bodybuilding competition were still very small. If that could be changed, if it could reach a level of popularity anywhere near those sports, bodybuilding's higher-ups stood to enjoy enormous financial gain.

In the 1970s and before, making bodybuilding truly popular had been Joe Weider's dream. In the 1980s it became his goal. Nevertheless, several obstacles stood in his way. One of the more important problems he faced was public awareness. Even with the rise of Arnold Schwarzenegger's action films, to the majority of the Western world's population bodybuilding was practically invisible. Most people still had only vague knowledge of what bodybuilding even was. Once that problem was solved, he reasoned, bodybuilding would sell itself: the public would become fascinated with the amazing physiques of modern bodybuilders and the excitement of their competitions; and an entirely new and massive fan base would emerge. That base of fans would be the foundation upon which bodybuilding would reach the big time. The rapid growth of bodybuilding in the first part of the '80s suggested that this was possible. The existing momentum of expansion would help carry it forward.

For this to happen, the public-awareness barrier would have to be smashed. Doing so would be no easy task. *Pumping Iron* had come as close to achieving that goal as anything yet seen; and even though the film effectively launched the acting career of Arnold Schwarzenegger, the wall separating the public from the world of muscle contests held firm. Apart from the undeniable bump in bodybuilding's popularity that followed the release of *Pumping Iron*, its expansion had been more or less incremental.

If bodybuilding continued growing at its current, accelerated pace, it would eventually hit the big time, but that day might not arrive for decades, quite possibly after Joe Weider's time had come and gone. That would not do. To break through in the near future, what he needed was a bold stroke; a solution that would once-and-for-all acquaint the world with physique competition. Weider's plan was simple: he would at long last get bodybuilding into the Olympics.

Weider's reasoning was equally simple: once bodybuilding became an Olympic sport, the world could not help but sit up and take notice. Along with other Olympic sports, there would be television coverage. Newspaper sports sections, whose long and steadfast view that bodybuilding had no place on their pages, would be forced to adopt a new policy. Nations would cheer their muscle-flexing countrymen and prize those who brought home medals. Bodybuilders themselves would be thrilled with the idea of achieving Olympic glory and fame, and the best of them would rise to the occasion. The world would become fascinated with the latest sport to joint the Olympic brotherhood.

Once this Olympic dream had come to fruition, Weider would be the biggest winner of them all. Muscle culture and competition, which he now truly dominated, would get loads of free advertising. Securing a place in the Olympic Games would arguably become the single most important event in the history of bodybuilding, and it would all be his doing. All that remained was to figure out how something like this is actually accomplished. That task was given to his brother Ben, President of the IFBB.

The younger Weider had dreamt of getting bodybuilding into the Olympics for decades, and had taken numerous steps to make that dream a reality. Following the advice of former Olympic organizer Oscar State, in 1971 Ben oversaw the restructuring and democratization of the IFBB, and he helped create strict new rules for competition. As a sanctioning body, the IFBB took on a professional, dignified appearance. However, all these efforts had thus far gotten him nowhere. The chief Weider publication *Muscle Builder* made much noise about the IFBB's efforts to secure a place for bodybuilding at the 1976 Montreal Olympics, but when the games came and went without a bodybuilder in sight, there was conspicuous silence.

Fans who paid attention to the Olympic claims wondered what the problem was. Unfortunately for those fans—not to mention the Weiders, the IFBB, and its members—the International Olympic Committee did not consider bodybuilding to be a sport. Nor did it consider its participants to be athletes. This was the first of two major obstacles faced by the Weiders in their attempt to secure an Olympic birth. According to the IOC, a sporting event should be a competition of physical skill. In any given event, whichever individual or team displays a greater amount of skill should be victorious.

In the eyes of the IOC, bodybuilding was more of a pageant, or perhaps even more like a dog show: in the event itself, there is no comparative demonstration of skill; the competition is simply won by whoever looks best. In an interview conducted years later, Ben Weider claimed to have convinced Olympic authorities otherwise—that bodybuilders are not only as skilled as athletes of other sports, but more so. According to him, what makes this true is that bodybuilders have the skills of proper training, eating, and posing.[1] Apparently the IOC authorities were less convinced by this line of reasoning than Weider thought. Their official stance didn't budge. To the IOC, bodybuilding was not a sport.

Regardless, the Weider brothers were still optimistic and enthusiastic about their chances. Nor was their hope without foundation. They had after all

[1]Interview with the Getbig.com website.

brought bodybuilding to a level of popularity that no one a half-century before would have dared imagine. They also had an unwavering belief in the power of persuasion. Surely, they believed, the IOC could be made to see the light. Once that happened, all that was needed was for the IFBB to conform to Olympic standards for sporting competition. Its 1971 restructuring was a major step in this direction. There was however one other important issue that needed resolution. Conforming to Olympic standards meant many things; most importantly, it meant implementing drug-testing.

Getting bodybuilding into the Olympic Games—a collection of sporting events governed by an association that strictly enforces drug-testing—was going to be a problem. Sometime around the early 1960s, bodybuilders began using anabolic steroids to reach previously-unattainable levels of muscular mass and conditioning. In the years that followed, steroid use became a fundamental component of bodybuilding contest preparation; the higher the level of competition, the greater the prevalence of drug use. Among bodybuilding's greatest specimens—IFBB professionals—drug use was an unwritten requirement. This was fairly well known. Even though those particular competitors would be out of the running for Olympic qualification due to their professional status, this would matter little. The strong association of bodybuilding and steroids was thought to be ample grounds for an IOC nix of the idea.

Regardless, the Weiders thought the problem was fixable. In the early-to-mid 1980s the awareness of steroid use among the at-large public was relatively low. It seems most people had heard of the drugs, but their knowledge was typically mired in ignorance, rumor, speculation and denial. Some bodybuilding fans, members of the public, and even a few lower-level bodybuilders thought of steroids as optional chemicals that would merely replace the demands of time and hard work. It was thought that competitors with superior character and drive could attain a physique similar to those of the "cheaters"; it would just take them longer and require more effort and dedication; it would demand a greater moral constitution. Others were not so naïve. A better-informed group knew that to become truly massive, like the stars in the magazines, the use of chemicals was mandatory.

The Weider magazines seized upon and embraced the former view, that steroids were for lazy cheaters who were looking for an easy way to build their bodies. Although this sentiment was used in *Muscle & Fitness* in an attempt to sway the opinions of its readership about drug use, it also became a convenient platform to promote Weider products like Anabolic Mega-Packs. In both cases, Weider would simply convince his magazines' readers that steroids were unnecessary. The "Steroid Free!" and "Steroid Replacement Kit" selling points on Anabolic Mega-Pack boxes suggested that the product was effectively equivalent to steroids, as did articles in *Muscle & Fitness* that cited studies supposedly confirming its effectiveness. Although Weider soon found himself in legal hot water over those claims, his campaign of misinformation was underway. If he was going to pry bodybuilding from its association with steroids, it seemed he was determined to make a few bucks in the process. But the important thing was the overall message: steroids have no place in bodybuilding.

For the Olympic goal to be realized, the bodybuilding world would need to visibly fall in line with that position. Yet fortune was not always on Weider's side. With time, tales of steroid use in various sports began to make waves in the mainstream press. From the perspective of someone trying to sell bodybuilding to the public—and to the International Olympic committee—any news about steroids is bad news.

These stories increased, as did the public's awareness of performance-enhancing drug use. By the summer of 1988 there was no escaping the specter of steroids, thanks to an event that would change the world of sports forever. At the Olympics held that year in Seoul, Canadian gold-medal and world-record-holding sprinter Ben Johnson tested positive for the drug stanozolol, also known by its brand name of Winstrol. His medals were stripped and he was banned from future competition. The world was shocked and mystified.

By 1988, very few people had ever heard of stanozolol. As part of their reports, media outlets described it as a water-based, injectable form of synthetic testosterone. Originally developed for veterinary uses, it became a favorite performance-enhancer for race horses. It was furthermore mentioned that stanozolol is a popular *bodybuilding* drug. Bodybuilding had long been suspected by much of the public as being a haven for steroid users, but this revelation bumped that notion tenfold. Bodybuilding was in fact no longer suspect. It was now guilty. OIC officials, being members of the general public themselves, were not immune to that judgment.

When Joe Weider kicked off his official anti-steroid campaign in 1986, the Seoul Olympics were still more than two years away—and things didn't look so bad. Granted, steroids had occasionally been in the news and in 1985 had even warranted a segment on the feature-news television show *20/20*, but they weren't yet grabbing big headlines. To Weider, it still seemed possible for bodybuilding to shake its association with steroids; and the best way to do so would be to clean it up, as it stands, right now. The decision was therefore made: at the soonest possible date, the IFBB would begin testing for steroids.

Through the first six years of the 1980s, anti-steroid sentiment in Weider's muscle magazines wasn't taken seriously, at least by the hardcore segment of his readership. After all, their line of reasoning followed, how could Weider simultaneously demonize steroid use and glorify obvious steroid users? It's unknown whether Weider was aware of these grumblings of his constituency. It's quite possible that he thought that people believed everything he told them. Whatever the case may have been, eventually the readers of his publications would be expected to take the anti-drug sentiments seriously. Drug-testing really was going to happen.

To prepare the bodybuilding community for what was going to be unleashed upon it, the first seeds were planted. The February 1986 issue of *Muscle & Fitness* featured an article written by Joe Weider himself called "It's My Turn: A Time for All Federations to Come Together!" in which he described plans to drug-test the amateur world championships, and eventually, the Mr. Olympia contest.

Ben Johnson. 100-meter finals, 1988 Olympic Games.

Getty Images

By the time that issue of *Muscle & Fitness* hit the stands, Joe Weider had acquired a steadfast belief that drug-free physiques would be the key to taking bodybuilding to the big time. Once testing was fully underway, his gamble was that everyone would be happy—the IOC, the general public, and the existing base of bodybuilding fans. The first two groups were at least theoretically safe bets. Yet once it became known that Weider's claim about testing the Mr. Olympia contest was no bluff, the world of bodybuilding experienced an immediate division of opinion. Some bodybuilders and muscle-contest fans loved the idea. Some hated it. A large segment simply didn't know what to think. After all, what would the world's top bodybuilders look like without muscle-building drugs in their systems? Fans were used to the steroid-enriched "look" of the best physiques of the recent past and present: the same ones lauded in the magazines, the same ones praised by Joe Weider.

Steroid-enhanced physiques were also the same ones to which up-and-comers aspired. A desire to copy muscle-world heroes was the reason why hardcore gyms of the 80s were bedecked with posters of top bodybuilders, and why young men often cut out and pinned up full-page photos of competitors from magazine spreads. Those young men wanted, often badly, to be famous, and to live what they perceived to be a glamorous life of IFBB professional bodybuilders. But more than anything, they wanted to look like the pros. They wanted to be massive and ripped. They longed to become pinup models themselves, to be weight-room idols. In the minds of these men, the IFBB was about to wreck their pastime. For the most obsessed young bodybuilders, it threatened to shatter their dreams.

Regardless, the plan was in place. The wheels were in motion. The 1980s were drawing to a close, and the new decade would usher in a new era. The 1990 Mr. Olympia, to be held in Chicago, would test all of its entrants for appearance-enhancing drugs. The world of bodybuilding was about to change forever. Weider was King, and if he wanted drug-testing, anyone that didn't like it could go elsewhere, perhaps to one of the federations his IFBB long ago dwarfed. In his mind, the 1990 Olympia would set things right. The specter of Ben

Johnson would be vanquished; and just like the Olympics, bodybuilding would punish cheaters. The International Olympic committee, it was hoped, would be pleased and impressed.

At the Chicago Olympia, fans witnessed a parade of their favorites, all in good condition, and most with a noticeable reduction of muscular mass from the previous year. The top six placings, in order, were familiar names: Lee Haney; Lee Labrada; Shawn Ray; Mike Christian; Rich Gaspari; and Francis Benfatto. Nevertheless, rumors circulated that 20% of the entrants had been disqualified due to positive drug tests. Speculation also made the rounds that at least one of the top six competitors had successfully used a blocking agent, a chemical with the ability to make steroid use undetectable. It was therefore wondered by fans and competitors alike whether bodybuilding would simply become a cat-and-mouse game of drug use and detection evasion. For the latter, this would add yet another dimension of worry to an already highly stressful occupation. The combination of hard training, precise dieting, and the use of illegal chemicals was no longer going to be enough. If the blocking agent rumors were true, in order to remain competitive an entrant would have to blatantly break the rules, do his best to cover it up, and then hope that he didn't get caught.

Although Weider's magazines featured statements by officials, competitors and fans that praised the event and the dawn of a new era, the reality of the situation was something rather different. To typical fans, the event represented regression, not progress. Over the years they had been asked to occasionally tolerate favoritism and fixed outcomes, which they did. But for some, this was too much. It was therefore no surprise that the contest and the months leading up to it revived an attitude not known since the days when Bob Hoffman wielded supreme power: fans wondered why there couldn't be an alternative to the status quo. More specifically, they wondered why there couldn't be an alternative to the Weider brand of bodybuilding.

Enter Vince McMahon. Whether his out-of-nowhere emergence on the bodybuilding scene was timed to coincide with IFBB drug-testing—like a proverbial shark smelling blood in the water—or whether that timing was just dumb luck, the king of professional wrestling boldly strode onto the scene, apparently in the nick of time. McMahon had recently gained an interest in bodybuilding, and he now decided that he wanted a piece of it. Actually, he wanted more than a piece. Much like what he had done with wrestling, McMahon wanted to take it over. He had every intention of using the might of his wrestling empire to crack the Weider stranglehold on bodybuilding.

McMahon's white-knight pledge to promote bodybuilding "the way it was meant to be" was a rallying call to those who had been quite happy with *the way things were*—before drug-testing, and before the IFBB's new obsession with public acceptance became official. His mega-bucks power base promised the firepower to make this happen, and as something that likely caused IFBB officials to lose no small amount of sleep, it threatened to level the walls of the Weider Empire.

Like Joe Weider, Vince McMahon was—and remains—an enigmatic figure. Though the two were about to engage in a direct struggle for leadership of the bodybuilding world, they were perhaps more alike than not. Both men were widely perceived to be self-made tycoons with unmatched drive, flexible scruples, and a carnival-show, ring-master mindset—much like a pair of modern-day P.T. Barnums. Depending upon whom was asked, each could be described as savior, usurper, saint or swindler. Each was the master of his own niche corner of the greater entertainment market.

McMahons's niche was big-time wrestling. The son of an absentee-father wrestling promoter—the two did not meet until Vince was 12 years old—McMahon decided early on that his destiny was to not only walk in his father's footsteps, but to dwarf them. In this he was successful. By the late 1980s,

Vince McMahon. c. 2005

Getty Images

McMahon not only dominated professional wrestling; he had propelled it into the big time. Though his rise to power began decades after that of Weider, it took less than half the time and yielded greater rewards. This may have had as much to do with the chosen endeavor of each man as with the men themselves.

Bodybuilding and professional wrestling are both forms of entertainment, and both could be described as pseudo-sports. Nevertheless, the fans, officials, and participants of both sometimes refer to their respective activities as full-blown, legitimate sports.[1] Since this is especially so with bodybuilding, comparisons with other sports are naturally invited. Athlete salaries, market share, advertising dollars and a host of other variables are used to compare professional sports to each other. One important point of comparison is attendance figures. In bodybuilding, these numbers are rarely presented as marketing items, for the simple reason that they don't match up well with popular sports or similar forms of entertainment. This is not the case with wrestling. A comparison of the biggest events of the 1980s for each genre amply demonstrates the disparity: the 1988 Mr. Olympia contest, held at the Universal Amphitheater in Los Angeles, was announced to have drawn more than 6,000 spectators—a modern bodybuilding record; WrestleMania III, held in 1987 at Detroit's Pontiac Silverdome, boasted ticket sales of 93,173.

Although the exact WrestleMania figure has been disputed, it's beyond dispute that on that evening the Silverdome, a prior host of the NFL Superbowl, was filled with wrestling fans, all eager to see McMahon's brand of entertainment. It wasn't until more than a decade later, when the Schwarzenegger Classic contest was renamed and made into a full-blown festival featuring 45 different sports, that similar numbers—albeit for the entire three-day gathering—could be claimed. However, in the '80s, convention-like bodybuilding-and-sports festivals had not yet been conceived.

Bodybuilding generated respectable dollars from magazine and nutritional supplement sales, but wrestling had everything else: sellout crowds, household-name stars, entertaining storylines, and a strong presence on television. Not only were wrestling pay-per-view events a hit, but wrestling could also be seen on broadcast television, during normal hours and at regular intervals. Bodybuilding had no such media presence. Apart from the rare televised contest or a low-quality, monthly "magazine"-type show that aired at off-hours on cable television channels, the most bodybuilding could muster was something called the *Flex Magazine Workout*.

The program showed top bodybuilders lifting weights. The physiques were impressive, but endless exercising, tiresome banter, and lack of a storyline ensured that the program would never get anything close to a top rating. Although the hosts pretended they were performing their actual everyday workouts, they lifted light weights, often without a great deal of effort. The show was therefore more a demonstration of how to exercise than a documentation of the actual training of a bodybuilding star. The decision to use fake workouts was due to the shooting schedule demands of television production: 40 shows were filmed in 10 days. The production team figured that fans of the show wouldn't know the difference or wouldn't care if they did.

While hardcore bodybuilders who wanted to see real workouts were left wondering what the point was, pure fans were satisfied. The *Flex Magazine Workout* fulfilled the basic of bodybuilding, the same purpose served by Eugen Sandow's very first posing performance: large, flexing muscles were put on display. After all, in bodybuilding, muscles are

WrestleMania III. 1987

[1]Since it's a poorly-kept secret that the execution and outcome of professional wrestling matches are scripted, the term "sports entertainment" is typically used to describe it.

merely for looking at; how one goes about getting them is a peripheral issue. On the *Flex* show, there was plenty of muscle to look at, and that was enough. Pure fans were quite willing to tune in at 2:00am to watch. This was the audience the show aimed to attract, the same one the Weiders hoped the general public would become. To them, the tastes and desires of the hardcore element were irrelevant. The United States was not going to be turned into a nation of such people. It was hoped, however, that it could be turned into a nation of bodybuilding fans.

The featured bodybuilders of the *Flex Magazine Workout* lifted weights together, shared training tips, and congratulated each other on a job well done. It was all rather harmonious. The general public meanwhile had little interest in it. By Vince McMahon's estimation, nor would they ever. The public was instead watching things they found to be exciting, like major-league sports or, occasionally, pro wrestling.

A relative lack of excitement has always been a fundamental problem with bodybuilding. The cast and crew of the movie *Pumping Iron* discovered this once they had shot enough reels of film. Even Arnold Schwarzenegger, reflecting on the experience several years later, admitted that early footage was turning out to be "boring." The cast and crew therefore contrived a plot to boost the film's watchability. Without that plot, the viewer would have been left with countless shots of flexing, posing, pumping and training. This wouldn't have been enough to make the film into the classic that it became. In real-life bodybuilding, unlike *Pumping Iron*, there really are no such plots. Other than occasional publicized disagreements between competitors or officials, there are few storylines, there's little excitement, and no action.

It's therefore the case that the expectations of a bodybuilding fan have to be limited. He's promised the opportunity to marvel at incredible physiques and pick his favorites, and he's given the chance to see how his opinions compare to those of the judging panel. There is little beyond that. Bodybuilding is arguably nothing more than performance art with an awards ceremony. It's not particularly enthralling, and there's no real action. In this regard, it's the opposite of wrestling.

Vince McMahon knew this. When he resolved to take over bodybuilding, he was undaunted by wrestling's 15-to-1 attendance advantage. Instead of seeing in bodybuilding a small pond of dedicated fans, he instead perceived a vast ocean of untapped interest. His own wrestling formula allowed him this vision. It also taught him that audiences could be drawn in by things outside the ring. McMahon became so attracted to the idea that his own, real-life persona was caricaturized and put into action. He built his body, called himself "Mr. McMahon," and got into the ring—not once or twice, but repeatedly. When he resolved to crush Weider like he had crushed his wrestling-promoter rivals, the storyline idea was not forgotten.

While there was never any indication that Vince McMahon had a personal desire crush any one individual, one thing was certain: taking over bodybuilding would require a knockout blow of Joe Weider. It was for this reason that McMahon's secret intentions would be made public in the most dramatic manner possible. He would come forth on bodybuilding's biggest stage, at its most important moment, in front of its greatest audience.

* * * *

The annual Mr. Olympia contest—*Joe Weider's* Mr. Olympia, as its full name reads—is without a doubt the principal event of the bodybuilding calendar. At the show, bodybuilding's greatest examples are showcased, a world champion is crowned, and everyone who's anyone within that world is present: IFBB officials with their badged blazers, platoons of magazine photographers and reporters, sponsoring companies and their executives, and even a few mainstream celebrities. Beyond the exclusive press circle is a packed house of fans, all eager to see the best of the best oil up and flex. The most important attendee is of course the man for whom the contest is named: Joe Weider, the self-proclaimed Father of Modern Bodybuilding, the one-and-only "Master Blaster." The Olympia is more than a contest; it's a celebration of his Empire. From the moment the ceremonies begin until the abominable "Joe Weider's Mr. Olympia" theme song closes the show, the audience is reminded of this. It's his stage, and it's his night.

The 1990 Olympia was an especially momentous occasion. The IFBB's new drug-enforcement policy was for the first time brought to the greatest event in bodybuilding. A full lineup of new, drug-free physiques was unveiled. Important speeches were made. *The dawn of a new era* was their theme, and praise was heaped on the idea and the men behind it.

Among the show's attendees were representatives from *Bodybuilding Lifestyles,* a new magazine owned and published by Vince McMahon's corporation, Titan Sports. Their official purpose at the event was the promotion of the magazine as well as Titan's new muscle-building supplement line, ICOPRO. In the months prior to the event, these ventures attracted the attention of Weider, who was immediately made uneasy. He astutely perceived McMahon to be a potential and quite powerful rival. For McMahon's plan to work, Weider would have to be mollified. McMahon assured Weider that he had no intention of promoting bodybuilding competitions or starting his own federation; he merely wanted to cash in on bodybuilding's growing magazine and supplement market. Though these declarations were received with skepticism, they were nevertheless plausible. By 1990, large markets had formed for both.

While assurances were offered to Weider, plans were hatched to overthrow him. Success would depend quite simply upon McMahon's ability to reproduce Weider's model of operation, which had four primary factors: gaining a large share of the magazine market; generating substantial merchantdise sales; securing the loyalty of high-quality individual competitors; and organizing popular contests. McMahon's magazine and supplement line were already in place and ready to expand once demand took off. He now merely needed to attract top competitors and assemble them into contests.

It was in the exploitation of the final two areas—competitors and contests—that McMahon planned to embellish the Weider model. Compared to wrestling, bodybuilding contests were small-time gatherings, something he attributed to the rigid, stoic format they all followed. As far as McMahon was concerned, this could be fixed. He would make them big. McMahon additionally planned to get bodybuilding on network television—not just contests and training segments, but also as part of "reality"-based shows. He furthermore believed that the Weider brand of bodybuilding didn't come close to tapping into the marketing value of individual bodybuilders. He had big plans for these people. First however, he needed to be assured of their loyalty.

Weider commanded the loyalty of bodybuilders through fear. IFBB bodybuilders who competed in other federations were handed official suspensions, but in practice their punishment rarely stopped at official penalties. After serving a suspension, especially after 1980, only in rare instances did a competitor again place well. Nor, it seems, was he later afforded much press in magazines. McMahon was in no position to rule by fear. For the moment, at least in bodybuilding, he ruled nothing. He therefore chose a better weapon: money. He would ensure the loyalty of bodybuilders the same way he did with wrestlers—by signing them to lucrative, exclusive contracts.

The first bodybuilder to sign on with McMahon was Tom Platz, who was in some ways the perfect representative for *Bodybuilding Lifestyles*. As an icon of '80s bodybuilding, a former top-three finisher in the Mr. Olympia contest, and the owner of the largest, most muscular thighs of all time, Platz's credibility was beyond dispute. Yet it was the combination of his rugged, almost cartoonish good looks, full head of flowing platinum hair, southern California tan, million-dollar smile, speaking ability and reputation for business acumen that sealed the deal.

Platz's portrait shot on the cover of *Flex* magazine in September of 1986 helped form that reputation. That particular issue broke free of what was thought to be the unbreakable formula of muscle magazine covers: it didn't show a shirtless and oiled bodybuilder flexing his muscles, and there were no attention-grabbing headlines about training or sex. What

Tom Platz. c. 1986

Courtesy of Michael Newman

the reader instead got was something more *GQ* than *Musclemag* or *Iron Man*: a photo of Platz, from the shoulders up, wearing a tuxedo. His hair was slicked to match the formality of his attire, and he wore the subdued smirk of a corporate raider. The cover had but a single headline: the name Tom Platz, and beneath it, the words "Mr. Midas." The title was clearly meant to imply that everything Platz touched turned to gold. Almost overnight, Platz's image was transformed. It seemed he was more than a mere grand champion of the squat rack; apparently he was a success in business too. The cover was an unusual ploy, maybe even a gimmick, but the reputation stuck. Vince McMahon, who was always keen to embrace and exploit clever alter-ego personas, offered Mr. Midas a high-level position at *Bodybuilding Lifestyles*. Among other things, Platz would be the magazine's official spokesman. Platz accepted; and with that, Joe Weider was about to be bitten by an object of his own creation.

Platz was present as part of the *Bodybuilding Lifestyles* contingency at the Olympia. In addition to the procurement of a lobby booth alongside the event's other sponsors, McMahon paid a few thousand dollars extra to secure a couple of minutes of time at the podium for his new spokesman. Once onstage, he was expected to promote the new magazine.

Tom Platz did indeed take the microphone on that fateful evening, but his message was something quite different from what was expected. He asked for the attention of the audience, saying he had an important announcement. All eyes were upon him. He continued: "We at Titan Sports are proud to announce the formation of the World Bodybuilding Federation. And we are going to kick the IFBB's ass!"

On that cue, representatives of Titan Sports—smiling and waving female models sporting the *Bodybuilding Lifestyles* logo on sashes—came streaming into the auditorium. Each carried an armful of fliers that were quickly distributed to the quite surprised and now very interested audience. The spectacle was unlike anything yet witnessed in the world of physique competition. The fliers announced the creation of the WBF, something that promised not only to infuse new life into the world of professional bodybuilding, but to change it forever. Through its guarantees of "dramatic new events and the richest prize money in the history of the sport," the new federation became an instant threat to topple the IFBB, along with all its personnel, competitors, and leaders. And with that, Vince McMahon's real intentions were finally made known: he would take over bodybuilding, just as he had taken over pro wrestling.

The Olympia's entrants were particularly interested in this development. After all, it was they who attempted to make a living out of bodybuilding. If the IFBB was indeed about to get clobbered, what then? If the WBF promised bigger and better things—and most importantly, more money for competitors—it would be difficult to resist switching federations. For the moment, the value of an opportunity with the WBF and the timeline for its materialization were cause for much wonder. Yet for several of the Olympia entrants, they didn't have to wonder for long. While the WBF announcement spectacle was in full swing, McMahon's henchmen were reportedly slipping big-money contract offers under their hotel room doors.

Following the shock-tactic publicity stunt of the Olympia, the WBF focused its energies on talent acquisition. If there was anything Vince McMahon learned from his experience with wrestling promotion, it was the value of attracting stars. Nothing more clearly demonstrated this value than the 1984 contract agreement he secured with a man named Terry Gene Bollea—otherwise known as Hulk Hogan. The deal was widely perceived to be the most important event in the rise of McMahon's World Wrestling Federation to pre-eminence. Hogan

Hulk Hogan. 2005

U.S. Department of Defense

had ability, star-power and his own brand of charisma, and fans loved it. They were quite willing to give their support—and their dollars—to whichever organization featured him. Meanwhile, lesser wrestlers were content to follow Hogan wherever he may go.

Seven-time Mr. Olympia Lee Haney might therefore have seemed a likely WBF acquisition target. While it would have been a massive blow to the IFBB to have its reigning world champion stolen, a few factors made that scenario virtually impossible. Haney's string of Mr. Olympia wins meant that from a financial standpoint, he was reasonably well taken care of. The first prize for that contest in 1990 had risen to $70,000, a decent increase from the $50,000 he brought home in 1985. He was also the recipient of substantial endorsement money and guest-posing fees. During his reign Haney made more money from bodybuilding than any of his peers, and certainly more than any past competitor.

Being Mr. Olympia had monetary perks, but nothing was more important that the title itself. The Olympia was the premier event and the most important title in all of bodybuilding. It was to muscle shows what the Super Bowl was to American football, or what the World Series was to baseball. In 1990, Haney was a single victory from breaking Arnold Schwarzenegger's all-time record for Olympia wins. Securing that victory would earn him the unofficial title of *greatest bodybuilder who ever lived*. Asking him to pass on that opportunity would not be realistic. There can also be little doubt that he felt deep gratitude and personal loyalty toward the Weiders. It's probable that Haney would not have abandoned the IFBB before the 1991 Olympia for any amount of money.

That may have suited Vince McMahon just fine, since it's unclear whether he had much interest in Haney anyway. McMahon was interested in promoting bodybuilding and making a lot of money from it. He wasn't necessarily interested in making sure that his champion really was the greatest living bodybuilder. Haney almost certainly wouldn't budge, but neither was Haney a must-have star the way Schwarzenegger once was. Haney was, after all, no Arnold. He was without Schwarzenegger's looks or quick wit, and possessed no trademark charismatic accent. Haney's likeable family-man persona was nice, but it bore no relevance to the type of entertainment that McMahon cared to promote. Besides, McMahon already knew who he wanted his champion to be.

Courtesy of Michael Newman

Lee Haney. c. 1989

Since Haney had become an immovable fixture atop Mount Olympia, other competitors had to be content with merely giving him a run for his money, or with settling for lesser titles. The creation of the WBF instantly made things different. The new federation would host an annual world championship contest. The winner would hold the title of WBF Champion, and if Lee Haney was not on hand to compete, so be it; the IFBB and its Mr. Olympia title might soon sink into obscurity anyway. At the same time, this line of thinking was not the WBF's primary draw for potential competitors. As future WBF stars would soon come to learn, the federation could afford to offer much more than glory for another lone champion.

McMahon's domination of big-time wrestling had given him deep pockets. He was therefore able to offer big-money contracts to all his bodybuilders, sums that dwarfed the earnings of many of the IFBB's top professionals. Yet before his targeted competitors even had a chance to see the contracts he had prepared for them, they were given a brief glimpse of what fame and fortune could bring. As part of his Chicago Olympia invasion, attractive female WBF representatives were instructed to mingle, flirt, and pose for photographs with the contestants. In the world of bodybuilding, this level of star treatment was unknown, so the gesture was not quickly forgotten. It was also only the beginning. Competitors were flown first-class to Connecticut, picked up in limousines, and taken to McMahon's headquarters in Stamford. There they toured Titan Towers, his state-of-the-art office complex and media center. They were shown the Titan Sports television studios and housed in five star hotels.

The entire gesture was meant to be an introduction to the life of a star. McMahon had learned enough about bodybuilding to know that this treatment was far beyond anything experienced by these men as IFBB professionals. Since Weider had long established himself as the only game in town, he saw no need to lavish special treatment upon his competitors, much less sign any of them to big-dollar contracts. After all, throughout the 20th century bodybuilders had demonstrated that they were quite willing to get in top shape and compete for little or no money. When McMahon presented contracts with annual figures of $200,000 per year—running as high as $400,000—most found the offer irresistible. Wide-eyed bodybuilders signed on the dotted line.

In 1989, the last full year before the WBF was created, the average annual salary in Major League Baseball was $489,539. Average annual salary figures for bodybuilding have never been recorded, since unlike major league sports, bodybuilding contracts are usually not made public. Nevertheless, it's believed that in 1989 the richest IFBB contracts did not exceed $50,000, and these were offered to a select few. In any given year, the majority of professional bodybuilders had no annual contract agreement, and non-endorsement earnings were therefore limited to contest prize money. At the 1985 Mr. Olympia, 24 entrants competed for cash prizes that totaled $100,000. To finish in the money required a top-ten placing. Since winner Lee Haney walked away with a check for $50,000 and runner-up Albert Beckles received $20,000, the average prize for the remaining eight finalists was $3750. Each of the 14 entrants that placed 11th or lower walked away with a nominal reward of $1500. The prize money for the 1988 show was $150,000, and in 1990 it had grown to $200,000. Regardless, in 1990 the majority of professional bodybuilders had to rely on other sources of income to survive. The WBF offered something vastly different.

McMahon could afford to be picky about which bodybuilders he would make contract offers to, so he was. As with the case of Haney, the judges' scorecards from IFBB events did not necessarily guide his selections. For the WBF to survive, prosper and dominate, it certainly needed to attract men with fantastic physiques, but by McMahon's estimation it was more important to draw bodybuilders who were "marketable." Of the current field of IFBB professionals, Gary Strydom fit this description better than anyone.

Three years earlier, Strydom's height, mass and good looks made him seem like the second coming of Arnold Schwarzenegger. While on paper the two were comparable, McMahon's wish was that the comparison would transcend mere measurements and titles. His hope was that Strydom would indeed become the next Arnold. The deal offered to him let this hope be known. At $400,000 per year, it was the largest WBF contract offer, and by far the largest ever put in front of a competitive bodybuilder. Strydom accepted; and with that, the WBF had a big star, and it had a face.

Of nearly equal importance was that the IFBB was now minus one top competitor. Yet a single star does not a bodybuilding federation make. The WBF needed to sign a number of such men. Throughout the fall of 1990 and into the winter that followed, the bodybuilding world therefore pondered a question that only a few months prior was unthinkable: who would defect from the IFBB?

By late January, McMahon was prepared to end the suspense. He arranged a press conference at the Plaza Hotel in New York City to introduce the group of competitors who had signed on with the World Bodybuilding Federation. Wearing matching neon green jackets, small tight shorts and tank tops, a total of 13 men marched onstage for the grand unveiling. All were accomplished bodybuilders with massive physiques and what McMahon considered to be the right look for his organization. All had been lured from the IFBB. In addition to Strydom, the WBF stable of competitors included Aaron Baker, Mike Christian, Vince Comerford, David Dearth, Berry DeMey, Johnnie Morant, Danny Padilla, Tony Pearson, Jim Quinn, Mike Quinn, Eddie Robinson, and Troy Zuccolotto. Together they would be called the WBF BodyStars.

McMahon further announced that the first-ever WBF contest would take place that June at Donald Trump's new Taj Mahal hotel and casino in Atlantic City. Tom Platz, now the WBF spokesman, took the podium and added a few comments. He declared that the WBF campaign of talent acquisition had just begun, and that many more great bodybuilders could soon be expected to join its ranks. He also offered a vision for the future: that soon a time would come when a WBF BodyStar would be on an airplane, and Magic Johnson would lean towards him and say "I saw you on television last night."

A number of IFBB competitors weren't so sure that McMahon's brand of bodybuilding would be able to produce such encounters. Many opted to stay put. Lee Haney's abstention was a given, but joining him were Lee Labrada, Vince Taylor and Rich Gaspari—men who occupied the next three placings behind Haney at the '89 Olympia. Also remaining loyal to the IFBB were Dorian Yates, Bob Paris and Shawn Ray.

Because of what had transpired at the 1990 Schwarzenegger Classic, Ray's decision to remain loyal was noteworthy. As a prelude to the Olympia, in 1990 the IFBB drug-tested the Schwarzenegger contest. Ray initially won the event but was shortly thereafter revealed to have failed his test. When he was stripped of his title and forced to return his trophy and prize money, Ray became living proof that drug testing was for real. The title and trophy were handed over to Mike Ashley, a top competitor who became famous for his controversial claims that he never once took steroids. However humiliating the incident may have been, Ray's faith in the IFBB and Weiders remained intact. Like other IFBB competitors who remained loyal, he had serious misgivings about the WBF.

After McMahon's press conference, it was clear that the IFBB had retained a pool of talent that was superior to that of the WBF. Although he had won the 1987 Night of Champions contest, the WBF's big star, Gary Strydom, could do no better than a fifth-place finish in his one and only Mr. Olympia contest in 1988. Berry DeMey, the owner of a more balanced physique, never finished better than third. The remainder of the WBF was made up of men with good physiques, but their collective placings over the prior decade were lower than those of Haney, Labrada, Taylor, Gaspari, Ray and Paris. The defectors were easily replaceable. Competitors like Ron Love, Andreas Munzer, Steve Brisbois, Thierry Pastel, J.J. Marsh, and Nimrod King were already waiting in the wings, ready to take their places.

All things being equal, it would appear that the WBF was attempting to win over bodybuilding's current and future fans by offering an inferior product. In early 1991, however, things were not equal. The IFBB's new drug testing policy changed everything. Unless rumors about chemical blocking agents used for beating drug tests turned out to be true, bodybuilders of the IFBB were going to be smaller and less muscular than their non-drug tested WBF rivals. Past contest results would therefore be irrelevant. The slate would be wiped clean. The WBF would soon overtake the IFBB. After all, a good bodybuilder on steroids is always more impressive than a great one who isn't.

* * * * *

Vince McMahon understood that bodybuilding's fans preferred to see bigger and more muscular physiques. He also had faith in marketing. Gary Strydom was beaten handily by Lee Haney in a direct showdown, but Strydom was also thought to have far greater potential to become a mainstream star. There was a big reason to believe this, and his name was Arnold Schwarzenegger. By the late 1980s the level of size, shape, and conditioning among bodybuilding's best competitors had advanced beyond what Schwarzenegger carried at the top of his game. However, even though by 1990 Haney had tied his record for Olympia victories, Schwarzenegger's marketability—even years after he retired—far outdistanced that of Haney. Through current times, Haney has appeared on the cover of 25 bodybuilding magazines. Schwarzenegger has been on more than 130. It was a plain demonstration of the fact that a bodybuilder's appeal by no means hinges solely on his muscularity.

The success of *Pumping Iron* was the first real indication of this phenomenon. Though the film had no shortage of flexing, posing and weight training, a greater portion was devoted to exploring the personalities of individual characters. Audiences became acquainted with the men behind the muscle, and they were taken in by the story that had been concocted to make it all watchable. This is what made the film—and to some degree, bodybuilding itself—interesting. People who were turned into bodybuilding fans by that movie were therefore sometimes faced with some disappointment. Muscle contests offer a barrage of muscularity, but there's little else.

By Vince McMahon's estimation, this was the most important factor limiting bodybuilding's appeal. His solution was to take elements from *Pumping Iron*, and to a greater degree, professional wrestling, and infuse them into an entirely new form of bodybuilding entertainment. The WBF would heavily emphasize the personalities of its competitors; by doing so, it would make bodybuilding more interesting, compelling, and marketable. Although there was no one among the WBF Body-Stars with the charisma or star power of a Schwarzenegger, he believed that problem could be got around. Just like with pro wrestling, bodybuilders would assume alter-egos.

Through drug testing and statements about Olympic aspirations, Joe Weider had made known his plans for propelling bodybuilding into the realm of public acceptance. Through his initial WBF press conference, Vince McMahon had made known his. Weider wanted bodybuilding to be a legitimate sport, something that could one day rival or even surpass the popularity of hockey or even football. McMahon wanted bodybuilding to be sports entertainment, like professional wrestling. Those who embraced Weider's vision were prepared to endure a slow, arduous journey; those who favored McMahon's thought of it as a fast track to success. The fulfillment of McMahon's plan would require no winning-over of the IOC, no cleaning-up of bodybuilding's image, and more specifically, no drug testing. For the WBF to succeed, all that was needed was effective marketing.

McMahon's federation possessed the potential to break the Weider monopoly and do away with drug testing forever. Those were by themselves powerful marketing points. As soon as rumors began to circulate about the riotous goings-on at the 1990 Mr. Olympia contest, a segment of bodybuilding fans began rooting for the WBF. This did not go unnoticed by the IFBB, who in turn declared that McMahon could be counted on to turn bodybuilding into a WWF-like circus. After the WBF's initial press conference, it now appeared that this conjecture might have real foundation. Many of the people who had jumped on the bandwagon right after the Olympia were now not so sure of it.

Over-the-top alter-ego personalities had certainly worked for wrestling, but the idea was something completely new to bodybuilding. Although both professional wrestling matches and bodybuilding contests were constructed around the exhibition of gigantic physiques, there were few other similarities. Bodybuilding considered itself to be a dignified endeavor. The production of IFBB events aimed to reflect this. Weider's federation had organized and conducted events that featured stoic formality, with clearly-defined rules and protocol. The proceedings were orderly. This contrasted sharply with pro wrestling events, where mayhem reigned. Since Vince McMahon was an outsider to the world of bodybuilding, his point of view naturally differed from those who had spent decades polishing IFBB decorum. He aimed to breathe life into something he thought was tedious and boring.

* * * * *

At least in the beginning, the Weiders opted to play it cool. Ben professed to be unmoved by the spectacle that unfolded before his eyes on that fall night in Chicago, on his turf, at the IFBB's greatest event. It was the correct posture to take, though he likely considered the WBF's Olympia invasion to be a personal affront. After the event, stern warnings were issued to competitors: anyone who crossed over into the WBF would be indefinitely suspended. Were the WBF to fail, this would spell doom for the defectors. Tom Platz, once a Weider favorite, was dealt with more harshly. The IFBB banned him for life.

Weider adopted the tactic of regularly updating IFBB competitors on the WBF; his language was derisive and mocking, and he reiterated his claim that the WBF would make bodybuilding into a pro-wrestling-like circus. The number and emphatic nature of Weider's memos betrayed his concern. In his autobiography, Bob Paris reflected on the IFBB President's behavior: "you could tell…that he was worried." If the WBF's inaugural event turned out to be a success, Weider had even more reason to lose sleep.

The IFBB meanwhile got on with business as usual, or close to usual. Although bodybuilders of the past had occasionally left to compete in other organizations—for example when 1983 Mr. Olympia Samir Bannout competed in and won the 1985 WABBA World Championships—the IFBB had never experienced anything like a mass defection before. Organizations like the WABBA posed no threat to the IFBB, but this was not the case with McMahon's federation. When it was able in short order to steal 13 bodybuilders, some of them high-quality, the WBF instantly became too big and powerful for the IFBB to ignore. Nor could the IFBB pretend that the defections weren't worth acknowledging.

Such were the opinions of those who organized the 1991 IFBB Night of Champions contest, held that May in New York City. Since its inception in 1978, the Night of Champions had become one of the bigger events on the IFBB competition calendar, boasting a slew of winners that included the likes of Lee Haney, Albert Beckles, Robby Robinson and Lee Labrada. Attendees of the 1991 installment included the usual band of IFBB officials, bodybuilding photographers and journalists, sponsors, and of course a packed house of fans. That particular contest was also the first major IFBB event following McMahon's press conference. Its organizers opted for a dramatic introduction, one that confronted the WBF specter head-on.

As the show began, theater lights were slowly dimmed to black. The audience, expecting the usual parade of muscle, was instead greeted with something completely different. Stage lighting came on. Atop the posing platform were 13 gravestones, each bearing the name of a WBF defector. Although Ben Weider had claimed "I'm not mad" after the 1990 Olympia spectacle, the second half of the Night of Champions opening act belied that statement. After the audience had enough time to read the inscriptions on the graves, IFBB competitors emerged and smashed the headstones.

Attending the contest that night was new WBF competitor Mike Quinn. Apparently feeling insulted by the scene, he was reported to have yelled "you wouldn't be doing that if I were on that stage." Regardless, the destruction continued. Quinn remained seated, the display came to an end, the headstone fragment markers were cleared off the stage, and the scheduled competition got underway. The remainder of the event was typical IFBB fare. At its conclusion, Herculean British newcomer Dorian Yates was declared champion. The IFBB had wasted little time in letting the bodybuilding world know what it thought of its new rival. The ball was now in the WBF's court. Exactly four weeks later, the curtain would go up at its first-ever event. The new federation had essentially been challenged to prove the career-death prediction of the Night of Champions stage show wrong, and Titan Sports was working overtime to meet it.

Since the WBF's inception, McMahon had aimed to cultivate mainstream interest in bodybuilding, much like he did with wrestling. He therefore looked to mainstream channels to generate excitement for the upcoming WBF World Championship. He signed well-known TV personality Regis Philbin to host the pay-per-view broadcast of the show. McMahon also inserted promotional pieces in his own World Wrestling Federation TV shows. Wrestling fans who tuned in to watch the *Prime Time Wrestling*, *WWF Challenge* and *WWF Superstars* programs got the usual mix of clotheslines and pile-drivers, but there were also workout and interview segments featuring WBF BodyStars.

Finally, McMahon was somehow able to convince the CBS network to run an unprecedented week-long segment of the game show *Family Feud* that pitted BodyStars (Gary Strydom, Jim Quinn, Danny Padilla and Eddie Robinson, as well as Cameo Kneuer—the sister of multiple Ms. Olympia winner Corinna Everson) against members of the WWF (The Mountie, Jimmy Hart, Brian Knobs, Bobby Heenan and Sensational Sherri).

Unfortunately for McMahon and the WBF, the *Family Feud* shows were the high point of his pre-contest promotional activities. He had tried to sell to the USA Network a weekly BodyStars variety show that would feature skits, brief action sequences and other material, but the network's executives weren't impressed. The idea was rejected. McMahon was therefore stuck trying to sell WBF bodybuilding to wrestling fans on his WWF shows, and to bodybuilders via his *Bodybuilding Lifestyles* magazine. He was meanwhile having trouble coming up with something to sell. Revenue for the contest would be generated by ticket sales, sponsors and vendors, and pay-per-view television subscriptions. The greatest potential source of dollars for the event would come from TV, but as the June 15th contest date approached, no pay-per-view providers had shown much interest in televising it. Unless he found an interested provider, there would be no broadcast.

It quickly became apparent that the best-case scenario would involve televising the contest as a discount "Hot Ticket" pay-per-view, with viewers paying five or maybe ten dollars for a subscription. A worst-case circumstance would mean no television coverage, with the competition immediately becoming available on video. In the end, a pay-per-view deal was secured with a provider. However, it became questionable whether the exist-ing base of bodybuilding fans—the core group McMahon was counting on to show interest—would even be aware of the broadcast.

While its marketing department grappled with this problem, Titan's production team was busy preparing for the contest. It was turning out to be far more complicated than anything yet seen in competitive bodybuilding. Since the BodyStars would be given alter-ego personalities, a method was required for WBF fans to become acquainted with them. McMahon and a few WBF staffers had busied themselves creating a character for each bodybuilder. At the evening performance of the contest, a video would be played before each posing routine, featuring that competitor in his new alter-ego role.

The WBF therefore had 13 short videos to produce, and time was short. Meanwhile, an impressive stage show was being planned and assembled. By bodybuilding production standards, it was an altogether massive undertaking.

Considering the elaborate nature of the show, a rehearsal was held the day prior to the event. Present at the rehearsal was Nelson Sweglar, the President of WWF Television, a man who had become well acquainted with the WBF and its competitors over the prior few months. Sweglar watched the run-through in quiet disbelief. He left that evening convinced that the WBF could not possibly hope to succeed. A complete revision of strategy might have reversed that forecast, but it was far too late to make any changes. Preparations had come to an end. Tomorrow was the big day.

* * * * *

Although a few Titan Sports insiders were secretly predicting disaster, the bodybuilding world was consumed with anticipation. Its eyes were firmly fixed on the Taj Mahal in Atlantic City when the day of the contest finally arrived. If the WBF's boasts were true, that this really was the beginning of a new era in bodybuilding—and the beginning of the end for Weider domination—no one dared blink.

As dawn broke over the Taj Mahal on June 15th, a tally revealed that pay-per-view purchases had been few and far between. Although there was still plenty of time for day-of-the-event orders, it was clear that any revenue generated by home viewing was going to be disappointing. Evidently Titan's marketing efforts had fallen flat. Ironically, the existing base of bodybuilding fans—those who were quite interested in the outcome of the event, and who McMahon was counting on for support—turned out to be a passive market. Few read *Bodybuilding Lifestyles* or watched the WWF shows, so not many had seen the pay-per-view ads. Perhaps most importantly, since bodybuilding had never been on live television, pay-per-view or otherwise, apparently no one had thought to go looking for it.

Taj Mahal hotel and casino, Atlantic City.

Getty Images

In the days before the internet and its near-instantaneous dispersal of information, bodybuilding fans were accustomed to learning of major contest results through one of five means: attending the contest; reading about it in magazines; talking to fans who had knowledge of the outcome; calling Gold's Gym in Venice; or attending a telecast event.

Beginning with the 1985 Mr. Olympia contest, the IFBB had arranged for live telecast feeds for a handful of international events. The competitions were shown on movie screens in small auditoriums or rented multi-purpose rooms in a few major cities in the United States. For an admission fee, bodybuilding fans could see the event live. To be present for the 8:00pm introduction ceremony of the '85 Olympia, held in Brussels that year, a fan on the US west coast needed to be in his seat at 11:00am. Telecast events worked reasonably well and drew modest crowds. Though they were probably more trouble than they were worth for Weider, those live feeds did successfully tap into the segment of fans who were eager to see the contest but would never have traveled to Europe for it—and who didn't want to wait three months and pay $50 for the official video. Those same fans would gladly have opted for pay-per-view had it been available. Since McMahon was essentially a newcomer to bodybuilding, it's likely he was unaware of this. Meanwhile, fans expected telecasts or nothing at all.

While a large majority of bodybuilding fans would not witness the contest, either in person or via pay-per-view telecast, not a single fan would witness prejudging, which was closed to the public. This was a modern bodybuilding first. Although there was speculation that the first two judging rounds never actually took place, rumors to that effect later proved unfounded. Another bodybuilding first was the decision to eliminate the evening show's posing round and replace it with an "entertainment" round.

Until the late 1990s the IFBB had strict rules regarding its posing round: competitors were not allowed to use props of any sort; they were forbidden to wear any jewelry save for wedding bands; and even posing suits had to be made of a certain material. The WBF had no such restrictions. To the contrary, elaborate presentations were meant to be one of the event's major selling points.

The other significant difference between IFBB and WBF contests was their scoring systems. The new WBF method was actually a return to the system the IFBB had done away with in the early 1980s. Rather than assigning each competitor a rank relative to other members of the field, each was given a score based on how he compared to an imaginary model of perfection. The main difference was that the WBF used 100 as a perfect score instead of 20. WBF judges were furthermore allowed to use decimal points; for example, at the 1992 WBF Championships judge Ed Corney gave Danny Padilla a score of 86.5.

In the afternoon lull between prejudging and the evening show, additional pay-per-view orders trickled in, but there was nothing close to a last-minute mad rush. By the time the Taj Mahal opened its doors to the public, it was certain that home-viewing orders would fall well short of what was anticipated. Titan Sports executives had to hope that home video sales would make up for the pay-per-view debacle, and that after-the-fact accounts of the contest would inspire fans to order future events. For that to happen, a good contest would have to be put on.

Expecting that very thing, fans filed in and took their seats. All were aware the show was being put on by the biggest of the big-time wrestling promoters. They were expecting an elaborate spectacle, and that's what they got. Whereas the stage presentation of the previous Olympia contest consisted of a single posing platform with an immense "Joe Weider's Mr. Olympia" logo as its backdrop, the WBF show featured a light show, a multi-tiered stage, and giant video screens and smoke machines. Above it all was a brilliant, multi-colored WBF logo, rendered in neon—a sign that perfectly captured the character of the new federation.

Introductory video segments, which had been completed just in time for the contest, were shown before each competitor took the stage. In each, the new alter-egos were finally revealed to the public. Jim Quinn became known as "The Future" and appeared in front of the audience in a space helmet and sunglasses. Johnny Morant was revealed as "The Executioner"; the beginning of his routine consisted of him stalking about the stage with a double-bladed axe. Tony Pearson's alter-ego was called the "Jet Man." Troy Zuccolotto's character was a surfer. He took the stage by handing a surfboard to women in bikinis and later, during a pause in his posing music, turned to the audience and lip-synched "totally radical, dude."

Zuccolotto's routine was typical fare for the entertainment round. Apart from the props, light show, smoke effects and women in bikinis, it was evident that WBF posing routines were different from what fans were used to. In all other bodybuilding competitions, entrants choreograph routines to the songs of their choosing. The songs are usually popular and easily recognizable. At the inaugural WBF Championships, none of the songs were familiar; in fact, they all sounded generic. This was done deliberately.

This practice of posing to recorded music has always carried the potential for copyright infringement claims against the promoters of contests. Since posing music constitutes a portion of the entertainment the promoter is charging attendees or video purchasers to witness, legally the songs' copyright holders are entitled to a percentage of that revenue. In what very well may be testimony to the obscurity of bodybuilding competition, copyright holders have never gone after contests promoters or sanctioning federations, not even ones with deep pockets like Arnold Schwarzenegger or Joe Weider. Apparently nobody noticed that the songs were being used; either that or the copyright holders figured that the money they stood to gain from filing a claim and winning a judgment wouldn't be worth the trouble.

Vince McMahon didn't want to chance it. He saw potential for copyright infringement claims against his enterprise. He expected his production to be big, popular and highly visible. He was also determined to not share any revenue, up-front or as part of a judgment. All WBF competitors were therefore issued generic posing music.

Berry DeMey, who in previous Olympia contests had posed to the likes of U2, Madonna and Bruce Springsteen, now flexed his muscles to a classical-and-rock fusion piece no one had ever heard, before or since. Likewise Zuccolotto was given a no-name guitar-rock song that vaguely matched his new surfer image. Gary Strydom posed to a rock anthem-type number with a heavy beat. All of the tunes came straight from studio sessions directly into the Taj Majal's sound system. This was yet another bodybuilding first, and it wasn't a particularly well-liked part of the show.

Since the time bodybuilders first began to synchronize poses to music, a wide variety of songs could be heard at any given competition. Bodybuilders chose music based on their personal tastes, manner of presentation and appearance. The interpretation of music through skillful posing, when executed by the owner of a superior physique, can sometimes border on artistry. A few such routines have become near-legendary, and represent the pinnacle of what can be achieved through physique display and bodybuilding itself. Lee Labrada's 1993 Mr. Olympia routine is among these, as is Mohammed Makkawy's 1984 interpretation of Modest Mussorgsky's *Great Gate of Kiev* from his *Pictures at an Exhibition* suite. Lee Haney's use of *Siegfried's Funeral March* from Richard Wagner's *Götterdämmerung* opera the same year reflected the differences in physique and personality between himself and Makkawy, and it was executed to even greater effect. These were among the inspired and sometimes great routines IFBB crowds had come to expect.

For at least a portion of bodybuilding fans, great bodybuilders performing great posing routines made contests worthwhile and memorable. However, such would not be the formula or vision of Vince McMahon's WBF. He believed bodybuilding and wrestling fans to be cut from the same rug. McMahon reckoned bodybuilding fans would want an upbeat display of flashing muscle, so that's what he gave them. WBF music was generic; and after each contestant's signature entrance, so were the routines.

Few things that took place on the Taj Mahal stage that evening would be remembered as positive contributions to bodybuilding. Berry DeMey's routine was certainly memorable, but for other reasons. As his theme music began, DeMey appeared on the theater's uppermost platform, at the top of a broad stairway. A blue towel was fitted about his waist, seemingly meant to imply that he had just stepped out of a shower. He slinked forward toward fit and attractive females who sat on the steps wearing pink towels. As DeMey strode by they gently pawed at him. After a last caress from each woman, the towel was slipped from his waist, revealing a regular posing suit. Most of the rest of his routine was pretty standard-fare physique presentation, mixed in with a decent share of hand-clapping and prancing. It was more striptease than serious physique display.

Bodybuilding had for a long time attempted to cultivate an image of dignity. This was especially true of the IFBB. This did not however prevent bodybuilding from teetering on the brink of raciness and overt sexuality. Its very nature set bodybuilding upon this edge: physique contests are a parade of nearly nude, exceptionally well-developed men. Competitors have periodically exploited this fact in order to spice up their free-posing presentations. Berry DeMey did so at the WBF Championships, and at least for the duration of his routine, the image of dignity that bodybuilding had for so long tried to project was tossed out the window.

At least in appearance, Vince McMahon belonged to the school of bodybuilding fans who never knew that dignity was something to be cultivated. Dignity didn't exist in wrestling, and wrestling brought in big bucks. He figured that the same must therefore be true of bodybuilding, or so the time and energy invested into his WBF venture would suggest. He therefore concocted images and routines like those of Berry DeMey and the remainder of the field at the first WBF championships.

Berry DeMey. 1991

Courtesy of Michael Newman

Gary Strydom's routine wasn't a striptease, but his introduction had similar theatrics. He appeared on the top tier of the stage, flanked by attractive females. He was holding a top hat and cane, which he handed to the women before launching into his series of poses. As the WBF's most important product and the favorite to win the contest, the intro was meant to impress upon the audience that they were being graced with the presence of their champion. The emcee's announcement just prior to Strydom appearing—"you've seen the rest; now get ready for the best"—left little doubt that Strydom was meant to win the contest, and strongly suggested that the outcome was pre-decided.

The pay-per-view broadcast and home video release of the contest featured play-by-play commentary by Vince McMahon and Bobby Heenan. Although they brought big-time wrestling enthuseasm to their descriptions and analysis, through most of the show they were struggling to find interesting things to say. Unlike wrestling with its ongoing action, save for anecdotes there isn't a whole lot that can be said about any one physique—especially when the commentators don't know much about bodybuilding in the first place. McMahon had clearly become interested in bodybuilding, but he was still pretty new to it. Heenan was a wrestling announcer and commentator whose knowledge did not go beyond the ability to name a few standard bodybuilding poses. To home-viewing physique contest fans who were used to the insightful and intelligent commentary of Frank Zane and Chris Dickerson, McMahon and Heenan were uninformed and annoying.

Gary Strydom. c. 1992

Courtesy of Michael Newman

Heenan's excitement peaked as Strydom's routine got underway. With his trademark, gravelly yell, Heenan's commentary consisted first of a long, drawn-out "*wow*," followed by "look at the mass!"; "look at the striations!"; "take a look at that double bicep!"; "Gary Strydom really knows how to strut his stuff!" With each synchronized flex of his muscles, the home audience was loudly encouraged by Heenan to "look at…!" what they were already, well, looking at.

And then nothing happened. The posing routine ended. The WBF wanted to instill big-time wrestling excitement into its championship event, but that style of presentation tempted its audience to expect something different than what it was witnessing. Those brief moments also reminded the world why pro wrestling had become much bigger than bodybuilding. Strydom's routine was staged in such a manner that it would be the climax of the evening's events. The combined assault of whirling lights, thunderous music, bulging muscles, and the roar of riotous fans[1] effectively conveyed the notion that this was the high point of the evening. Yet all the while even the purest of bodybuilding fans couldn't help but expect to see another competitor come running up behind Strydom, sending him crashing off the stage with a blow to the head from a folding chair.

Everything about the WBF reminded its viewers of the WWF, except for the one thing that fills arenas for pro wrestling events on a regular basis: the action. In bodybuilding, there is no action. Physique competitions are won or lost based solely on appearance, with consideration sometimes given to presentation. In that respect bodybuilding really isn't much different from a dog show. The scant WWF fans curious enough to order the pay-per-view were momentarily impressed by the massive, near-perfect physiques, but they quickly lost interest in something which is, at its core, an artistic display. After all, the thinking goes, what good is 250 pounds of rock-hard muscle if you're not body-slamming someone with it? Bob Hoffman would have applauded the sentiment.

Nevertheless, this was still a bodybuilding contest, and when all was said and done, Strydom's 250

[1]The 1991 WBF Championship video appears to have a soundtrack of cheering fans added in.

pounds of muscle were enough to carry him to victory. He was made the very first WBF World Champion. Following him in the placings were Mike Christian, Berry DeMey, Jim Quinn and Eddie Robinson.

At its earliest stage, when rumors of the Olympia invasion made the rounds through gyms, a number of bodybuilding fans found themselves rooting for the WBF. Many wrung their hands at the thought of a new and powerful federation shattering Weider's monopoly. Other organizations with professional divisions had been around for years, but compared to the IFBB, they were small, inconsequential, and sometimes shady. The WBF promised something entirely different. If any organization was capable of ending Weider domination, this was it. Yet the hope proved to be a false one. To bodybuilding fans, the WBF version of physique competition was far too overblown, overhyped, silly and fake.

The pro-wrestling-style fake-persona gimmick was met with eye-rolling disapproval from bodybuilding fans who followed their favorites into the new federation. That same group felt their intelligence was being insulted by the glitz, storylines and comic-book personalities. For all the faults ascribed to traditional bodybuilding, it's still "real." The competitors who appear onstage are real people using their real names, the judging is real, and the outcomes are meaningful.

The outcome of the first WBF Championships meanwhile looked very much fixed. Not only was Strydom's introduction a giveaway, but the final placings corresponded exactly to the value of each competitor's annual contract with the WBF. The event's judging practices were questioned, and fans voiced their displeasure. It's possible Vince McMahon didn't anticipate this. His experience was with wrestling, where fixed outcomes are fully expected. The world of bodybuilding was entirely different. Results mirroring contract values were a major turn-off to fans who wanted to see a fair fight, not a fancy pseudo-contest.

McMahon's plan had been to simultaneously entice existing bodybuilding fans by showcasing top-notch competitors and to lure new fans by making bodybuilding contests more entertaining. To that end, he poured a lot of time and money into something that had never been tried before. As he quickly discovered, just because something is new doesn't mean that people will like it.

* * * * *

In the end, the poor reception of the event proved to be of little consequence. The historical significance of the first WBF Championships is owed merely to the fact that it took place. Even though reviews were mostly bad, fans were disillusioned and the contest was a financial failure, the Weiders still feared the WBF. It's possible that they weren't fully aware of the event's failings, that they believed WBF propaganda, or that they became conscious of the grumblings of those who opposed IFBB drug testing. But there was one thing they did know for certain: they had lost 13 good bodybuilders to Vince McMahon's enterprise. Fearing they might lose many more, the Weiders took action. Several months before the 1991 Mr. Olympia contest, competitors were discretely informed that the IFBB was going to stop testing for drugs.

With a single, silent stroke, five years of drug-free posturing and fanfare were erased from official memory. The IFBB professional division and most importantly the Mr. Olympia contest would return to the ways of old, the way fans and competitors liked it. The WBF's greatest advantage over the IFBB had been its lack of drug testing. That advantage had now been eliminated. The scales had been tipped.

For the moment however, this fact was largely unknown. Joe Weider certainly wasn't going to make statements in his magazines or over auditorium PA systems about the abolishment of drug testing. Nevertheless, word would get out. The rumor-mill would churn. Once contests had taken place, savvy fans would draw the correct conclusions. Most critically, IFBB bodybuilders would all be in top form. The photo spreads of the 1991 Olympia would tell the tale. The event's competitors would appear massive, in excellent condition, and quite chemically-enriched.

Although the elimination of drug testing at professional contests theoretically placed the Weiders' Olympic dreams in jeopardy, their official stance on the Games did not waver. The IFBB would continue to drug test its amateur world championship contests. It was hoped that this gesture would be enough to convince the IOC that bodybuilding and drugs are not inseparable. Meanwhile, Ben Weider had made no tangible progress with the IOC since the 1990 Olympia. While an Olympic birth was still fantasy, Weider's very real IFBB pro division was vulnerable and threatened. The playing field needed to be leveled. Drug testing had to be abolished.

Once that happened, the WBF would be outclassed. The IFBB had a superior stable of competitors, it had a tried-and-tested formula for successful contests, and it had Joe Weider's strong-selling magazines to prop it up. On top of all this, to insure that defections would halt, Weider began signing bodybuilders to contracts, something he had little need or desire to do in the past.

WBF did have one remaining advantage: television exposure. Vince McMahon was finally able to convince the USA Network to run a weekly bodybuilding variety show called *WBF Bodystars*. Hosted by McMahon, Cameo Kneuer and wrestler Lex Luger, the show would feature competitors performing skits and imparting training advice. *BodyStars* would also directly advertise for the WBF, *Bodybuilding Lifestyles* magazine and the ICOPRO supplement line. Wrestling-centered variety shows had done well, so there was hope for one that featured bodybuilders.

Unfortunately for McMahon, the entire WBF venture had begun to reveal one important fact: things that work in wrestling can totally flop in bodybuilding. The *WBF BodyStars* show was no exception. Yet before the new TV show even had a chance to fail, prospects for the WBF worsened.

Vince McMahon owed his fortune to professional wrestling. It was that fortune which allowed him to come crashing into the bodybuilding scene, turning heads and frightening the Weiders. Ironically however, it was his association with wrestling that set in motion the undoing of his bodybuilding venture.

Less than two weeks after the first WBF Championships, steroids once again made headlines. A man few had ever heard of, a Dr. George T. Zahorian, achieved overnight infamy when he was convicted on a dozen counts of distributing anabolic steroids to professional wrestlers. Not only were the wrestlers members of McMahon's WWF, but McMahon himself was named as a buyer. Zahorian's ties to the WWF were clear and direct; he was previously the state-appointed physician for that organization in Pennsylvania. Zahorian was sentenced to three years in prison, and McMahon quickly became an object of close official scrutiny.

To take some of the heat off, in July McMahon called a press conference to announce that the WWF would begin testing its wrestlers for drugs. By November the program was put into effect. However, the WBF was not subject to the new policy. McMahon hoped that testing wrestlers would appease those who threatened to come down hard on him. Also, in spite of McMahon's efforts to the contrary, the WBF was still small-time compared to the WWF. The WBF had not been mentioned at Zahorian's trial and federal agents had not inquired about it. Because of this, McMahon thought he was still in possession of his primary advantage: a lack of drug-testing. He wasn't yet aware that the IFBB professional division had done away with testing and his advantage was lost.

* * * * *

Though the WBF was off to a shaky start, Vince McMahon remained determined and hopeful. There was plenty of time left before the 1992 WBF Championships, and he was resolved to inject momentum into the federation before that event. He would continue to promote the WBF and its associated ventures through television programming and magazines; and as far as he knew, he was still competing with a handicapped federation. As McMahon prepared to witness what he assumed would be the second installment of a drug-tested Mr. Olympia contest, a potential blockbuster marketing device fell into his lap.

16 years after unofficially retiring from competition, Lou Ferrigno made it known that he was ready to once more step onto a bodybuilding stage. His last contest had been the 1975 Mr. Olympia, famously documented in *Pumping Iron.* A Ferrigno comeback would be the biggest news to hit bodybuilding in recent memory, even bigger than the IFBB's decision to begin testing for drugs. The reason was simple: Ferrigno was one of the biggest stars bodybuilding had ever produced. After Arnold Schwarzenegger, he was the only modern bodybuilder whose name the general public recognized; and among hardcore bodybuilding fans, he was a living legend.

Some of the dialogue in *Pumping Iron* makes reference to Ferrigno's not-yet-realized potential. Part of his desire to return was based on feelings that he had unfinished business in the world of physique competition. In the film, his showdown with Arnold Schwarzenegger ended up falling flat, mainly because Ferrigno was unable to achieve peak condition. Ever since the film's release, he had been associated with that condition. As a life-long hardcore bodybuilder, Ferrigno could not be satisfied with that, especially when he knew he was capable of much more. In *Pumping Iron*, he had not given a definitive account of himself. He had demons to exorcise.

Ferrigno was also in a position to turn a comeback

into financial gain. He knew full well that in 1991 bodybuilding was far bigger than when he left. Regardless of how he might actually place in competition, there was money to be made. His commitment to return would soon reveal how true that was. But whatever Ferrigno's true motivations may have been, he clearly wanted back in.

Although he was an icon from a past era, Ferrigno was only 40 when he declared interest in returning to competition. The viability of his comeback therefore served as a reminder of one important way that bodybuilding differs from most competitive sports: unless he has suffered some type of serious training injury, a 40-year-old bodybuilder is by no means over the hill. Albert Beckles famously placed second in the 1985 Mr. Olympia contest at the age of 55 (or, by the reckoning of some, 47). Chris Dickerson won the Mr. Olympia in 1982 at the age of 43. A legitimate Ferrigno comeback was certainly plausible.

At least in the beginning no one expected Ferrigno to compete in any organization other than the IFBB. Weider's federation was still very much the supreme power in bodybuilding, and it was on an IFBB Mr. Olympia stage that Ferrigno's score stood unsettled. Ferrigno also had a long-standing, personal relationship with Joe Weider. A mid-80s piece in *Muscle & Fitness* even made the strange claim that he and Weider had become training partners. It was well known that Ferrigno was a Weider favorite, but up until 1990 so was Tom Platz. Vince McMahon caught wind of Ferrigno's desire to return and immediately recognized the value he could bring to the WBF. McMahon knew Ferrigno was loyal to Weider, but his dollars had already proven that such loyalties came with price tags.

Weider naturally recognized the value of a Ferrigno comeback as well, but he stood to gain less from it than the WBF. Even after its first contest—or more likely because of it—the WBF still wasn't generally perceived to be a credible organization. If Ferrigno signed on with the new federation, that perception could only improve. It might even improve dramatically. Ferrigno could bring credibility and press coverage, two things the WBF was badly in need of. Weider's IFBB already had both of these things. Any benefit for that organization would be incremental rather than dramatic. Weider was therefore left to ponder several unknowns: how much additional press coverage Ferrigno would actually bring; if the comeback would attract significant mainstream interest; and most importantly, how much money he would have to lay out to keep Ferrigno loyal.

Earlier that year McMahon had lured some very decent IFBB bodybuilders with his checkbook. He would no doubt try to do the same with Ferrigno. A token bidding war with Weider ensued, but the cards were clearly stacked in favor of McMahon. He had more money to throw around and more motivation to do so. Weider meanwhile wasn't convinced that Ferrigno's cost-to-benefit ratio was attractive. The fairly recent and ho-hum return of Sergio Oliva had not been forgotten. The war therefore didn't last long. Ferrigno reportedly signed a two-year, $900,000 contract with the WBF. As part of the agreement, he would compete in the WBF Championships. His showdown with 1991 WBF champion Gary Strydom would be billed as the greatest clash of muscle the world would ever see.

Since he became a part of the WBF, it was certain that Ferrigno would not be competing in the Mr. Olympia contest. Although he had auctioned off his chance to claim something which 15 years prior might have been his for the taking, times had changed. Considering the ever-rising quality of the IFBB competitive field, he may have understood that his chances of coming out of retirement and winning the 1992 Mr. Olympia title were less than realistic. Whatever the case, Ferrigno's after-the-fact comments suggested that he was more interested in laying to rest the ghosts of the'75 Olympia than in competing with the pros of the '90s. This could be accomplished at the WBF Championships.

The showdown was hyped. The December 1991 cover of *Bodybuilding Lifestyles* featured a picture of a shirtless, flexing and smiling Gary Strydom, wearing his WBF Championship gold medal. Over his left shoulder towered Ferrigno, simultaneously glaring and grabbing the medal with a massive flexed arm. The headline was brief and to the point: "Ferrigno vs. Strydom."

Even though it was only a magazine cover, the top billing given to Ferrigno suggested what fans could expect to see: Lou Ferrigno, the Incredible Hulk, coming out of retirement and winning a world championship title. Though at the time true bodybuilding fans would only recognize a Mr. Olympia winner as a legitimate world champion, this was far from the case with general public. The limitless masses who were unfamiliar with physique competition, those whom it was hoped would soon take interest, were by no means bound to distinguish the WBF from the IFBB, the WABBA, the NABBA, or any other of the organizations that have hosted contests whose proceedings produced so-called world champions.

The gears were set in motion. For the 1992 WBF Championships, McMahon booked a giant 12,000-seat arena in Long Beach, CA. To fill it, every ounce of publicity was going to be milked from the impending Ferrigno/Strydom confrontation. The professional wrestling mogul had secured an expensive but important draw. For the moment it seemed the scales had tipped his favor. But the perception wouldn't last long. Two events were about to throw things wildly out of balance.

* * * * *

The 1991 Mr. Olympia contest was going to be held that fall in Orlando, Florida, disrupting the IFBB's tradition of hosting the event outside of the United States in alternating years. The exact motivations for staging the contest in the US that year were not advertised, though there were several reasons why it was a sensible move. Chief among these was that an American location would guarantee a large audience and substantial coverage. This was important for the 1991 installment of the contest. Barring any sort of major upset, in '91 Lee Haney would break Arnold Schwarzenegger's long-standing record of seven Olympia wins. For bodybuilding fans, this was a big deal. Drug-testing or no, attendees could expect to see the greatest contest ever held, or certainly the most significant.

The evening show went off without a hitch. Haney returned to a previously-used, majestic Richard Wagner/Carl Orff combination for his theme music,[1] though the physical interpretation of his soundtrack seemed a little less inspired than in previous competitions. The man who turned out to be Haney's chief competition, rookie pro Dorian Yates, used what had by then become an old posing round standard—the *Conan the Barbarian* theme—in an unimaginative but effective routine. Vince Taylor brought a far higher level of showmanship to the contest, posing and mimicking robotic movements to a custom-made soundtrack, all done as part of a Terminator-inspired presentation. Unfortunately for him, it wasn't enough to best Haney or Yates, the bringers of more massive physiques.

The crowd that gathered that night expected to see history made, in grand fashion. When the matter was settled, few walked away disappointed. Haney did in fact win his eighth Sandow statue. The remainder of the top six, in order, were Yates, Taylor, Lee Labrada, Shawn Ray, and Sonny Schmidt. Yet the significance of that year's Olympia by no means began and ended with the crowning of a new all-time great. Unlike the prior year, the lead-up to the 1991 Olympia included no bold talk or magazine articles about drug-testing or the continuation of a new era. Once the contest was underway, the reason became obvious. 1991 would not represent the continuation of a new era. It would mark an immediate return to an old one. The competitors all looked chemically-enhanced as ever.

Bodybuilding fans who understood what it takes to achieve the look of a top professional soon put two and two together. The lack of anti-drug rhetoric combined with the appearance of the 1991 Mr. Olympia field could only mean one thing: the IFBB had abandoned drug-testing. Vince McMahon may have caught wind of the IFBB decision to halt drug-testing before the Olympia. If he hadn't, that evening's events would have come as a rude shock. The advantage of showcasing non-drug-free bodybuilders no longer belonged exclusively to the WBF. When Haney was handed his final Sandow statue, it seemed the 1991 Mr. Olympia had been the greatest muscle contest ever held.

A post-Olympia inventory of the WBF's selling points revealed that it was now clearly offering an inferior product. Even though Haney was expected to retire after winning his eighth title, the IFBB would still have a superior field of competitors and a traditional, tried-and-true contest format. Its structure also guaranteed that several top amateur bodybuilders would turn professional each year. The WBF could only rely on enticing competitors to desert other organizations. After the reception of the WBF's first event, the IFBB's abandonment of drug-testing, its increased contest purses, and the new contracts that Weider began doling out, it appeared that the WBF would have trouble adding bodybuilders other than Lou Ferrigno to its 1992 roster.

The WBF's future was looking dim. Nevertheless,

[1] 1982 Mr. Olympia Chris Dickerson, a trained opera singer, six years earlier commented that Haney's decision to use the music of Wagner was "very interesting." Wagner and Orff were both favorites of the Nazi Party of Germany in the 1930s and 40s; combining the two for Haney's posing routine deepened an irony that went almost entirely unrecognized.

Vince McMahon was still holding a few cards. Through his wrestling events and TV shows, he possessed the ability to reach a lot of potential bodybuilding fans. Although that had been the case for the prior year as well, for its 1992 championships the WBF would have much more time and far more television coverage and build-up. It also now had The Incredible Hulk as its main attraction.

McMahon knew Ferrigno was a potential mainstream draw; and signing him to a Titan Sports contract inspired his next move. McMahon hatched plans to directly cash in on the popularity of some of his wrestlers by convincing them to compete in WBF physique contests. Foremost among those who might inject life into the WBF was Larry Phofl, a wrestler known by the stage name of Lex Luger. Phofl had been one of the top stars of the WWF rival World Championship Wrestling organization. Feeling that his career was going nowhere with the WCW, in 1992 he negotiated his release from the federation so that he could sign on with Titan Sports. Because a no-compete clause prevented Phofl from wrestling in the WWF until 1993—and since he was the owner of large, muscular, and defined physique—he was an obvious choice to cross over into the WBF.

There were also rumors that McMahon was trying to lure James Brian Hellwig, otherwise known as the Ultimate Warrior, over to the WBF. Hellwig was an even more obvious target than Phofl. Apart from being massive and defined, he was a former competitive bodybuilder and winner of the 1984 Mr. Georgia contest. In 1985 a chance introduction to the world of pile drivers and clotheslines proved fateful, as Hellwig abandoned both bodybuilding and chiropractic school to become a professional

The Ultimate Warrior. c. 1989

Courtesy of Steve Harris

wrestler. Within a few years he would be an icon of the ring. He would also make a salary that far exceeded anything seen in bodybuilding. Unfortunately for McMahon, the Ultimate Warrior's return to bodybuilding was not to be. The same rumor-mill that told of McMahon's effort to bring him to the WBF later declared Hellwig would have nothing to do with it; apparently he worried that a foray into muscle competition would damage his credibility as a wrestler.

Other attempts to boost the WBF's popularity didn't fare much better. The *BodyStars* show was groping for interesting material. Phofl now co-hosted the program, but this didn't help the show's ratings; nor did it enhance the program's quality. Apart from his antics, lots of ICOPRO commercials and a smattering of bodybuilding training tips, viewers were left to ponder segments like swimming pool chicken fights and tug-of-war contests.

The tug-of-war drew particular attention to the fact that bodybuilders and wrestlers are breeds apart, and that the whole idea of promoting bodybuilding through wrestling channels was ill-conceived. In the event, a handful of WWF and WBF stars went head-to-head in a traditional rope-pulling contest. Just before it began, each side was given the opportunity to taunt and insult the other. This was standard fare for professional wrestling. Once the shouting began however, it quickly became clear that the bodybuilders either didn't know how to do the loud, in-your-face shtick at which wrestlers excel, or they simply couldn't bring themselves to try.

The WBF was generally perceived to be going from bad to worse. Chicken fights and tug-of-war contests contributed to these perceptions. While future program content was being mulled, worse had become dismal. When Vince McMahon first brought the WBF to life, the high visibility of professional wrestling, in particular his own WWF, was imagined to be his greatest advantage. Barely a year into the WBF's existence, it became a giant liability. When McMahon and several wrestlers were identified in court as customers of George Zahorian's steroid-distribution business, McMahon's entire wrestling enterprise was placed in jeopardy. Shortly thereafter, the entire WWF was drug-tested. Meanwhile, WBF bodybuilders had been given a temporary free pass. McMahon needed to let his bodybuilders slide, because the WBF's competitive edge was based on the absence of drug tests.

That free pass expired more quickly than anyone

at Titan Sports hoped. Drug-testing wrestlers did not spare McMahon from further investigation by federal authorities. He was forced to realize that promoting bodybuilding contests which featured highly steroid-enhanced physiques produced risks that far outweighed any potential benefits. A few months before its second championship event, he therefore announced plans to subject WBF bodybuilders to rigorous steroid testing. Shortly thereafter *Bodybuilding Lifestyles* began running articles about the health risks associated with steroid use. In short order, McMahon's would-be bodybuilding empire became a half-baked copy of the real one he had attempted to overthrow.

In one of bodybuilding's great moments of irony, the competing federations' roles had been reversed: Vince McMahon's WBF would enforce strict drug-testing, while Joe Weider's IFBB would allow its competitors complete chemical liberty. Except for the Lou Ferrigno signing, all of the WBF's advantages had vanished; and alas, even that was not to be. Several weeks after the drug-testing announcement was made, Ferrigno backed out of the WBF. The federation's death-knell had sounded.

It was widely assumed that Ferrigno dropped out of the WBF specifically because of drug-testing. After all, his reputation, persona and success had everything to do with his massive physique. Stepping onstage in drug-free condition would hurt his image. Moreover, if Ferrigno was truly going to lay the ghosts of 1975 to rest, he needed drugs to do it. Although he never admitted that any of these things factored into his decision to leave the WBF, the rationale for his departure mattered little. He was gone. The WBF was left with its original cast of 13 bodybuilders, all of whom were scheduled to appear in the 1992 WBF Championships in drug-free condition. Larry Phofl was placed on the evening's bill as a guest-poser. It was hoped—or more likely prayed—that his Lex Luger alter-ego would help draw fans to the event, in-person or on pay-per-view.

Meanwhile, the IFBB was more popular than ever. The 1992 Night of Champions contest was won by stunning newcomer Kevin Levrone; the '92 Schwarzenegger classic by the now-veteran Vince Taylor. The quality and depth of competition at both events had been nothing short of sensational. Since Joe Weider's IFBB had returned to giving fans what they want, the near-mutiny sparked by drug-testing and the WBF's emergence had entirely dissolved. Bodybuilding fans no longer clamored for Weider's overthrow.

As the IFBB spring events came to a close, all eyes that cared were fixed on the second installment of the WBF Championships. Since few fans now expected the new federation to survive for much longer—and most viewed the contest as something entirely peripheral to legitimate physique competition—interest in the event came only from fanatics or the morbidly curious.

Additional bits of news preceded the competition. According to reports, at least one WBF competitor was fined $25,000 for failing a drug test. Due to the heat brought down on him by federal authorities, McMahon's program was not a day-of-the-event urine or blood test, like other drug-tested bodybuilding contests. Instead, a full cycle of tests was administered, beginning months before the contest. It was by far the most stringent drug-testing program bodybuilding would ever know.

As the contest approached, the rumor-mill kept churning. Word was that one WBF competitor simply opted to pay fines and accept a short suspension rather than halt his drug regimen. (The suspension ended, rather coincidentally, right before the contest.) Another piece of gossip was that Gary Strydom was ready to split from the WBF and that Vince McMahon was able to secure his return only after making a personal plea. Finally, Larry Phofl crashed his motorcycle just days before the contest, badly fracturing his arm. Although this appeared to be a ploy to keep him away from what was shaping up to be a terrible evening of entertainment, the accident did in fact happen.

Such was the state of the WBF as it limped into the second installment of its World Championships. Despite running a much larger volume of magazine ads and TV promos, pay-per-view sales for the contest were actually worse than the prior year. It was later reported that a mere 3,000 households ordered the event, with San Diego County—a short drive from Los Angeles, the center of the bodybuilding universe—accounting for a mere 30 buys. Considering that more than 40 million American households were then capable of ordering pay-per-view, the 1992 WBF Championship telecast could not be described as anything but a monumental failure.

The significance of the first WBF Championships was owed merely to the fact that it took place. The same can be said for the contest's second installment, though for entirely different reasons. Taking into account the total dollars spent versus up-front revenue generated, the IFBB's resurgence, the Ferrigno resignation, a mutinous talent pool, the Phofl accident and the looming threat of prosecution by federal authorities, it's surprising that McMahon didn't just cancel the show. Nevertheless, he didn't—and with disregard for all these things, the auditorium doors opened on time, fans took their seats, and the contest got underway.

It quickly became obvious that drug-testing had taken its toll. Compared to the prior year's event, or especially to recent IFBB contests, most of the competitors looked small, with less hardness and definition. There were however a couple of notable exceptions. Mike Quinn turned up for the show so overweight that he would have needed to lose at least 30 pounds before he could be described as being smooth. As part of his contest preparation Quinn had enlisted the help of someone named Dr. Mario Dipasquale, the inventor of a special "anabolic diet." The nutritional plan was similar in many ways to the Atkins Diet that gained popularity a few years later. Dipasquale's approach called for the ingestion of very large amounts of protein and fat, with minimal carbohydrates. According to him, the diet would trigger a physiological state whereby its follower would simultaneously build muscle and shed fat. Unfortunately for Dipasquale, Quinn, and anyone who dared watch his dance-filled posing routine in the show's entertainment round, the diet didn't work.

McMahon had originally hired Dipasquale to oversee the WBF's drug-testing program. According to claims later made by Quinn, McMahon became so convinced of the merits of Dipasquale's secret-weapon nutritional approach that he was forced (by a clause in his contract) to eat whatever foods Dipasquale mandated. Although some found this excuse to be far-fetched, there was clearly some reason why Quinn, a man known previously for competing in excellent condition, had shown up so horribly out-of-shape.[1] Ironically—or perhaps appropriately—Quinn's on-stage condition became the thing for which the event was best remembered. Obviously this did not bode well for remainder of the show.

Few people other than Vince McMahon know how much pressure federal authorities applied to him once his involvement with George Zahorian became known. McMahon was apparently dangling over some rather hot water. The small viewership that witnessed the 1992 WBF Championships was given an inkling of its temperature as they sat through an intermission segment featuring the event's drug-testing physician. In yet another bodybuilding first, Dipasquale explained the extensive nature of the federation's new testing efforts and even read off a list of chemicals that could be detected. Although an information segment like this was quite contrary to what originally drove many fans to the WBF, Dipasquale's spiel may have been the true motivation behind going through with the show. Canceling the show outright may have seemed suspicious to any interested party whose job it was to be distrustful.

After the intermission, the contest labored on. Gary Strydom was the sole bodybuilder to hit the stage in above-average condition. This immediately gave credence to rumors that he had have been subjected to drug-testing standards which differed from everyone else. Some wondered whether Strydom was tested at all, and whether the threat of his departure got him special treatment. Whatever the case, his was clearly the best physique on stage that night.

Not surprisingly, Strydom was crowned WBF Champion for the second time. Mike Christian was reported to have shown up for the contest at under 200 pounds—a full 40 pounds below his peak condition—and therefore did not repeat as runner-up. Apart from needing to pass the WBF's stringent drug tests, it was widely rumored that Christian was suffering from substance abuse problems. The remainder of the 1992 top five were DeMey, Robinson, David Dearth and Aaron Baker. Unlike the previous year, contest results did not correspond to contract values. Considering Christian's condition, having him in second again would have been outrageous. Nevertheless, Christian might as well have placed second, for the simple reason that none of the results mattered anyway. The WBF's downhill slide had been picking up momentum, and by the time the lights went up that night, virtually no one still considered it to be a serious or legitimate bodybuilding organization. Few expected it to survive long enough to hold another contest. It certainly no longer posed any threat to the IFBB.

[1]Despite Quinn's condition, WBF judge Ed Corney gave him a higher score than third-place finisher Eddie Robinson.

* * * * *

Upon which day Vince McMahon awoke and realized that the WBF dream had become a nightmare is known only to him. Regardless, at some point reality set it. The IFBB—the federation that had produced the legends of Larry Scott, Sergio Oliva, Arnold Schwarzenegger, Frank Zane and Lee Haney—would not be easily toppled. It's not clear whether McMahon ever grasped the folly of his actions, if he ever really knew where he went wrong, but a quick check of his bottom line told him all he needed to know. The WBF was a money pit. It was reported to have lost upwards of $15 million.

Thanks to his wrestling empire, McMahon was no stranger to success. He was also the owner of a few ideas that flopped hard. The XFL of a decade later is one of the more famous examples. He knew that profitable ventures are not built by clinging to unrealistic dreams, and that on occasion one must raise the white flag.

Less than two years prior McMahon had declared war on an unsuspecting foe, threatening complete destruction. Yet as he now surveyed his position, it became clear that it was his own WBF that had been destroyed. Anxious to move on, he was reported to have offered unconditional surrender. When he decided to officially disband the WBF, he called the Woodland Hills office of Joe Weider, who was given the courtesy of being the first to know the news. As part of the call, McMahon pronounced Weider to be the true King of bodybuilding. Weider was surprised and impressed with the gesture, and a truce was declared. Shortly thereafter, the official announcement was made. The WBF no longer existed.

Bodybuilding Lifestyles printed a few more issues before going the way of the dinosaurs. Meanwhile, Titan Sports still had its *WBF BodyStars* time slot on the USA network. Since companies were no longer interested in buying commercial time for the program, its format had to be revised. Under the new name of simply *BodyStars,* the show became an infomercial for the previously dismal-selling ICOPRO line of supplements. Eddie Robinson was retained as its spokesman and was allowed to keep his WBF annual salary of $225,000 for two additional years. Considering the total amount of money paid to him, television production costs, and ICOPRO's continuing poor sales, it became clear that Titan Sports' venture into the nutritional supplement market was an unmitigated failure.

Robinson may have made out better than any single person associated with the WBF. Combined contract earnings and contest prizes put his total take in the neighborhood of a million dollars. Though he placed tenth in his one and only Mr. Olympia contest in 1990,[1] by the time his Titan payments stopped coming in he was one of bodybuilding's all-time highest-paid competitors.

Meanwhile, the WBF aftermath left stranded 12 other professional bodybuilders. All of them had known that leaving the IFBB for the WBF entailed huge risk, and now that move's worst-case scenario came to pass. Out in the cold and still banned from the IFBB, all were now left to ponder their futures. Fortunately the episode found Joe Weider in a conciliatory mood. His prudent business sense tempered any ill will he may have harbored toward the group. At his mercy were 13 good, humbled bodybuilders with hopes of returning and a willingness to make amends. While Weider was interested in getting them back, he also figured he may as well dish out some punishment and make a few bucks in the process. He allowed WBF bodybuilders to return to the IFBB, so long as they paid a fee equivalent to 10% of their annual Titan contract salaries.

Weider wisely made one exception and levied no sanction again Lou Ferrigno. Since Ferrigno never actually competed in a WBF contest, the decision was easy to justify. Now that there was no one to bid against, Weider could also get him for free. Considering Ferrigno's mindset at the time, he probably would have paid Weider for a chance to get back onstage. Ferrigno was also given a special invitation to compete in the 1992 Mr. Olympia contest, something which otherwise requires a top-three placing in a qualifying event.

Quite a few WBFers wanted back into the IFBB as well, so checkbooks were pulled out and fines were paid. Repatriated bodybuilders began entering the contests of Weider's federation. Unfortunately for all of them, the IFBB field of competitors was now bigger and better than it had been just a few years prior. The early-to-mid 1990s saw the rise of phenoms like Dorian Yates, Flex Wheeler, Kevin Levrone, Ronnie Coleman, Paul Dillett, Chris Cormier, Andreas Munzer, Mike Matarazzo, Nasser El Sonbaty and Roland Cziurlok. Against this lot,

[1] Although the 1990 Mr. Olympia was a drug-tested event, Robinson's web site declared the 1992 WBF Championships to be "Eddie's first drug free show."

Courtesy of David Moore

above: Aaron Baker, c. 1996
right: Tony Pearson, c. 1983

Courtesy of Michael Newman

average WBF competitors like Troy Zuccolotto or Tony Pearson stood little chance.

Apart from that, in a world where the level of competition had risen so high—and fields were so deep—it's often the case that a judge will be forced to give a relatively low placing to the owner of a good physique. The judge may have little choice, simply because there are better physiques onstage. Sometimes one physique will best another by only the slightest of margins, but such is often the difference between second, sixth or ninth place finishes in modern professional bodybuilding contests. In an environment like that, it can be easy for judges to give low placings to men who were previously banned for disloyalty.

Whatever the real causes may have been, nearly all former WBF competitors fared poorly after returning to the IFBB. Their contest placings were lower than what they had been before joining the WBF. Only Aaron Baker, who joined the WBF before he ever had a chance to compete in IFBB events, had a post-Titan Sports competitive career that could be described as successful. As the owner of what some have called one of the greatest physiques ever to grace a bodybuilding stage, it would have been difficult for judges to consistently assign him low placings. However, like all of the other WBF defectors, he never again won a contest.[1]

[1]Frank Zane, in his commentary for the 1994 Schwarzenegger Classic contest, pointed out that Baker's relatively low placings did not correspond to the quality of his physique.

At age 32, Gary Strydom decided to retire a winner. Not long after the WBF collapse he officially announced that his competition days were over. After a few years he changed his mind however, and in 1996 Strydom chose the Night of Champions contest as the site of his return. As a prior NOC winner, Strydom may have anticipated a glorious and heralded return. The actual outcome was something rather inglorious. He finished a distant 12th.

Because Strydom won both WBF Championships, IFBB judges may have been eager to give him a low placing; doing so would invalidate whatever level of quality the WBF was thought to have possessed. In the end though, Strydom made their decision easy. He was simply outclassed. A narrow back, which had always been a problem with his physique, caused him to vanish in a lineup featuring the likes of Wheeler, Coleman and Matarazzo. More importantly, the world-class definition he had brought to a number of contests was absent. Having suffered the worst defeat of his career, Strydom promptly went back into retirement. After a full decade had passed he emerged once more, at the 2006 IFBB Colorado Pro contest, and at 46 years of age finished a respectable seventh. Afterward he retired for a third and (possibly) final time, making his WBF adventure the uncontested high point of his career.

Meanwhile, in some cases the once-mighty had truly fallen. Berry DeMey's last IFBB contest before joining the WBF was a third-place finish at the 1988 Mr. Olympia. At the 1994 Schwarzenegger Classic DeMey finished in 15th. He called it quits for good after that. Mike Christian, who also once finished in the top three of an Olympia, apparently figured that a return wouldn't be worth the time, money and effort. He and Vince Comerford never returned to competition. The remainder of the former WBF talent pool struggled their ways into a slew of bottom-half placings at second-tier competitions, and none won contest prizes that equaled the fines they paid to return.

It's tempting to conclude that the WBF effectively ruined the competitive careers of everyone who signed on with it. However, considering the depth and quality of talent unleashed upon the bodybuilding world in the first half of the 1990s, those who joined the WBF might consider themselves lucky to have made such a good living from it for a couple of years. Few bodybuilders are able to financially break even from their competitive endeavors. To have enjoyed the lifestyle and income of a professional athlete was for most of the BodyStars a once-in-a-lifetime experience. Gary Strydom made far more money in the WBF than he could have in the IFBB.

As for Berry DeMey, the contract offered to him by Vince McMahon early in 1991 was a godsend. He had torn his right pectoral muscle after the 1988 Mr. Olympia contest, missed the next two Olympias, and was thought by many to have been tempted into retirement by the injury. Considering that the level of competition in the IFBB was about to rise significantly, he was almost certainly better off going out with Titan Sports paychecks in his account. The lone exception was Aaron Baker, who was still able to consistently place reasonably well in IFBB shows for another six years. The WBF did not end his competitive career, though it almost certainly hindered it. The remainder of the WBF talent pool soon called it quits.

* * * * *

Today, the rise and fall of the WBF is mainly remembered—when it's remembered at all—as a one-off effort by a famous wrestling promoter with big bucks, zany ideas and inferior talent. In the minds of those who ponder the history of bodybuilding, it's rarely recognized as being anything other than footnote-worthy. Nevertheless, the opposite is true. Although the events surrounding the swift invention and sudden collapse of Vince McMahon's professional bodybuilding venture were heavily influenced by the financial ambitions of its major players, the end result revealed far more than who was willing to spend what. Before the WBF came along, there was a disconnect between Joe Weider's perceptions and reality. McMahon's blitzkrieg shocked him out of his dream.

Weider's decision to eliminate drugs from bodybuilding would quite inadvertently trigger a sequence of events that would result in a completely opposite effect. Once those events had run their course, drug-testing would be dropped and bodybuilders would be more chemically-enhanced than ever. Bodybuilding as a whole would be no closer to public acceptance than in the days when the covers of bodybuilding magazines pictured nude men wearing fig leafs.

Weider and McMahon were both led astray by hope and greed. Both had ideas about how to make bodybuilding truly big, and both were willing to gamble on untested ideas. McMahon had the luxury of being able to lose interest in muscle contests and return to his established, mega-profit wrestling venture. Weider had the luxury of having his new rival fail miserably. He might have been bludgeoned into obscurity had McMahon only copied the formula that fans wanted—and had George Zahorian not gotten caught selling steroids to the WWF.

Although bodybuilding competition had always appeared strange to the general public, there was most certainly a method to its madness. The decorum lecture given to judges and photographers prior to the church-quiet prejudging of the 1975 Mr. Olympia contest revealed this to the world in *Pumping Iron*. The film's narration explained the criteria of physique judging while studious and serious-looking judges thoughtfully considered each physique. Prejudging audiences have become far rowdier since the mid-1970s, but fans still favored and expected rigid structure in physique competition.

Bodybuilding fans were on hand to marvel at extremely muscular physiques, but they also wanted a clear-cut methodology for choosing the winner. The structured and methodical rules and procedures for judging physiques in federations like the IFBB and the NPC gave bodybuilding fans a sense that they were witness to something more than just a parade of muscle.

This notion seems to have been completely lost on Vince McMahon, who thought that turning bodybuilders into comic book characters and muscle contests into rock concerts was the key to making bodybuilding big. He was quickly proven wrong but gave no indication that he knew it. Regardless, it became an era of unmasking: gone were the character-propped bodybuilding shows of the WBF; gone was Vince McMahon's pretense of bodybuilding mogul; and gone was Joe Weider's new role of crusader.

In the end, Weider revealed himself to be little more than a businessman masquerading as a champion of goodness. McMahon's venture turned out to be a giant bluff, though even McMahon himself didn't know it. Weider certainly didn't know it, and he folded. Fearful of the WBF's potential to continue stealing his stars—the people whose images Weider relied on to sells magazines and supplements—and correctly fearing that his fan base would opt to show more interest in chemically-enhanced physiques, he pulled the plug on his healthy-lifestyle, drug-free marketing campaign. He hung up his make-believe cape, rolled up his sleeves, and got on with the business of promoting Weider bodybuilding, in all its forms. Before the next year passed he was heralding the arrival of a new champion, a man whose physique smashed through what was supposed to be the limits of human muscularity—and this was just the beginning of a new era.

Joe Weider may have believed in promoting a healthy lifestyle, but he definitely believed in money. His bold declarations of the recent past about drug use in bodybuilding were swept under the rug, and he proceeded as if his tough talk, drug-testing, and the WBF had never existed. George Orwell would have found Joe Weider interesting indeed.

Joe Weider is guilty of many things. Regardless of whatever his true motivations may have been, one thing for which he must accept guilt is his attempt to save bodybuilding from itself. What he didn't count on is that bodybuilding didn't want to be saved. Above all, individual bodybuilders certainly didn't want to be saved from themselves. To understand this, all one need do is observe the large numbers of them who have no interest in competing but who use steroids anyway.

Nevertheless, a large number of users are competitive bodybuilders. After the Olympic goal was hatched and before the WBF threat emerged, there opened a wide chasm between the aspirations of that group and those of Joe Weider. His plan was to vastly expand his empire by cleaning up bodybuilding and selling it, in its wholesome and repackaged glory, to the rest of the world. His minions meanwhile wanted merely to succeed within its existing framework. They wanted to follow in the footsteps of Arnold Schwarzenegger. Though his goal was to gain multitudes of new constituents, to conquer new territory, Weider was instead forced to quell unrest within his own domain. At least at first, he incorrectly judged the security of his overlordship, the loyalty of his subjects, their willingness to forgo the use of chemicals, the tastes of bodybuilding fans, and the potential interest level of the general public.

The immense popularity of Schwarzenegger during that era should have given him clues about at least some of this. It cannot be denied that the rapid growth of bodybuilding correlated directly to the success of Schwarzenegger's action movies. Bodybuilding's all-time greatest marketing tool was a man who had clearly benefited from—and freely admitted to—steroid use. A lot of people got into bodybuilding because they wanted a physique like Arnold's. On one hand was witnessed the enthusiastic marketing of a man whom the bulk of bodybuilders aspired to emulate. On the other were warnings that to do so would result in punishment or expulsion. This policy was understandably met with confusion, frustration and resentment.

The mixed messages were everywhere, and in some instances these were rather blatant. In the very same issue of *Muscle & Fitness* where Weider declared that the IFBB would not put up with steroid use, there was a 24-page spread covering the 1985 Mr. Olympia contest. The top six competitors were as follows, in order: Lee Haney; Albert Beckles; Rich Gaspari; Mohammed Makkawy; Mike Christian; Berry DeMey. In addition to the fantastic assortment of full-color photos, the accompanying article praised the level of muscular mass, definition and hardness each was able to attain. They all possessed amazing physiques, and all had mass and conditioning significantly beyond what can be achieved without the use of drugs. After all, in 1985, these were the top six bodybuilders in the world.

For those who aspired to possess such a physique but who liked the anti-drug stance, Weider himself offered a solution: Weider-brand supplements that were implied to be as effective as anabolic steroids. This appeased at least a fraction of the confused crowd, but the appeasement lasted only until the same group realized the supplements didn't work. Weider was taken to court over these claims, exposed as a fraud, and forced to pay back money he had bilked from his customers. It was a hopelessly shortsighted strategy, a shabby attempt to steer bodybuilders away from drugs while making a few dishonest bucks, and it failed. The specter of drugs remained.

The reality of the situation was far more simple than what the Weiders had supposed. Promotional rhetoric about the new-age, healthy lifestyle that had become an ongoing theme in *Muscle & Fitness*—which projected bodybuilding as its nucleus and promised a clean and fit public image—had fallen wide of the mark. Most bodybuilders didn't care to look at natural physiques, they wanted to get huge, they weren't concerned about their health, and they were ready, willing, and able to jump ship if something better than the IFBB came along. The days of Physical Culture had long-since passed. In its real-world manifestation, and by definition, the bodybuilding lifestyle is constructed around the goal of muscular enhancement, not increased health. Granted, there are those who perform bodybuilding training as part of an overall health and fitness program. However, these are the types of people who normally have, at most, a passing interest in bodybuilding competition. This is not the hardcore crowd.

What ultimately saved Weider and his corporation was the strength of the foundation he had established over the prior few decades, the tradition of excellence in his champions, and his willingness to return to a tried-and-true formula. This was enough to make good his recent miscalculations. Of equal importance were the perceptions and ideas of Vince McMahon, which turned out to be far worse than his own.

In what was to be a giant learning experience, it was made clear that although bodybuilding is capable of sustaining a loyal following, it would not be perceived by the outside world as anything more than an unusual pastime—not in the near future, and maybe not ever. The International Olympic Committee, mainstream news sources and the great bulk of the general population remains unconvinced that bodybuilding is a real sport. Nothing Joe Weider or anyone else said or did was able to change that. Bodybuilding would continue to proclaim its status as a sport, but this would count for little. Like a tree falling in the middle of a vast forest, nobody on the outside would hear it. With no credibility as a sport, and no Olympic presence, bodybuilding would remain insular.

Once this was realized, consciously or otherwise, the evolution of bodybuilding was allowed to resume. This accorded well with a big part of bodybuilding's fan base, who didn't share Weider's Olympic dream. It didn't want a return to the days of Steve Reeves. It wanted to behold ultra-muscularity. It wanted no less than a freak show. That particular group was about to get its wish. Bodybuilding was about to get so freaky that concerns over the degree of its transformation would become commonplace; so drug-infested that a number of bodybuilders would soon find their find their ways into prison; and so unhealthy that, in their quest to attain the ultimate physique, a few would actually drop dead.

Before long the smoke cleared. Vince McMahon stepped over the pile of ashes that had been the WBF and got on with the business of promoting professional wrestling, something he understands and is good at. He never looked back. With his WWF (and later WWE) leading the charge, wrestling would continue to dwarf bodybuilding events, in attendance and especially television viewership. Joe Weider meanwhile regained his position as unchallenged overlord of bodybuilding. However, his long reign was approaching its final decade. Aging, and maybe having seen enough of what he had helped bodybuilding become, the new millennium would see him sell his magazines to publishing giant American Media. As for the IFBB, it would most certainly put up with steroid use. It rolled out the red carpet for it.

The 1990s

The rise and fall of the World Bodybuilding Federation was but the opening act of a decade that would become one bodybuilding's most important. While the episode was characterized by upheaval and much bad noise, it did produce a simple, significant outcome: there would be no turning back of the clock. Bodybuilding and science would continue their waltz through weight rooms and across posing platforms and onto the pages of muscle magazines. Because of this, the 1990s became as critical to bodybuilding's evolution as the 1960s: it was during these two decades that the physiques of top bodybuilders underwent the most dramatic changes. By the time the final decade of the 20th century had run its course, bodybuilding had mainly reached its present state.

1991 saw Lee Haney win his eighth Mr. Olympia title, giving him the record for most wins and bolstering the argument that he was the greatest of all time. As expected, he retired after the competition. Much like the '91 Olympia, the following year's contest attracted special attention, though for a different reason: it would be the first time since 1983 that someone other than Haney would capture bodybuilding's greatest title. Top professionals, weary from fighting over scraps from Haney's table, were lined up and eager for the chance to take his seat.

For 1992, Helsinki, Finland was chosen to host the Olympia. Of the long list of potential locations for the contest, Helsinki was an especially curious choice. Situated in the northeastern corner of the Baltic Sea and occupying the land mass between Scandinavia and northern Russia, for most bodybuilding fans Finland was a remote location. Many would have been hard-pressed to point it out on a map. Although a segment of bodybuilding fans have always been willing to travel long distances, even thousands of miles to see the Olympia, a large local fan base helps to drive up attendance. It's true that Finland and nearby countries have produced a few good bodybuilders over the years, but the region is not known for any such base of fans.

Considering that the Olympia had been held in places like Essen, Pretoria, Gothenburg and Rimini, the decision to stage the event in Helsinki was perhaps not so surprising. The choice of venue on the other hand was rather unusual. A large multi-purpose arena had been booked for the contest; although that wasn't terribly out-of-the-ordinary for a physique contest, the schedule of events for the day was a different story. In what was a first for professional bodybuilding, a hockey game was played between judging rounds. The contest's prejudging was normal enough, but once it ended the audience was quickly ushered out so that the venue's main floor could be removed, exposing the ice rink below. After the game was played, hockey fans were hurried out, the rink was recovered and floor seats were repositioned. All this was done in time for the Mr. Olympia evening show attendees to file back in.

Such an arrangement probably wouldn't have raised eyebrows at a regional AAU contest, but for the 28th installment of the IFBB's greatest event, the bodybuilding-then-hockey-then-bodybuilding format seemed shoddy. In his after-action report for *Flex* magazine, Julian Schmidt cited the unlikely pairing to suggest that Helsinki probably wasn't the best locale for the contest. The quote "we hate bodybuilding" was selected to describe the mood of thousands of Finnish hockey fans who witnessed the strange crowd that came, then left, then came back again.

It was in this location and in front of this crowd that the IFBB was going to crown a new champion for the first time in eight years. This would also be the arena and crowd that would bear witness to the return of Lou Ferrigno. Less than a year prior, Vince McMahon had banked heavily on Ferrigno's return, signing him to what was by far the biggest contract the world of bodybuilding had ever seen. His comeback was highly publicized. The WBF had since vanished, but Ferrigno images were still fresh in the minds of bodybuilding fans. By doing nothing other than welcoming him back, Joe Weider had placed himself in a position to take full advantage of all the comeback publicity. Unfortunately the event itself was in no such position. Had the Olympia been booked for Los Angeles or New York, it could have broken modern attendance records. In Helsinki there was no such chance.

Meanwhile, judges got down to the business of picking a new champion. For northern European bodybuilding fans and those outside the region who had made to the trip to Finland, the contest didn't disappoint. The depth and quality of that year's Olympia field was excellent. Dorian Yates, the previous year's runner-up, was the obvious favorite to take the title. As the owner of a thickly-muscled and rugged-looking physique with excellent definition, a gigantic back and a level of hardness that made it seem as if bullets would bounce off of him, Yates had come as close as anyone to defeating Haney. Now that Haney was gone, the smart money was on Yates going home with a Sandow. At the same time, by no means was a Yates victory a forgone conclusion. He first needed to compare favorably to the likes of Shawn Ray, Lee Labrada, Vince Taylor, Mohammed Benaziza and a host of other top competitors. The man who ended up giving him the most trouble, however, was newcomer Kevin Levrone.

Due to the competitive depth of the pro-qualifying contests, it's often the case that a bodybuilder will earn the privilege of competing as an IFBB professional only after several attempts. The most famous example exists in the personage of Bob Cicherillo, a man who required more than a decade to break into the pro ranks. At his first qualifying event, the 1987 NPC National Champions, he placed a respectable fifth. 13 years and nine national contests later, his goal was finally realized. Although no one who eventually succeeded competed in as many qualifying events or over a greater span of time than Cicherillo, even the best professionals often had to enter two or three national shows before winning. Such was not the case with Levrone. He burst onto the national bodybuilding scene with a physique of such high quality and size, with such pleasing lines and long muscle bellies, that he won an invitation to turn professional on his first attempt. Only a year later he was a legitimate threat to take the IFBB's greatest title.

At the prejudging, competitors were situated on tiered platforms, with a stairway down the middle. When called out for comparison, a competitor made his way down the stairway and onto the main stage floor. The tiered arrangement allowed the judges to get a good look at the entire field, something which isn't always the case at bodybuilding contests, even at the highest levels. Added to the front-runners Yates, Levrone, Benaziza, Ray and Labrada was an array of great physiques, all positioned in good view of the audience: Ron Love, Francis Benfatto, Porter Cottrell, and several others. Within the group was Samir Bannout, back for another try at reclaiming the title he won in 1983. Unfortunately for Bannout, next to the bodybuilders of the 90s he looked outclassed. In spite of the confidence projected by his trademark beaming smile, he did not factor into the fight for the 1992 title. His unusual choice of baby-blue coloration for his posing suit didn't help, and he eventually tied for last place with six other competitors.

For Bannout, '92 would be one of his last attempts to win the Mr. Olympia title. Of the remaining bottom six, for one man it would be his first. Throughout most of the prejudging, on the top tier stood a little-known, tired and dejected-looking new pro named Ronnie Coleman. He was out of his league and he knew it. The show was barely underway, but Coleman already looked beaten. However, the world had not seen the last of him.

Kevin Levrone. c. 1999

Courtesy of David Moore

One man bodybuilding fans had thought they had seen the last of was Lou Ferrigno. The minute the Olympia competitors filed onto the prejudging stage that day, those same fans were delighted to have been proven wrong. For the first time since he had held Arnold Schwarzenegger's hand up in victory at the 1975 Mr. Olympia, Ferrigno was in a real-live bodybuilding show. Fans, judges and even some of his fellow competitors were thrilled to finally see him back in shape, and back in action. If Ferrigno was determined to give a definitive account of himself on that day, he succeeded.

The *Pumping Iron* version of the same physique was a tad smooth and pale. In his 1992 return Ferrigno left no stone unturned. He showed up in the best shape of his life—bigger, harder, and more defined than in the past. From the moment he struck his first double-biceps pose he had, at long last, proved that he was capable of much more than what he had achieved in 1975. He instantly became a living tribute to himself, and the fans loved it. The modern-era Ferrigno was clearly better than the Golden Age one. Being competitive in the new era was another matter however. There was an entire field of world-class bodybuilders for judges to place, and before long it became clear that several men would finish ahead of him.

Since Yates and Levrone had never competed against each other, their side-by-side comparisons marked the high point of the contest. Levrone was the owner of better lines, deeper cuts and a smaller waist. Yates was bigger, harder-looking and taller. Of the entire field he most closely fit what had become the expected profile of a Mr. Olympia physique. Except for the years between Schwarzenegger and Haney, Mr. Olympias were specimens of stunning, herculean muscularity rather than fine lines and graceful symmetry.

The IFBB and its judges seemed quite interested in finding a man who fit that bill to carry the Olympia torch. Gary Strydom was at one time thought to be the next Mr. Olympia, but his physique had too many flaws. In a few of his mandatory poses Strydom looked no better than average. This wouldn't have been good enough. A Mr. Olympia needed to look dominating in most if not all of the required poses. Dorian Yates possessed such a physique. At five-foot-ten—slightly tall by bodybuilding standards—Yates appeared to tower over the closest of his rivals. Lou Ferrigno of course towered over everyone, but as the prejudging wore on it seemed evident that he was more of a curiosity than a threat to take the title or even break into the top six. Yates was the man to beat. No one was more thickly-muscled or better conditioned.

The 1992 Olympia therefore became a fight for lower placings. In particular third place was hotly contested, since both Shawn Ray and Lee Labrada had shown up in the best shape of their careers. Although Ray appeared to have a slight advantage in muscularity, shape, definition and hardness, Labrada was declared to be superior. Ray settled for fourth. Fifth place went to Mohammed Benaziza. Since turning professional in 1987, Benaziza had gone on an absolute tear, winning six IFBB contests and placing in the top five in nine others. A fan favorite who was much-liked by fellow competitors, height was the only factor that kept him from legitimately threatening the title. Although Kevin Levrone had made a spectacular debut, Dorian Yates was determined by to be the appropriate successor to Lee Haney. He was handed the '92 Sandow award, and with that, for the first time in more than a decade bodybuilding again had a white champion.

By winning the greatest title in existence, Yates was indeed bodybuilding's champion. Because of that, he also became a divisive figure. Yates had dominating mass and incredible hardness, but those attributes were not without compromise. He also possessed a rather thick midsection that by itself destroyed any pretense of Classical aesthetic appeal.

Dorian Yates. c. 1995

Courtesy of David Moore

While the color of Yates' skin was thought by some to be the true reason behind his victories, IFBB judging panels had much ground to declare otherwise—including what had become the all-important factor of precedent.

Yates defeated opponents in a fashion quite similar to Franco Columbu: both men possessed torsos with world-beating thickness and muscularity, and both had back development that far exceeded that of their competition. Yates meanwhile didn't have to use muscularity to make up for a height disadvantage. He was taller than most competitors. His limbs were also considerably more developed that Columbu's, especially his legs. Most importantly, the Olympia had a long history of rewarding beast over beauty. Columbu was a beast. As the 1990s got underway, Yates was the greatest beast yet seen.

The IFBB once more proved its consistency. Precedent was observed. After the upheaval of the '80 and '81 Olympias, this was important. Although precedent worked again Kevin Levrone at the '92 Olympia, the rookie sensation left the stage satisfied. He had gone from virtual unknown to world's second-best in just over two years. Almost out of nowhere, he promised to be a force to be reckoned with for a long time to come.

For the first time in its 28-year history, the Olympia was won by a man who resided outside the United States. This became part of Yates' appeal. His physique, method of operation and life story all together painted a picture of a tough, gritty, working-class Brit. He was very much the antithesis of the decades-old bodybuilding image: the tanned and smiling muscle-god who trained at Gold's gym in Venice and frolicked on beaches in southern California with beautiful women in bikinis. Yates' magazine image was something completely different, and it was also more honestly portrayed. He was a mover of heavy iron. He trained at a "dungeon" gym in Birmingham, an industrial city in central England known for urban blight, bleak skies and Black Sabbath. The equipment he used was old and simple but functional. The walls of his gym had few mirrors. Most pictures of him were in black and white. He was stoic, almost quiet.

In a way Yates therefore possessed a bit of the mythical aura that was wanted for Olympia champions. Between contests he would descend into his dungeon. Beyond its walls could be heard the sounds of creaking steel, slamming iron, and echoes of loud shouting with occasional gasps of agony. Reports of his progress would trickle out, along with intermittent photographs, previews of what the world could expect to have unleashed upon it come contest day. On its eve, the dungeon doors would fling open and out would march the King, a one-man wrecking machine, ready to brush aside all those who stood before him. Of course no one thought this to be a literal reality, but the mention of Yates did conjure such visions; and these images were more fact than fiction. He was the owner of a phenomenal physique, but he was also mysterious. His nickname of "The Shadow"—so called because his immense size was thought to throw a shadow over his competitors—could only add to this air of mystery.

Schwarzenegger certainly had a mythical aura, though it was of a much different hue. He *was* the guy in Venice who frolicked with beautiful women on the beach. He was just the best at it. His aura also came from his accent, his confidence, his charisma, and the impression of Teutonic invincibility that he crafted into an important weapon. In his day, Sergio Oliva's mythical aura was based mainly and simply on his otherworldly physique. His signature hands-over-head arm pose from 1972 remains to this day one of the most impressive sights ever witnessed in bodybuilding. Above all, Oliva's nickname was "The Myth." Lee Haney had an aura, though it stemmed more from his untouchability than anything else. He lived in Georgia, was raising a family, espoused Christian values, and seemed genuinely gregarious. He was an open book. There was no mystery to him. He just happened to be the best bodybuilder of his era. After only his first victory Yates seemed a worthy addition to this list of greats.

The crowning of a new champion was the big story heading into the 1992 Mr. Olympia. The next-biggest was the return of Lou Ferrigno. Although he had given a good account of himself, in the end Ferrigno placed a disappointing 12th. The most highly anticipated comeback in the history of bodybuilding had come and gone. Fans loved having him back, but his return clearly hadn't lived up to the hype. With the Ferrigno comeback in the books, the final page had also now been written on Vince McMahon's WBF adventure. McMahon had badly overestimated the potential of bodybuilding's appeal. By signing Ferrigno to a monster deal, he showed that the Incredible Hulk's return had been overestimated too. Ferrigno defeated the lower end of the lineup, a cast that included no one better than Alq' Gurley, Henderson Thorne and Francis Benfatto. This did not however stop Ferrigno from declaring that in his present condition that he would have beaten the 1975 version of Schwarzenegger. It was a final reminder that Ferrigno mainly came to do battle with the ghosts of the '75 Olympia.

Meanwhile, few were aware that above the head of Dorian Yates lingered phantoms of a different sort. These were the ghosts of 1980, the year of Schwarzenegger's infamous comeback. In 1992 Yates was the big winner, but with his victory came some vindication for a man who had long-since disappeared from the competitive bodybuilding scene. Mike Mentzer, who was perhaps the most notable victim of the Schwarzenegger's return and victory, had been advising Yates on his training. Instead of the usual pre-contest bodybuilding routine of spending anywhere from two to four hours per day in the gym, Mentzer had Yates using a variation of his high-intensity training, a method which called for short bouts of extremely intense exercise. In preparation for the Olympia, Yates reported to be training with weights a mere three and a half hours per week. The results were beyond dispute, Mike Mentzer once more became a topic of conversation in bodybuilding circles, and his personal training business got a gigantic boost.

Having lost all faith in judging practices after the 1980 Olympia, Mentzer quit bodybuilding at the zenith of his career. He never returned to competition, but through Dorian Yates his advocacy of high-intensity training, the centerpiece of his life's work, became much better known. Mentzer died in 2001 of heart failure, but he went to his grave knowing that the unusual and controversial style of training he promoted—the same one Arnold Schwarzenegger declared to be a farce—had produced a world champion.

In the fall of 1992, onstage at a hockey rink in southern Finland, that champion was crowned. Joe Weider hung a Gold Medal was around his neck, gave him a Sandow trophy, and held his arm up in victory. The crowd cheered, the Mr. Olympia theme music was cued and the evening came to an end. Dorian Yates was the new Mr. Olympia. Most of the remaining field swore to come back bigger and better. Shawn Ray complained about his placing while Lou Ferrigno resolved to give it another go. After the audience left, the stage was torn down and the arena was made ready for the next game. Bodybuilding's greatest show packed up and left town. It would be the last time the Mr. Olympia contest was ever held outside the United States.

* * * * *

The 1990s became one of bodybuilding's most important eras. Those years formed a bridge between the optimistic, burgeoning and naïve '80s and the dawn of the new millennium, an era characterized by nearly opposite attributes. The most significant change to take place during the decade was the physical appearance of its top competitors. By the mid-'90s they were bigger than ever, and they continued to grow more massive each year. Bodybuilding continued to gain new fans, but the events of the prior few years all but proved that it would never hit the big time. Changes in the appearance of bodybuilders as the decade wore on insured this.

Beauty truly is in the eye of the beholder—and nowhere is this maxim more true than in the world of muscle contests. Failed attempts to take bodybuilding mainstream revealed two important problems with the idea: few consider it to be a legitimate sport, and many believe it to be a haven for drug use. Meanwhile, there exists a third problem, possibly the most important of them all: a lot of people think bodybuilding is ugly. This is a cold hard fact that members of the muscle subculture often have a difficult time understanding or accepting. According to conventional physical tastes, an ideal male should possess slight-to-moderate levels of muscularity and relatively low body fat levels—an appearance the general public refers to as "toned." Mainstream magazines exalt the bodies of tennis players, swimmers, and even United States President Barak Obama. The "sexiest celebrities" lists are comprised of actors, bicyclists and soccer players, not professional bodybuilders. Bodybuilding certainly has its share of fans, but random-sample surveys show that most people rate extremely muscular physiques as unattractive or worse.

Pure bodybuilding fans tend to steer clear of the term "attractive" when assessing competition physiques, especially when heterosexual men evaluate male competitors. The terms "impressive" or sometimes "pleasing" are substituted. To the general public however, a scantily-clad body—especially one that's fit and deliberately posed—carries sexual connotations. As the 1980s drew to a close, bodybuilders became very scantily-clad indeed.

The posing outfits of the 70s and before resembled Speedo-type swimsuits, but the explosion of bodybuilding in the 80s brought with it a gradual change in style. Competition attire began to shrink. By the end of that decade all competitors were wearing a suit with string-thin sides and minimal coverage elsewhere.

For a few competitors however, minimal was still too much. Before the decade was out a few high-level bodybuilders were pulling much of their suits' rear area into their nether regions, turning conventional posing attire into makeshift thongs—a trend that has refused to die and hasn't been outlawed by the IFBB.[1] Official condonement of the practice contrasts with the vilified "moon" pose—an onstage ploy that was banned by the IFBB and its amateur affiliates in the late 1980s. The pose involves facing the rear of the stage, bending over at the waist and grabbing the ankles. Although the moon pose brings attention to the various muscles of a competitor's lower body, it was deemed crude and offensive.

The IFBB stance on stuffing a posing suit into one's rear end is more forgiving. While the practice was invented to show off highly developed and striated gluteus muscles, its users were now mere square inches of material away from complete nudity. To the public, a body with its rear end almost completely exposed invites of the question of attractiveness, whether it's on a 110-pound bikini model or a 280-pound bodybuilder.

Until the end of the 1990s, such displays were known only in female bodybuilding. Nevertheless, bodybuilders were getting bigger every year—and in the eyes of the public, the bigger they got, the less attractive they became. In the '80s the physiques of top bodybuilders were typically described by their fans as being *massive, symmetrical,* and even *beautiful.* During the same era much of the public described the same physiques using terms like *gross, ugly* or *disgusting*. That same public often perceived bodybuilders and their fans to be mired in narcissism and weirdness; as physiques became more muscular, those opinions intensified. Images of extremely muscular men wearing thong bikinis did nothing to help this.

The physiques bodybuilding had begun to produce may have widened the chasm between its fans and the general public, but by the mid-'90s this point was moot. Bodybuilding no longer had the people of the outside world to worry about. It wasn't going to attract them. "Public acceptance" was a vague goal anyway. Ben Weider would continue to bang his head against a wall trying to get

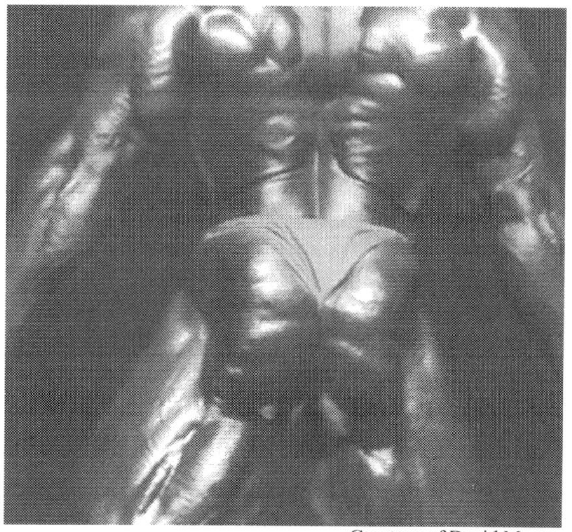

Courtesy of David Moore

Kai Greene. c. 2008

bodybuilding into the Summer Games, but it was never clear how many bodybuilders really cared if that happened. They appeared far more interested in the Olympia than the Olympics.

Public acceptance may have been a vague goal, but to bodybuilding fans, pushing the limits of human muscularity was not. Physiques were getting bigger and freakier, and fans ate it up. For the countless hours Ben Weider devoted trying to get bodybuilding into the Olympics, the visible appreciation he received from fans was altogether dwarfed by a single display of freakiness, in a lone photo spread in one of his brother's magazines.

After the Helsinki Olympia, Dorian Yates chose not to rest on his laurels. He returned to his dungeon gym and got to work forging the 1993 version of his body. Reports from the few bodybuilders and fans who were able to get a glimpse of him that summer suggested that he had already made drastic improvements to the physique that conquered the world of professional bodybuilding in '92. *Flex* photographer Kevin Horton was directed by the magazine and invited by Yates to visit his Birmingham gym and take a few pictures of the champ in his pre-contest condition. Horton obliged the request. He packed his cameras and flew to the UK. He arrived at Yates' gym at the agreed time. Yates disrobed, Horton took a few shots, and twenty minutes later he was out the door and headed back to the US.

The resulting photo spread, published in the December issue of *Flex,* became the most talked-about

[1]Kai Greene and Ronnie Coleman are among the trend's worst offenders.

collection of pictures the world of bodybuilding has ever seen. The cover-page headline advertising "shocking" new photos of Yates was altogether accurate. The biggest and most thickly-muscled man on the planet was now significantly bigger and more muscular. No one had ever seen anything like it. There was not a single photo where Yates didn't look like something from another planet, like some frightening, armor-plated new species. None of his body parts were anything less than amazing. When put together, the physique they created nearly defied description. The issue hit the stands in October, a few weeks before the Mr. Olympia contest.

Elite bodybuilders had been collectively making only gradual increases in overall size since the days of Sergio Oliva's dominance, but that all came to an end a generation later, in the fall of 1993. Once that issue of *Flex* hit the stands, the bodybuilding world knew this to be true. What was unknown to that world was that it was also being given a preview of what bodybuilding had in store for the years ahead. At that moment however, there was no one close to Dorian Yates. Nearly 100 years to the day after Eugen Sandow wowed the world with his first muscle-display performance, there emerged a man whose muscularity was equally ascendant.

Yates' peers were as impressed as his fans. In a subsequent issue, *Flex* even ran an article that documented the reactions of other pro bodybuilders to the images. The photo spread was that sensational. Its release bore similarity to some of the sudden and significant historical events of the outside world: anyone who was a bodybuilding fan at the time remembers where he was when those images were first shown to him. History was being made, and everyone knew it.

A Yates victory at the 1993 Mr. Olympia, to be held in Atlanta, seemed a forgone conclusion. It was like a replay of the recent past: throughout much of the 80s, the dominance of Lee Haney almost made the Olympia boring. It now seemed as though the 90s were shaping up for a similar era of dominance. There was, however, one man with the ability to make things interesting.

* * * * *

The 1990s will forever be remembered as a decade that saw the emergence of several IFBB professionals with truly great physiques. The first couple years had already witnessed the emergence of Dorian Yates and Kevin Levrone, a pair who wasted no time securing the top two spots in the world's greatest contest. Yates won the Olympia on his second try and Levrone was runner-up in his first. In both instances no one has ever done better—and in no other Olympia has this dual feat been accomplished. The 1992 version of the contest was in fact so rich in quality and depth that it added a new complexion to a debate almost as old as bodybuilding itself: Which is the best physique of all time?

In the mid-1980s it was popular to compare the best-ever build of retired legend Arnold Schwarzenegger to that of current world champion Lee Haney. Haney was pound-for-pound the larger competitor, though Schwarzenegger was thought to look better in certain poses. Schwarzenegger also had seven Olympia titles under his belt while Haney by that time only had a few—something that was imagined to be an advantage in a straightforward comparison of muscle. Regardless, Schwarzenegger was thought to possess irresistible charisma and a certain *je ne se qua* that would carry to him victory over any other competitor. Although this argument was not universally bought, especially by those who hadn't witnessed the 1980 Olympia, it was soon moot.

The '92 Olympia mercifully killed the Arnold-versus-Haney debate. There were now too many other great bodybuilders worthy of consideration, Dorian Yates being chief among these. Yet another name had recently been added to the discussion. Among the new wave of IFBB professionals one man truly stood out; like Yates, his build was otherworldly, though it seemed to be from an entirely different part of the Universe. His transition from amateur to professional ranks was much hyped, yet he lived up to every bit of it. The best-bodybuilder-of-all-time debate may indeed go on until the end of the world, but to some fans the issue has been decided; and the quest to find the ultimate physique has ended. From the very moment he was handed a pro card many believed the owner of that physique was a man named Flex Wheeler.

Kenneth Wheeler, as his 1965 birth certificate reads, was the latest member of the steady parade of phenomenal physiques that became professional in the 1990s. His turn came in 1992, when he won the overall title at the NPC USA Championships. At 5-foot-9, Wheeler's height was slightly above average for a bodybuilder. Nothing else about him warranted that description. Despite having a frame composed of exceptionally small-diametered bones—the trademark of lightly-muscled "ectomorphic" body types—he was able to pack on an astonishing amount of mass. The result was a physique of billowing muscles and flowing lines the likes of which the world had never seen, before or since. His light frame brought with it a particularly small waist; when combined with his characteristic sharp definition, Wheeler's 235 pounds looked like far more. The size ratio of his upper arms to that of his midsection—possibly the most critical attribute of an impressive physique—was unrivaled.

In his IFBB professional debut, the 1993 Iron Man contest, Wheeler won easily. A victory at the Schwarzenegger Classic came next. No one had ever won his first two professional competitions; nor had any new professional generated so much press; and most certainly, no one had ever produced a physique like Flex Wheeler's. The few months between the Schwarzenegger Classic and the release of Dorian Yates' *Flex* photo spread issue were therefore filled with doubt and wonder. Wheeler seemed a legitimate threat to make Yates a one-time champion.

Dorian Yates was the first new Mr. Olympia in eight years, yet barely six months after collecting his Sandow trophy all eyes and all momentum were shifted away from him and toward Flex Wheeler. 1992 had turned into a showdown between Yates and Levrone, yet that confrontation hadn't nearly generated the level of pre-contest hype as that which preceded the impending Yates-Wheeler faceoff. Yates had a few advantages: he was bigger, an inch taller, and thicker. The giant slabs of muscle over his torso covered a deep ribcage, which made him appear extra-thick in side shots. His back and calves were also far superior to those of his competitors. In any lineup he stood out. Finally, Yates was the reigning Mr. Olympia. Because of this, judges would be reluctant to unseat him; and since he hadn't competed since the last Olympia, he would be well rested.

Flex Wheeler, c. 1993

Courtesy of David Moore

Wheeler meanwhile had a combination of graceful shape and bulging muscles that seemed to leap off of his frame when he flexed them. It was a combination of strengths that had never truly been witnessed. Bodybuilders tend to have one or the other. Men known for their shape—competitors like Frank Zane, Bob Paris and Lee Labrada—as a rule do not possess the muscles-on-top-of-muscles look that characterized the physiques of men like Bertil Fox and Albert Beckles. Fox and Beckles were known for stunning muscularity but not elegant form. Wheeler incredibly had both attributes. Together they gave him a physique with excellent shape, amazing mass, and separation so deep he almost looked like something out of a comic book. His presentation skills were better than Yates, though this would likely account for little. Yates presented himself effectively and competently, which was good enough.

Battle lines having been drawn, fans prepared for something not usually seen: a closely-contested Olympia. Such was the feeling as the countdown to that event wore on. Such was the feeling, until of course the December issue of *Flex* magazine hit the newsstands. Photographer Kevin Horton recalled his thoughts upon seeing Yates disrobe and strike poses that day in his Birmingham gym: "F—ing hell. They don't stand a f—ing chance against that." His sentiments were echoed by the multitude that finally saw the images in print.

Thus, with a single stroke, momentum veered sharply back to Yates. The psychological value and impact of anticipation was advertised by Arnold Schwarzenegger in *Pumping Iron* when he declared that his superior power of persuasion would ensure victory over Lou Ferrigno. After his ill-intentioned counseling, Schwarzenegger boasted, Ferrigno would be "ready to lose." In 1993, a far more real anticipation consumed the visions of IFBB competitors and officials. After all, the Yates piece in *Flex* was more than a simple photo spread. It was a demonstration of complete dominance.

* * * * *

With the *Flex* issue stirring the bodybuilding community and leaning hard against the objectivity of IFBB judges, eager fans swarmed into the Atlanta auditorium that played host to the 1993 Mr. Olympia. In addition to Yates and Wheeler, a fantastic array of physiques were ready to unveil their latest incarnations. Among them were the previous year's other top finishers: Levrone, Labrada and Ray. Ferrigno, who knew he still had more in the tank, was present as well.

Before long it became obvious that the event's top six placings would differ significantly from '92. Wheeler wasn't the only rookie with the potential to do serious damage in his Olympia debut. Joining him was another first-timer, a Canadian behemoth named Paul Dillett. At 6-foot-3 and 285 pounds, on paper Dillett was comparable to Ferrigno. However, Dillett appeared far more massive—with Yates-like size at nearly a half-foot taller. His gargantuan build and stern demeanor gave him an intimidating, almost frightening presence. In a pound-for-pound contest of muscle Dillett probably would have beaten anyone, but a subpar back and terrible presentation skills threatened to limit him in a field of polished and complete bodybuilders. Nevertheless, with his size and condition it would be difficult for judges to keep him out of the top six.

Another change in the event's final placings also now seemed likely. A mere five months before the Olympia, Kevin Levrone suffered a complete tear of his right pectoral muscle. Although it had become normal in bodybuilding to leave torn muscles unfixed,[1] Levrone prudently opted to get the immediate surgery required to return the muscle to a near-original state. Considering the injury and surgery, few expected him to materialize. Regardless, he was in the lineup.

Courtesy of David Moore

Paul Dillett. c. 1993

Two men from the previous year's top six were not present. Vince Taylor sat out the event, while Mohammed Benaziza was no longer among the living. He met his end in a hotel room in an obscure town in the Netherlands, shortly after the final Grand Prix contest that followed the 1992 Olympia. In what turned out to be a pre-contest appearance-tuning regimen gone horribly wrong, he had accidentally dehydrated himself to death. As shocking as this revelation may have been to members of the general public who learned of it, the reaction of the bodybuilding world—though mournful and somber—didn't exceed surprise. They knew that there was method to Benaziza's madness, and that with the rising standards of physique competition, pre-contest rituals were becoming more and more hazardous.

Bodybuilding had come a long way since the days of Bernarr Macfadden and the Physical Culturalists. Rather than immersing themselves in a lifestyle that aimed to enhance normal physiological functions, modern bodybuilders began performing rituals that were designed to combat them. In this spirit, before

[1]The combination of heavy weights, lengthy workouts and growth-inducing chemicals has resulted in a large number of muscle tears among bodybuilding's elite. Top competitors who have over the years joined this club include Lee Priest, Johnny Fuller, Tom Platz, Rich Gaspari, Francis Benfatto, Alex Federov, Milos Sarcev, Jean-Pierre Fux, Shaun Crump, Toney Freeman, Adorthus Cherry, Branch Warren, Markus Ruhl, Ronnie Coleman and Chris Dickerson. Although he did not perform lengthy workouts, Dorian Yates also suffered muscle tears. He attributed this to his decision to ignore the minor injuries that preceded major ones.

contests bodybuilders regularly declare war on the largest organ in the human body: the skin that envelops it.

Human skin has several purposes, one of these being water storage. Although it's an extremely useful physiological function, water storage is also the worst enemy of bodybuilders on contest day. Just like the layer of fat that bodybuilders spend patient months stripping from their bodies, subcutaneous water blurs definition and hides muscular hardness. Competitors have therefore been known to rely on any number of methods to dehydrate themselves—most notably water restriction and the use of diuretic drugs—so that they might appear "dry" on contest day. The problem is that any warm-blooded animal can only withstand a certain level of dehydration before being overwhelmed with sickness, or in the worst of cases, death. The trick with bodybuilding pre-contest dehydration is to lose as much subcutaneous water as possible without precipitating either.

In this bodybuilders have not always been successful. There have been numerous instances at all levels of competition of bodybuilders becoming critically ill because of severe dehydration techniques. In nearly all cases, paramedics are summoned, IV fluids are administered, the competitor is saved, and the unfortunate event is chalked up to experience. Benaziza's case was different. He appeared visibly ill throughout the day on which he eventually died but was nevertheless able to maintain consciousness. He was also reported to have turned down several offers of medical care. Meanwhile, the clock was ticking. Benaziza was unaware that the abuse being inflicted upon his body was about to reach its limit. As the Dutch Grand Prix show went through its paces, every pose he struck brought him closer to it.

Benaziza made it through the contest and shortly thereafter returned to the hotel that housed federation staff and competitors. There, in his room, he finally collapsed. New IFBB pro and fellow competitor Porter Cottrell, a career firefighter and trained paramedic, was quickly summoned to his room, where he found Benaziza in a state of full cardiac arrest. Although Cottrell did everything in his power to resuscitate him, the dehydration ritual had been too severe and it had gone on for too long. At approximately 6:00pm on October 4th, 1992, in that hotel room, Benaziza died. He was 32 years old. Incidentally, he won the contest.

The episode was without precedent. Bodybuilding's uppermost tier had suffered a tragedy that was directly caused by contest preparation. What made the incident even worse was that it involved limited consequence. At the 1993 Olympia, the death of Mohammed Benaziza had but a single practical effect: the fifth-place spot from the previous year was left vacant. With a formidable competitor removed from the lineup, most of the Olympia field was given a chance to move forward in the placings. With the arrival of new phenoms Wheeler and Dillett, this fact became more significant. It may have been grim and terrible to find a silver lining in the death of a competitor, but such was the scratch-and-claw world of professional bodybuilding for the majority of its members throughout the 1990s and beyond.

For the third straight year, that world was about to push its level of competition to a new height. From the moment the '93 Olympia field filed onstage for prejudging, this much was obvious. Among the almost bewildering array of top-quality physiques, Yates and Wheeler were scrutinized most closely. For the better part of a year bodybuilding fans had been waiting to see the two, side-by-side, being matched pose-for-pose. The judging panel, being fans themselves, quickly ended the suspense. The two were called out early for comparisons. Wheeler without question had the more aesthetically-pleasing physique, but Yates was bigger, thicker and harder. This was especially so in back poses.

At the time of his *Flex* magazine photo shoot, Yates weighed 269 pounds. The furor caused by those shots had everything to do with him shattering the perceived limits of human muscularity. Yet what truly made the images so amazing was the definition Yates possessed at that weight.[1] In the *Flex* spread, he looked nearly ready to step onstage. When contest day arrived, a 257-pound version of the same physique was unveiled. With the subtraction of those 12 pounds, every last bit of unnecessary tissue and water had vanished.

Yates thus brought to the Olympia stage world-class definition and hardness combined with barrier-shattering size. A package like that simply could not be denied, no matter how wonderful the

[1]The photo shoot was a faint reminder of Eugen Sandow's unveiling. Even though Yates was more than 80 pounds heavier than bodybuilding's originator, it was the level of definition each man displayed that made their images most remarkable.

proportions of his nearest rival may be. It therefore appeared that the contest was all but over only minutes after it had gotten underway. Yates and Wheeler looked certain to finish first and second respectively. Lee Labrada and Shawn Ray once more appeared locked in a battle for third place.

The previous year's runner-up Kevin Levrone was the contest's most important unknown variable. If Yates had never taken up weights, in 1993 Levrone would be the reigning Mr. Olympia. However, his recent pec tear promised to impact his appearance and threatened to drop him from contention. Yet few took into account that Levrone was out to show his body who's boss. His recovery and return to serious training is permanent testimony to the power of medical science and the might of his own will. In five short months he had gone from world-class bodybuilder to major injury victim to patient to convalescent—and then back to world-class bodybuilder again.

Levrone wasn't just back in the lineup. He was back in the lineup, and he was good. At the same time, this was the Mr. Olympia contest. Five months hadn't been quite enough time to get back to top form. Levrone was at least as massive as the previous year, but the ultra-sharp lines that characterized his recent form weren't quite in order. Although it was clear that he deserved to finish somewhere near the top, there were too many other great competitors in career-best shape for him to repeat as runner-up. By allowing his condition to regress, Levrone was nearly assured a lower placing than in '92.

Paul Dillett was the contest's other major unknown variable. Although he lived up to his reputation for being a bad poser, his enormous and detailed physique promised to keep him in front of most of the field. Within that field and not far behind was another group of outstanding physiques. Among them were Charles Clairmonte, Sonny Schmidt and Andreas Munzer. That bodybuilders of such high quality looked unable to crack the top six spoke volumes about the rising level and depth of the IFBB's ranks.

Munzer especially was a fan favorite, due in large part to the extreme definition which characterized his build. He displayed muscular striations of unmatched depth and sharpness. Unfortunately for him, the overall lines of his physique were no match for bodybuilding's top tier. With the shape of a Bob Paris or Mohammed Makkawy, Munzer would have been a certain threat to take the Olympia title.

Among this second-tier group was Lou Ferrigno. After his 1992 comeback, Ferrigno apparently felt that he still had unfinished business. Besting his '75 form had not left him fully satisfied, especially since his recent condition had only been good enough for a 12th place finish. He was out to improve upon that; by doing so he would also treat an American audience to an encore performance of bodybuilding's most highly anticipated comeback. The moment he stepped onstage it became clear that he had done his homework. Ferrigno was bigger and harder than the previous year, so it was likely he would move up in the placings. A top-ten finish would be a minor victory and it would make good press, so he may have privately hoped for little more than that. Judges appeared willing to oblige.

In the end, that's exactly where Ferrigno wound up. He smiled, waved, shook Joe Weider's hand, and bowed his head so that the top-ten medal could be placed around his neck. A bodybuilding audience had never cheered so loudly for a 10th-place contestant. Similar medals were next presented to Munzer, Schmidt and Clairmonte. Kevin Levrone may have torn his pec a month too late, but in the end his combination of mass, balance, extraordinary lines and competent presentation were too much for Paul Dillett. The pair finished fifth and sixth, respectively. The image of the relatively small but shapely and polished Lee Labrada standing next to the gigantic Dillett, whom he had just beaten, reminded fans that bodybuilding was still about more than just sheer size.

Meanwhile, the hair-splitting that had produced the three-four finish of Labrada-Shawn Ray in 1992 created an opposite result in '93. Labrada was given the fourth-place medal and Ray the third. Ray appeared visibly upset by the announcement, which suggested he thought he was better than Flex Wheeler, or Dorian Yates, or both. Nevertheless, Ray and Wheeler enjoyed a protracted embrace, with Wheeler offering words of support and condolence. It was now he and Yates who were left standing. The bodybuilding world waited and watched, but expected no surprises. They were not given one. Wheeler was announced as runner-up, and again Dorian Yates was Mr. Olympia. Once more Joe Weider's theme music was cued, flash bulbs went off, and fans cheered. At that point in time, some thought it had been the best bodybuilding contest ever held.

The 1993 Mr. Olympia contest produced a result that was significant to the historical progression of bodybuilding, the fourth in a row to earn this distinction. At the contest, size was once more rewarded over shape. Yates had overwhelming mass, and this was enough to carry him to victory over those who finished in places two-through-five, all of whom had far more aesthetically-pleasing lines. By winning, Yates also demonstrated that he would be no one-off champion like Chris Dickerson or Samir Bannout. More importantly, he had now brushed aside the greatest of his rivals, in convincing fashion. A mere two victories into his streak there was now little doubt that Yates owned the greatest physique of his era. At least for the foreseeable future he would continue to reign, the only man capable of beating him being the King himself. Most critically, at the '93 Olympia fans had witnessed, onstage and before their eyes, the unveiling of a new standard of muscular mass. The retirement of Lee Haney may have brought with it the next phase of bodybuilding's modern era, but the big jump in size that became the hallmark attribute of that period had its true beginnings in '93.

Finally, that year's contest made far more real the perils of bodybuilding's drug regimens. A top-five finisher from the previous year was conspicuously absent; he met an early end, all because of rituals he performed in pursuit of the ultimate physique. That tragedy inspired a single professional bodybuilder, Steve Brisbois, to call it quits. The remainder of the IFBB's pro ranks were saddened but undeterred. With full knowledge of bodybuilding's risks, they chose to face them head-on. For nearly a third of the 1993 Mr. Olympia's field of contestants it was a fateful decision. Of that group of 21 men, three would soon find themselves at death's door while another three would pass through it.

* * * * *

As a direct result of Mohammed Benaziza's death, the IFBB's Grand Prix concept was overhauled. The one-show-a-week format that filled the post-Olympia schedule had been good for each event's bottom line, but for competitors a full month or more of maintaining peak condition was a merciless grind. In the modern era, achieving top form meant performing hazardous and draining water-reducing rituals. Staging contests only on Saturdays virtually guaranteed large crowds for both the prejudging and evening shows, but every week that went by increased the chances of catastrophe. To reduce the strains placed on bodybuilders that had already resulted in the death of a seven-time Grand Prix winner, the IFBB mandated that the contests would thereafter be much more closely spaced, with only a day or two separating each. The events were scheduled such that the IFBB, with its officials, events staff and competitors were given enough time to check into hotels, make last-minute preparations, stage the contest, pack up their gear, and head to the next city. Pleasantly, the bottom line generated by these events did not dip. Bodybuilding fans didn't care that the show was being held on a Monday or Thursday instead of a Saturday. If the Mr. Olympia lineup was coming to their town, they would be there to see it, come hell or high water.

Benaziza's death had also prompted the IFBB pro division to consider instituting a diuretic testing program. The idea was found viable and tests were first administered in 1996. Unlike the short-lived steroid testing program of 1990, diuretic tests have remained in effect. However, the ability of these tests to stamp out or even deter the use of dehydrating chemical cocktails has been a subject of much dispute.

Meanwhile, diuretic use has certainly remained rampant in the amateur contests of the NPC, which feature no drug-testing at all, and which have witnessed numerous little-known competitors falling ill from dehydration. Most bodybuilding fans never hear of these incidents; and since any drug-testing program is expensive and cumbersome, national or lower-level amateur contests haven't bothered with it. After all, it's the professionals who are scrutinized by the bodybuilding press. Regardless, as '92 drew to a close, the idea of diuretic testing was but one of many things the world of bodybuilding had been left to ponder

The very last contest of 1992 was immediately followed by the death of its winner. Some wondered whether the event might define the years to come. Benaziza'a former peers meanwhile felt secure that a similar fate was not in store for them. Much like the view held by soldiers heading off to war for the first time, getting killed was something that happened to *the other guy*. It was also widely believed that Benaziza's diuretic routine was of an extreme variety. Rumors had him going without water for days at a time—only absorbing whatever happened to be in the foods he ate—all the while taking powerful diuretic pills. If true, it was a testament to his constitution that he hadn't died sooner.

Apart from moments-of-silence held in honor of Benaziza at a few muscle contests, few things had changed. His death gave bodybuilding magazines something controversial to write about and fans plenty to talk about, but the bodybuilding world was ultimately more interested in the emergence of Flex Wheeler and the "shocking" new images of Dorian Yates. It turned out the *Flex* magazine choice of terms was entirely appropriate, since hardcore fans found the Yates photo shoot to be more shocking than Benaziza's dehydration death.

As time wore on there would be more tragedies to ponder, though the reactions of the bodybuilding world varied little for each: some sadness, many condolences, lots of what-went-wrong conjecture, and general acceptance; there were few reactions from the public, since these events were rarely newsworthy. The American public couldn't be expected to care about an unknown Algerian dying in Holland under circumstances they wouldn't understand after a type of competition few knew anything about. Thinking about it in these terms may have precipitated Steve Brisbois' moment of clarity, when he decided that life was about more than bulging muscles, thin skin and double-biceps poses.

Nevertheless, for every Steve Brisbois there were scores of top-level bodybuilders—and many thousands of men who wished to join them—whose pursuit of muscle-contest glory would not be so easily abandoned. Brisbois was a good friend of Benaziza and refused to think of him as an acceptable loss. He withdrew from competition forever, unlike other members of the pro ranks who counted their fallen peer as a friend, and unlike the legions of aspiring competitors who were willing to risk sharing his fate. The group's collective attitude was summed up afterwards by one of its faceless members: "I know he died an unfortunate death, but he sure looked great." It was an opinion easily and sincerely understood by hardcore bodybuilders. To non-bodybuilding fans who knew of it, the event was merely a bizarre tragedy.

Some however did wonder: what it is about bodybuilding that makes these people so willing to risk everything? From the moment it was first invented, bodybuilding became a pool into which a select group of men completely immersed themselves. To them, nothing was more important; it was a passion and a compulsion; it was a way of life and much more. It consumed them and guided their every move. These men later earned for themselves the name "hardcore"; they were characterized by unmatched passion and a willingness to do anything to achieve bodybuilding glory. Yet it wasn't until the 1990s that the world was given an inkling of what that really meant. In what must be regarded as one of its most significant effects, the '90s proved that bodybuilders exhibit a level of dedication exceeding what anyone had imagined. After all, a willingness to risk everything might be thought of as the ultimate expression of dedication.

Yet ultimately it may not have been bodybuilding per se, but rather human nature, that guided these men through the valley of the shadow of death. Competition bodybuilding is but one of many scores of activities man has concocted for himself that carries the potential for disablement or death. For example, the question could be posed: what it is about *big-wave surfing* that makes these people so willing to risk everything? The same question could be asked about mountaineering, skydiving or any number of motor sports. Granted, in all of these activities there are people who participate at a lower level, where the risk of calamity is practically nil. The highest levels however are occupied by those who are willing to stare death in the face. Their answers might include reasons like *the thrill, the rush, the feeling of power,* the *it-lets-you-know-you're-alive* feeling, or similar experiences. For some of these activities, fame and fortune is also a draw.

Through its magazines and contest gatherings bodybuilding has been good at suggesting that its top competitors live lives of fame and fortune. For those at the very highest level, this image is not without some foundation—and for the best of the best, there's a little of both. Lower-tier competitors make incrementally less, and almost all of the amateur ranks—and a fair number of professionals—eventually put more money into bodybuilding than they pull out of it. Most of the time it's little more than an expensive hobby. Although becoming rich through bodybuilding is an attractive notion to all competitors, for the large majority it's little more than fantasy. Many seem to know this, and few cite riches as a reason for devoting their lives to bodybuilding.

Muscle-contest fame is a far more realistic ambition, since even amateurs can get decent coverage in the bodybuilding press. This fame is limited to notoriety within the bodybuilding community however. The new millennium aptly drove home this reality, since at one point the reigning Mr. Olympia and a mediocre NFL quarterback shared the same name of Jay Cutler. Members of the football-centric American public were aware of the Cutler who led his team onto the gridiron on Sundays in the fall; but they had never heard of the bodybuilding world champion with the same name. Yet this fact does not subtract from the efforts of bodybuilders or the lengths to which they'll go in order to win. The bodybuilding pond may be a small one, but it's a pond nevertheless. The drive to be the best in the world at something, no matter what that something is, is enough to elicit an at-all-costs attitude.

After 1992, high-level bodybuilders very much knew what they were getting themselves into. Graphic accounts of Benaziza's final moments were printed in major muscle magazines. In less than two hours he had gone from trophy-holding champion to corpse, his last moments spent convulsing on the floor of a hotel room in a foreign land. Nevertheless, detailed descriptions of his death didn't stop bodybuilders from engaging in potentially deadly dehydration practices.

Less than two years after the Netherlands tragedy Paul Dillett had a near-fatal incident, from similar causes, at the 1994 Schwarzenegger Classic. Since he was in the throes of competition when dehydration overwhelmed him, medical care was immediately available. Dillett was actually onstage posing when his body sent its distress signal: as his last pose was struck, he became the victim of multiple severe cramps. Unable to unflex his muscles, Dillett remained stationary, literally locked in place, and event officials had little choice but to carry his 285-pound hulk offstage in its posed position. In the often strange history of physique competition this stands out as a particularly surreal moment. Scenes like this could never have occurred to Joe Weider when he predicted that bodybuilding would save the world.

On that day, the only thing saved was Dillett. He received proper medical care in a timely manner and lived to fight another day. Had he been alone in a hotel room when dehydration overwhelmed him, the same might not be true. The significance of Dillett's episode was that the IFBB's proposed diuretics-testing program found new urgency. When his competitive career was finally concluded and its story was told however, the event was unimportant. It didn't stop him. His brush with death may have elicited thoughts similar to those of a big-wave rider who comes within seconds of drowning, or to those of a race car driver who walks away from a fiery crash; Dillett may have considered calling it quits, even for just a moment. But just like the thrill-seekers who narrowly avert death, bodybuilders who flirt with disaster and emerge intact are rarely apt to bow out. It's those who don't come through unscathed who retire, since much of the time they simply have no choice. In the world of bodybuilding, such forced endings are fairly common. Starting mainly in the 1990s men began to drop out of competition because of less-acute health problems, presumably brought on by long-term drug use.[1]

Not only were competitors of the 1990s ingesting more chemicals than those of the previous decade, but new drugs, many rather powerful, were regularly becoming available. Year by year, contests were being won by bigger and freakier men. It was becoming clear that some of the more important events in the history of bodybuilding had taken place not on the posing platforms of physique contests, but within the laboratories and boardrooms of pharmaceutical corporations. The most basic of all bodybuilding drugs, synthetic testosterone, was developed in 1935. Its derivatives—drugs like Dianabol, Winstrol, Deca-Durabolin, Sustanon, Anavar, and Anadrol—had been available for several decades. Yet relative to the current state of high-level bodybuilding, 1985 must go down as a banner year. It was then that biosynthetic human growth hormone first became available. Before that discovery, all HGH had been extracted from the pituitary glands of cadavers. It was therefore in short supply and difficult to obtain. Biosynthesis changed all of that, and by the early mid-1990s, bodybuilders were getting their hands on synthetic HGH.

Growth hormone by itself only causes minor growth of skeletal muscular tissue. When used in conjunction with anabolic steroids however, the end result can be dramatic. This is because HGH makes anabolic steroids more potent. It also significantly increases the body's fat-burning capabilities and generally helps it to recover from exercise and injury. This collection of attributes quickly made growth hormone a must-have weapon in any top-tiered professional's arsenal. From the standpoint of those who wished to build as much muscle as possible—and to showcase it under a paper-thin layer of skin—HGH was a dream come true. Unfortunately for these people, it was also expensive. Bodybuilders who had been accustomed to spending at most a few thousand dollars per year on their drug regimen were now shelling out up to ten times that.

[1]See p. 203 for more information.

The end result was that bodybuilders, and bodybuilding itself, had taken on a new look. Bodybuilders of the 1990s were steadily growing larger, but their proportions were not necessarily improving. The new-era cocktail of growth-producing drugs was extremely effective, yet entirely indiscriminant. The combination of chemicals that allowed bodybuilders to become so large had the consequence of causing substantial growth of all their muscles, voluntary and involuntary alike. While competitors were busy training the voluntary muscles of their skeletal systems with weights, the involuntary muscles of their internal organs, without any intentional prodding, were doing their own growing. The practice of combining the newly-discovered anabolic chemical IGF-1 (insulin-like growth factor) with insulin, which began sometime mid-decade, exacerbated this effect. New-era bodybuilders were therefore bigger, inside and out. The midsections of top bodybuilders of the 1980s and before were trim; those of their later-era counterparts often appeared bloated. Of the bodybuilders who bridged the eras, substantial size gains almost always came at the expense of increased midsection thickness.

By the beginning of the new millennium, the large-waist look had become common. Unfortunately for fans of the small-waist aesthetic, precedent dictated that massive physiques should prevail, especially at the highest levels of competition. At the '93 Olympia, Wheeler without question had better proportions than Yates, but IFBB judges had long-since made up their minds about the type of physique they wanted to see holding a Sandow statue.

IFBB professional competitor. c. 2003

Courtesy of Steve Harris

The beauty-versus-beast question was first posed in the 1940s. Its pre-1993 zenith was witnessed a few decades later, when Frank Zane placed ahead of Bertil Fox at the '83 Olympia. The judgment was about evenly lauded and despised. Since the Olympia judges had been presented with two physiques that were different in every possible way, deciding which one was better became a matter of philosophy. Is an ideal physique shapely or massive? According to major-federation standards, a bodybuilder should be both. Flex Wheeler, Shawn Ray and Kevin Levrone were all massive and near-perfect, hence their rapid ascent to the highest levels of bodybuilding competition. Unfortunately for them, their path to bodybuilding's pinnacle was blocked by an immovable object—a man so massive his lack of perfection was rendered irrelevant.

Bodybuilding drifted further from the once-hoped-for land of public acceptance. The at-large public had long considered it to be a giant freak show, and the emergence of ultra-massive competitors with bulging waistlines only intensified that opinion. For all the accolades laid at the feet of Dorian Yates, he also must be recognized as one of the trend's leaders. No one but him knows what supplementation regimen fueled his ascent to 257 pounds of granite-hard muscle, but in 1993 he appeared to have the thickest midsection of the entire Olympia field. That attribute became his detractors' main source of ammunition. But this mattered little. Yates' physique was so overwhelming that his not-so-pleasing waistline was, for all intents and purposes, completely forgiven. IFBB judges certainly forgave it, and his march through history continued.

* * * * *

With a third consecutive Olympia win looming large on the horizon, the Champion once more descended into his dungeon gym and got to work. In his quest to gain entrance to the next circle of bodybuilding's most elite fraternity—that of the three-time Olympia champions—his aim was to improve on something that was already unbeatable. Yates' resolve was unmatched; his drive vehement; his training legendary.

Sometimes however, resolve and drive can become too powerful; and sometimes they can block good sense and cloud judgment. This is certainly not a problem particular to bodybuilding, although numerous bodybuilders have famously suffered consequences from unabated enthusiasm. After all, the human body has limitations. In some senses it's like a well-made car: it will often operate trouble-free for many years, even if abuse is heaped upon it, and even if its limits are continually being tested. Yet neither can indefinitely withstand both.

A major problem with bodybuilding is that humans were not designed to be bodybuilders. We were designed to be efficient hunter-gatherers. Inasmuch, we humans were constructed to carry out tasks relating to both means of survival: we're equipped to perform large amounts of low-intensity activity, which includes things like walking; our physiology also allows us to occasionally perform short bouts of highly intense exercise, for example sprinting or lifting heavy objects. Bodybuilding training is comprised primarily of lifting heavy objects, something we humans are good at. However, that type of training is neither occasional not short. It's done regularly, with great effort, and often in sessions that last multiple hours.

Bodybuilders would like the toughness of their bodies to match that of their minds, but this attitude often leads to crushing disappointment. Multiple years of high-effort weight training have left many of them with broken parts and worn-out frames. Torn muscles are among the most common of the severe injuries suffered by bodybuilders, and they're certainly the most noticeable. The highly intense contractions that take place during a bodybuilding workout often damage the tissue of whichever muscle is being trained.

Microtrauma, as this damage is called, is the microscopic tearing of this tissue. Shortly after it occurs, the body will begin repairing the damage. It's actually an extremely efficient arrangement: considering the physical demands placed upon the hunter/gatherer by his environment, his body is able to repair itself quite nicely and without missing a beat. Unfortunately for the late 20th-century hardcore bodybuilder, his body did not anticipate the introduction of brutal weight-training sessions and strength-boosting drugs—two things that combine to increase microtrauma. Since both things are also unnatural, it isn't surprising that the body's damage-control mechanisms sometimes can't keep pace.

Although Dorian Yates was one of the very few bodybuilders who did not perform lengthy workouts, he regularly lifted heavy weights with great effort. He experienced some aches and pains, but he couldn't be bothered with them. After all, he was the greatest bodybuilder in the world, and fans were expecting great things from him. Yates also truly loved hard training. He needed to keep going. However, his body disagreed. Like everyone else, he had a breaking point. After storming his way to the top of the professional ranks with such a powerful physique, Yates might have wondered whether he even *had* a breaking point. Nevertheless, he did. Months spent ignoring his body's warning signals—aches and pains in his left arm—proved fateful. In the late summer of 1994, he suffered a complete bicep tear. The Mr. Olympia contest was only six weeks away.

There are a number of muscles in the human body that are susceptible to tearing: pectorals, hamstrings, triceps and quadriceps are all at risk. In addition to these, there's a particularly high incidence of torn biceps among bodybuilders. This isn't surprising, because the biceps are typically where a bodybuilder's physiology and his psychology most dangerously intersect. The muscle itself has a relatively fragile construction; it's held in place at either end by somewhat thin tendons. Meanwhile, building big biceps has always been a primary goal of just about anyone who ever took up weight training for its visual effect. For a lot of bodybuilders, it's the reason they started lifting weights. Although it has been proven that weight-training workouts need not be long or frequent to be optimally effective, this fact is often incongruent with the mentality that drives men to build extremely muscular physiques. Bicep workouts are often long and brutal, and they're often done far more frequently than is necessary.

Arnold Schwarzenegger preached the benefits of long, frequent and brutal bicep workouts. He happened to have some of the greatest biceps the world has ever known, so a legion of hopefuls accepted this correlation as cause and followed suit. The large majority ended up disappointed. More than a few ended up injured, their biceps broken and withered, with countless hours of their lives lost forever and dreams of bodybuilding glory dashed along with them. For those who act quickly, there is hope. Often a muscle tear is surgically correctable, as long as the affected region is operated on within a day or two. Past that, the muscle will have atrophied too much to repair.

Dorian Yates may have been performing much

shorter and less frequent bicep workouts than those praised by Schwarzenegger, but all of that matter little now. What matter was that Yates was faced with a decision: he could get his torn bicep surgically repaired and miss the upcoming Mr. Olympia contest, or he could keep training, knowing full-well that the bicep would forever be small and misshapen. On the line was a chance to win a third straight title. If Yates bowed out that opportunity would vanish. Also gone would be the winner's check; in 1994 that amount was $100,000. Yet it was a risky proposition. There was no guarantee Yates would win now that his physique had a blatant flaw. If he entered but only placed fourth, his prize money would be a mere $25,000. Placing second would get him $50,000, a much better take, though in light of his past success it would be little more than a consolation prize. He would still have been unseated. Viewed in this light, anything less than victory would be a disaster.

Fortunately for Yates, history was on his side. In the contest's 29-year history up to that point, only twice had a reigning multiple Mr. Olympia been beaten, and both times the benefactor was Arnold Schwarzenegger. Bodybuilding had come too far and Schwarzenegger was too old for a comeback to be fathomable. Also, Chris Dickerson was able to win the contest in 1982 with a pectoral muscle that had been at least partially torn. Dickerson didn't know it at the time, but he had set a precedent that would become more and more important as the years passed. Meanwhile, a bit of off-stage news rocked the bodybuilding world: Flex Wheeler had been in a serious car accident that left him severely injured. It looked as though the career of bodybuilding's brightest new star had suddenly and violently flared out. Images of a bruised and comatose Wheeler lying in a hospital bed in bandages and a neck brace were printed in the magazines, and he was crossed off the list of men who might give Yates trouble at the upcoming Olympia.

Yates took inventory of the current situation. He may have had a torn bicep, but he still had the remainder of his physique to rely upon, including an entire backside that was still leagues ahead of his competition. The prior year also saw the emergence of no new threats. The choice was made: he would compete.

For 1994, Atlanta was once more picked to host the Olympia; and for the first time in 15 years the contest would be held in the same city on consecutive occasions. Apparently the Helsinki experiment wore heavily on IFBB tastes. After all, why gamble on an international location when American crowds with American dollars were a sure thing? It was an argument that found few opponents, and the debate would soon fall from fashion. Just like the prior year, a big crowd was on hand to witness the greatest muscle contest yet conceived.

With the exception of his left bicep, at the Olympia Yates was bigger than ever. He still looked dominating from almost every angle. His posing routine was living testimony to how much a weak muscle can be "hidden" by selecting the right poses and deleting others. Nevertheless, the bicep was noticeable when Yates faced the judges straight on, in the so-called semi-relaxed pose. Competitors assume that particular posture more than any other, by far, and it may well be the most important in all of bodybuilding. If the '94 Mr. Olympia contest had been judged solely on that pose, Yates most likely would have lost. In addition to the problematic left arm, his midsection looked even thicker than the previous year. In comparison to the top men with smaller waists who flanked him—Levrone, Ray, Dillett, Cottrell and newcomer Chris Cormier—he almost looked outclassed. Nevertheless, Yates won the symmetry round, a decision that provoked the recurring ire of Shawn Ray.

Yates found the muscularity round to be smoother sailing, since only in his front double biceps pose was the disfigured muscle a distraction. What may have been more distracting was the glossy appearance of Yates' face. It glistened with a deep sheen, almost as if he had purposely oiled it. For some reason the everything-shines-but-the-face mantra of bodybuilding photographers escaped him and his helpers. In the end however, Yates' imperfections were happily forgiven. IFBB judges were unwilling to unseat him. At the end of the evening performance he was handed his third Sandow trophy, with Ray, Levrone, Dillett, Cottrell and Cormier finishing behind him. Finishing seventh was a little-known competitor named Nasser El Sonbaty, a man with designs on greater fame.

Much like the aftermath of the 1980 or '90 Olympias, fans were left with much to ponder. While both Shawn Ray and Kevin Levrone looked stunning and near-perfect, they had been beaten by a man with crushing mass but obvious flaws. Nevertheless, the outcome was predictable. In an activity where being called a "freak" is taken as a compliment; where the abandonment of drug testing was met with relief by most fans and competitors;

Courtesy of Steve Harris

Kevin Levrone, Dorian Yates and Shawn Ray. 1994 Mr. Olympia contest.

and in a decade where the size of bodybuilders and the sales of muscle magazines rose hand-in-hand, the trend of rewarding mass over perfection should have surprised no one.

Though the outcome of the '94 Olympia may have been predictable, this doesn't mean that fans were universally happy with it. Some made clear they were not. But for every fan who found fault and disillusion in what contest judges were rewarding, another two became enthralled with the spectacle. These fans of the new era were content to bicker over contest placings so long as they were able to feast their eyes on competitors who were huge, and shredded, and when possible, "symmetrical." This became the character of the modern era, and it has since remained locked in place.

* * * * *

Though few recall Chris Dickerson's 1982 Mr. Olympia triumph, much less what his flaws may have been, the partially torn pectoral muscle he brought to the stage that evening set an important precedent. Throughout bodybuilding's history, judges had no choice but to tolerate and give de facto reward to genetic imperfections. As the 20th century entered its final decades, they had proven themselves willing to do the same for self-imposed abnormalities. At the '82 Olympia they showed they would do so even at the highest levels of competition. In Dickerson's case, his tear was noticeable but not horrendous. To IFBB judges, the rest of his physique made up for it. As time passed and bodybuilding grew, more and more visibly injured bodybuilders entered muscle contests. In the case of each, the judges were faced with a quandary that had no clear answer: how should these men be judged? This basic question quickly became more complicated, since visibly torn muscles are but one of a handful of common self-imposed imperfections that judges routinely look past.

Contest placings are often considered in the context of reward and punishment. At the 1994 Olympia for example, some felt Shawn Ray was rewarded with second place. It was the second consecutive time he moved up one place from the prior year. In '94, Ray also beat Kevin Levrone—who had gotten the better of Ray in '92, and who was now better than ever. An equivalent argument could be made that Levrone was punished with third place. In 1994, Dorian Yates was given the ultimate reward of first place. A Gold Medal at the Mr. Olympia contest means that there is no one better anywhere.

By handing Yates the Gold Medal, the IFBB declared him to be the world's greatest bodybuilder; and it also therefore put a shining seal of approval on his physique. An inventory of that physique revealed what exactly was being approved. Yates had barrier-smashing mass and world-class conditioning. The thickness of his torso and the size and quality of his back and calves far exceeded those of his rivals. His overall physical form was indeed outstanding, but he also had a torn bicep, a large waistline, and tattoos. By making him Mr. Olympia, the IFBB sent an important message: this is what we reward.

With the crowning of each year's Mr. Olympia, that same message of reward is sent. It was sent for Scott, Oliva, Schwarzenegger, Zane, Bannout and Haney. By rewarding the physiques of some of the Olympia's other champions, judges also proved themselves willing to look past the three common self-imposed abnormalities that are now witnessed routinely at all levels of bodybuilding competition: torn muscles, tattoos, and gynecomastia. In physique contests, torn muscles present judges with an obvious problem: how should a disfigured and atrophied muscle affect an otherwise complete competitor's final placing? The other two abnormalities raise similar issues.

Tattoos came into vogue at about the same time the current phase of body-building's modern era got underway, so it became inevitable that they would be seen on physique competitors. The most memorable precedents had actually been set a few years earlier, by two of the 1980's top competitors. Berry DeMey sported a simple, innocuous rose on his left shoulder, while Mike Christian displayed his own signature on his left pec (copying the convention used by artists to identify their work). Yates turned things up a notch with tattoos from his youth: a Union Jack and bulldog above the words "My England"[1] on his right forearm, and a pair of red boots with the word "skins" on his left. The latter was a skinhead tattoo that he later had removed, and any association he had with that group was likewise disavowed. Regardless, as he began to rack up Olympia victories, it was still there. As the years passed, more and more competitors of all levels adorned themselves with "body art." Meanwhile, the tattoos themselves became bigger and more numerous.

[1]The Union Jack is actually the flag of Great Britain, not England. The English flag is a red cross on a white field.

The presence of tattoos became a minor divisive issue within the bodybuilding community. Purists held fast to the idea that physique competitions are contests of appearance; that tattoos detract from or deface the bodies they cover; that they are rarely better than cheap and trashy; that Sandow's century-old "good skin tone" criteria should be applied in the strictest possible sense; and that any and all physical attributes should be taken into account when judging a competitor. The opposing faction considered tattoos to be attractive and unique art that often displays deeply personal subject matter; and they furthermore declared that even the most extensive tattoos do not obscure a competitor's lines, definition or muscularity. Bodybuilding officials tasked with determining judging guidelines were left to consider each viewpoint.

If judges were to penalize tattoos, a new sub-set of evaluation criteria would emerge. Judges would have to consider the size, placement and subject matter of tattoos when judging each competitor, and when comparing all competitors together. For example, Berry DeMey's rose would theoretically count less against him than would a skinhead tattoo; and if the majority of his back was covered with designs, that would further impact his placing.

Dorian Yates, guest posing exhibition. c. 1995

Courtesy of Steve Harris

An important question was raised by all of this: how much should tattoos matter relative to other criteria? It appeared there could be no easy answer. Tattoos are not a single variable. They're a variable with myriad sub-variables. In a selection process with perpetual disagreement[1] over how much any particular attribute should factor into a competitor's assessment, further complication would not be happily welcomed.

In high-level contests where hair-splitting often determines placings, finer hairs would have to be split, and judges would have a more difficult task. Nevertheless, modern NPC rules mandate that judges should take the following attributes into consideration:

> Skin tone, skin texture and quality, skin color tone and evenness, blemishes, stretch marks, scars, tattoos, cellulite, skeletal defects and proper application of oil.

Nothing more is said about the topic. Although they are listed here amongst a number of unsightly attributes, the section nevertheless fails to specify whether tattoos should be viewed as positive or negative. It should therefore be no surprise that tattoos are for the most part ignored by judging panels of the NPC and IFBB—and tattooed competitors are judged as if their permanent ink designs did not exist. This became each federation's de facto policy, and a politically correct one at that. As the new era progressed, a growing number of competitors and their fans began to sport tattoos. Judges and the federations they represented risked alienating much of their patronage if body art was penalized. Bodybuilding purists would have to be left unsatisfied. That may have been just as well, since many purists were losing interest anyway.

As the years passed, it became clear that the 1991 IFBB decision to abandon drug testing had not returned things to the way they had been. It instead propelled bodybuilding in a new direction and toward a new group of fans. To those fans, tattoos, bulging waistlines and the occasional torn muscle were fairly normal attributes of physique competitors. New fans also became accustomed to the rising incidence of gynecomastia—a condition where men develop female breast tissue. Although torn muscles are typically seen more at higher levels of competition, gynecomastia is prevalent and widespread.

Commonly referred to as "bitch tits," the condition is characterized by the presence of fatty deposits of female breast tissue behind and around the nipples of its victims. Among otherwise very lean bodybuilders, gynecomastia is quite noticeable and visually distracting. Ironically, the condition is precipitated by the use of artificial male hormones. The process is fairly simple: the presence of substantial amounts of anabolic steroids often triggers a reaction called aromatization, whereby any unused testosterone or testosterone derivative is converted into the female hormone estrogen. That estrogen in turn triggers the development of female breast tissue. Fortunately, the condition is reversible through a simple surgical procedure that removes the tissue. Gynecomastia can also be prevented with the use of estrogen-blocking drugs. However, once the tissue has grown, surgery is the only remedy. Unfortunately for audiences and bodybuilding in general, more and more competitors were stepping onstage with unaddressed gynecomastia. As with muscle tears and tattoos however, competitors with gynecomastia suffered few penalties. Major titles—from the NPC California State Championships all the way up to the Mr. Olympia contest—have been won by men afflicted by the condition.

As the 1990s progressed, the three self-imposed physical abnormalities became less and less abnormal. It appeared that the trend of emphasizing maximum muscle made judges more tolerant of imperfection. Since by the mid-1990s bodybuilding's public-acceptance goal was little more than rhetoric, contests and magazines could afford to cater to the large faction who wanted muscle, lots of it, and not much else. In a subtle way, the relationship between that goal and the growing incidence of physical imperfections served as a reminder of the muscle culture's place in the greater world: to much of the public, bodybuilding is itself one giant self-imposed abnormality.

That public had no idea who Dorian Yates was, or that he had just won his third Mr. Olympia title. It therefore could not have known that he had every intention of extending his streak far into the future. The outside world also had no clue who Flex Wheeler was, that his brilliant young bodybuilding career appeared ruined forever in the twisted metal

[1]Bodybuilding contest organizers recognized early on that there would never be agreement about which physiques are best, hence the creation of seven or nine-member judging panels.

of a car wreck, or that the following year he mounted an incredible comeback. Indeed Wheeler suffered no irreparable damage in the accident that could have as easily taken his life. By early 1995, he was back in action.

The bodybuilding community was delighted to hear that Wheeler was okay, although his peers probably would have been happy had he stayed away from competition. He quickly regained top form and resumed his position as Dorian Yates' heir-apparent. Even when he wasn't at his best he was still close to unbeatable. Despite suffering from a severe intestinal bug at the 1995 Schwarzenegger Classic—a condition that left him looking relatively flat and soft—he was still able to defeat the entire field save one.

Thus far a single competitor, Dorian Yates, had been able to beat Flex Wheeler in an IFBB contest. There was now a second: a man named Michael Francois. Francois was yet another of the handful of top-quality bodybuilders who turned professional in the 1990s. As much as Wheeler was off his top form at the '95 Schwarzenegger Classic, Francois was on his. At a height and weight similar to that of Wheeler, with above-average lines and particularly impressive limb development, he was an instant threat to win almost any contest he entered.

The Schwarzenegger Classic also happened to be held each year in Francois' hometown of Columbus, Ohio. He was therefore presented with a rare opportunity: the chance to win a major professional bodybuilding contest in the city where he grew up and lived. With this in mind, Francois trained for the contest with unmatched vigor and determination. He showed up in his all-time best condition, with incredible fullness and sharp lines; and he needed every bit of it to defeat an under-the-weather Wheeler. Had Wheeler been at or near his best, the decision would have been a hands-down reversal of fortune. In the eyes of a heavily pro-Francois gathering, the judges made the right choice.

Bodybuilding judging panels have historically given special consideration to hometown products, and Wheeler's subpar condition made it easy for them to oblige that tradition. The custom was alive and well in 1998, when popular New Yorker and brand-new IFBB pro Johnny Moya placed fourth out of 47 competitors at that year's Night of Champions contest. The NOC was always held in Manhattan, and that year a large contingent of Moya fans were in attendance. They knew he had beaten a huge field of middleweights in Dallas at the previous year's National Championships, and they were hoping to witness similar success against some of bodybuilding's best physiques on his home turf. Whether judges were influenced by the reaction of the prejudging crowd to Moya's callouts, or they were already inclined to award special consideration to the hometown hero, the end result suggested there may have been a little of both. Moya also happened to train at competitor-turned-IFBB-judge Bev Francis' gym on Long Island, which likely didn't hurt his chances.

In the end Moya found himself ahead of a slew of excellent competitors, including Porter Cottrell, who had previously earned a top-six finish in the Mr. Olympia contest, and Gunter Schlierkamp, who would later reproduce that feat twice. Like Francois in Columbus, Moya came into the show with his best-ever shape. By all accounts he owned an impressive physique, with particularly good chest, back and thigh development, topped off by world-class definition. It was therefore reasonable that he should earn a spot near the top of the lineup. However, had the contest been held in another region it's likely that Moya would have been lost among the scores of competitors who surrounded him. Such is often the reality of modern-era amateur middleweights who become professionals, since the upper levels of the IFBB pro ranks are dominated by men who competed at the amateur level as heavyweights.

The remainder of Moya's career followed this script, and accordingly he later had trouble cracking the top ten of any show he entered. Even his home-turf Night of Champions contest later found favor elsewhere. Apparently the hometown-hero fervor that characterized his first crack at the show had worn off; and NOC judges found themselves more interested in men like Paul Dillett and newcomer Dexter Jackson.

For all that's it's made out to be—for the lofty, world-saving hopes of Joe Weider and the bold nation-building claims of his brother Ben (p. 205), and for the life-consuming efforts of those who place physique competition at the center of their universe—the fact cannot be escaped that bodybuilding is a form of entertainment. The purpose of a bodybuilding contest is to entertain its audience; and ultimately all other factors are subordinate to that end. Vince McMahon grasped this concept, though he didn't have the foggiest idea how to apply it. Because of this, his WBF promptly collapsed in a fit of silliness. The Weiders on the other hand had always known how to apply it. As a result, their IFBB prospered and dominated.

New-era bodybuilding audiences are entertained by muscle—gigantic, striated, rippling mounds of flexing muscle. That's what fills seats. They appreciate competent presentation and occasionally delight in skillful posing routines, but as long as long as the beef is onstage and before their eyes, they're happy. They also like to see the right competitor win, though there is almost always disagreement over who that might be. When a large contingent shows up to see a local hero take on the world, there are few doubts about which man they would like to see prevail. If he wins or does well, or at least secures a better-than-expected finish, the crowd has been entertained.

* * * * *

The 1995 Schwarzenegger Classic and the 1998 Night of Champions were feel-good stories, brief chapters in the lives of two men whose bodybuilding careers would eventually end in disappointment. Unlike the celebrated, spot-lit onstage retirement of Arnold Schwarzenegger, vividly documented in *Pumping Iron,* most final exits from competition are quiet and lonely affairs. A tale which became somewhat common was that of the accomplished bodybuilder whose run had neared its end; of him being excluded from posedown groups; of later struggling to secure a place among the 15 men who were allowed to pose at the evening show; of the hollow feeling he experienced watching other competitors called out for prejudging comparisons, one after the other, until he was given his obligatory chance to flex for the judges. Larry Scott, Arnold Schwarzenegger and Lee Haney had gone out with a bang. Most others, including a few major titleholders, went out with a whimper.

Beginning in 1994 the IFBB sought to remedy the yearnings of men whose time had passed but who still wanted to compete. The cure came in the form of a "masters" division, a separate category exclusively for competitors who had passed the age of 40. The new Masters Mr. Olympia contest attracted some big names of the past, including Lou Ferrigno, Chris Dickerson, Robby Robinson, Ed Corney, Samir Bannout, Boyer Coe and several others which would be recalled by bodybuilding's older devoted fans.

Masters categories had long-since been a staple of amateur physique contests, so for the IFBB, the formula was in place and ready to copy. Creating the division was a relatively easy way to generate more interest in its shows.

Pitting bodybuilding's old-timers against each other didn't necessarily translate into greater profits however. Professional contests don't base their bottom line on the simple the-more-the-merrier strategy followed by their amateur counterparts. It was questionable whether money spent—prize money and competitor expenses—was offset by the additional dollars generated by the new division. Older competitors loved the idea of an over-40 professional world championship, but love cannot be deposited into a promoter's bank account. The Masters Mr. Olympia was therefore done away with after a ten-year run.

Older competitors who were still intent on gathering snatches of past glory would have to find some other means by which to accomplish this. Unfortunately for them there were few opportunities. Some became sideshow staples of local amateur contests, sitting in the auditorium lobby and hocking 8x10 photos for anyone who wanted a personally-signed memento from the former bodybuilding star and was willing to cough up the $10 asking price. This became a way to remain connected, however faintly, to the glory of the past while making a few bucks in the process. For some former greats it seemed merely a sad epilogue to a storied career.

Except for those who die first, all bodybuilders eventually call it quits. A fair number excuse themselves from the world of competition with their heads held high, resolved to move on to bigger and better things. Others leave the scene with few opportunities, and few feelings other than bitterness and disappointment. They loved bodybuilding, but they made the fatal error of thinking that bodybuilding would love them back. Like a great magnet, bodybuilding can pull devotion, sacrifice and love out of those who offer these things, but to only a tiny fraction of competitors will these things be returned. Neither does bodybuilding promise fair treatment, a level playing field, or prosperity. Nevertheless, many dive headlong into the world of physique competition expecting them all.

The excitement of nearing or achieving IFBB professional status will often at least temporarily blind up-and-comers to the realities of modern high-level muscle contests. Many of these same people later find out that bodybuilding can be unfair, uncaring, unsympathetic and even ruthless.

The judging guidelines of major federations have

always been put into writing, but there's no guarantee that they won't on occasion be subject to liberal interpretation or ignored altogether. (There are several reasons why Las Vegas casinos do not take bets on the outcome of bodybuilding contests, and this is the most important.) There is also no recourse for competitors who feel victimized by unfair judgments, other than quitting. Mike Mentzer saw this quite plainly, so after the 1980 Olympia, that's what he did. Those who elect to stick around are certainly free to complain, but by doing so they may place their competitive futures in jeopardy.

Bodybuilding competition is entertainment, and its ultimate goal is to generate an entertaining product. If creating an entertaining outcome for a particular contest requires that one or more competitors get treated unfairly, bodybuilding federations have proven themselves ready, willing and able to do that. This has caused a good deal of bitterness among competitors who expect no less than the faithful application of judging guidelines. That bodybuilding is interminably referred to as a "sport" by all layers of muscle culture has no doubt added to this thinking.

In a sport like soccer, a bad judgment call by a referee can make headlines in the world's major news outlets, as was proven by the 2010 FIFA[1] World Cup. A pair of such calls by referee Koman Coulibaly gained worldwide attention and prompted federation officials to relieve him of his position, with little delay. There is no such quality control in bodybuilding, even at its world-championship level. When judging panels collectively render decisions that provoke widespread protests of favoritism, fans have no choice but to accept those decisions. Major bodybuilding federations have also yet to admit that in any of their contests the right man might not have won.

The image bodybuilding created for itself didn't reflect its reality. Its competitors are very much real people however, and they are very much subject to the perils of illusion. Bodybuilding fans in 1995 saw the rise to prominence of a competitor who seemed to have bought into that illusion, at least for a while, before angrily snapping out of it. When he had finally called it a day, his legacy became one not of glory and accolades, but of outspoken bitterness and disenfranchisement. First however, he would become known as the one man with the potential to beat Dorian Yates at his own game.

Nasser El Sonbaty—or simply *Nasser*, as he was later commonly known—was yet another outstanding bodybuilder to turn professional in the 1990s. His admittance to the IFBB pro ranks actually came before that of Wheeler, Levrone, Dillett, Francois, and nearly the entire remainder of his future rivals. Unlike those men however, El Sonbaty's debut was entirely without anticipation or fanfare. Since he wasn't American (being German-born, with a Serbian mother and Egyptian father), as a high-level amateur he hadn't been given nearly the same press coverage as his stateside counterparts.[2] The beginning of his career was more of the same, as he competed in a number of events throughout the early 1990s with mild success and to limited acclaim. Though he possessed the strengths of above-average mass, balance and definition, with decent lines, El Sonbaty was barely noticed by the bodybuilding press. Around 1993 his career began to pick up some steam, and in 1994 he was able to secure a respectable seventh-place finish at the Mr. Olympia contest. What happened after that caused a small stir in the bodybuilding world.

At a height of five-foot-eleven, El Sonbaty was 250 pounds at the '94 Olympia. Six months later, at the 1995 Houston Pro Invitational and Night of Champions contests, he was about 20 pounds heavier—with a level of conditioning that was at least as good as anything he had yet brought to the stage. El Sonbaty had managed to pull off a Yates-like increase in muscular mass, and the rewards were immediate. He won both shows. Suddenly the perennial also-ran was the talk of the bodybuilding community. On paper he now even had a slight edge over Yates: El Sonbaty was a little taller, a little heavier, and with comparable sharpness. With his rapid increase in mass also came the significantly expanded abdominal area that characterized men who had reached this level of mass, but judges had proven themselves willing to look past this.

Olympia judges had already proven themselves unwilling to favor lighter and shapelier competitors like Flex Wheeler or Shawn Ray over the more massive Yates. With El Sonbaty, they were suddenly confronted with a competitor who was more

[1] Fédération Internationale de Football Association

[2] Although they typically enjoy far less press coverage, non-US amateurs have the advantage of not having to battle their ways through the tough NPC ranks in order to turn professional.

like Yates than not. Comparing photos of Yates to the new-look El Sonbaty told the tale. In certain poses—his front double-biceps in particular—El Sonbaty looked superior to the reigning Mr. Olympia. He also sported no visible injuries. A showdown was therefore in the making, though of a different sort than that of 1993; the Wheeler-Yates confrontation pitted beauty against beast. With El Sonbaty, Yates now had another beast with which to contend.

Because of this, the 1995 Olympia had no shortage of pre-contest buzz. The biggest question was whether Yates, despite his compromised left arm, could maintain or even improve upon his physique while simultaneously holding off El Sonbaty and the monstrous cast of runners-up who surrounded him. The event itself did not disappoint. Yates had resolved to not let the injury deter him in any way; and bad arm notwithstanding, the '95 version of the champion was generally considered to be the best yet witnessed. However, when his first muscularity-round comparison with El Sonbaty was called for, it appeared that Yates would need every bit of that condition to prevail.

After the 1995 spring contests, *Musclemag* declared that El Sonbaty's version of the front double-biceps pose "took the sport to a new level." When the new-look El Sonbaty finally struck that pose in a Mr. Olympia contest, next to the reigning champion no less, the claim rang true. No one could touch him in that pose. Fortunately for Yates, El Sonbaty's domination ended there. When the comparison group was asked to face the curtain, the

Nasser El Sonbaty, c. 1995

Courtesy of Steve Harris

competition no longer appeared close. Much like the highly anticipated Lee Haney-Gary Strydom showdown of 1988, the challenger was badly outclassed in the all-important back poses. The audience was quickly reminded why Yates had already won three titles. Yates' back, which had always been his trademark body part, was considerably larger and far more defined than El Sonbaty's.

Throughout its history, most Mr. Olympia winners have had show-stopping backs. Yates and especially Haney had learned to skillfully exploit this strength while posing, and few things in bodybuilding are more dramatic or impressive than a well-timed and well-executed series of rearward-facing poses from a man with superior back development. IFBB judges had unofficially decided upon the type of physique they wanted to see prevail at Mr. Olympia contests, and added to the list of required attributes was truly great (if not "best in show") back development. El Sonbaty didn't have this. When Haney and Yates faced the curtain, their dominance was given a large exclamation point. When Strydom and El Sonbaty did the same, they raised question marks. For this very reason, the latter pair hit few back poses during their posing routines. In the muscularity round however, there's no hiding.

El Sonbaty's primary strength was his pace-setting mass as seen from the front and sides. In the end it was good enough to land him in the top three of the '95 Olympia, a significant jump from the seventh he earned just one year prior. Kevin Levrone was too massive, shapely and complete to be overtaken, and he resumed his position as Yates' runner-up and heir-apparent. Meanwhile, and to the surprise of no one, Yates won his fourth Sandow. The issue of his bad arm was all but dead, and he once more appeared unstoppable. His march through the history books became an assault. In '95, Yates joined the ultra-exclusive company of Haney and Schwarzenegger as the only men to win more than three Olympia titles.

An El Sonbaty victory at the '95 Olympia was not to be. He did however manage to defeat Shawn Ray, much to the latter's chagrin, and Flex Wheeler. By all accounts Wheeler was not in top form. It had already been proven that in a modern Mr. Olympia contest, only in the rarest of circumstances can a competitor show up in subpar condition and expect to finish near the top. The level of competition had risen far too high. The man who had formerly threatened to wrest the title from Yates would this time have to be content with eighth place. He would be back.

El Sonbaty was undeterred by his loss to Yates and Levrone and was furthermore determined to one day take home a Sandow trophy. He continued to roll. Throughout the remainder of the decade he amassed more than two dozen high-level placings, culminating in a runner-up finish at the 1997 Olympia and a win at the '99 Schwarzenegger Classic. He was never able to win an Olympia title, though he became known as one of the decade's greats. He also demonstrated early on that Dorian Yates would not be the only competitor to bring breathtaking mass and world-class conditioning to bodybuilding's biggest stage. In time quite a few men would follow his example, and by the dawn of the new millennium the groundbreaking size of Yates and El Sonbaty became almost commonplace at bodybuilding's highest levels. El Sonbaty's slew of top placements demonstrated that the ultra-massive, thick-waisted look would continue to be rewarded at the highest levels of competition.

According to El Sonbaty's later boasts, it was not rewarded enough. El Sonbaty declared that his physique should have earned him the Mr. Olympia title, and in fact El Sonbaty refers to himself as "The Uncrowned Mr. Olympia." His protest over never being officially recognized as the world's greatest bodybuilder was but the tip of a mountain of complaints he later aired about the IFBB and its judges, and what he deemed to be their unfair, racist and conspiratorial practices. Inasmuch, he also calls himself "a foe of injustice."

In a lengthy series of post-retirement internet interviews,[1] El Sonbaty portrayed himself as a victim of not only unfair judging practices and backstabbing by fellow competitors, but outright conspiracy. His tirade was lengthy, and countless aspersions were cast. He offered myriad details to support his allegations, but the true significance of his rant was found in its overall theme. El Sonbaty made himself into a highly visible worst-case example of how bodybuilding is sometimes perceived by its competitors, especially at its highest levels. He asserted that the IFBB is essentially crooked, that titles are dispensed as much for political reasons as physical merit, and that important parts of the federation are populated with people of low moral standing. He went so far as to claim that some IFBB judges are drug addicts, while others become intoxicated before judging contests. He was by far the most accomplished bodybuilder to come forth with such a list of complaints. Shawn Ray also made public a number of complaints, though his rants were without the damning personal allegations or venom of El Sonbaty's.

The post-Golden Age expansion of bodybuilding brought with it a small parade of future muscle-contest icons. It also created a small army of disgruntled and disillusioned competitors. At one time that group wanted fame, fortune, and onstage glory; and through the allusions of muscle magazines, they were lulled into believing that if they merely tried hard enough, those things could be had. However, since only a tiny minority were able to make that dream a reality, the remainder either graciously accepted failure or looked for someone to hold responsible. For those who chose to dispense blame, the most obvious targets were the people who decided their placings in contests. Judging panels, their practices, and the federations themselves were naturally called into question.

The gripes of unhappy competitors were heard mainly by their friends and gym acquaintances, or by anyone who was willing to listen. These complaints seldom received any press coverage however, especially since for the better part of four decades a single body controlled both the major fed-

Nasser El Sonbaty, guest-posing exhibition. c. 1996

Courtesy of Steve Harris

[1]With Bodybuilding.com's David Robson.

erations and bodybuilding's biggest news outlets. Grievances were therefore isolated, and the greater bodybuilding community was in turn unaware of the scope of dissatisfaction coursing through its ranks. With time, and the rise of the internet, that gradually changed. Through the searing comments of El Sonbaty, disgruntled and disillusioned competitors now had a real voice. He spoke for a small legion of them when he declared that bodybuilding was corrupt. Yet all of this—the tirades, the complaints, the aspersions, the host of unhappy competitors—it all raised an important question: did any of this matter?

There wasn't much reason to believe it did. El Sonbaty's grumblings were posted on the internet for anyone to read, and they supplied a little extra, word-of-mouth proof for bodybuilders and fans who thought the IFBB and its judging practices were suspicious. Nevertheless, El Sonbaty's insistence that he was the best bodybuilder in the world and that contest judges simply refused to acknowledge it did not win him much sympathy, especially when a lot of fans simply did not agree. Nor did El Sonbaty's ad nauseum name-calling and mudslinging enhance his credibility, since those tend to be tactics of the sore loser. Rather, his message and manner of delivery brought further to light two of bodybuilding's more poorly-kept secrets: only in the rarest of cases will the life of a professional bodybuilder resemble that of a major league athlete or a movie star; and some make rather unhappy exits.

That being said, the greatest significance of El Sonbaty's loud-and-clear tirade about the IFBB, its members, and his own experiences may be found in its result: bodybuilders who had been made aware of the snakepit over which they peered chose to jump in anyway. Despite the warnings in El Sonbaty's diatribe and mood of departure, competitors didn't stop competing.

Above all else, fans didn't turn away. They wanted to see muscle, and lots of it. If there was unfairness, politics and back-stabbing going on behind the veil of beef, so be it. For some fans, juicy gossip only made things more interesting. Certain members of the IFBB were no doubt chafed by El Sonbaty's accusations, but nowhere is it more true than in modern bodybuilding the old saying which declares: there's no such thing as bad press. Federation coffers were undamaged by his bomb-throwing.

While El Sonbaty intended to discredit the IFBB, he inadvertently revealed a few things about the motivations and need for acknowledgment displayed by many bodybuilders. He calls himself the Uncrowned Mr. Olympia; although he portrays the IFBB to be disreputable and shady, El Sonbaty nevertheless dignifies that organization by coveting its titles. He could have as easily labeled himself "World's Greatest Bodybuilder," washed his hands of any IFBB affiliation, and moved on. He instead chose to dwell on the past, and on his belief that he was unjustly denied victory at the Mr. Olympia contest. His statements became a clear demonstration of the fact that for many competitive bodybuilders, building an impressive physique is not enough. For them, a muscular body is also a means by which they might satisfy a strong, twofold desire: the need to be recognized as superior to others; and the longing for official recognition, even if it comes from a governing body which is thought to be unfair and illegitimate.

A large number of competitors of all levels believe that unfair judgment is sometimes or even often passed. Regardless, most continue to compete anyway. In essence they enter contests hoping that unfair practices on the part of the judges will not affect their placings, or that they will be the lucky benefactors of unfair judgment. Many competitors will thus devote a large amount of time, energy and money, and sometimes jeopardize their health, in order to prepare for an event whose outcome they believe may very well be influenced by luck. "Luck" may be defined as events or circumstances beyond someone's control that nevertheless work to his advantage. In bodybuilding competition, those events and circumstances are found in the whims of those who wield power. Bodybuilders who enter contests submit themselves to that power. As the stakes get higher the power becomes greater and the submission deeper.

Quite a few men dead-set on achieving bodybuilding greatness have few skills, little education,[1] and no other real means by which to be successful. When they're given what they perceive to be an opportunity to achieve glory, and to become rich and famous in the process—all by doing something they love—they will go to great lengths to make that dream a reality. They submit themselves to the

[1]El Sonbaty is apparently not among this group, since he claims both to have a bachelor's degree and fluency in several different languages.

whims of those who decide their fate because they have little choice. They can accept it or quit. El Sonbaty eventually quit, and he resolved to never accept the judgments of the IFBB or the way they were handed down. He later declared himself a Foe of Injustice in bodybuilding. Yet anyone who assumes that role faces an uphill battle. After all, bodybuilding never promised to be a bastion of fairness and justice.

* * * * *

Bodybuilding may have never guaranteed fairness and justice, but as the 1990s wore on it was promising to be an endeavor fraught with risk. Mohammed Benaziza had died. Scores of other competitors, many of them little-known amateurs, required paramedic help after falling severely ill from dehydration. Numerous others were stricken with less urgent but equally severe medical conditions. Except for incidents involving big-name competitors like Paul Dillett, these affairs went largely unnoticed. Few are remembered. It's the more dramatic and terrible events which live in infamy and survive in memory. 1992 ended with one such episode. 1996 began with another.

Andreas Munzer continued to roll after his top-ten finish at the 1993 Olympia. He earned top-six finishes at the next three Schwarzenegger Classic contests, and another ninth at the '94 Olympia. Like many of the men who competed at the '96 Schwarzenegger, he decided take advantage of his peak condition by entering the following week's San Jose Pro contest, one of the circuit's minor events. He placed seventh, and shortly afterward flew back to his native Austria. He then became gravely ill.

Andreas Munzer. c. 1995

Courtesy of Steve Harris

Four days later he was dead. Although the exact cause of Andreas Munzer's death was never conclusively determined, the doctors who last examined him discovered massive internal bleeding and multiple organ failure. Munzer had previously avoided consulting with physicians, being perhaps afraid of what they might tell him. The level of conditioning he had brought to bodybuilding's biggest stages, contest after contest, may have made him a living legend, but the drug regimen he was rumored to have used to get that way gave him notoriety of another type. Encouraged by his own success, Munzer ignored the risks. He was not however able to ignore the severe abdominal pain that overwhelmed him on his final day. He was taken to the closest hospital emergency room, but by then it was far too late. Munzer's body had suffered far too much damage. When puzzled surgeons finally cut into his abdomen, he was in a full physiological tailspin. Years of daredevil drug use had taken its toll, and numerous bouts of severe, self-induced dehydration may have played a role as well. He died on March 13, 1996, at the age of 31. Like Benaziza, he was at the peak of his career when time ran out. Arnold Schwarzenegger, a hero of Munzer's who hailed from the same hometown, sent flowers to his funeral.

The Benaziza tragedy and tales of competitors who survived their own brushes with death had significantly jaded the bodybuilding world. Considering the state of high-level competition and Munzer's unofficial title of *world's most shredded man*, to many, his death wasn't even surprising. Further taking into account the amount and variety of drugs that were rumored to be in his system, it seemed as though a catastrophe was inevitable. Once Munzer's death became known, there was naturally a good deal of speculation and rumor in bodybuilding circles about the exact cause. The significance of the tragedy was not to be found in the specifics of his cocktail however, but in the fact that once again a competitor had been killed by his own contest-preparation drug regimen.

Since Munzer was from Schwarzenegger's hometown of Graz, it's easy to image that he wanted to follow in his hero's footsteps. In fact a huge number of bodybuilders at one time wanted something similar. Although the star-power and eventual fame of Schwarzenegger was arguably the greatest thing ever to happen to Joe Weider and his burgeoning

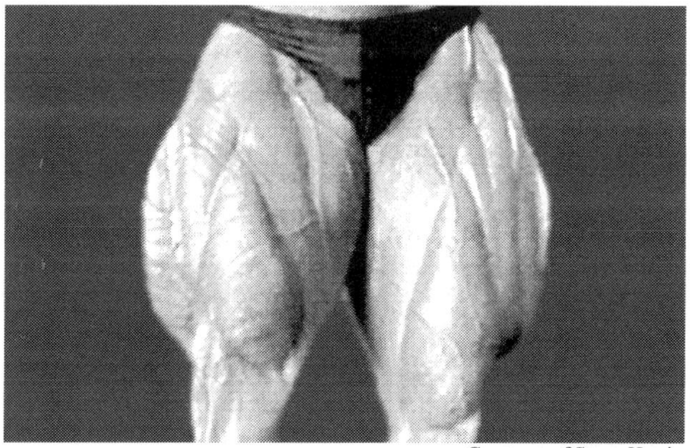

Courtesy of Steve Harris

Andreas Munzer. c. 1993

empire, for a host of run-of-the-mill bodybuilders the opposite may be true. Schwarzenegger's fame helped foster the false belief that bodybuilding could be a viable path to legitimate stardom. In time his movies fell from fashion; he entered politics and quit working out. His muscles gradually vanished, as did visions of mega-stardom dreamt of by a fading legion of bodybuilders.

Meanwhile however, the number of new competitors and the size of contests continued to swell. The world of bodybuilding had grown enough to create its own version of a big-time star. Unlike Schwarzenegger, a new-era star wouldn't appear on the silver screen. His image would instead grace magazine covers and posters advertising him as the featured guest-poser at local bodybuilding contests. Apart from his own competitions, these personal appearances were the star's primary means of experiencing fame. They were also where the star came most closely into contact with fans. At the event he would stride onstage to booming music and the howls of a crowd that had been goaded to cheer by raucous emcees and—in a departure from past eras—his own gestures.

By the mid-1990s it became common for competitors and guest-posers to elicit crowd response by cupping their hands next their ears and waving their hands in "let's hear it" motions. Gone were the days when audience applause was owed solely to the merits of the men who stood onstage flexing. Posing routines in many instances had become orchestrated cheering exercises. John Brown made crowd interaction an important part of his groundbreaking '85 Olympia spectacle, and the Brussels audience who witnessed it was understandably enthralled. Up to that point, the biggest change in bodybuilding presentation had been the addition of musical accompaniment. The crowd got a big kick out of Brown's routine, and his gestures in a small way allowed them to be part of it. Considering the context, it all made sense.

Although Lou Ferrigno was a product of an age where such antics would have been completely out of place, he used a variation of the ploy to whip the '93 Olympia audience into a frenzy. As a beloved competitor and living tribute to bodybuilding's greatest era, the crowd felt he deserved loud and sustained cheers and applause. His sincere prodding was enthusiastically received. With Ferrigno's de facto seal of approval, the trend had officially begun, and a trickle of copycats later became a flood. Kevin Levrone incessantly waved his hands near his ears at the '94 Schwarzenegger Classic, the audience mainly obliged him, and within a few years such onstage gestures were commonplace. Levrone never again hit the stage without motioning for the audience to cheer for him. During his 1997 Mr. Olympia posing routine, he did so no less than 25 times.

New competitors naturally assumed cheer-goading to be part of a normal posing routine, and by the turn of the 21st century attendees of all levels of competition could expect to receive cheering requests for up to three straight hours. Some longtime fans found the trend to be immodest and narcissistic, but since the general public often describes bodybuilding as a whole with similar terms, it can perhaps be said that cheer-goading was bound to happen.

For guest-posing professionals, the new audience-interaction trend had arrived with convenient timing. Unlike the previous decade, during the 1990s many were showing up for exhibitions in deplorable condition. Although posters advertising upcoming appearances showed featured performers in best-ever, contest-day shape, what audiences got was, with increasing regularity, something altogether different. Guest posers often took the stage at the peak of offseason condition, which frequently meant that they just looked fat. The distended waistlines of many modern-era competitors looked especially bloated when they were out of shape, and the term "pregnant" was increasingly used to describe their appearance.

It was common for top competitors of the 1980s to stress the importance of staying relatively lean year-round. The 1990s saw that practice lose importance. Bodybuilders whipped themselves into world-class condition when they needed to, but as the years passed it seemed that they let themselves become more and more overweight when it didn't matter. Cynics alleged that new-era chemicals made getting in shape easier than ever, and that a competitor armed with the right precontest drug cocktail need not bother with efforts to stay lean in the offseason. Whatever the reasons for the trend may have been, guest-posers were looking less and less like the men advertised on event posters. Crowds howled with approval anyway, delighted to see world-class size onstage and before their eyes, even if it was encased in a thick layer of soft tissue.

Before and after performances, visiting stars sat at lobby meet-and-greet stations, selling and signing 8x10 photographs, videos, and other memorabilia. Beyond having their images in bodybuilding magazines or being invited to the "VIP" parties that followed major competitions, such was the recognition upon which famous bodybuilders could rely. The Arnold action-movie era had ended, as did any false hope for greater fame held by those who wished to follow him. Like the bodybuilders whose time preceded *Pumping Iron,* physique competitors of the new era would have to be content with anonymity; with being big fish in a small pond; with being unknown to the outside world. Regardless, to the truly devoted, this would be enough. After all, bodybuilding *is* their world. To them, the rest of the planet is populated with people who simply don't get it. Along with an at-all-costs commitment to their cause, the prevalence of this attitude helped transform bodybuilding from culture to cult.

IFBB professional competitor,
guest-posing exhibition, c. 2006

Courtesy of Steve Harris

*　*　*　*　*

In the first half of the 1990s that cult saw the emergence of a number of outstanding new professsional bodybuilders, along with an era-changing bump in the muscular mass of its greatest examples. The second half of the '90s was characterized by a series of high-level battles between what was more or less that same group of competitors. It became a situation similar to the second half of each of the prior two decades: a small, mainly unchanging group of closely-matched competitors, year after year vying for the top spots in bodybuilding's biggest shows.

The 1996 Olympia simply saw a reshuffling of the previous year's top placements, with Yates once again finishing on top. The biggest news story to surface from that particular competition was Nasser El Sonbaty's disqualification for failing the new diuretics test. Not surprisingly, El Sonbaty would later cry foul. Some professionals quietly sided with him; they were guided by the belief that the testing program was a farce and that the IFBB was out to make an example out of somebody big, to give the illusion that testing was for real. The continued widespread use of water-shedding drugs and a lack of future disqualifications gave credence to these opinions. Nevertheless, in '96 El Sonbaty was forced to surrender his $35,000 third-place prize money, and he will forever be noted in IFBB historical records as having been stripped of his bronze medal. Some who recalled the incident lent a sympathetic ear to his later tirades.

For at least the time being, El Sonbaty kept his nose to the grindstone. He resolved to both triumph in contests and avoid detection, and to keep improving. Before six months had passed he came close to winning another major competition. In fact the 1997 Schwarzenegger Classic title would have been his had Flex Wheeler not returned, finally, to the condition that had so quickly catapulted him to the top of the IFBB ranks. The federation's judges lived up to their words and added legitimacy to their judging guidelines when, at least in this instance, pure mass did not carry the day. Beauty was chosen over beast. When the two stood side-by-side, El Sonbaty certainly looked more massive, but Wheeler had far better lines. Sonbaty's inferior back development also once more came back to bite him. He may further have done himself a disservice in the posedown by relentlessly following the more complete Wheeler around the stage and standing in front of him at every opportunity. El Sonbaty evidently had strong doubts about whether he would be able to beat a well-condition Wheeler by matching him pose-for-pose. However, he knew for certain that he could block Wheeler from view by standing in front of him. He therefore opted for the latter strategy. It didn't work. Only on the rarest of occasions will a posedown affect the outcome of a contest, and this wasn't one of them; nor was El Sonbaty's strategy consistent with the spirit and purpose of the posedown round, which is to create additional side-by-side comparisons with rival competitors, not block them from view at every opportunity.

The 1997 Schwarzenegger Classic gave IFBB judges an easy opportunity to prove that contests would not always be won by the most massive competitor. Recent versions of the Mr. Olympia contest, '94 in particular, had suggested otherwise. But since this wasn't an Olympia and judges weren't constrained by what appeared to be that event's special criteria for its winner, they had the freedom to create such an outcome. The decision also kept professional events slightly unpredictable, something that naturally generates more interest from fans. As much as anything however, the contest proved that an in-shape Flex Wheeler was still close to unbeatable.

Wheeler therefore factored heavily into 1997 Mr. Olympia predictions. Barring any mishaps, for the second straight year it appeared that Yates, Wheeler, Levrone, Ray, Dillett and El Sonbaty would be onstage together at an Olympia, with all of them in top form. Added to the mix would be Lee Priest, Jean-Pierre Fux, Chris Cormier, Ronnie Coleman, Mike Francois, Charles Clairemont, Milos Sarcev and Mike Matarazzo, making the collective quality of the '97 Olympia field no less than incredible.

Of this second lot, Swiss national Fux perhaps had the most potential to break through to the top six. He possessed mass that was on par with that of Yates and El Sonbaty, and his back development surpassed that of the latter. Nevertheless, he was able to finish no better than eighth in the previous year's Olympia, and ninth at the Schwarzenegger Classic. The relative lack of sharpness in his entire backside had been his downfall, as may have been his gargantuan midsection. IFBB judges had quickly proven themselves ready to ignore the thick waistlines of Yates and El Sonbaty, but Fux's stomach may have pushed itself too far into their line of sight.

Next to men like Shawn Ray, Kevin Levrone, Flex Wheeler and Charles Clairemont, Fux looked positively bloated through his middle. Nevertheless, as a third ultra-massive perennial top-ten contender for bodybuilding's greatest title, his presence officially made the thick-waisted look a trend. In the years to come scores of others joined him, and the prevalence of distended midsections eventually became an official topic of IFBB concern. For the moment however, there was no policy to punish those who sported that look.

While IFBB officials pondered the issue, competitors prepared for the Olympia. At the eleventh hour it was made known that the contest's phenomenal assemblage of physiques would be short one its finest examples—none other than the resurgent Flex Wheeler—thanks to a mishap of the most unusual variety.

According to Wheeler, six days before the event two men menaced him at a traffic light. One brandished a firearm. Quick to recognize his peril, Wheeler unleashed upon them the full might and fury of his martial arts expertise. The bodybuilding champion exited his vehicle and delivered unto the gun-wielding assailant a blow so potent that the man was rendered unconscious. Wheeler then turned to the second attacker, who produced a pair of nunchucks—a classic martial arts weapon and an unlikely accessory for a modern crime. Wheeler dispatched his attacker, but not before suffering wounds to his left arm that were serious enough to force him out of the upcoming competition.

Jean-Pierre Fux, c. 1997

Courtesy of Steve Harris

Unable to compete, Wheeler showed up at the Olympia anyway, with a cast on his arm and a tale to tell. Few believed it. Most figured the story had been concocted as a means to bow out of the competition without penalty. Speculation held that Wheeler had not properly prepared for the show, and that compared to the damage stepping onstage in poor form would have done to his career, he preferred to be known as a teller of tall tales. Despite his repeated insistence that the confrontation was real, no police report was filed, and the episode—sarcastically dubbed "the ninja story"—was conspicuously absent from the pages of Wheeler's 2003 autobiography.

In later years details of the assault were occasionally rehashed by amused fans who found camp value in the affair. The story itself has little value beyond that. Flex Wheeler claiming to be the victim of a random attack by a nunchuck-wielding assailant was not an event that factored into the historical progression of bodybuilding. However, by bowing out of the Olympia, he did unwittingly deny fans a final chance to see all the great physiques of the 1990s together on one stage. Few of them knew it in advance, but a very real arm injury sustained by another competitor was about to end the current phase of bodybuilding's modern era.

* * * * *

Three weeks prior to the '97 Mr. Olympia contest, Dorian Yates suffered another major muscle tear. This time it was his left tricep that came almost completely detached. In what was later described by Yates as a "miracle," he was nevertheless able to prepare for and enter the show. Being completely unable to train for the final few weeks, Yates instead opted for aggressive therapy in an effort to reduce swelling and bruising in the damaged area. Predictably, his training methods were called into question. He denied that there was any danger inherent to high-intensity training, and that it was instead his decision to train "gung-ho all the time and with no break" that caused his injuries. Summing up an attitude that has prevailed in bodybuilding for the better part of a century, he said: "I'm not really good at knowing where 85 or 90 percent is. I only know where zero and one hundred is." Numerous bodybuilders—most of them unknown—who have suffered severe injuries lament having possessed the same mindset.

Just like in 1994, Yates made up his mind that the injury would not stop him. The decision was consistent with his reputation; that he was a man who possessed both unwavering resolve and a steadfast determination to prevail. Although it can truthfully be said that countless bodybuilders share these qualities, what separated Yates from most of them was that he had the physique to back it up. For the sixth straight Olympia, even with a left arm that was now compromised front and back, that physique carried him to victory. The three-week layoff that preceded the contest somehow ended up not affecting Yates' overall condition, and even more remarkable was that his recently-torn tricep was only somewhat noticeable. Afterward, considering himself fortunate to have not only competed but to have won the show, and possibly fearing what other surprises his body might have in store, he called it quits. Based on his competition record alone, Dorian Yates retired as the third-greatest bodybuilder of all time.

Since Flex Wheeler wasn't in the 1997 Mr. Olympia lineup, most competitors were given the opportunity to move up a notch in the placings. In the end, the remainder of the top six were, in order, El Sonbaty, Ray, Levrone, Dillett, and Priest. Fux and Cormier occupied the next two spots. Yates therefore left competitive bodybuilding with the satisfaction of having defeated, for a final time, a truly amazing field of competitors. Like the aftermath of the '91 Olympia, much talk centered on who would next ascend the throne.

One man who wasn't seriously considered a threat to take the next year's title was ninth-place finisher Ronnie Coleman. Now a veteran competitor, Coleman had turned into a bit of a stalwart pro. After his disappointing Olympia debut in 1992, faith was not lost, and he managed to gradually and steadily improve. Coleman was able to consistently finish in the top six of lesser events like the Niagara Falls and Chicago Pro Invitational contests, and he was almost always good enough to qualify for each year's Olympia. Although his first few appearances at that contest resulted in double-digit placements, the '96 version saw him crack the top six. At the time that finish was generally thought to mark the pinnacle of his career, and the consensus was that Coleman's destiny was to remain a fixture of pro bodybuilding's second tier. That notion was confirmed at the '97 Olympia, where he dropped back to ninth. Few expected much more from him.

What Coleman expected of himself, meanwhile, was merely to reach his potential. While some of his peers publicly complained about their placings, Coleman accepted his and moved forward. As a career police officer, he had the luxury of not needing to rely on contest earnings or product endorsements for income. He also didn't seem to take low placings personally. Like Yates and Haney before him, Coleman saw no need to move to Venice and train at Gold's. His off-the-beaten-path warehouse gym in Texas would do just fine. It had a large supply of 45-pound plates under its roof, which was good, because Coleman needed a lot of them to train. Videos released later testified to this.

By the mid-1990s, training videos became a cheap and easy way for bodybuilders to generate income. All they needed to do was have someone with a camera film their workouts, get the footage edited, release it on video, and advertise for it in the muscle magazines. Each video had a different flavor. The Yates video was appropriately shot in black and white, with brutal training and weights clanging, all done to the trademark yelling of his training partner. Kevin Levrone's video showed workouts that were more like that of the *Flex Magazine* TV show, with lighter weights and more banter. The video also had lots of flexing, along with several reminders to "pump up the volume." Craig Titus' video showed regular training, but included shots of him driving around, cooking food and eating. In fact it had become common in training videos to include scenes of the bodybuilding star engaging in non-workout activities. Yates was seen walking his dog; Levrone showed himself helping underprivileged children by handing them Levrone t-shirts; and cameras followed Coleman on the job, in his squad car, even making an arrest. Mainly though, Coleman's video showed him training. It was a remarkable sight.

At his peak, Ronnie Coleman was a man of mind-blowing strength. He favored basic exercises like barbell squats, used very heavy weights, and in general lifted like a man possessed. He offered no garish reminders to "pump up the volume," nor was there a lot of close-up flexing for the camera. Viewers were instead treated to his sincere battle cry of "light weight!" before thrusting himself under an 800-pound barbell or heaving 180-pound dumbbells.

In the months following the 1997 Mr. Olympia contest however, scenes like these were unknown to the great majority of the bodybuilding world. Ronnie Coleman was a fairly popular pro, but he hadn't really broken through yet. Since he hadn't grabbed big headlines, and had but a single professional victory under his belt—the 1997 Russian Grand Prix—not a great deal of attention was focused on him. In that regard he was a bit like Aaron Baker: both were nice guys with incredible physiques who didn't do all that well in IFBB contests. While Baker's entire post-WBF competitive career was characterized by punishment for having switch loyalties, Coleman had been penalized for purely physical reasons.

Although Ronnie Coleman was always one of the bigger and better-conditioned competitors, he didn't have the shape of a Flex Wheeler or a Shawn Ray. He didn't even have the shape of an Aaron Baker. Coleman's lines certainly weren't bad, by any standard; but his physique was without a narrow, straight-lined and symmetrical midsection, like those possessed by men who were known for exceptional shape. In that regard he was a bit like Lee Haney. Coleman's great strength was that he was one large collection of fantastic body parts. His thighs were massive and full, with excellent sweep. His biceps displayed an incredible peak. His entire back was both massive and deeply cut. His glutes were beyond shredded, and although his manner of displaying them started an unfortunate trend (p. 157), they nevertheless made the entire backside of his physique something to behold. Like Yates and Haney, when his comparison group faced the curtain, Coleman stood out.

When viewed in these terms, Ronnie Coleman suddenly seemed like a good candidate to one day take the Olympia title. He displayed nearly all the characteristics the IFBB wanted in its world champion: he was tall; at five-foot-eleven he was taller

Ronnie Coleman. c. 2005

Courtesy of Steve Harris

than nearly all of the contest's top contenders; Coleman also possessed what could be described as a herculean physique, one known more for brutal, rugged size than graceful shape; he had no weak body parts, and his back development was show-stopping. Despite all this, he did lack one critical characteristic: dominating overall mass. Coleman was certainly big, and throughout his six years on the professional circuit he was known as one of the larger competitors, but he didn't possess the stand-out mass that separated Haney, Yates, Schwarzenegger and Oliva from their competition when each was in his prime. The minority of fans who grasped the scope of Coleman's potential knew that if he could ever achieve a significant bump in his overall size—something like the famous growth spurts of Yates and El Sonbaty—he would be a legitimate threat to win the Olympia. Until then, he would merely be a good pro.

Other than that he was a part-time pro bodybuilder and a full-time police officer, little was known about Ronnie Coleman. Even less was known about just what he was up to when he went back to Texas after taking part in the whirlwind Grand Prix tour that followed the '97 Olympia. Since the release of his first training video was still a few years away, the bodybuilding world also had no real idea about the brutality of his training sessions, the poundages he was lifting, or the sharpness of his focus. They would soon have full knowledge, however, of what kind of effect that training could have on a man with one-in-a-million genetics and state-of-the-art supplementation.

Dorian Yates, in an act of well-timed publicity, had broken the unofficial mass barrier in 1993. Nasser El Sonbaty joined him in '95. Ronnie Coleman's turn came three years later, and it was made known the moment he stepped onstage at the '98 Night of Champions. Just like the ascent of El Sonbaty, in less than six months Coleman had catapulted himself onto bodybuilding's top tier; and significantly, he defeated El Sonbaty upon arrival. Especially considering that Coleman could do no better than ninth place at the Iron Man show that preceded the NOC, it was a stunning victory—pulled off by a perennial also-ran from whom few expected great things. Satisfied for the moment, Coleman returned to Texas and resumed his life as a beat cop with an immersive hobby.

Shortly thereafter Flex Wheeler won the Schwarzenegger Classic. He therefore also became the odds-on favorite to finally win the Mr. Olympia contest, to be held that year in New York. When the list of men who had committed to compete in the Olympia was released, a quick scan revealed a list of men whom Wheeler at one time or another had already defeated: El Sonbaty; Levrone; Priest; Cormier; Dillett; Fux; Ray; and Matarazzo. The presence of the name Coleman on the list of competitors surprised no one. Once the event got underway however, the physique he presented surprised everyone.

* * * * *

Ronnie Coleman had again returned to Texas after the Night of Champions, and got back to work improving upon a physique that some though had no remaining room for improvement. He was eager to show them what he was capable of. Concerning his prospects for the Olympia, comparison rounds told the tale. He was sharp, balanced and massive. His size was now of a dominating variety. His back, which had for years been among bodybuilding's best, was bigger and better than ever. Like Yates before him, when his comparison group faced the curtain, Coleman's ascendancy was evident. A contest that previously figured to be a four-way fight between Levrone, Ray, Wheeler and El Sonbaty—men who had all at one time worn a Silver Medal on an Olympia stage—was suddenly made more interesting by a familiar face who had never placed higher than sixth. That familiar face was now, out of the blue, a legitimate dark horse and a threat to pull the rug out from under them all.

A review of the 1998 Olympia's top competitors at least partially suggested the outcome. Kevin Levrone was a tad less sharp than normal. At a level of competition where any regression in form is almost always punished, without mercy, it seemed doubtful that he would become the first new Mr. Olympia in six years. Nevertheless, his combination of size and lines promised to land him somewhere near the top. Chris Cormier, as always, was big and defined, with tremendous thigh development and excellent overall balance. He also had a trim waistline, something that was becoming rare at bodybuilding's highest level. He just didn't have the necessary overall mass to seriously threaten some of the men who flanked him. Nasser El Sonbaty meanwhile had enough size and separation to threaten the entire field, at least when viewed from the front. He still had the same old problems with his back development however; and combined with his recent losses to Coleman and Wheeler, few expected him to exit the building with a Sandow trophy. Nevertheless, since El Sonbaty had already defeated the entire Olympia lineup at various times over the prior few years, he theoretically had a shot to take the title. Finally, there was the perennial threat, the ever-perfect Shawn Ray. Although it was certain he would finish somewhere near the top, it was equally doubtful that he would win. For better or worse, the Olympia was now a big man's contest. Since at least four inches of height and 25 pounds of muscle separated Ray from the next-smallest top-tier competitor, he had little chance of prevailing.

Unlike a few of the giants who surrounded him, Shawn Ray never became a specimen of freakish transformation. In fact he had added only a moderate amount of muscle to the physique that earned him an easy victory at the 1987 NPC California State Championships, where he was a 21-year-old, 198-pound light heavyweight. Few who witnessed his National Championship win later that year imagined that there was any room for improvement on his physique, yet over time, he found some. His strides were gradual. He didn't mess with success, and he never tried to fix anything that wasn't broken. His strengths were excellent balance and shape. His physique was as close to perfect as anything that had yet been seen, and he knew it.

Shawn Ray was also one of the few bodybuilders of the new era who wasn't sold on the idea of becoming as massive as possible, regardless of the costs. Nor did he quietly accept judging decisions that favored shocking mass over subtle perfection. He nevertheless placed well enough over the years to stay motivated, winning a few big contests along the way, and all the while suffering few penalties for his protests. Most competitors were too afraid of any repercussions criticizing their judges might bring, but not Ray; he either knew something they didn't, or he was just too good to be denied top placings, or both. Whatever the case, he had a brilliant career in bodybuilding. He just didn't have the type of physique that the new-era IFBB wanted holding its Sandow statues.

The IFBB wanted tall men with rugged, herculean lines and dominating mass to leave the stage with its most important trophy. The big question of 1998 was whether an exception to that unwritten rule would be made for Flex Wheeler. While Shawn Ray was short and light enough for judges to unofficially disqualify him from consideration, the same couldn't be said of Wheeler. He was shorter than El Sonbaty and Coleman, but only slightly. Although he also weighed considerably less than either, a light frame and ultra-deep separation mostly made up for it.

Over the years, direct comparisons between Wheeler and Coleman showed some similarities but revealed more differences. Going into the '98 Olympia, judges didn't anticipate the significance of once more comparing the two. Nor did they consider Coleman to be a threat to win the Olympia until he stepped onstage—or more accurately, until almost halfway through the first round of judging.

It's typical in professional bodybuilding contests to call out first for comparisons whichever three men are considered to be the best of the field. Although the determination of who those three might be is sometimes based on the appearance of each man as he files onto the stage, it's far more often the case that the first callout is based on the competitors' contest histories. It was therefore no surprise that the first three men asked to step forward for semi-relaxed quarter turns at the '98 Olympia were El Sonbaty, Wheeler, and Levrone. The second group of comparisons typically includes men that are expected to finish closely behind the top three. In '98, those men were Coleman, Ray and Priest. Subsequent early comparison round callouts are based on similar predictions for lower finishes. After that, members of earlier callous are mixed and matched so that the judges might adjust their placements. For example, a direct comparison of two men of subsequent groups might show that the judges initially guessed wrong about the top three. This happened in the first round of the '98 Olympia.

Ronnie Coleman was in the second callout group, where he seemed to have gotten the better of Lee Priest and, unexpectedly, Shawn Ray. He was then called back in the fourth, fifth, and eighth groups—a sign that the judges weren't quite sure what to do with him. Based on his long professional contest history, Coleman wasn't supposed to be comparing favorably against bodybuilding's best competitors, yet he was. They stood Coleman next to El Sonbaty and Levrone, and he got the better of them too. It was in the ninth group called out that he was therefore, finally, asked to stand next to Flex Wheeler. The judges looked long and hard at the pair.

It was realized halfway through the first round that Coleman and Wheeler were the top two men in the contest, even though both possessed completely different builds. Much has been said elsewhere concerning the strengths of each, but the gist of the struggle for the top spot at the '98 Olympia can be described in the simplest of terms: Coleman had mass, and Wheeler had shape.

The second round's comparisons reinforced the conclusions of the first. This time, right off the bat, Coleman was compared to Wheeler, with El Sonbaty thrown in for good measure. Unlike the first round, there was now much less uncertainty about Coleman's prospects. The first call-up suggested he was in the top three. The remainder of the field was then shuffled to and fro, as the judges busied themselves assigning their placings. The judging was made slightly easier due to the early withdrawal of Paul Dillett, who once again had a frightening dehydration episode. He lost consciousness between rounds, and was yet again hospitalized. As always however, the show went on. A total of ten comparison groups were called forward as Wheeler and Coleman mainly waited and watched. The pair, again with El Sonbaty, was called out one last time as the round's final set. This was a sign that the judges wanted to be sure of the decision they were about to make. They had to decide not only which man was better, but which type of physique was superior. Few who witnessed the event may have realized it, but the future of professional bodybuilding hung in the balance.

Seldom had bodybuilding been presented with so clear a crossroads as at the 1998 Mr. Olympia contest. This time, there was no reigning champion to whom judges would give special consideration; nor was there an issue of race, as had been supposed by some when Dorian Yates pulled off a couple of his more controversial wins, or when Arnold Schwarzenegger in 1972 defeated Sergio Oliva. This time, the two top men were black. The stage was therefore set for a pure and simple judgment of whichever physique truly was best. All that remained was for the judges to tell the world what that meant.

The evening's proceedings were typical late-90s fare, with a few contestants following the growing trend of injecting dance moves into their routines. By the end of that decade it had become common at bodybuilding contests for at least one competitor, midway through his routine, to abandon flexing and posing altogether in favor of dancing. The notable example from the 1998 Olympia was Johnny Moya.

John Brown wowed the 1985 Mr. Olympia audience with a lengthy display of posing and dancing, and he was given much credit for his originality. Brown's ideas later reached their apex in the routines of his understudy Melvin Anthony. While Anthony was still clawing his way to the top of the amateur ranks, a fair number of competitors of all levels decided to jump on the posing-and-dancing bandwagon. A trend was born.

Unfortunately for the imitators and their audiences, few had the talent to pull it off or the ability to recognize that they couldn't. Although by 1998 the dancing-bodybuilder novelty had already worn off, the trend grew in popularity. The Olympia audience sat through a few routines that were part flexing and part dancing, and it responded favorably.

Meanwhile, suspense continued to build. Fans after all didn't come to see a muscular dance recital. They came to see the world's greatest living bodybuilders, at the top of their game, in a battle for a now-vacant throne. Those who saw or were briefed on prejudging now paid special attention to Ronnie Coleman, as did those who witnessed his unexpected victory at the Night of Champions. When the first phase of the awards ceremony was concluded and Coleman was left standing among the top six, few were surprised; when that top six was instructed to execute their mandatory poses in unison, any remaining doubters were silenced; and when the comparison group faced the curtain to display their backs, a new wonder filled the auditorium. With Dorian Yates gone, the 1998 Mr. Olympia title was thought to be Flex Wheeler's for the taking. Yet here next to him was a veteran competitor, vastly improved, threatening to ruin his date with destiny.

The posedown having been completed, the announcement of awards began. In sixth was Chris Cormier, followed in ascending order by Shawn Ray, Kevin Levrone and Nasser El Sonbaty. Each man accepted his awards and exited stage left. At Olympia contests in the 1990s standard procedure dictated that each competitor leave the stage after receiving his placement and award. Previously each man was expected to stay in the lineup. As the stakes in bodybuilding got higher, competitors' emotions ran deeper and their reactions to placings became more pronounced. It was decided that the occasional scowls and grave faces of disappointed competitors were best moved offstage. The new tradition also drew more attention to remaining competitors and raised the level of drama of the announcements.

The two men left standing, as expected, were Coleman and Wheeler. IFBB Vice President Wayne DeMilia, who traditionally took the microphone and announced the awards at professional contests, had over the years developed a simple method for creating suspense at those events. After each successsive award, the gaps between announcements would lengthen. This was especially true of the '98 Olympia. After El Sonbaty was awarded third, a full two minutes went by before the runner-up position was announced. It was almost as if DeMilia knew the true significance of the announcement he was about to make. After torturing the audience and especially the two competitors long enough, he made it known that Flex Wheeler finished second.

With the announcement, Coleman dropped to the floor. There he lay, completely prone, head resting on his arms, and apparently sobbing. It was as if his decades of toil and seven years of frustration at the professional level had all come crashing down directly on top of him, heavier than the 800-pound barbells he shouldered, and with greater might than his own force of will. His own humility left him pinned to the dais, unable even to acknowledge the congratulations of Wheeler, who bent over him, spoke into his ear, and patted him on the back. When he was finally roused, he came down the ramp from the second tier to accept his award and offer heartfelt and sincere, teary-eyed thanks to the audience, his girlfriend, and his diet advisor. Coleman also thanked his mother, who now stood next to him, for supplying the Olympia-caliber genetics that made the win possible. She smiled and flexed her arm for the audience. It was the most touching scene yet witnessed at a Mr. Olympia contest.

*   *   *   *   *

The 1998 Mr. Olympia contest had finally come to an end, and a tenth Mr. Olympia was crowned. In the process, the IFBB reminded the world what type of physique it wanted to see prevail at its greatest contest. In accord with past standards, Coleman had a Mr. Olympia physique, through and through. His victory provided a seamless continuity from the two champions that came before him. Viewed from this perspective, the contest could have had but one outcome.

Above and beyond his delivery of an appropriate physique, Coleman had a few subtle traits that may have helped his cause. He was a humble, soft-spoken and religious man with a feel-good story. In a way, he became the new Lee Haney; a living reminder of the recent past, of happier times before bodybuilding was faced with wrecked Olympic dreams, the public's education on steroids and the deaths of a few champions. Coleman's unprecedented, seven-year ascent from last to first place added an inspiration tilt to his image. Here was a true die-hard, a man whose tireless efforts were at long last rewarded.

Flex Wheeler was also most certainly a die-hard, though he left the stage that night with disappointment rather than a Sandow trophy. The correlation of massive champions and the overall growth of bodybuilding over the prior 14 years could not be denied, but in 1998 it raised an important question: would bodybuilding have lost fans and money if Wheeler had been declared Mr. Olympia? It seems the answer would have to be no.

At the same time, no one could know long it would be before the contest's gargantuan mass standard would return. It might have returned the moment Wheeler's reign came to its end. As the modern era of bodybuilding fermented, fans proved time and again that they wanted to see a "freak show." Plus, for all the praise heaped upon Wheeler for being a man of fantastic shape, he himself was rather massive. He wouldn't have won so many other contests, or so often threatened the Olympia title, if this was not the case. But like Shawn Ray, he just didn't have the imposing mass judges wanted in their Olympia winner.

*   *   *   *   *

As the 1990s drew to a close, the bodybuilding world was a much different place than just a decade prior. While the evolved appearance of bodybuilders was the most obvious change, the magazines showcasing them underwent a transformation as well. Publications of the '90s were bigger and more slickly-produced than their predecessors. Ten years prior, the formatting of bodybuilding magazines resembled those of other areas of interest: articles and photographs were interspersed with advertisements that ranged from tiny, 10-word classified ads to full-page, full-color displays. While this basic format remained largely unchanged, by the end of the '90s magazines began to take on the appearance of muscle-building supplement catalogues.

The thickness of individual magazines swelled. Page after page displayed product after product, each one suggesting it was a fast track to muscular growth. Advertisements themselves grew, as full-page ads on occasion grew to two or even four pages. Later ads sometimes had more than 12. A typical multi-page advertisement included a faux-article describing the featured product, citing studies and alluding to results, all alongside pictures of the bodybuilding star who endorsed it.

In the '70s and '80s, Joe Weider's false advertising claims got him in trouble. In the new era, advertisers were more cautious, and promises were less specific. This made little difference to men hell-bent on coaxing every last ounce of muscular growth out of their bodies. Since the days of Charles Atlas and even before, a legion of such men had proven themselves quite willing to buy anything that might help. Fueled by their dollars, the supplement industry had long since taken off. In the '90s it continued to streak skyward. The once-dominant Weider supplement line now had dozens of competitors, some of them multi-million dollar powerhouses. In later years Twinlab became a publicly traded company with over $300 million in annual revenue. Met-Rx, which made a bit of a splash in the early '90s with its complete meal replacement product, was sold in the new millennium for over $100 million.

The willingness of new-era bodybuilding hopefuls to pony up for new supplements was heavily influenced by one important factor: some of the products lived up to their claims. It was a bit of a revelation when, in the early 1990s, Creatine monohydrate became available. Creatine gets its most immediate and visible effect by causing the body to store extra water within individual muscle cells. This in turn makes the users' muscles appear larger and more full. Creatine additionally promotes protein synthesis and deters protein breakdown. The end result is bigger, stronger muscles. Once word got out, bodybuilders lined up to buy creatine.

Buyers naturally then wondered what other great undiscovered legal supplements might one day become available. The supplement industry got to work, eager to oblige their curiosity. What followed was a free-flowing exchange of money and product, one that supported the burgeoning supplement industry, filled bodybuilding magazines with impresssive and often lengthy advertisements, and provided endorsing bodybuilders with a new, significant source of income.

Most of the big supplement companies began to sign professional bodybuilders to endorsement contracts. In exchange for approving statements and use of the bodybuilders' image, companies gave them money and free products. Since the overall amount of prize money in IFBB contests was still very small compared to major individual sports, and a significant portion of that money was gobbled up by the handful of men who occupied the competitive top tier, endorsement contracts became the primary means by which a professional could make a living from bodybuilding. Pro bodybuilders jumped at opportunities to sign them.

It could never be known how many young men bought particular supplements because of the imagery and testimonials of their endorsers. To older and wiser bodybuilders, any purchase driven by these selling points was an exercise in naïveté. They understood that top bodybuilders achieved their size and condition through dedication, hard work and nutrition—but they also knew achieving world-class development required the combination of rare genetics and powerful growth-producing drugs. Over-the-counter supplements only minimally factored into this equation. Besides, top bodybuilders got their endorsement contracts by first achieving world-class physiques; afterward they were approached by supplement companies and asked to endorse their products. To those who understood bodybuilding's realities, top-tier new-era competitors were instead a collective endorsement for anabolic steroids, growth hormone, and a variety of other drugs.

More so than ever, here was an activity that thought of itself as a sport that also held illegal drug use as an absolute requirement. When those who knew little about it asked bodybuilders whether they had to pass drug tests in order to compete, some were met with a facetious response: "Yes. If they find you're not on any drugs, you're disqualified." The association of drugs with bodybuilding was stronger than ever. Unfortunately for a few individuals, this did not go unnoticed by authorities. The United States Drug Enforcement Agency, keen to punish the trafficking and possession of any and all illegal drugs, in the 1990s began paying attention to certain high-profile bodybuilders and their activities. Before that, drug busts typically involved unknown individuals and generated little or no press.

In the 1970s and before, bodybuilding was small and obscure enough that authorities for the most part paid no attention to it. Once its rapid rise in popularity began, and steroids started making headlines, all of that changed. Starting in the mid-1980s, some bodybuilders found themselves facing charges for drug possession, often after being singled out for searches upon crossing the Mexican border into the US. Since Mexican pharmacies sold anabolic steroids without requiring prescriptions, cross-border shopping sprees became common. Cheap prices and abundant supplies often made these trips into sources of income for those who knew enough end users. Weightlifting gyms where those men congregated served as convenient distribution centers, and it wasn't unheard-of for small-time gym owners or their employees to turn back rooms into clandestine steroid dealerships.

Police raided some of these. However, by the mid-1990s no "big fish" had yet been taken down.

Top NPC amateur bodybuilder Craig Titus changed all that, when in April of 1995 he became the first high-profile bodybuilder to face drug charges. Notably however, the drugs he was accused of possessing weren't steroids. Titus was arrested for conspiring to distribute the recreational drug Ecstasy—a fairly significant event, because it reinforced the idea that bodybuilders weren't always the wholesome, health-conscious lot advertised in *Muscle & Fitness*. Recreational drugs, especially ecstasy and GHB[1], had in the '90s gained a fair amount of popularity in certain bodybuilding cliques.

In the 1990s, these cliques began converging on Las Vegas with every intention of letting Sin City live up to its billing. Ecstasy use was a staple. The increasingly popular trend of holding physique contests in the gambling Mecca was therefore well-received, as it allowed bodybuilders, in town to see a big show, to kill a few birds with one stone. Craig Titus in later years had his hand in this pot, when he gained a small amount of fame for organizing contest after-parties. In 1995 however, he was merely out to make a few bucks off the Ecstasy trade. His became the familiar tale of a mid-level dealer: all went according to plan until he got busted. In exchange for a guilty plea, Titus was offered house arrest and supervised probation.

Titus had gotten off easy. Significantly however, under the terms of his probation he was forbidden from taking any illegal drugs. Although this included anabolic steroids, Titus decided to risk detection and continue taking them. After all, his career aspiration—and indeed his life's goal—was to become a professional bodybuilder. It's true that countless bodybuilders share that ambition, but for Titus it was entirely realistic. After placing second in the heavyweight division of both the 1994 USA and National Championships, he was at the cusp. Since the men who defeated Titus at those shows had joined the IFBB professional ranks, the way was now cleared for victory. Either title was his for the taking. There was no way he was going to stop. He just needed to keep taking steroids.

Since Titus was convicted of conspiring to distribute recreational drugs, he assumed his probation officers wouldn't spring a steroid test on him. At first his gamble seemed to be paying off. At the '95 USA Titus once more showed up in top condition. A much-improved Phil Hernon ruined his day however, winning the heavyweight division and taking the overall title. Though disappointed, Titus vowed to return. He did, a year later, and with the desired result: he won the heavyweight division and overall title at the '96 USA Championships.

His short-term goal having been achieved, Titus created new ones. He was now a professional, and would soon be competing against the best of the best. His program intensified. Unfortunately for him, so did the scrutiny of his probation officer. While preparing for his first pro contest, Titus was required to take a steroid test, which he failed. The terms of his probation having been violated, Titus was sentenced to 21 months in prison. It would not be his last brush with the law. Nor would this be the last bit of negative press involving bodybuilders or steroids. Meanwhile, a far more sinister event had already overshadowed the Titus story.

Pro bodybuilder Ray McNeil, another member of the ill-fated 1993 Mr. Olympia field, was shot twice by his wife Sally on Valentine's Day of 1995. Unlike Sergio Oliva, McNeil didn't survive. Ray was a mid-tier competitor who had earned a handful of top-ten placings at lesser IFBB shows. Sally was a top amateur who appeared close to gaining professsional status. Both were former US Marines.

At her trial, Sally said the shotgun blasts delivered to her husband's abdomen and face had been an act of self-defense. She portrayed herself as a victim of domestic abuse, and that at least in this final incident, she feared for her life and therefore had no choice but to resort to deadly force. Police reports did in fact show that the pair had a number of violent episodes, although the same reports sometimes described Sally as the initiator. She also had a long history of violent episodes outside their relationship, including assaulting a police officer and bashing in the window of her first husband's car with a crowbar. In a later interview, the former spouse said that Sally became "unhinged" after taking up bodybuilding. A jury of her peers didn't buy the self-defense story. She was convicted of second-degree murder and sentenced to 19 years in prison. Reflecting on the episode years later, she was without remorse or regret, and maintained that Ray was a steroid-enraged wife-beater.

The mainstream press for the most part finds little about bodybuilding to be interesting or newsworthy. When a major crime is committed by a bodybuilder,

[1]Gamma-hydroxybutyrate

that changes everything. The Ray McNeil murder was one such occasion. Murder is always newsworthy, especially if it involves celebrities; and although professional bodybuilders may be celebrities of the most minor degree, they're noteworthy individuals nonetheless. By 1995, anabolic steroids and the apparent evils of their use had been making headlines for more than a decade. The McNeil murder therefore came to press loaded with two newsworthy topics: murder and "roid rage."

As top bodybuilders, it was naturally assumed that both McNeils were taking steroids. Rumors circulated that Ray had several different growth-inducing drugs in his system when he was killed—and therefore, at least at first, many believed Sally McNeil's shotgun blasts were an act of self-defense. Statements made by her daughter gave this idea some credence. According to her, from the next room she could hear the sounds of gurgling, as if her mother was being choked. A gunshot followed shortly thereafter. However, according to testimony, Sally loaded a second round into the gun so that she might finish off the already mortally wounded Ray. Since the jury found the second shot to be an act not of self-defense but of revenge, it was reasonable for news sources to suppose that both parties had been in the throes of 'roid rage.

The whole terrible episode made for a juicy mainstream news story: a dramatic, steroid-fueled domestic killing. The public image of bodybuilding, low already, sunk further. The McNeil murder also served as an unfortunate reminder that the world of bodybuilding had its share of lethal domestic episodes.

The first famous incident involved a man named John Riccardi. Although Riccardi never appeared in a physique contest, he was known to be an avid bodybuilder. When his girlfriend Connie Navarro left him in 1983, he became obsessed with getting her back. Riccardi, who earned a living as a burglar, had no problem breaking into her apartment. Navarro wasn't home at the time, so he laid in wait. When she finally returned with an out-of-town female friend who just happened to be visiting, Riccardi confronted her. A brief argument ensued, and moments later both women were dead from gunshot wounds. Riccardi went on the run, and was at large for several years before time and the law finally caught up with him. His capture initially didn't draw much attention to the world of bodybuilding, mainly because Riccardi wasn't a competitor. Rather, the crime was most notable because it was solved by a series of tips generated by the TV show *America's Most Wanted*; and because the victim's son Dave Navarro was a member of the rock band Red Hot Chili Peppers.

The next famous domestic killing did involve an active competitor. San Francisco-based amateur Gordon Kimbrough was a low-level competitor with a successful personal training business and a beautiful fiancée named Kristy Ramsey. Reports indicated his relationship with Ramsey was turbulent, though it was apparently nothing like that of Ray and Sally McNeil. Nevertheless, Kimbrough had episodes of 'roid rage, and on a few occasions Ramsey caught him with other women. In July of 1993 she decided that she had enough, and told Kimbrough that the relationship was over. He became enraged. Unlike Sally McNeil, Ramsey did not run to the closet to grab a shotgun; she instead ran for the front door, trying merely to get away.

Kimbrough stopped her. The scene that followed was one of unspeakable horror. Kimbrough choked her with an electrical cord before grabbing a knife and repeatedly stabbing her. Within moments of her attempt to escape, Ramsey lay motionless in a pool of blood; and by the time police arrived she was dead. Kimbrough briefly staved off arrest by threatening suicide, but he was soon taken into custody. His conviction for first-degree murder came exactly two weeks before the McNeil incident.

Unlike "ordinary" murders, the McNeil and Ramsey tragedies owed a good deal of their notoriety to the people involved, both perpetrators and victims. To the public who consumed these news stories however, it wasn't important *who* exactly these people were; what mattered was *what* they were. It directed the media's wandering spotlight back onto the insular, strange, cult-like world of bodybuilding, the fringe group that lived to build their muscles and loved to take steroids. Bodybuilding had always fought an image problem, and the few newsworthy episodes of the modern era—gruesome murder scenes created by jealous, drug-crazed hulks topping the list—did little to reverse its gradual downward spiral. In time, similar tragedies would follow.

Before the decade was out, a final bloody rampage would rock the bodybuilding world and further sully its reputation—and it would involve one of the biggest names of the prior era. Although he competed in a few events in the 1990s, Bertil Fox rose to prominence and became one of the most celebrated competitors of the early '80s. Known for an extremely thick and muscular upper body topped with deep separation, and for one of the most impressive "crab" poses ever witnessed on a bodybuilding stage, Fox was a favorite of the mass-loving hardcore crowd. To a segment of devoted fans, he was exactly what bodybuilding was meant to be: gargantuan, rippling mass, excellent conditioning, and little else. He was not "pretty" by any stretch of the imagination. Fox was, as his nickname aptly made clear, *Brutal*.

Bertil Fox was one of the greatest bodybuilders ever to call Great Britain home. Though he was born on the small island of St. Kitts in the Caribbean, Fox was only a year old when his family relocated to the UK. He later disavowed the Caribbean-native label that had been attached to him. "I'm one-hundred percent British," he declared. "I think, I act and talk like an Englishman, not like someone from the West Indies." Nevertheless, more than 40 years after his original departure from St. Kitts, Fox returned. He opened a gym and became engaged to a 20-year-old local beauty queen named Leyoca Browne. Their relationship soon ended. On September 30, 1997, Fox went to the shop where Browne and her mother Violet were working. Shortly thereafter both women were dead, killed by bullets fired from a .38 caliber pistol owned by Fox. According to Fox, it was actually the elder Browne who was in possession of the gun; she threatened him with it, a struggle ensued, rounds were accidentally discharged, and both women were killed. The St. Kitts court did not believe the story. Fox was sentenced to death by hanging, though this was later commuted to life in prison.

By the end of the 1990s, the bodybuilding subculture had witnessed killings by four of its members. This unfortunate trend would by no means end with the 20th century, and some bodybuilders of the new millennium would produce more death, sorrow and ruined lives. The most famous murder of them all was yet to come. To bodybuilders however, these events were anomalies. It was a tiny fraction of the bodybuilding community that committed violent crimes; and the rate of incidence of domestic killings among bodybuilders might not have been any higher than that of the general population. Unfortunately it would be impossible to compile any statistics to show this, since no one really knows how many true bodybuilders walk the Earth. People of the outside world couldn't be expected to care about such comparisons however. They had for the most part already labeled bodybuilders to be narcissistic, depraved and sometimes dangerous, and there was little reason to believe that any statistical comparison would change that. In the public's mind, news stories the mainstream media ran about bodybuilding crimes were all it needed to know. Each gory detail confirmed its suspicions.

Few stood up to defend bodybuilding's image. Nor did anyone challenge the presumption that bodybuilders commit violence against their domestic partners at a higher-than-average rate. After all, bodybuilders are often the first to admit that they periodically become extremely aggressive.

The passion required to undertake a lifelong campaign of hard weight training can come from a variety of places. Many who take up weights and never let go are inspired by what they hope will be the end result. Some love the physical challenge supplied by ongoing training. To many of that same group, training itself is cherished for its therapeutic effects. Some bodybuilders freely admit that deep-seated frustration or even anger supplied their impetus; that bodybuilding became a positive outlet, a way to dispense negative psychological energy through intense physical output. It can be excellent therapy.

However, becoming a competitive bodybuilder can change all that. It can revive latent aggression and amplify it. It can produce consequences of the most serious degree. A typical pre-contest training and diet regimen can turn levelheaded and friendly people into surly, combative introverts. Such transformations are common, and fellow bodybuilders will often give a wide berth to their pre-contest peers. It is also known that the greatest mood-modifying variable in the entire pre-contest bodybuilding mix is the presence of anabolic steroids.

Although synthetic testosterone and its derivatives are necessary for building a modern championship-caliber physique, those drugs feature a number of unwanted and potentially dangerous side effects. Markedly increased aggression is one of these. In one important way it's also the most unique effect of anabolic steroid use, since its risks are undertaken not only by the user, but by those around him. Among those who might already be inclined toward domestic violence, steroid use can be akin to lighting a match in a gunpowder factory. 'Roid rage can be explosive, and explosions always have a blast radius. The worst-case results have been made public, and a small ring of bodies testify to the dangers.

Nevertheless, none of this—the killings, the partying, the drug busts, the 'roid rage—none of it directly factored into the historical progression of bodybuilding, except when viewed from one perspective. Throughout its evolution, bodybuilding has been in a perpetual state of self-measurement. Its yardstick has been the opinions and attitudes of the public, the greater world that lay beyond its shell, like a child looking to its parents for approval. Many years after it had been produced, when the cast and crew of *Pumping Iron* reflected on the significance of that film, the common theme of their analyses was public reception.

The film was written and produced for public consumption, and rightly so. When Charles Gaines and George Butler, both of them non-bodybuilders, became fascinated with the bodybuilding subculture, they wanted to share their findings, and their insight, with the world. It worked. The film was a small hit, and it later earned for itself, rather appropriately, "cult classic" status. True fans of film could appreciate its merits as a documentary. For its viewership as a whole, the movie was a quick and interesting lesson about bodybuilding.

For bodybuilders themselves, the film was an affirmation, if not a vindication. What they were doing, the film told them, was legitimate. It was with a self-congratulatory attitude that the *Pumping Iron* cast and crew shared their memories of the production, and few could blame them. It was very much a job well done. Maybe most importantly, the world now knew who they were; and the world now knew what bodybuilding was.

With time however, the influence of that film waned. Two decades after its release, it was not widely known. Most of the new generation of bodybuilders had never seen it, and a large portion of their non-bodybuilding peers had never heard of it. As the new millennium approached, outsiders' opinions about bodybuilding were often based on what they had noticed on the covers of muscle magazines in supermarket checkout lanes, or what they had seen in TV news stories about steroid-crazed murders. Other than Schwarzenegger's action movies, they had little else to go on.

Meanwhile, the year 2000 was looming large on the horizon. Joe Weider's lofty visions for the future described in his still-trumpeted *Your Physique* magazine piece were about to turn 50, yet the world of bodybuilding was fixed on a path quite unlike what he had predicted. Perhaps the next 100 or 1000 years would see a straighter course, and a muscle culture that—if it could be not viewed as a savior—could at least be appreciated, or even dignified. Time would tell. Meanwhile, the old millennium was not through quite yet. The 20th century IFBB still had one last big contest to put on, and one last issue to decide.

* * * * *

The beginning of the 1999 competitive season saw both Nasser El Sonbaty and Paul Dillett finally hit paydirt. Dillett triumphed over 42 other men at the Night of Champions, winning his first non-Grand Prix event. El Sonbaty meanwhile got the better of a deep field at the Schwarzenegger Classic, making him the winner of the world's second-biggest contest. He would later admit to having mixed feelings about the win, saying that a victory at the Schwarzenegger Classic was a consolation prize given to top competitors who were not deemed worthy of the Mr. Olympia title. Winning the Schwarzenegger contest, El Sonbaty said, by itself guaranteed that he would never be allowed to win the Olympia. IFBB officials had a different view. They maintained that it was El Sonbaty's inability to produce the world's best physique that barred him from claiming that title. It's true that by 1999 no one had won both titles; however, in its 11-year history, a reigning Mr. Olympia had never entered the Schwarzenegger Classic. Regardless, by the judgment of an IFBB panel, in 1999 El Sonbaty had the best physique at bodybuilding's second-best contest; and unless his theory about judges conspiring against him was true, he remained on the short list of viable threats to take the Olympia.

In 1999, the Olympia was at long last moved to Las Vegas, a locale perfectly suited to the convention-like gathering the contest had become. Unlike cities like Columbus or far-flung locations like Pretoria and Helsinki, Las Vegas had unlimited side attractions for fans who flew in to see the contest. In all 17 men were on the bill, including what had become pro bodybuilding's perennial top tier: Coleman; Wheeler; El Sonbaty; Levrone; Ray; Dillett; Priest; and Cormier.

Making his Olympia debut was a German national named Markus Ruhl. With dimensions similar to Jean-Pierre Fux, but with shoulders and pecs that were perhaps the most massive ever carried on a human frame, Ruhl threatened to place near the top of any contest he entered. Unfortunately, he shared the same midsection problems as Fux, as did all men who were able to achieve similar levels of development. Regardless, the audience was pleased to see another monster added to the Olympia lineup. It readily forgave his faults. As an energetic poser onstage and a gentle giant off, it didn't take long for Ruhl to become a crowd favorite.

Prejudging callouts immediately demonstrated that judges of the '99 Olympia were picking up where '98 left off. In both comparison rounds, Coleman and Wheeler were in the first callout group. In the all-important muscularity round, just like the previous year, they were also in the final group. It was therefore obvious which men would occupy the top two positions. Coleman and especially Wheeler had both improved since the prior year, but their relative strengths and differences remained intact. Judges were therefore faced with the same quandary: which would carry the day, beauty or beast?

Coleman merely hoped that judging standards would stay the same, and that the IFBB would honor its unofficial policy of embracing Olympia dynasties. A first win was already under his belt. A second would almost certainly lead to more. Wheeler on the other hand hoped that standards would change; or, more accurately, revert to what they had once been. He also had to hope that the IFBB would divorce itself from its love of long Olympia reigns. Yet this hope was faint, and everyone knew it. If Wheeler was going to beat Coleman and win the Olympia, it needed to be *now.* Otherwise, he would be faced with the challenge of unseating a multiple winner. In the 34-year history of the Mr. Olympia contest, only Arnold Schwarzenegger had been able to do that. More than anything though, Wheeler hoped judges would simply make the right choice—because, without reservation, he believed himself to possess the superior physique.

Markus Ruhl. c. 1999

Courtesy of Steve Harris

The usual evening show festivities were held in a packed Mandalay Bay Events Center. The contest overall showed few marked changes from the prior year, with perhaps the exception of some notable posing routines. Ronnie Coleman's was far more polished than the previous year, and he used a ploy that Lee Haney had so skillfully made part of his repertoire: he withheld back poses until the final stages of his presentation. It was dramatic, effective and well received. In contrast, Flex Wheeler decided to forgo the slow and fluid posing typical of the first half of his routines. His presentation was instead of a high-energy variety, with rapid transitions and near-violent pose-strikes. His previously humble demeanor had also vanished entirely, something that may have worked against him.

The contest's outcome had a few surprises. Markus Ruhl was disqualified for failing a diuretics test. He was nevertheless able to compete in the English Grand Prix that followed, finishing seventh. Jean-Pierre Fux finished dead last, behind an American rookie named Jay Cutler. Fux had not conditioned himself properly. As for Cutler, he was undeterred; and like Coleman in 1992, he resolved to keep plugging away. Another rookie, Dexter Jackson, finished ninth. His physique was somewhat reminiscent of Wheeler's: a light frame, very good shape, and deep separation. However, at five-foot-six, his dimensions were more like that of Shawn Ray. A top-ten finish in his Olympia debut was entirely encouraging. Like Cutler, he would be back.

The evening's biggest surprise came when Nasser El Sonbaty finished sixth. In a situation somewhat similar to that of Rich Gaspari a decade earlier, here was a competitor with an impressive albeit unusual physique, one that judges were growing weary of. Like Gaspari, each year would see him slip further out of contention, until frustration overwhelmed him and he quit. In bodybuilding, just like any field of human endeavor, the greatest falls come from the very top. Each man's high point was a Mr. Olympia Silver Medal. Gaspari's gradual descent into irrelevance and final retirement cost him eight years of his life and a torn lat muscle. El Sonbaty kept at it for five, emerging physical intact but with scars of a different sort. Both learned the hard way what the ancient Romans knew all too well: all glory is fleeting.

Some top competitors walked away from bodybuilding with the feeling they never really experienced glory anyway; that anything short of the Olympia title was a failure; and that the system was

Courtesy of Steve Harris

Shawn Ray, Ronnie Coleman and Flex Wheeler. Mr. Olympia contest. c.1999

was to blame. The "system" was indeed responsible for picking its winners, and for picking the criteria with which to do so. Throughout the 1990s, criteria were debated as much as results. Judges may have grown weary of El Sonbaty, but weariness is not a criterion for judgment; however, the physical balance of a competitor most certainly is. Judges could easily justify his slip in the placings by pointing out the lack of balance between the front and back of his physique, especially relative to that of his competitors. Previously that criterion may have been less important, simply because El Sonbaty had such Earth-shaking mass. On the eve of the 21st Century however, Earth-shaking mass was not such a rare commodity.

The next three placings, in ascending order, were Ray, Levrone and Cormier. For Chris Cormier, the event marked one of the high points in one of pro bodybuilding's most successful careers. He showed up with no expectations of victory, and gratefully accepted his bronze medal. Flex Wheeler grabbed him first, and the two stood hugging while the crowd looked on. Wheeler had become famous for such displays. Cormier was given his medal and check, and was directed to exit the stage.

Just like the year before, as expected, there stood Coleman and Wheeler. Wayne DeMilia once more took the microphone to announce awards, and his slow-tempo delivery again added suspense to the event's most critical moment. After a pause that seemed even longer than the year before, DeMilia made the outcome known. Wheeler again finished second. What followed was a scene that would not be soon forgotten.

In a near-replay of his first win, Coleman dropped to his knees, and then laid facedown on the floor, his head resting on his folded arms. For a brief moment he appeared to weep. Meanwhile, Wheeler's reaction was nothing like the previous year. His head dropped. When the awards presenters came forward, Wheeler turned away from them. He walked to the rear of the stage's lower level and stood motionless, hands on hips, facing away from the audience. The display was met with a chorus of boos. Before long Wheeler returned to the presenters; he received his medals and had his arms raised for the cameras. He did not smile. Flashbulbs went off, and as soon as Wheeler's hands were released he removed the medals, took his check and left the stage.

Flex Wheeler was a veteran professional. Of the tiny handful of competitors from that era who were thought of as heirs-apparent to the Mr. Olympia throne, he arguably possessed the most potential to pull it off. Nevertheless, seven long years of hard work and intermittent adversity had thus far not brought him that title. At the 1999 Olympia, Wheeler considered himself to be at his all-time best, which to him and many others meant he should have been unbeatable. Yet there he was, beaten. The decision did not go his way. Countless bodybuilders have a similar tale to tell. Yet this was no ordinary contest, and no ordinary decision. He was denied glory. Bodybuilding glory—which for some simply means the glory of the Mr. Olympia title—had eluded him. Now, with the official beginning of the Coleman Dynasty, it would most likely continue to elude him, indefinitely, possibly forever. Viewed in this light, Wheeler's reaction was perhaps more understandable.

By winning a second Sandow statue, Ronnie Coleman put himself in a position to collect many more. His dynasty had indeed begun. Bodybuilding's best days had come and gone under the watches of long-reigning kings, and the IFBB would be quite happy keeping another great champion crowned. Based on what the IFBB had determined to be the criteria for its winners, Coleman was deserving of victory, title and crown. When he dropped to the floor after his first Olympia triumph, it was from the shock and awe of having actually won. When he did so at his second, he was humbling himself before what the future likely had in store; and it was on a humble, grateful brow that the crown was worn. Meanwhile, for the all the excitement Flex Wheeler generated at the beginning of the decade, by its end, it appeared that he was destined to remain another disappointed prince.

* * * * *

The English Grand Prix, the decade's final contest, was also won by Coleman. The competitive history of the 1990s was now complete. In a decade of many lessons, the greatest was learned early on: bodybuilding fans wanted to see gigantic men; the bigger the better. Most competitors were happy to oblige that wish. Physical perfection would still carry anyone to victory, in any contest, so long as the owner of a perfect physique was also the biggest man onstage. At bodybuilding's highest level, after three and a half decades of Mr. Olympia contests, no such scenario had yet come to pass. The ancient Greeks had a clear idea of male physical perfection, but among late 20th century bodybuilding fans, there was no such consensus of opinion. In a modern context, it was a vague term. Meanwhile, there was nothing vague about dominating size; nothing unclear about overwhelming opponents with superior muscular mass. In bodybuilding's newest era, such was the mark of an Olympia champion. Starting in 1984, there had been an uninterrupted succession of such men; and since 1967 there had been but a handful of exceptions.

And now, on the eve of the new millennium, bodybuilding had a great new champion; a man who very much fit this bill, and whose reign figured to extend far into the next decade. In an arena that embraced so dearly the concept of precedent, the situation was almost ideal.

Such was the state of affairs when the 1990s came to an end. The unrealistic dreams, uncertainty, upheaval and fragile loyalties that characterized the decade's beginning had, by its end, given way to something that was, for the most part, unified and orderly. This did not spare bodybuilding from controversy. It was far too late for that. Bodybuilding's main product had always been its visual spectacle; this was now more true than ever, thanks to a rapid and significant change in its physical standards. That transformation was not without important and often destructive consequences however, and it did not come about by accident. The emergence of powerful new growth chemicals, judging standards which rewarded their use, and fans who loved their effects set bodybuilding on a clear path. Uncertainty had vanished. As the seconds counted down to the new millennium, bodybuilding now very much knew where it was, and where it wanted to be. When the clock struck midnight, there was no turning back.

For these reason and others, 1999 marked the end of the road for the once-mighty bodybuilding division of the Amateur Athletic Union. The AAU announced that starting in 2000 it would no longer hold muscle contests.

The Weiders

No discussion of bodybuilding's evolution can be considered complete without devoting words to two of its most influential figures: Joe Weider and his brother Ben. It was under their leadership and domination that bodybuilding was transformed from its classic to post-modern forms. When their instruments of power were first put into action, Steve Reeves was the world's greatest bodybuilder. Half a century later, long after those instruments had secured Weider dominance, Ronnie Coleman was supreme. Many of the events and circumstances that fostered and enabled that transformation were devised by the Weiders. Some were not; but none escaped the scrutiny of the two brothers. In other words, it all happened on their watch.

While the brothers proved to be eminently successful in taking bodybuilding to the limits of its potential, they were ultimately unsuccessful in their bid to push it into the realm of mainstream acceptance. Through drug-testing, the WBF adventure, and the events of the years that followed, a simple fact was revealed: no matter what, bodybuilding can only get so big. Its potential popularity always had built-in limitations.

Though it had been long-blessed with the enigmatic Arnold Schwarzenegger, a man destined to become one of the world's biggest stars, to the rest of the world bodybuilding was little more than something that he *used to do*. Efforts that took place in the early 1990s attempted to change this. Two wildly different strategies were tried, and both were complete failures. Although the rise and fall of the World Bodybuilding Federation is vaguely remembered by older generations of bodybuilders and fans and largely unknown to newer ones, it became one of bodybuilding's most pivotal episodes. When it is remembered, Vince McMahon is almost universally thought to be its central figure. When all was said and done however, the battle for domination of the bodybuilding world centered on—and revealed much more about—the Weiders.

The Weiders were for a long time certain that bodybuilding's limits lay within the realm of public acceptance. Without this certainty, they wouldn't have spent so much time and energy trying to make that dream a reality. The question was how to get there; how to make bodybuilding into something as big and commonplace as any of the major-league sports; how to bring muscle to the masses. Yet in the end it was revealed that the wrong question was being asked. The question was not how to breech the wall of public acceptance and allow bodybuilding to flow outward. The question was how to pull as many members of the general public inward. The wall, after all and with hindsight, could never be breached. Bodybuilding was just never going to be that big. Once this was finally realized, all real efforts to bring it into the mainstream were dropped and forgotten. These had amounted to little more than wasted time and resources.

It's true that Ben Weider never gave up in his efforts to get bodybuilding into the Olympics. He was able to get bodybuilding officially recognized by the IOC, but since that organization refused to make it an Olympic sport, the gesture was, in the end, meaningless. When the younger Weider's high-water mark came on the day the OIC said that they "would consider it," it has to be realized that the effort was always futile.[1] Maybe he himself grasped this, and it's possible that all of his efforts which came after the IFBB professional division abandoned drug-testing were little more gestures to save face. After all, giving up would have been no different from admitting defeat. Such was not the Weider way.

Yet whether the Weiders realized it or not, it became clear that the popularity of bodybuilding had

[1]By Ben Weider's own admission, on a separate occasion the IOC President, Baron Killanin, told him that bodybuilding would be allowed to become an Olympic sport "over my dead body." (Getbig.com interview.)

real limitations. The outside-world influence of Joe Weider proved to be limited as well. The IOC would not budge. Plans for public acceptance and Olympic glory would have to be labeled as dreams and shelved. The real-world goal could now only be to optimize bodybuilding in its current form.

It was therefore no surprise that the Olympic style of operation, so long imitated by the IFBB, began to be abandoned. Drug testing was out. Copying the Olympic-model internationalization of championship contest venues was a nice idea, but profits lay elsewhere. This applied mostly to the Mr. Olympia contests: the long-standing rule was that like the Olympics, the event would always be held at a different location. The IFBB variation mandated that about every other year the Olympia would be held at a location in the United States; in alternate years, somewhere else. The contest thus found itself in places such as Pretoria; Columbus; Sydney; London; New York; Munich; Brussels; Los Angeles; Rimini; Chicago; Orlando; and Helsinki. Throughout much of the 1990s the contest was held in Atlanta. In 1999 the Olympia moved to Las Vegas.

It took the powers-that-be a long time to realize this, but Las Vegas is the perfect locale for the event. It has large venues and the infrastructure to easily support convention-like gatherings; unlimited accommodations; and a host of other draws. After all, Las Vegas is an adult vacation spot. For the adventurous, it's an adult playground. The Sin City ambience of the town somehow meshed well with the throng of bodybuilding fans who descend upon it every year for what became known as the Olympia Weekend. There was also no language barrier for the English-speaking IFBB staffers to contend with; no international travel headaches, at least for most competitors and event personnel; and a ready-made venue with a guaranteed full house. Most importantly, holding the show in Las Vegas gave the show a greater potential for profit. Thus, from 1999 forward, Sin City had a new annual attraction; and the Mr. Olympia contest had a permanent home. For its pro-qualifying shows, the NPC followed suit. The annual USA Championships would now always be held in Las Vegas; the National Championships, Altanta.

It had become an era of consolidation and optimization. Once Vince McMahon withdrew his ill-conceived bid to wrest power away from the IFBB, the last of Joe Weider's rivals was gone, and Weider was king. His was therefore a remarkable story: a classic rags-to-riches tale of the kid with nothing but a dream, a determination to work hard, and a willingness to do whatever it takes to get ahead. In the end he did more than just get ahead. Before his reign had come to an end, he was the last man standing. Some people let success like this go their heads. To this group Joe Weider belonged. He promoted his brand, and himself, like no other man in history. He did more than congratulate himself. Articles heaping praise on him would regularly run in his magazines, and these quite often tested the limits of vanity and pretentiousness. In an article titled "In the beginning was…JOE" from the June 1985 issue of *Muscle & Fitness,* Weider visited a recurring theme of divine association. It begins with the following passage:

> In the beginning the earth was without form, and void; and darkness was on the face of the bodybuilding world…and God said: "Let there be Joe."

Since every page, headline, photograph, and word of *Muscle & Fitness* was subject to his approval, it may as well have been Weider himself who wrote this line. Really though, the identity of the person that came up with it out doesn't matter. What matters is that Weider was running serious articles in his own magazines with these types of messages. Suffice to say he wasn't bashful about letting the bodybuilding world know his true feelings about himself. Apart from his resolve to ensure that bodybuilders should not ever forget to whom they must pay homage—by putting his name in front of every possible product, magazine, contest, and exercise method—he appeared equally determined to transcend mortality. Whereas in the above passage Weider is content to portray himself as a gift from God, apparently he more often wished to be seen *as* a god.

All Joe Weider logos and contest medals portray him as being hewn from gold, a god-like figure, complete with the physique of a Greek deity. Although in the above article the reader is later assured that "he does not like…to be admired as an idol," his product logos quite deliberately depict him in the form of a golden statue, indeed very much like the idols warned about in the Old Testament. Due to his Semitic heritage, Weider should have been familiar enough with the Ten Commandments to recognize the irony. Similar irony can be found in his self-comparison, in a now-infamous quote, to Jesus Christ:

> They grumble about Jesus. They grumble about Ghandi. Lincoln, they killed him…I don't wanna be an egotistical person, but if it weren't for me, bodybuilding would still be in the cesspool.[1]

Granted, since Weider here compares himself not only to Christ but also to Abraham Lincoln and Mohandas Gandhi, it's arguable that although he apparently fancied self-deification, he wasn't necessarily fixated on it.

At the same time, the construction of his Greek-god image was certainly about more than just deification or simple ego-feeding. It also had a practical purpose. Since Weider had given himself the title of "Father of Modern Bodybuilding," he obviously figured it would be appropriate for him to be marketed as an actual bodybuilder. After all, real bodybuilders would be more inclined to accept his authority if they saw him as one of *them.* He therefore instructed the illustrators and sculptors who came up with his logo images to give him a rugged, muscular physique and a chiseled, square-jawed face. Though the real-life Weider had a diminishing jaw line and a physique that looked nothing like that of Robbie Robinson, whose body the sculpture depicts, the images resembled him just enough to work. His magazines were loaded with them.

Since it takes years of hard work and dedication to become a legitimate bodybuilder, Weider's claims and depictions were sometimes met with ire and resentment, at least in the decades before he established dominance over the muscle world's business side. The one-time Weider rival Dan Lurie decided enough was enough, and publicly called him on his real-bodybuilder claims. The top headline of the January 1967 cover of Lurie's magazine, *Muscle Training Illustrated*, read: "Dan Lurie Challenges Joe Weider to Public Bodybuilding Contest." Weider wisely ignored the challenge, opting instead to compete with Lurie in the area of his true expertise, business. Unfortunately for Lurie, Weider eventually won that contest, and won it handily. Lurie's magazine went the way of the way of the dinosaurs, Weider prospered, and the pedaling of his Greek-god image continued.

By the time bodybuilding's popularity peaked, Weider enjoyed a comfortable lead over all other publishers and promoters. Run-of-the-mill bodybuilders, especially beginners, typically didn't give him much thought. They passively acknowledged his position of authority, since Weider's magazines were quite successful in portraying him as bodybuilding's leader. Just as there was no reason to doubt Weider's domination of the business side of bodybuilding, there was no real cause to question the authenticity of his physical portrayal. Naysayers like Lurie had moved on, and by the '80s Weider's age—he billed himself as "Trainer of Champions Since 1936"—clearly implied that he was beyond his prime. The bodybuilding community was asked to believe that the paintings and statues of Weider depicted him at his physical peak.

Apparently a lot of people bought it. In the age before the internet, a great majority of future bodybuilders introduced themselves to the milieu by thumbing through the pages of *Muscle & Fitness* or *Flex* magazines. They accepted the virile, muscular depiction of Joe Weider, since for those who had never seen the real Weider, the image was entirely plausible. After all, he *was* the father of modern bodybuilding, the face on the Mr. Olympia logos and medals, the source of countless food supplements and workout devices—and a more-or-less behind-the-scenes guy anyway. Until bodybuilders actually got a glimpse of this father figure, there was no reason to be skeptical.

For many, *Pumping Iron* provided that first glimpse. Although that film became the single greatest marketing tool the world of bodybuilding had ever experienced, it was an independent creation. It was therefore one of the few sources of information about bodybuilding available to the general public that didn't require—or even seek—the approval of Joe Weider. He has a small part in the film—so small, in fact, that he's not identified or mentioned. Yet there he is, giving instructions at a photo shoot. We hear his voice (like "an out of tune accordion under the rear wheels of a dump truck," as Bob Paris would later describe him) and—although he's clothed—we see his physique.

Many in the bodybuilding crowd never saw *Pumping Iron* in the theater. It was seen a decade or two later, as a television movie-of-the-week, or afterward on a video tape or disk. This group was certainly aware of Joe Weider, the "Master Blaster." The typical bodybuilder had seen his name thou-

[1]Klein, p.100

sands of times. They had taken in the Joe Weider logos and the Joe Weider contest medals. They had been told, over and over, that he was the Father of Modern Bodybuilding. And there he was, in *Pumping Iron,* directing one of Arnold's photo shoots. But somehow, none of it matched up. The voice was certainly a head-scratcher. A man like the one depicted in his logos should also have had the booming, commanding baritone of Zeus himself.

The body was even more puzzling. The official image of Joe Weider had become so pervasive, so ingrained, that it became a part of the bodybuilding subconscious—a testimony to a remarkable ongoing marketing campaign. Yet for many who had just seen him for the first time, the whole episode required a double-take. Here, before everyone's eyes, was someone who resembled a typical middle-aged businessman. Just what was going on here?

For many the first clue to the real Joe Weider was revealed: in real life he bore little resemblance the god-like figure depicted in his medals and product logos. For those who became curious enough to look more closely, there were other indications of what might lay beyond the golden statues and gushing praise. A series of advertisements he was forced to run in his magazines was one of these: after being found liable by the US Government of making misleading marketing claims about his Anabolic Mega-Packs and Dynamic Life Essence products, he was required to post ads directed at the victims of these scams, instructing them how to get their money refunded. To the average *Muscle & Fitness* reader who happened upon those ads and read the fine print, it was made clear that the self-described Father of Modern Bodybuilding was not above making false advertising claims.

There was more. The number of times the name "Weider" appeared in his magazines—often more than 200 in a single issue—was yet another clue about the man lurking behind that name. By making certain that his name was displayed that many times, it was evident that his ego needed feeding. At the same time, Weider understood that this repetition could help convince his audience that he was not only their provider of information, but their unchallenged leader.

Beyond this massive repetition may have also been simple business strategy. Weider must have known that in the most remarkable instances, names stop being people and become institutions. For example, in an era long since past, seeing a Ford automobile caused people to think of Henry Ford. Over time, as the company grew larger and larger, the buying public unintentionally allowed the man to be superseded by his creation. After a while, the public no longer thought of him, but of the cars. Ford was probably quite happy about this, since in business reaching that level of notoriety is a strong indication that you've truly made it. "Ford" now means the company; the institution; the entity; the products. The same can be said for McDonald's, Macy's, Harley-Davidson, Jacuzzi, Milton Bradley, Sears, Gucci, Honda; and scores of others. Weider no doubt hoped to join this elite club. To those who saw all of this, the proliferation of his name was more than mere vanity. He appeared consumed with a desire to dominate.

In an industry whose dollars revolved around magazine sales, name-proliferation was made easy. The rest of the Weider magazines were product catalogues, interspersed with training articles, contest reports, and lots of pictures of bodybuilders. Articles like "In the beginning was...JOE" were little more than advertisements for Weider, disguised as journalism. Of all the sections in the piece, the following stands out as most telling. Author Joyce Verdal describes the following interaction with him:

> Looking at his determined face, and detecting the kindness twinkling through his sagacious eyes,[1] I asked, "What is your secret, Joe? How do you manage to remain the leader of the bodybuilding world after all this time?"

Verdal clearly wasn't out to produce a piece of hard-hitting journalism. At the same time, the tone of the interview would not have been hers to determine. After all, this was *Muscle & Fitness*, Weider's flagship magazine. In his response to the question, Weider cited a love for bodybuilders and a desire to help them. Considering the legal problems he faced due to his attempts to defraud bodybuilders, his answer is interesting. Regardless, Verdal's question is not based on imaginary premises. By mid-1985, Weider was indeed the leader of the bodybuilding world. This was becoming more true every day. Some might charge that a more honest and accurate answer about how he remained

[1]Sagacious is typically defined as "possessing or showing sound judgment and keen perception."

the leader of that world would cite the value of an effective marketing campaign. Others have had more stern words. The 1968 Mr. America and former Weider acquaintance Bob Gajda had this to say:

> …Joe was the only New Jersey Jew that read Goebbels (Hitler's Minister of Propaganda). He did. And he (Goebbels) said, "Tell the lie over and over and people will believe it as the truth." And I see this. He (Joe) just took it in.

Goebbels controlled the flow of information for an entire nation, and was instrumental in convincing it that the war it waged was justified. Next to him, Weider was a tiny fish in an obscure pond. Regardless, he knew that through his virtual monopoly of the magazine market he controlled the flow of bodybuilding's information. Whether or not it was the case that Weider ran a purposely-constructed campaign of lies will almost certainly never be known. Nevertheless, on a few occasions he was caught lying and was punished for it.

Apart from these episodes, not many people in the outside, non-bodybuilding world knew he even existed. As long as he wasn't breaking the law, the billions of people who existed beyond the muscle microcosm paid little notice of him. The outside world didn't care that he portrayed himself as having the physique of a Greek god, or that a single issue of *Muscle & Fitness* mentioned his name no less than 224 times.

In the nether-regions of bodybuilding, meanwhile, Weider was the ultimate power, and perhaps more like a godfather than a father. He ran the show. His brother was the president of the IFBB. Together they could very easily blackball whomever they chose, and didn't hesitate to remind competitors of this fact—as was the case when worries of WBF defections shook the IFBB. There's no reason to believe that bad-mouthing of Weider or the IFBB would have been tolerated either. Of course non-Weider magazines could report and comment on whatever facts they liked, although upsetting the people in power could easily have damaging repercussions. The bodybuilding world therefore showed deference. Before and after the WBF, aspiring competitors had no choice. Current competitors or anyone with business interests in bodybuilding knew better than to risk offending the Boss. Meanwhile, a few disenfranchised and bitter former IFBB competitors occasionally took parting shots at Weider, through books or published interviews. Former friends often couldn't resist speaking their minds either. Years before Dan Lurie was challenging Weider to bodybuilding contests, the two were close friends and business partners. Lurie later made no bones about his former cohort:

> All I can say is he was an extremely hard worker, but very ruthless in business. He would put a knife in your back. He would use people, and throw them out. There were lawsuits. He did a lot of bad things. But that was him. That was his character. I introduced him to his first wife.

It had also been reported that Lurie was puzzled by Weider's obsession with not only Joseph Goebbels, but Adolf Hitler.[1] Nevertheless, in the end Weider prevailed, regardless of whom he may have admired. He was therefore in a position to label his detractors as sore losers and to attribute their criticisms to jealousy.

Weider's own words and actions are on record, however, and these paint the portrait of a hypocrite. Despite the ad nauseum repetition of his name, the grandiose imagery which honored him, and articles like Verdal's, Weider claimed to be entirely modest: "The idea of being singled out for attention and praise fills me with discomfort," he declared in his autobiography.

Even Weider's staunch, passionate position on the acceptance of bodybuilding as a sport was, when convenient, amendable. The AAU had always enforced a strict policy of disqualifying athletes who achieve professional status, regardless of their sport. When that organization in 1947 threatened to disqualify weightlifters for participating in non-AAU bodybuilding contests, Weider feared that competetors would avoid his new IFBB events. In the December 1947 issue of *Your Physique* magazine, Joe Weider asserted, in an official statement, that any such ban would be groundless:

> Bodybuilding is not a competitive sport in any sense of the word.

[1]Both Lurie and Weider are Jewish. Weider was reportedly fascinated with Hitler's absolute power and was willing to look past Nazi efforts to eradicate European Jews—even though he had distant relatives in Poland during the Holocaust.

This declaration was, of course, in direct opposition to Weider's later agenda. But just like his 1986 announcement about drug-testing, Weider would later just pretend he never said it.

The post-2000 IFBB information machine still churns out Joe Weider propaganda. The organization's official stance is that Weider should be looked upon with respect and reverence, for a simple and important reason: "he made bodybuilding what it is today." That he played a critical role in transforming muscle culture and competition from a fairly small, obscure activity into a billion-dollar industry—with accompanying strides made by competitors, in sheer numbers as well as degrees of size, muscularity, and conditioning—cannot be reasonably disputed. He did in large part make bodybuilding what it is today. However, it's been increasingly fashionable to ask whether this is a good thing. This is a bit of a complex question, since the growth of bodybuilding has had a large number of effects.

Joe Weider didn't create the bodybuilding industry, but he played an instrumental role in its growth. He is therefore responsible, directly or indirectly, for providing occupations and income to people who would otherwise have to make a living in some other field. These people include magazine staff personnel like writers, editors, photographers, and a myriad of support positions. The expansion of bodybuilding also gave occupations to gym owners, their employees, and personal trainers. Food supplement and workout apparel manufacturing enterprises likewise required employees, and these industries needed help from a variety of other positions, including executives, managers, marketing agents, factory and warehouse workers, and even truck drivers. Additionally, there was new work for contest promoters and events staff. Finally, and most visibly, bodybuilders themselves were sometimes employed by the industry. Before Joe Weider's organizations reached maturity, no one had been able to make a living solely from physique competition. Previously there had been a small handful of bodybuilders who were able to make a living from their bodies—like Steve Reeves, who got plenty of work acting in B movies—but none had ever made a living purely from bodybuilding. Weider changed all that.

The official IFBB website includes a page dedicated to Weider, with quotes from a dozen or so individuals who heap praise upon him. Since nearly all were at some point on the Weider payroll, it's quite reasonable to expect this group to pay tribute. He gave numerous people means with which to make a living. That, by itself, is a good thing.

Some of the quotes praising Weider are from famous bodybuilders. They have him to thank for endorsement contracts, prize money, and other favors. Without Weider's money it's highly unlikely that they would have been able to compete in bodybuilding for as many years or with such high-level muscularity. Without the IFBB structure, Weider marketing and Weider prize money, the ranks of top competitors would also be thin, or possibly nonexistent. His efforts therefore influenced the number of competitors in the upper tiers of competition as well as their size and conditioning. And really, if Weider had never entered the business of bodybuilding promotion, there's a good chance a lot of top bodybuilders might never have competed. Some might never have picked up a weight. He was that influential. Among the elite competitors who pay tribute to Weider, the remarks of Jean-Pierre Fux are typical:

> He is the father of modern Bodybuilding. His dedication to the sport is outstanding. A man that devoted his entire life to make the sport better and more acceptable towards the public eye. Bodybuilding would not be where it is today without Joe.

All the above points considered together, Weider at first does appear worthy of great praise. Because of his efforts, bodybuilding experienced immense growth. At the same time however, bodybuilding's effects are not limited to revenue-generation and employment opportunities. There's much more to it.

Today, there's a large pool of competitors in both the professional and top-level amateur ranks who display both immense size and stunning definition. Many in the industry and subculture feel that this alone is a good thing—a positive effect of bodybuilding's growth. Contrary opinion asserts that the existence of this army of massive bodybuilders is something quite negative. To some, the ultra-massive appearance of today's pro ranks is unpalatable.

It's also no secret that it's impossible to be competitive in the upper echelons of bodybuilding without ingesting large doses of anabolic steroids and other appearance-enhancing chemicals. It's further commonly agreed that neither Joe Weider nor anyone else can be held accountable for the actions of those who choose to follow this path. Bodybuilders have every right to quit competition, stop taking drugs, and lead a different life. No one is being forced to live a life of daredevil drug use.

Rather, something quite the opposite is true: top bodybuilders relish attaining high or even "freaky" levels of muscularity and definition. After all, this is often the primary reason bodybuilders set the goal of competing at a world-class level. Moreover, their actions indicate that these people are okay with taking large quantities of illegal drugs.

For many of those making their way through the ranks, competing in the IFBB professional division is a dream come true and therefore worth whatever risks that may entail. Most who achieve professional status got there from a combination of great genes, very hard work, lots of chemicals, a burning desire to win, and a willingness to do whatever it takes to reach the top. Freaky muscularity is what the fans want to see, and freaky muscularity is what the competitors want to deliver. In this sense Weider and the IFBB are guilty of no more than giving bodybuilders and their fans what they want. However, many do not agree that this is a compelling or even reasonable argument for the assertion that bodybuilding, in its present form, is a good thing.

It's further worth considering that every bodybuilding contest, website, magazine, video, 8x10 photograph, and even every top bodybuilder—all of these act as advertisements which successfully lure young men into bodybuilding every year. Many of these people merely want to put on some muscle, which by itself is good. It has been proven that weight training has several benefits, ranging from increased athletic ability to better overall health.

However, some of these men and boys begin to dream of leading what they believe to be the glamorous life of a pro bodybuilder: of being huge and "ripped"; of working out for a living; of being admired and feared; of making big money; of being fawned over by beautiful women. Before long they learn—through sources of information like internet articles, online forums and word-of-mouth—that none of this can be obtained without the use of large amounts of drugs. This revelation scares away some, but not all. Thus every year an untold number of new bodybuilders begin taking growth-enhancing drugs, often with little or no attention paid to potential consequences.

For a large number of those who eventually make it anywhere near the top of the competition ladder, and even for many who never even compete beyond the local amateur level, the glamorous life alluded to in bodybuilding magazines never materializes. For some, a much different reality awaits. Heavy drug use can bring a heavy price. Bodybuilding drugs have the potential to cause serious health problems, and in the very worst of cases, there is evidence to suggest that they can contribute to an early death. There have been no official records compiled of those who retire from bodybuilding due to health problems, since for the most part the reasons for these departures are kept private and are usually only made known through rumors. For example, it's common to notice that a particular bodybuilder simply stopped competing, with no publicized explanation, and then hear gossip that wellbeing issues prompted the exit. Occasionally a health-related departure is made public by the bodybuilders themselves, as part of a coming-clean, *don't-do-what-I-did* diatribe. Mike Matarazzo, a top professional of the 1990s who possessed both a massive physique and a reputation for making candid statements, not surprisingly had frank revelations after health problems forced him into retirement:

> Worst were the chemicals. I have so many memories of being alone in a hotel room the week, five days or two days before a contest, and doing unspeakable things to my body—steroids, growth hormones, diuretics—anything and everything that we as bodybuilders do to achieve a certain look.

In Matarazzo's case, his body issued various warnings, including a heart attack, that maintaining this type of lifestyle could result in early death. He thus bowed out and walked away with his life. Flex Wheeler was forced to retire at age 37 due to kidney disease, a condition which required transplant surgery. There are numerous additional acknowledged instances of health-related forced retirement, with the departure of a host of others subject to rumors. Professional bodybuilders whose competitive careers were cut short by illness include Dennis Newman, Mike Francois, Don Long, Tom Prince, and Marko Savolainen.

Arguments have been made that those who quit competing due to medical reasons could have had pre-existing medical conditions, and that at worst, steroid use did little more than aggravate the situation. Wheeler insists his malady was not caused by drug use, and several others have made similar claims. For many this very well may be true.

However, acute biological trauma—damage that is not dependent on any pre-existing condition—is regularly self-inflicted by the use of "accessory" bodybuilding drugs or pre-contest dehydration rituals, or both, with dire and occasionally fatal consequences. Prominent competitors who have reportedly visited hospital emergency rooms because of conditions related to contest preparation include Edgar Fletcher, Paul Dillett, Milos Sarcev, Nasser El Sonbaty, Bob Cicherillo and Mustafa Mohammad. Matarazzo, Wheeler and Dillett were all members of the ill-fated 1993 Mr. Olympia field of competitors. Lesser-known competitors are not immune to the effects of risky contest-preparation methods, and it's not unheard-of for local amateur competitors to find themselves in an ambulance receiving intravenous fluids on the day of a contest. In most cases, immediate medical care can save the lives of competitors suffering from self-induced trauma. Regardless, occasionally some don't make it.

The two most famous examples of competitors who were killed as a direct result of taking bodybuilding drugs are Mohammed Benaziza and Andreas Munzer. Both were top professionals in the prime of their careers when they died, and both were in their early 30s. Concerning their deaths much is said elsewhere,[1] but it should be noted that their highly-publicized deaths are but two additions to a growing list populated mainly by men who met quieter ends. A number of notable (and in some cases, famous) bodybuilders have died prematurely, from less immediate causes. These include BJ Johns (age 34), Curtis Leffler (36), Erik Fromm (36), Derrick Whitsett (37), Eric Otero (38), Fannie Barrios (41), Charles Durr (44), Hans Hopstaken (45), Edwardo Kawak (47), Ray Mentzer (47) Denny Gable (49), Don Ross (49), Mike Mentzer (49), Sonny Schmidt (50), Don Youngblood (51), and Paul Grant (60). Although the individuals listed here died from a variety of ailments, the reasonable and widely-held conclusion is that long-term effects of bodybuilding drugs either precipitated or aggravated eventually fatal medical conditions.

Another way of looking at it is to observe a simple correlation: All of these people competed at a high level in bodybuilding, and all died early deaths. Since everyone on the above list is male except for Fannie Barrios, and most were born in the United States, a comparison to the life expectancy of US males (75) demonstrates that bodybuilding could potentially be one of the world's most dangerous occupations.

Since drug use is necessary for achieving elite status in bodybuilding, it's reasonable to expect that more deaths will follow. Since there are no competitors from the new (post-1990) era who have yet to reach 75 years of age, it's not possible to tell how the overall life expectancy of bodybuilders will compare to that of the general public. There are however a few top bodybuilders from preceding eras—where drug use, muscularity, and especially size were considerably less extreme than what's witnessed today—who have made it to advanced age. The longevity of men like Albert Beckles, Chris Dickerson and Ed Corney, all competitors born in the 1930s, prove that the use of bodybuilding drugs alone does not have to be a sure path to an early exit. The long lives of early competitors like John Grimek (88), Clancy Ross (84), George Eiferman (76), Armand Tanny (90) and Jack LaLanne (96) would support this assertion, except that they all competed in the pre-steroid era.

Like other types of chemicals that humans ingest, type and quantity factor heavily into the extent of damage that takes place. For example, smoking two cigarettes a day probably won't lead to a smoking-related death. Smoking two packs a day is a different story. Anabolic steroids and most other bodybuilding drugs were developed for legitimate medical purposes. There's no evidence that moderate use of any of them will shorten someone's life expectancy. But as with cigarettes, heavy use is something altogether different. It remains a fact that a number of former competitors of recent eras died early deaths, and that many have suffered life-threatening episodes.

An obvious way to prevent further calamities would be for bodybuilding federations to ban the use of any and all appearance-enhancing drugs. After all, without them bodybuilding can is a healthy activity. A variation of this policy was attempted by the IFBB in 1990. A tear later it was recognized to be a failure and dropped. Once testing was done away with, all concerned parties knew that it would never return. The genie was out of his bottle and running amok. IFBB professionals went right back to taking traditional size-boosting drugs. All the while the wheels of science kept turning. The 1990s saw the emergence and increasing availability of new and more powerful drugs. Though nearly all of

[1]Benaziza: pp. 160-1; Munzer: p. 178.

the new drugs were invented for legitimate medical applications—chemicals like synthetic growth hormone and IGF-1 (insulin-like growth factor)—any drugs that are able to increase the size or definition of bodybuilders eventually will.

Because of this, even more drugs were added to the cocktail of the elite bodybuilder. In short order competitors became much larger and freakier; by the early 2000s the average professional carried approximately 30 more pounds of muscle than his 1980s counterpart. The pressure to keep up with the Joneses increased as well. Competitors were copying each other's chemical regimens. In 2005 former top professional Shawn Ray placed blame for the increasingly reckless drug-taking of competitors squarely on the shoulders of the Weider-run IFBB:

> The bodybuilders don't make up the rules. The federation does. The bodybuilders are like race cars on a track. Until somebody puts a pace car out there in a form of a drug test, the bodybuilders are going to run on all cylinders. They are going to do and use whatever they can to get an edge. That responsibility does not fall on the bodybuilders, but the federation.

Ray's claim that bodybuilders cannot be held responsible for using "whatever they can" to get an edge is not easily defensible. He is however correct in stating that unless restraints are put into effect, bodybuilders will stop at nothing in order to succeed. However, this has become part of bodybuilding's appeal. Although the list of casualties from drug use continues to grow, and although modern-era drug cocktails tend to produce immense midsection measurements, hardcore fans have been delighted. After all, bodybuilders are now bigger and more muscular than ever.

The Weiders instituted drug-testing as a gamble, apparently because they believed in the long run the move would make them more money. When they realized that they more likely stood to lose money from the decision, the policy was promptly dropped. It therefore became apparent that there were never any serious designs to clean up bodybuilding because it was "the right thing to do"; nor were there genuine intentions to look after the well-being of bodybuilders, from Joe Weider, his brother Ben, or Ben's federation, the IFBB. If the opposite were true, drug-testing would have remained in place.

These moves were also entirely consistent with Joe's apparent attitude toward the community as a whole. If Weider truly cared for the legions who bought his magazines, as he claimed, he would not have been found liable, repeatedly, by the United States government, of attempting to deceive them through misleading marketing claims.

Joe Weider no longer operates in bodybuilding in any official capacity, but his actions when he was in charge heavily influenced its current state. Weider did not invent bodybuilding, nor did he invent bodybuilding drugs. He certainly did not give a small percentage of mankind the at-all-costs determination to attain incredible levels of size and muscularity. Rather, he was presented with, and capitalized on, the opportunity to exploit a combination of these things. In doing so, he built a large fortune. He also fostered the development of an activity with a strong correlation between fanatical participation, health problems, and early deaths.

The question here isn't whether Joe Weider is responsible for these deaths, since he clearly is not. He is in fact no more responsible than Leopold Ruzicka, the inventor of synthetic testosterone. The question is what the effects of bodybuilding's growth have been. When the famous competitors listed on p. 203 have dropped dead at an early age; when a substantial number dropped out because of chronic health problems; and when all participated in an activity where the heavy use of potentially dangerous drugs is rewarded with success and notoriety—all of these things make controversial the claim that the expansion of bodybuilding has made the world a better place.

However, that isn't the end of the story. The effects of modern bodybuilding do not begin and end with the rise of a new industry and a trail of bodies. Nor is bodybuilding merely a tale of the evolution from the ideal of physical perfection to the preponderance of bloated midsections carried by a small army of mass monsters. In spite of these things, it's possible that some good has come out of the growth of physique competition and culture. The Weiders insist they've created something which is a positive influence on the rest of the world.

Although bodybuilding itself is mainly invisible to society as a whole, it is nowhere close to being a fully self-contained entity. Its effects are not limited to members of the subculture or the industries that rely on their dollars. As the general public's awareness of health and fitness began to grow in the last few decades of the 20th century, Weider magazines were quick to point out and eager to maintain that bodybuilding was responsible for this. Without bodybuilding, we are told, the fitness craze of the 1980s would never have existed; and without the ongoing inspirational effects of bodybuilding, the public would be less healthy. If this increased health was absent, society itself might operate less efficiently. The influence of bodybuilding was declared by the Weiders to be so great, and so transcendent, that Ben famously made the following pronouncement part of IFBB letterhead:

> Bodybuilding is important for nation building.

It was a bold, grandiose claim. If it turns out to be true, the importance of bodybuilding becomes far more real, and its growth far more momentous. "Nation-building" is commonly defined in the following way:

> It is the process of constructing or structuring a national identity using the power of the state. This process aims at the unification of the people or peoples within the state so that it remains politically stable and viable in the long run. Nation-building can involve the use of propaganda or major infrastructure development to foster social harmony and economic growth.

Let there be no doubt that Ben Weider displayed drive and enthusiasm which rivaled that of his brother. One of his self-appointed jobs as head of the IFBB was to involve as many nations of the world as possible in the Weider brand of bodybuilding. To this end he worked tirelessly, and his efforts were met with great success. At the time of his death in 2008 the IFBB had 177 member nations. However, neither Weider nor any other source has explained how bodybuilding has played an important role, or any role, in the "constructing or structuring a national identity" of a single nation.

Ben, who gained a small amount of notoriety for his interest in historical subjects, was smart enough to know that getting bodybuilding organizations within various countries to sign on with the IFBB does not constitute nation-building. It is in fact difficult to imagine how staging exhibitions where muscular men oil their bodies and flex their muscles could possibly bolster any country's nation-building efforts. The idea is generally thought to be hopelessly far-fetched. Granted, brother Joe's adventures in self-deification may also be described this way, so if nothing else, the result is a sort of bizarre symmetry of delusion: Joe saw himself as the God, and Ben the Nation-Builder. As a student of history, the younger Weider must have been familiar with the exploits of the fifteenth-century figure Richard Neville, the 16th Earl of Warwick, famously known as the Kingmaker. He may have fancied himself a similar character.

Regardless, and with fantastic declarations about nation-building aside, Ben Weider played a big and serious part in bodybuilding-building. In the world of muscle contests, the IFBB is the real deal. Introducing it to the four corners of the globe strengthened the Weider monopoly, but it also helped bodybuilding grow. And grow it did.

Meanwhile, since the fitness industry and participation in fitness activities experienced rapid expansion at around the same time, it was tempting for the Weiders to claim responsibility for the movement in general. So that's what they did.

The explosion of interest in fitness and exercise became one of the 1980s' trademark pop culture attributes. Like just about all pop culture movements, the rise of fitness did not materialize out of thin air. Its causes were many and varied. Throughout the 20th-century Western world there had always been at least some interest in exercise, since it naturally and necessarily accompanied athletics and sporting events. Exercise for the sake of pure self-improvement existed during this time as well, though throughout most of the century it was never particularly popular. That all changed in the 1970s, when exercise and fitness gained greater popularity. However, physical activities during that period were mainly limited to things like "jogging" (a now-dated term) and roller-disco (which is doubly-dated).

The big breakthrough came in the early 1980s, when interest in exercise rose dramatically. Although a number of personalities and events have been associated with the fitness explosion, its rapid rise in popularity correlates most directly to the efforts and products of two people: Richard Simmons and Jane Fonda. By 1982 Simmons had a hit television exercise program and a number-one best-selling book about diet and exercise. Fonda likewise had a number-one bestseller, plus a bestselling workout video; between the two she had sold four million copies by 1986.

Before those two broke through, the fitness industry was a model of slow, steady, and unspectacular growth. Its biggest name was Jack Lalanne, the exercise guru who had been pitching fitness since 1930s, and who by 1980 had already been a household name for decades. His TV program had been broadcast every weekday morning since 1951, several years before most people had TVs. Even if they didn't get up for the before-dawn calisthenics, a huge number of people at least knew the show existed. Likewise anyone who had ever picked up a Marvel comic book had seen the Charles Atlas ads. But never had fitness products or personalities created a fad worthy of mainstream national attention.

The new video cassette boom no doubt played a huge part in the instant success of both Simmons' and Fonda's products—and in the success of a growing variety of exercise videos of all types. No longer did people need to wake up with Jack Lalanne and his dog. A video tape could be exercised to at its owner's convenience. Media itself therefore began to play as big a role as the workout stars who appeared in them. Fitness-related themes even influenced the soundtrack to which people exercised. Prominent among these was the 1981 song "Physical" by Olivia Newton-John. A Billboard number-one hit for ten weeks, the tune instantly became synonymous with the new surge in synchronized exercise-class participation, or what soon became known as "aerobics."

Of course there was also a big spike in interest in weight training. This was inevitable. The idea that a comprehensive fitness program should include exercises for the entire body was eventually going to be accepted, by experts and the exercising public alike. The most direct and efficient way to subject all parts of the body to exercise is through a resistance training program that makes use of weights and specialized weightlifting machines. Thus, as the 1980s began, for the first time a consensus of opinion about the benefits of weight training was reached.

Moreover, exercise could not have become nearly so popular without there being a variation that appealed specifically to men. Although Fonda and Simmons sold huge numbers of books and videos, their products were more or less marketed toward women. The large majority of men were just not going take part in what was essentially a synchronized dance class. Of males who wanted cardiovascular-type exercise, most were willing to run, ride bikes and swim. Beyond that, men have historically and naturally gravitated toward what is often regarded as the most masculine form of pure exercise ever invented: weightlifting.

As the '80s got underway, more and more people began training with weights. Because training with weights also happened to be the method of exercise used by bodybuilders to increase the size of their muscles, a rapid transformation of attitude about that group came about. Bodybuilders and bodybuilding trainers regained some of their lost relevance. Bernarr Macfadden's 70-year-old vision of physical culture began to come back into view. The entire bodybuilding industry suddenly seemed more important—and all of a sudden, it began transforming itself to exploit this fact.

* * * * *

If nothing else, Joe Weider was a master of the art of business. He built a multi-million-dollar corporation from the ground up. Some would say his perceptive abilities have rarely been matched; others might say he was merely in the right place at the right time. Whatever the case, he recognized the prospects for bodybuilding and understood the importance of things like star-power. He cultivated personalities he perceived to be stars, and later profited from their growth. In the case of Arnold Schwarzenegger, he struck gold. He also knew that the real potential for bodybuilding, and the real money, lay beyond the lair of dungeon gyms and underworld heroes. Weider knew that if bodybuilding was going to be big, it would need to transcend itself. He saw the rise of fitness as the path upon which bodybuilding could claw its way out of the darkness.

At least in this one critical instance, Weider felt the winds of change blowing before most others detected a breeze. After his discovery of Schwarzenegger, maybe his most important business decision ever came in 1980, when he decided that his magazine *Muscle Builder* should change its name to *Muscle & Fitness*. After this simple switch, the magazine went from being a leader in a niche genre to the first and perhaps only-ever publication to successfully bridge the gap between mainstream fitness and hardcore bodybuilding. Although realistically it was essentially the premier bodybuilding magazine with some general fitness-related articles thrown in, its name, cover imagery, high-quality appearance and content were sufficient to drive distribution well past the five million monthly reader mark by the late '80s. The success of the magazine was so great that it sometimes appears for sale in the checkout isles of supermarkets. If there ever was a mark of successful magazine publishing, this was it.

As the '80s began, the public was hungry for information about how to get fit. A lot of people wanted to build their muscles while they reduced their waistlines. The name *Muscle & Fitness* promised both of these things before the reader even opened the magazine, before he even read a single word of its content. The actual content, meanwhile, centered on exercise and diet advice, profiles of bodybuilders or the occasional celebrity who lifted weights, and the reporting of professional or high-level amateur bodybuilding contests.

What Weider was selling was inspiration. To thumb through a copy of *Muscle & Fitness*, two things stand out most prominently: the huge number of advertisements for muscle-building supplements, and a large number of photographs of bodybuilders and fitness models. For most bodybuilders and weight-training enthusiasts, the decision to immerse themselves in the discipline can be traced to a single moment or incident, a contest, or something as simple as a picture in a magazine. Many can recall a moment when they first told themselves "I want to look like *that*."

Soon the impact of the new emphasis on weight training could be observed in various forms of media, often in areas where it wasn't expected. When the characters of *Saturday Night Fever*—the 1977 film which is one of most important pieces of '70s pop culture—are compared to that of its 1983 sequel, *Staying Alive*, it's easy to notice a physical difference. In the first film, the actors were thin. In the second, they were lean and more muscular. Although the physique of leading man John Travolta in the sequel could be attained by dancing alone (as long it's the rigorous and highly physical kind which involves lifts), an easier and more direct route to get a body like the one he displayed involves lifting weights. However, large numbers of people probably did not start lifting weights because of movies like *Staying Alive*. If anything, it was the new popularity of weight training that influenced the equally new look Hollywood wanted for its actors.

With action movies it was a different story. In the '80s, it was often no longer enough for the hero-figure to supplement his firepower with guts, heart and brains. Now he needed muscles too. Movie audiences loved it. It was through these films that the greatest impact of the new standard of muscular development could be seen. The movies of muscular actors Schwarzenegger and Sylvester Stallone (and to a lesser degree, Jean-Claude Van Damme) became trademarks of the era. Schwarzenegger's success in particular had relevance and impact, since before anything else, he was a bodybuilder—and a product of Joe Weider. His move to the United States was financed by Weider; his image was exalted by Weider; and it was Schwarzenegger who came to dominate Weider's brand of bodybuilding. To most everyone, even those who knew very little about the activity, Arnold Schwarzenegger *was* bodybuilding. To this day he is the only bodybuilder a typical member of the at-large public can name.

It would be a disservice to say that Joe Weider created Arnold Schwarzenegger. It's perhaps more accurate to say that Weider discovered, launched, or even unleashed him. Schwarzenegger was one of those rare people destined for success in whatever field he chose to apply himself. Most fortunately for Weider, he chose bodybuilding. He took it up early in life, and before long realized that that he had what it took to become the world's greatest bodybuilder. There's a good reason why 1975 Mr. Olympia emcee Reg Park more than once referred to him as *the one and only*. He truly was the one and only, a man that possessed the ambition and ability to not only dominate bodybuilding, but to transcend it.

Weider's single greatest business move was buying Schwarzenegger a plane ticket to America. A parade of famous bodybuilders had come before him, but none had Schwarzenegger's rare combination of attributes. Mesmerized young men saw his movies and then went straight to local gyms and signed membership contracts. Soon they were reading muscle magazines and buying muscle-building supplements. For many young men, their initial push into the world of bodybuilding was really that simple.

Not only had Schwarzenegger become the world's greatest bodybuilder, he was also bodybuilding's greatest-ever marketing tool. Without any real inkling of the dividends that would one day be paid, Weider had put himself in a position to take full advantage of this. Without Weider's assistance, there's a chance Schwarzenegger would never have been able to reach a level of notoriety worthy of big-budget movie stardom. It's possible he may have never progressed beyond films the caliber of *Hercules in New York*. He may have never appeared in any. Yet he did go on to star in blockbusters, and because of this bodybuilding enjoyed a massive free advertising campaign. Weider had sown the magic seeds of Arnold Schwarzenegger, and by the mid-'80s he was reaping the rewards.

It can therefore be said that through a variety of means, Joe Weider attracted a lot of people to bodybuilding. But it remains debatable if a significant share of these people could be counted as part of the growth of health and fitness. In spite of magazine cover headlines that made bold assurances to the contrary, hardcore bodybuilding and healthy living are two different things.

Regardless, Weider did make concerted and successful efforts to launch himself into the realm of pure fitness, without using bodybuilding as the direct propellant. Through his bodybuilding ventures, by 1980 Weider had built a small fortune. Yet he was hungry for more. While bodybuilding was bigger than ever, the mainstream fitness craze loomed large and just beyond his grasp. Although the newly-renamed *Muscle & Fitness* was soon to reach one million readers each month, its bodybuilding-centric theme was always going to limit the scope of its appeal. The reason is simple: there will forever be a large majority of the exercising, health-conscious public who have zero interest in bodybuilding.

Those interested in general health and fitness in general won't spend money on a magazine whose core focus is maximum muscle-building, and which features a large number of photos of massive, chemically-enhanced bodies. This audience was Weider's next target. He therefore began publishing *Shape* and *Men's Fitness*—"vanilla" fitness magazines aimed at a mainstream readership, and slanted toward the novice or beginning enthusiast. Once these hit the stands, he was covered in all areas: *Flex* would concentrate on hardcore bodybuilding; *Muscle & Fitness* would do the same, but with the addition of fitness articles; and *Shape* and *Men's Fitness* would appeal to the non-bodybuilding fitness-minded segments of women and men, respectively.

Weider's success publishing bodybuilding magazines and selling muscle-building products gave him the wherewithal to expand his horizons, something conditions of the time almost begged of him. Whereas Vince McMahon's brief foray into bodybuilding a decade later was built upon an untested foundation that was soon revealed to be beyond flimsy, and which lasted less than two years, Weider's venture into fitness was almost a sure thing. After all, by 1980 two things had been proven: fitness was growing rapidly; and Joe Weider knew how to publish successful magazines. His most logical next-step was to combine the two into one, and with that, his mainstream fitness magazines were born. It's not unreasonable to speculate that their very existence may have encouraged people to become more fit and healthy. It could be further postulated that for people who had already decided to become more fit, these magazines were, at the least, able to help them realize that goal.

It could therefore be argued that the Weider brand of bodybuilding, through the dollars it generated, did in fact influence the rise of fitness: some of those dollars were at least initially put into the publication of magazines with legitimate health and fitness themes. Meanwhile, there is no direct evidence that Weider's fitness magazines by themselves drove people into fitness or made them more fit. By publishing them, he may have been merely throwing his hat into the fitness publication ring and bringing competition to existing health and exercise magazines. Whatever the case, if nothing else the publication of *Shape* and *Men's Fitness* demonstrated that as a business entity, the Weider corporation was interested in promoting pure fitness—and that it was not just going to concentrate on bodybuilding, which often masquerades as a form of fitness.

* * * * *

Though the healthy lifestyle image was the façade behind which hardcore bodybuilding lurked, at least in the pages of *Muscle & Fitness*, it's not like bodybuilding was one big lie. It is by no means always or necessarily an activity plagued with death and destruction. In its purest form and when properly executed it can in fact become the foundation of a healthy lifestyle. Drug use is certainly not a requirement, and a significant number of bodybuilders and dedicated weight-trainers know and abide by this maxim.

From the moment that steroids became available to anyone who wanted them, there were bodybuilders who chose not to partake. Contrary to what some people may think, it's possible to build an impressive physique without the use of drugs. This is, of course, a relative and subjective judgment. A member of the general public can sometimes be both impressed with the appearance of a top drug-free bodybuilder and horrified by images of IFBB professionals. Meanwhile, hardcore bodybuilders and their fans will often pay little attention to a drug-free physique, other than to occasionally recognize its "potential."

During the 1980s something called natural bodybuilding came into existence. It's exactly the same as regular bodybuilding, except that it's accomplished without the use of any appearance-enhancing drugs. Natural bodybuilding federations emerged, and they began to sanction and sponsor drug-tested contests. Relative to the IFBB and its amateur-league affiliates (such as the American NPC), these federations are small. Although this type of bodybuilding is entirely consistent with the healthy-lifestyle image promoted by *Muscle & Fitness*, that magazine ignored natural federations and their contests. This is mainly because Weider never had a hand or financial stake in either. Also, a magazine covering any contest with the word "natural" in its name suggests that the participants of other competitions—like IFBB professional events—are "unnatural."

The formula that worked for *Muscle & Fitness* throughout the 1980s was to revile drug use while exalting drug users. The 1990 experiment to condemn both use and user caused a significant revolt, a "never mind" official reversal, and a cue to return hardcore bodybuilding to its modern form. Weider's stars and his brand of bodybuilding were fueled by drugs. It is however still reasonable to give him credit for attracting those who elected to remain natural to bodybuilding. It's normal for drug-free types to have discovered bodybuilding through normal channels (magazines, websites, movies and contests), to become fascinated with it, but then to decide that it's not worth it to take the drugs. Natural bodybuilding is a healthy activity. If Weider helped attract people into it, this at least partially fulfills his claims about being a positive influence on the health of the public.

Weider's bodybuilding-oriented magazines and his stars got people involved with lifting weights. There's no question about that. Without the existence of these two things, the idea of weight training may never have even crossed their minds. At the same time, lots of bodybuilders don't opt for the natural route. Hardcore bodybuilding, which had always been Weider's main product, was an ongoing advertisement for itself. In order to look like a star from the magazines, more was required than hard work, dedication and good genes.

The examples on p. 203 demonstrate how certain versions of the bodybuilding lifestyle can easily be as dangerous as smoking or obesity. Granted, compared to the huge readership of *Muscle & Fitness*, their number is insignificant. At the same time however it must be realized that these are only the famous cases. Like any other sort of activity, the fraction of people who become famous from bodybuilding is destined to be small.

There are untold numbers of bodybuilders who never became famous but who nevertheless suffered similar maladies. Whereas Weider credits himself with bringing the healthy benefits of the bodybuilding lifestyle to masses, these unfortunate people prove that the consequences of such a lifestyle are often something quite the opposite. So the question remains: how many people have truly become healthy and fit as a result of the rise of bodybuilding?

It cannot be denied that Weider played at least some role in the fitness movement. However, it may be the case that bodybuilding latched onto the rise of fitness rather than vice-versa. The average fitness enthusiast still knows very little about bodybuilding, often no more than non-exercising members of the general public, despite being in much closer physical and cultural proximity. If he or she were inspired to live a fit lifestyle because of the influence of bodybuilding, this would not be the case. Moreover, some fitness enthusiasts who are familiar with bodybuilding are among its most vocal critics. Since they're versed in the requirements of a legitimate health and conditioning routine, they're also able to fully appreciate the hazards to which hardcore bodybuilders sometimes subject themselves.

Bodybuilding itself, meaning modern hardcore bodybuilding, represented by the professional ranks of the IFBB, was probably never really any kind of advertisement for general fitness. It therefore makes sense that there is now a wide discrepancy between the popularity of professional bodybuilding and the general health of the Western world. In some ways professional bodybuilding is more popular than ever. Its contests draw substantial crowds. Contest prize money continually inches higher. The bodybuilding industry has experienced growth to match this, and then some. At the same time, the general population has been experiencing declining health.

The overall health of the United States—where bodybuilding is bigger than anywhere else—has deteriorated so much that for the first time since such records have been kept the life expectancy of Americans is threatening to drop below that of the previous generation.[1] In other words, as bodybuilding has grown, the public's health has declined. If bodybuilding had as big an influence on fitness and well-being as the Weider publications claimed, this should not be the case. It's therefore reasonable to conclude that, when all is said and done, bodybuilding has little or no influence on the health and wellbeing of the general public. Although it's possible that the public would be even worse off without bodybuilding or Joe Weider, this can never be known; Weider has made too deep a mark, and barring some calamity, bodybuilding will never disappear.

* * * * *

While it was hoped by the Weiders that the public-at-large would look upon bodybuilding with wonderment and admiration, the opposite is now true. The public never really "got" bodybuilding in the first place, and as time marched on and the physiques of top competitors grew larger and freakier, it seemed apparent that it never would. There is also a pervasive sentiment that bodybuilding is more than a strange cult; it's not unlike the trouble-making kid your parents told you to stay away from. Put another way, it's viewed as a bad influence. This has everything to do with bodybuilding's hand-in-hand association with steroid use.

If a typical member of the general public is shown a picture of a professional bodybuilder, onstage, in top shape, and flexing his muscles—and is asked to comment on it, the word "steroids" will almost certainly come up. Although the public-at-large has been given by the mainstream media an incomplete, uninformed and sensationalized education on the effects of anabolic steroids, if nothing else it has become widely aware of that class of drugs. It also knows that unnatural-looking physiques must be the product of unnatural recipes. At least in this the public is correct.

Meanwhile, at least within the American media, one of the biggest news stories of the new millennium concerned the infiltration of steroids into major-league sports. Predictably, bodybuilding has been handed its share of blame for this. It's true that strength athletes began using steroids before bodybuilders; however, bodybuilders have always been far more visible, their bodies were far more muscular, and their ranks were swelling.

[1]U.S. Department of Health and Human Services, National Institute on Aging 2005 report.

Although it should be assumed that sooner or later all types of athletes were going to learn of the performance-boosting effects of synthetic testosterone, it's reasonable to suppose that bodybuilding accelerated this realization. It's long been known that a bigger muscle is a stronger muscle, and vice-versa. It furthermore became evident that added physical strength can be beneficial in nearly all sports. Once it was also proven that steroids do not cause physical skill or agility to diminish, athletes lined up to use them. All that was left was to figure out what to take and how much.

When venturing into uncharted territory, it's always wise to consult the experts. Although the new steroid underground produced a few self-styled gurus—*Steroid Nation* author Dan Duchaine being one of the more famous examples—by the mid-1980s there was a small army of bodybuilders armed with a wide variety of black-market drugs and enough knowledge to put them to use. By the time professional baseball players started using these drugs in the late 1980s, bodybuilders had already been using them for decades. Since more than a few bodybuilders supplemented their incomes or even made a living selling steroids, the inevitable exchange of ideas, money and drugs with athletes commenced. Athletes wanted performance-enhancing drugs, and bodybuilders had them.

It's true that athletes received performance-enhancing drugs from a variety of sources. However, in at least a few instances a bodybuilder directly influenced the drug use of a professional athlete. The most famous example is witnessed in the claims of Jay McGwire, the former heavyweight amateur bodybuilder whose older brother is Mark McGwire, the baseball player who shattered Roger Maris' long-standing single-season home run record. According to the younger brother's 2010 book *Mark and Me: Mark McGwire and the Truth Behind Baseball's Worst-Kept Secret*, Mark's decision to use performance-enhancing drugs came about as a result of Jay's urging.

Despite Mark's claims that he only took steroids in order to heal from injury, he could plainly see the effects these drugs were having on Jay. Mark in fact attended at least one of Jay's contests, the 1995 NPC Contra Costa Bodybuilding Championships, where the 240-pound younger brother flexed his way to third place. Mark later admitted to taking anabolic steroids. The idea that this use came about due to Jay's urging is therefore entirely plausible. Though the younger McGwire's motives for pub-

Getty images

Ben Weider. 2008

lishing the book have rightly come under heavy fire, the episode became a high-profile example of a bodybuilder influencing the drug regimen of a famous athlete.

For those who were aware of him, the younger McGwire was a walking advertisement for the combined effects of weight training and steroids. This came with the territory. No exceptionally muscular bodybuilders escape this association. For all his charisma, fame, and otherworldliness, even before he publicly admitted taking them, Arnold Schwarzenegger was perhaps the greatest advertisement for steroids the world has ever seen. That he was also the greatest-ever advertisement for bodybuilding merely draws closer the association between the two.

Athletes certainly made the association. That group has never had problems getting its hands on steroids. The reason is simple: there's a large supply available on the black market. It's no accident that this is the case. After all, although the distribution of steroids is illegal in most places, it's still a business. The same is true for all illicit trade. Since the steroid trade is a business, it must abide by the law of supply and demand.

As bodybuilding grew, so did the demand for steroids. This demand exists in all 177 member nations of the IFBB, in both eastern and western hemispheres, on all six habitable continents. Supply has steadily risen to match this. Photographs taken every year at hundreds of contests throughout the world prove that there is no shortage of drugs. If Jean-Pierre Fux was correct when he said that "bodybuilding would not be where it is today" without Joe Weider, then it is also true that Weider is responsible, however indirectly or unintentionally, for the hefty bump in the worldwide supply of steroids. As a result of this bump, bodybuilders who decide they want steroids, plain and simple, get them. The same is true for athletes. Weider directly addressed the drug issue in his autobiography. He disavowed any responsibility for the hand-in-hand association of bodybuilding and steroid use.

* * * * *

The growth of bodybuilding to its present-day form has produced the following effects: a huge increase in the number of bodybuilders and their fans; the massive expansion of an industry that caters to these individuals; a large rise in interest in weight training; an increase in the supply and use of steroids and other growth-producing drugs; and for some individuals, severe health problems and early death. The growth of bodybuilding is also at least partially responsible for two other important effects: the fitness explosion of the 1980s, and the performance-enhancing drug problem in major league sports. The degree to which bodybuilding is owed responsibly for these two consequences remains open to debate. Despite his claims to the contrary, Joe Weider was not responsible for the fitness boom. He partially fostered it and partially latched onto it.

Weider marketed magazines, muscle-building products and bodybuilders themselves. Perhaps more than anything however, he marketed an idea: the steadfast belief that there's something inherently good about competitive bodybuilding. It wasn't Weider's intention that bodybuilding should produce negative effects. However, it did; and in the end he did little to prevent any of them. It can as easily be said that he encouraged them. His drug-testing policy turned out to be nothing more than a short-lived, half-hearted experiment. His contests rewarded highly chemically-enhanced bodybuilders, and his magazines glorified them. It's true that Weider never forced anyone to take drugs, and that he was really only giving people—the competitors and their fans—what they want. At the same time, for all his self-propping as the man responsible for bringing health and fitness to the masses through bodybuilding, if he were to be honest, he would also have to admit accountability for all other things that have come from his creation.

Kevin Myles

Samir Bannout, Franco Columbu and Joe Weider. 2010 Mr. Olympia contest.

The official IFBB web site lists numerous accolades heaped upon Weider by a prominent cast of characters. These include current and past business partners, federation officials, competitors, and others in his employ—in other words, people who have benefitted from him financially. His greatest benefactor and favorite son decided to do one better. In 2007, the bodybuilder-turned-governor of the state of California, Arnold Schwarzenegger, declared that July 9th should be "Joe Weider Day." The following reason was stated:

> Joe Weider has, for over sixty-five years, promoted a healthy bodybuilding and fitness lifestyle, his passion and vision becoming a force that changed the lives and bodies of millions of men and women worldwide.

Weider brought Schwarzenegger to America. He gave him money, fame and contest titles; most of all, Weider gave him opportunity. Schwarzenegger, a man of rare ambition and ability, took the ball and ran with it. He went from penniless immigrant to champion bodybuilder to movie star to multi-millionaire to the Governor of the State of California. His was one of the most spectacular ascents in history. All of it began with the help of Joe Weider—something that can be counted as one of the most significant favors the world has ever known. Few would argue otherwise. By making bodybuilding what it is today, whether Joe Weider has done a favor for the rest of the world has not enjoyed any such consensus of opinion.

The New Millennium

"God put me here to be Mr. Olympia."
-Ronnie Coleman, *Flex* magazine
October 2005

When Ronnie Coleman's hands were raised in victory for a second time at the 1999 Mr. Olympia contest, the evolution of bodybuilding had nearly reached its climax. Its actual zenith occurred a few years later, in 2003, when a razor-sharp, 287-pound Coleman won his sixth consecutive title. At a similar height, he was 40 pounds heavier than Lee Haney at his peak. Clearly he had come a long way. Bodybuilding had come a long way too—a very long way. By 2003, bodybuilding had existed for 110 years. During that time, it evolved into something its originators would not have recognized.

Coleman gained admittance to the exclusive group of Olympia winners in 1998 by producing a physique deemed worthy of its standards. Except for the years 1976-1983, those standards dictated that the winner should possess a complete physique, passable lines and above all else, dominating overall mass. Overwhelming size became Coleman's calling card, and he rested on few laurels. He did win the Mr. Olympia contest in 2001 and again in 2002 with a physique that was lighter—he was in the 250-pound range—but because of this his reign nearly came to an end. The scare produced by consecutive close calls with Kevin Levrone and Jay Cutler inspired him to substantially increase his size. He successfully did so, and the payoff was additional titles. Coleman once again overwhelmed his opponents. By 2003, 287 ripped pounds was required to do this. Bodybuilding had progressed that far.

How bodybuilding transformed itself so dramatically from the time of its inception made for a fascinating tale. That it should even exist was an intriguing matter. The invention of bodybuilding was was neither preordained nor inevitable; and once it did come about, bodybuilding was by no means fated to assume its present form. The image of a 287-pound Ronnie Coleman winning his sixth Olympia title could have easily never materialized. Few realize it, but the current state of bodybuilding—and the existence of bodybuilding itself—is owed to a rather remarkable collection of whims, chance encounters, and instances of pure, dumb luck.

Things might have been turned out quite differently, for example, had Vince McMahon not elected to enter bodybuilding the same year the IFBB began testing its professional division for drugs. Nevertheless, McMahon did come crashing onto the scene at precisely the right moment. As a result, the Weiders feared losing their empire; drug testing was quickly abandoned; and for better or worse, bodybuilding was allowed to resume its transformation.

Vince McMahon became an important figure in the evolution of bodybuilding because of that episode. At the same time, McMahon and countless others may have never even become interested in bodybuilding had it not been for another matter of chance: the early-'70s decision by *Sports Illustrated* to not only cover unusual subject matter, but to send out two people with the foresight, passion and talent to take their assigned topic, bodybuilding, and turn it into a book and feature-length film. Charles Gaines and George Butler were those individuals, and *Pumping Iron* was their creation. Other journalists might have submitted their story and moved on, but not Gaines and Butler. Their film had a large, almost immeasurable impact on bodybuilding's growth, and it all began with a chance mission generated by a whim decision. Had the movie never been made, bodybuilding would not be as it is today. In the film, audiences were allowed a glimpse into the previously mysterious world of competitive bodybuilding.

above: Eugen Sandow. c. 1894
below: Ronnie Coleman. c. 2003

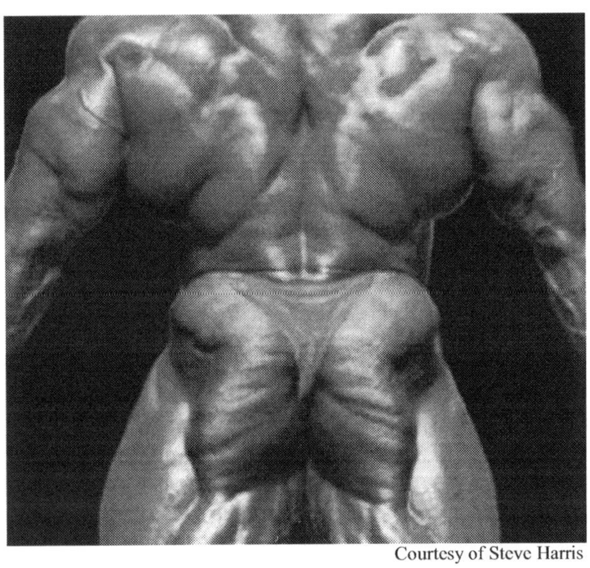

Courtesy of Steve Harris

The film's viewers were treated to images and words of a man who would become bodybuilding's greatest ambassador, Arnold Schwarzenegger, and they saw him triumph in bodybuilding's biggest contest. They also saw the federation that staged that contest in action, and they got an insider's look at bodybuilding as a whole. What they weren't shown is that most of those things were owed to the hard work and cunning of the man behind it all, Joe Weider. Had Weider not risen to dominate bodybuilding, Gaines and Butler would have peered into a different world. They might not have peered at all. It's anyone's guess how bodybuilding might have developed had a young Joe Weider not made his fateful trip to drop off garbage at a local dump, where he found the discarded muscle magazine that set him upon his life's course.

In the magazine, Weider was struck by pictures of the greatest bodybuilder of the Great Depression, John Grimek. Like many of his day, Grimek had been inspired by the world's very first bodybuilder, Eugen Sandow. In the entire of history of bodybuilding, no single figure is more important. After all, it was Sandow who got the ball rolling. Yet that ball might very well have never moved; and Sandow could easily have lived out his years in obscurity. His life was heading in that direction until two chance encounters and a one-off whim changed everything.

Although Sandow's strongman act was a success in Europe, his first trip to the United States had turned into a disappointment. As he began a particularly dreary performance before a sparse crowd one evening in New York City, Sandow caught the eye of future entertainment promoter Florenz Ziegfeld—a man who, on impulse, had entered the theater and taken a seat. A mesmerized Ziegfeld negotiated a contract to manage Sandow shortly afterward, and soon the pair found themselves at the 1893 Chicago World's Fair. There Ziegfeld had a whim. He asked Sandow to perform a "muscle display performance" as part of his act. Sandow complied, the crowd loved it, and bodybuilding was born.

Eugen Sandow became the world's first bodybuilder, but just a few years prior he was nothing, other than displaced and unemployed. He didn't remain that way for long. In order for the most important chance encounter in all of bodybuilding history to take place, fate intervened. By sheer luck, the circus Sandow worked for as an acrobat ran out of money in Brussels, not far from the residence of famous strongman Louis Attila. The two soon met. In the wiry young Prussian Attila saw potential. He took the youthful Sandow under his wing and taught him the finer points of strongman showmanship. Most importantly, Attila showed him how to build his muscles. The results were astonishing. The world had never seen anything like Eugen Sandow. His physique was unrivaled. By the time he left Europe, he was a full-fledged bodybuilder—except that the world, and Sandow himself, didn't know it yet. By the time he and Ziegfeld parted ways, bodybuilding had become his identity.

Had Sandow's circus not run out of money, or had it run out in any other town, it's highly unlikely he and Attila would have teamed up. Sandow would probably never have created the physique that stunned the world, and Ziegfeld definitely would not have seen any out-of-this-world specimens of muscularity on that night in New York. Granted, there were other strongmen to promote. Nearly all of them had fairly large muscles, but none had the lines and proportions of the Prussian sensation. Most critically, none had the fine muscular definition that made Sandow, by himself, a visual spectacle. Had any of them given muscle-display performances, audiences would have shown little interest. With this considered, it seems only Eugen Sandow could have pulled off being the world's first bodybuilder. Yet he almost wasn't there to do it.

* * * * *

Eugen Sandow almost wasn't the world's first bodybuilder, and because of this, bodybuilding almost wasn't invented. Its creation was neither predetermined nor necessary. However, it can be said with equal truth that the 20th century was destined to produce some very muscular men. This is so because of two inventions which, unlike bodybuilding, were bound to appear. The first was sporting competition. In his "Monday Night Hunters" essay, Carl Sagan makes a compelling argument that humans are hard-wired to compete against each other. According to him, once mankind progressed past its nomadic hunter/gatherer phase, the impulse was still there. An outlet for competitiveness was required, and sports provided one. With a few rare exceptions, all human societies developed sports.

The second invention was synthetic testosterone. Even if Leopold Ruzicka, the man who first accomplished this synthesis, had never been born, others would have solved the problem. German scientist Adolf Butenandt independently completed his own synthesis only days after Ruzicka. A steady flow of scientific discovery had led both men to the breakthrough. It was not accidental.

It is furthermore certain that athletes were going to realize the performance-enhancing capabilities of synthetic testosterone and its myriad derivatives, and they were going to put that realization to work. In the early 1950s, that's exactly what happened. At the 1954 World Weightlifting Championships in Vienna, the Soviet team completely dominated, with several members setting world records. Onlookers were shocked and mystified by the display. American team doctor John Ziegler was anxious to learn the Soviets' secret. In an era when such a thing could be declared treason, with all its invitations of peril, the Russian team doctor nevertheless told it to him. Soviet weightlifters had been given testosterone injections.

With the cat now out of the bag, Ziegler return to the States and began administering a steroid program of his own. His lifters were now once more competitive with the Russians. Word spread quickly and soon others followed. In 1956 the oral testosterone derivative Dianabol became available, and use escalated. Within two decades steroid use had become so prevalent that the International Olympic Committee banned them and began administering drug tests.

Due to the sheer number of muscular men created by the combination of performance-enhancing drug use and weight training, it's entirely possible that bodybuilding could have come into existence sometime after 1954. However, it would have been without the history—and the charm—of bodybuilding's first six decades. This history and charm created bodybuilding's initial base of support, and critically, its most important leaders. Because of this, no one can know how bodybuilding would have turned out if it had been created later rather than sooner.

Meanwhile, some things might have turned out about the same. Although the contests, federations and magazines would all have different names, barring the establishment of a successful drug-testing program, bodybuilders would still partake of a growing variety of appearance-enhancing chemicals. However, the degree and prevalence of this practice would depend on how bodybuilding was organized and marketed. With no Joe Weider, *Pumping Iron* or Arnold Schwarzenegger in the picture, bodybuilding could be expected to remain small.

Additionally, had bodybuilding come into existence in the 1950s or later, the perpetual struggle of beauty versus beast would likely have become a less important theme. Much more so than their modern-era counterparts, early bodybuilders were inspired by the concept of perfection. It's for this reason that so many old photographs show them imitating Classical Greek sculpture. At the time of their creation, those objects were meant to demonstrate perfect human form. Early bodybuilders knew this, and they aspired to copy those statues. Yet a division was about to form. The idea of becoming living sculpture was neat, but not everyone could relate to it. There were other contexts in which to view muscular bodies. Before long, the exact purpose of bodybuilding became a matter of individual opinion. The highly successful Charles Atlas marketing campaign, for example, hocked bodybuilding as direct means by which to assert dominance over other males.

In some ways bodybuilding became a battle of absolute versus abstract. Size is an absolute. It's something that can be quantitatively measured and understood by all. Perfection is abstract. It's subjective and open to interpretation. The very name "bodybuilding" is partly to blame for the struggle between the two. Upon seeing for the first time a video of Frank Zane defeating Bertil Fox at the 1983 Mr. Olympia contest, one outraged fan entered into his web log "Zane should never have beat him! This is body BUILDING!" In his eyes, and those of the group he represents, the Ancient Greeks got it all wrong: perfection is not determined by proportion. To them, he who can fit the most muscle on his frame is most worthy of the term.

Of all places, the historically troubled women's divisions of the IFBB and NPC can be credited with solving the dilemma inherent to the name "bodybuilding." This was accomplished in the late 1990s when an entirely new type of muscle contest was created. Sensing that women's bodybuilding had gone much too far, and that its current champions had taken on an appearance that was shocking and distasteful even to seasoned fans, the federations added a category known simply as *figure*.

Even though figure is a type of bodybuilding, that name was dropped altogether. In figure contests, entrants are marked down without mercy for displaying too much muscle. It was a huge success. The number of amateur female bodybuilders plummeted, figure ranks swelled, and figure competition became the biggest draw of many amateur shows.

Kevin Myles

Branch Warren. 2010 Mr. Olympia contest.

In 2011 the NPC experimented with a men's figure class. The organization didn't hope to deplete the men's open ranks like what had happened with the women's. It wanted instead to create a large new class of competitors, and to attract more people to bodybuilding shows. It was also the latest attempt to repair bodybuilding's image.

It was a tall order. Because of the colossal strides in muscular mass that had taken place since 1992, a portion of fans wondered if bodybuilding had gone too far. Another segment was sure it did. Top professionals possessed staggering amounts of muscle, but it seemed only a select group aspired to actually look like that.

At the 2004 Mr. Olympia contest, Ronnie Coleman won his seventh title at a bodyweight of 295 pounds. Although his physique was slightly less sharp than the year before, the fact that he was in good enough condition to win, at that weight, said enough. The previous generation, and all generations that came before it, would never have thought such a physique was possible. Considering the standards the IFBB had set, and what fans wanted to see, Coleman had to be picked as the winner. That did not however mean that IFBB higher-ups were happy with the current state of bodybuilding. Coleman and a large number of competitors who chased him in the rankings possessed the new-era, large-abdomen look that now seemed as if it was here to stay. While the most hardcore of bodybuilding fans didn't mind a large waistline, as long as it was accompanied by a glut of overall muscle, there existed among others a prevailing fear that "GH guts" had wrecked bodybuilding.

The IFBB knew that a lot of fans had been turned off, many had simply turned away, and that new fans were not a familiar breed. In his autobiography, Joe Weider characterized typical attendees of the Mr. Olympia contest as being "true aficionados, like those who go to the opera or ballet." The closest thing bodybuilding had come to anything like that was the 1976 fund-raising event for *Pumping Iron*, held at the Whitney Museum of American Art in New York. New-era professional contests were something quite different. Regardless, in the same book Weider declared "I wanted to push muscular development to the limits." Considering the current state of bodybuilding, his two statements seemed more incongruent than ever.

The IFBB looked for a solution. Following the 2004 Mr. Olympia contest it issued a memorandum describing amendments to judging standards. More specifically, it declared that distended stomachs would be penalized. Those who decried the preponderance of large waists were vindicated but skeptical. In an interview piece with Ronnie Coleman for Flex magazine, Peter McGough didn't dance around the topic. He reminded Coleman that his midsection was distended, and then asked how he would be affected by the new directive. Coleman replied: "just about everybody has an extended gut…people want to make a big thing of it (the directive), but it don't affect me."

IFBB professional competitor. c. 2006

Courtesy of Steve Harris

Kevin Myles

Darrem Charles. 2010 Mr. Olympia contest.

At the 2005 Mr. Olympia contest, Coleman was proved correct. There were a few men in the lineup with relatively small waists and classic proportions—Darrem Charles being chief among these—but none could compete with the extraordinary mass of those who finished at the top. Charles finished ninth. The bloated-stomach directive had been a nice gesture on the part of the IFBB, but since judges couldn't bring themselves to actually enforce it, nothing had changed. The freaky, shocking muscularity of Coleman and others like him simply could not be denied. This was the new look of professional bodybuilding, and it very much appeared here to stay. Ronnie Coleman was awarded an eighth Sandow statue, tying him with Lee Haney for most wins all-time.

* * * * *

Proportion and shape had always been factors in physique contest judging. Once the new millennium got underway, that did not change. IFBB professsional division judging panels were given the same task that had befallen their predecessors. They just had an entirely new set of physiques to judge. As a whole, those physiques were far bigger and more muscular, and with different proportions, than those of previous generation. This suited current competitors and their fans just fine. As far as they were concerned, the more muscle the better. Since bodybuilding no longer sought public approval, it wanted monsters.

This naturally chafed longtime fans, some of whom were now fed up. A vocal element lashed out at the current state of bodybuilding, those who supported it, and those who had collectively allowed it to materialize. In an article called "Bodybuilding is Dead" on the T-Nation website, author Chris Shugart gave his own take: "Today, people go to the Arnold Fitness Weekend and don't even attend the bodybuilding show, unless they want to laugh at the carnival freaks."

The public had always been divided in its attitudes toward bodybuilding. On one end of the spectrum were people who admired the hard work and dedication of bodybuilders. Those same people appreciated and even liked bodybuilding physiques. On the other were those who thought it was wasteful; that it was the ultimate expression of narcissism and self-absorption. When Craig Titus and Kelly Ryan[1] joined the list of bodybuilders convicted of murder following the death of their roommate Melissa James, the public was reminded that bodybuilding can also be destructive. While the public otherwise scarcely noticed the world of bodybuilding, it was nevertheless treated to every bit of bad news that came out of it. It wasn't fair that bodybuilding was being defined by the actions of a depraved and desperate few, but neither did anyone care. It made for juicy news stories.

The mainstream press had an affinity for running negative stories about bodybuilding. A slew of bad news in the 1990s kept it rolling. The Titus/Ryan story, with all its botched cover-up and flight attempts, made for yet another. Meanwhile, and quite unexpectedly, the trend toward massive physiques and shocking muscularity had also come swerving headlong into the mainstream media's path, courtesy of an unusual trick for adding inches to upper-arm measurements.

In 1986, something called "site enhancement oil" was invented. Otherwise known as Synthol, the compound is a sterile oil solution that's injected into the bellies of skeletal muscles in order to make them appear larger. While it's normal for about 30% of the oil to be metabolized, the remainder stays at the injection site. The body, recognizing it as a foreign substance, forms a capsule around it. The capsule forces surrounding tissue outward, causing the muscle to appear larger. Additional injections will make it appear larger still. The muscle tissue itself does not experience any increase in mass, as it has merely been stretched. It's a concept similar to that of other bodily implants.

Bodybuilders began using Synthol in the 1990s, mainly as a means to add size to visually weak bodyparts. Before long however it was used in an attempt to make large bodyparts appear even larger. Neither idea was without flaws. Synthol does not evenly increase the size of muscles. It makes them appear swollen and lumpy, often as if an injury had taken place. This apparently did not deter its users, whose numbers multiplied. Bodies soon appeared on IFBB professional stages with tell-tale bulges, inviting conjecture and accusations to competitions that already had no shortage of problems.

Anonymous users meanwhile began to experiment with Synthol, to test the limits of its capabilities. In time they realized that vast amounts of it could be injected into a single muscle. Because the ageless allure of big arms was stronger than ever, biceps and triceps were chief targets. After repeated injections, as much as ten full inches could be added to an upper-arm measurement, far outstripping what could be achieved through weight training. This fact was unknown to the world, and even to most of the bodybuilding community, until the dawn of the new millennium—when a single news story brought it to light.

In 2001, a New Jersey man named Greg Valentino was arrested on suspicion of distributing steroids. News cameras caught him being escorted out of his local police station. While that alone was an episode worthy of minor news coverage, Valentino's appearance made the event one of infamy. He wore a short-sleeve shirt, and he was handcuffed in front. From out of his sleeves jutted two arms that were positively gigantic. They were in fact more

[1]Because of a plea-bargaining arrangement, Ryan was found by a Nevada court to be an accomplice to murder. Titus was convicted of second-degree murder.

than gigantic; they were the biggest arms ever seen on a human. Yet something was amiss. Valentino's arms looked not like something carved by a Renaissance master. They more resembled a piece rendered by a sarcastic surrealist. He possessed neither the magnificent triceps of a Kevin Levrone nor the transcendent biceps of an Arnold Schwarzenegger. His individual components did not even so much resemble muscles. They were more like monstrous sacs of pus or immense tumors. To the tiny segment of viewers who knew about such things, they looked like they were filled with Synthol.

Cable TV networks got hold of the footage, and soon not just local New Jersey news-watchers but millions of people throughout the United States became horrified by images of Greg Valentino. While he quickly became the poster-child for humor-based anti-steroid campaigns, to the public he was simply an example of extreme steroid use. After all, the public had never heard of site-enhancement oil, and it was therefore certainly not aware that a small minority of bodybuilders had begun to fill their muscles with pockets of foreign matter. The public only knew two things: that yet another bodybuilder had gotten busted; and that due to the extreme measures he inflicted upon himself, that particular bodybuilder had a revolting appearance. It was not however a public-relations disaster for bodybuilding, which had already fallen too far to be broken by any new calamities. It was just another news item that promised to help keep bodybuilding, for the time being at least, pinned close to rock bottom.

Greg Valentino. 2001

MediaWeb Images

MediaWeb Images

Greg Valentino. c. 2001

Valentino denied ever using Synthol. Legions of bodybuilders didn't believe him. He was mocked, despised or both. The unofficial title "the most hated man in bodybuilding" was bestowed upon him. While Valentino did no physical harm to anyone other than himself, clearly he was perceived to be a bringer of damage. Without doubt he had touched a nerve. It may have been that some members of the subculture were fed up with the ongoing deterioration of bodybuilding's image. They considered Synthol to be a public-relations catastrophe, and they furthermore shuddered to think that the biggest name to come out of bodybuilding since Arnold Schwarzenegger could be Greg Valentino.

There were some who didn't care about bodybuilding's public image, but hated Valentino anyway. They imagined him to be someone who got big muscles not from the hard work of lifting weights, but from injecting large amounts of chemicals into them. Because of this, that group of bodybuilders found Valentino's very existence to be a personal affront. This revealed a few things about their own psychology.

The large majority of people who devote themselves to bodybuilding do so because of the end result. But bodybuilding also gives them satisfaction—and often a feeling of superiority—because of the work ethic and strong moral character they believe it represents. Building a championship-caliber physique requires a tremendous amount of hard work. Most bodybuilders are happy this is the case. They don't want it to be easy. If it were easy, they reason, a lot more people would do it. Individual bodybuilders would be less unique. This would not do. After all, part of bodybuilding's appeal has always been that it allowed those who were dedicated enough to belong to a group that cannot be accessed or imitated by the general public.

When bodybuilders became aware of people making their muscles large by injecting oil rather than lifting weights, many became perturbed and even incensed. It didn't matter that Valentino looked misshapen and disgusting (even Valentino admitted he looked disgusting), or that he could never hope to win or even place well in a bodybuilding contest. It didn't matter that Valentino actually did lift weights, or that he had for many years before his site-injection bombardment began. They didn't care. In image and purpose, he was screwing up bodybuilding.

Yet there may have been a touch of unwitting brilliance—if there can be such a thing—to Valentino's injection regimen. The point of bodybuilding is to create a muscular, aesthetically-pleasing physique. The fact that this happens to require hard work is ultimately peripheral to the true purpose of the activity. If other means were to become available to achieve bodybuilding's end result, regardless of anyone's opinion about those means, they would be fair game. On rare occasions, for example, an individual bodybuilder possesses a bodypart that's so well developed that he doesn't train it at all. Even though that part did not come about from hard work, the bodybuilder nevertheless possesses it, and is often complimented on it. At least with that one bodypart, the purpose of bodybuilding has been achieved without any effort whatsoever. It follows that bodybuilding's purpose is independent of the means used to fulfill it.

Few people feel this way however. For the large majority of people who do it, bodybuilding is about more than just building a muscular, aesthetically-pleasing physique. While Valentino's physique could not by any stretch of the imagination be described as aesthetic-pleasing, he did create his build for its visual impact. More specifically, he wanted to make himself into a "freak." Valentino admitted being deeply troubled by his short stature—he's five-foot-five—and that "small-man complex" was his primary motivation. Yet regardless of whatever impetus drove him to do it, his personal bodybuilding goals were fulfilled. Valentino turned himself into a freak, and he was hated for it.

Were he brought back to life in the first decade of the 21st century, former AAU weightlifting kingpin Bob Hoffman would no doubt have a few "told you so" moments. Bodybuilding, broken free from his control and left to its own devices, had produced abominations like Greg Valentino and small flock of wannabes who tried to imitate him. That alone may have been enough to vindicate Hoffman. He despised the idea of building a physique for no purpose other than its visual effect, and tried everything in his power to make sure bodybuilders did something other than stand in place and flex. Joe Weider disagreed, he and his IFBB rose to dominate bodybuilding, and Hoffman faded into obscurity. Few new-era bodybuilders know his name.

Nevertheless, Hoffman may be owed the satisfaction of a posthumous last laugh. By the beginning of the decade, bodybuilding shows had been largely replaced by strongman contests on cable TV sports networks. The World's Strongest Man contest—the same competition that destroyed Franco Columbu's knee in 1977—had slowly but surely gained fans and fame. By 2003 segments were regularly shown on TV. They were aired during the afternoon, rather than late at night, as had been the case with bodybuilding-related shows in the 1980s and '90s. Declining interest in bodybuilding had finally taken those shows from the witching hour to the grave.

Meanwhile, top World's Strongest Man competitors enjoyed modest fame. While strongmen rarely had the refined physical shape of bodybuilders, to the expanding base of World's Strongest Man fans this mattered little. Their muscles were put to work

World's Strongest Man competitor
Zydrunas Savickas. 2010

Getty Images

in exciting, fiercely-contested strength matches. It really wasn't that far from what Hoffman had envisioned, more than 70 years earlier, when he began organizing weightlifting competitions.

The IFBB had originally distanced itself from Hoffman and his AAU by, among other things, promising a bodybuilding-only format. With the exception of adding fitness contests in the '80s and bikini contests a generation later, that held true. Nevertheless, one of the big draws of major IFBB professional contests in the new era was the strongman contests and exhibitions that had been added to the bill. In one way it was a return to the late 1890s: onlookers were given a chance to marvel at muscle-display performances and spectacular feats of strength, all under one roof.

In all other ways it was nothing like the 1890s. The most obvious change was that both types of men looked vastly different from their predecessors. Concerning the then-to-now change in the appearance of bodybuilders, much has been said elsewhere. Suffice to say it was a quantum leap. Strongmen had meanwhile undergone a substantial though less-dramatic transformation. Both bodybuilding and strongman shows were now also full-fledged competitions, overseen by highly organized governing bodies. For strength shows, the change was definitely warranted and enthusiastically received. For bodybuilding, organized competition became the very backbone of its evolution.

*   *   *   *   *

On May 11, 1996, eight mountain climbers died in a single day while attempting to summit Mt. Everest. All eight belonged to two separate professionally-led expeditions: "Adventure Consultants," and, ominously, "Mountain Madness." In an attempt to take advantage of the small window of opportunity afforded each May by Everest's otherwise unpermitting weather systems, both groups planned the 11th to be the climactic day of their assault. Climbing Everest is an endeavor fraught with risk. Because of the deadly, blizzard-like conditions that let loose upon the mountain late every afternoon, even on the best of days, and because climbers can carry only limited stores of critical bottled oxygen, both groups were to observe a strict turn-around time: regardless of success or failure, all climbers had to begin their descent by no later than 2:00 pm. Rival expedition leaders Rob Hall and Scott Fischer had the duty of enforcing the turn-around rule.

As the day progressed, a number of problems surfaced. Among other things, a critical climbing rope that should have been fixed in place was not. After a long delay, the situation was resolved and the climb continued. Nevertheless, by 2:00pm, only a small handful of climbers had actually reached the top. This did not bode well for either Hall or Fischer, whose livelihood depended upon successfully getting clients—who had dished out $50,000 each to participate in the expedition—to the peak. Due to a variety of technical considerations, a missed attempt on a planned summit day would most likely mean the entire trip would be a failure.

Hall and Fischer also had each other to worry about. If one got his clients to the top while the other did not, the unsuccessful guide could very well have problems attracting future customers. He might soon find himself out of business. The presence of journalist John Krakauer, who was covering the ascent for *Outside* magazine, made success even more imperative. Although both guides had a sincere desire to see their individual clients succeed, each also had personal pride on the line. Yet perhaps above all else, their very nature as adventurers inclined Hall and Fischer toward competitiveness. It was for these reasons that when 2:00 pm arrived and few climbers had reached the summit, neither guide ordered his group to head back. The ascent would continue. It was hoped that all climbers would summit and begin their descent—soon.

Unfortunately it was not turning out that way. Although bad weather was seen approaching at 3:10 pm, by 4:00 pm there were still climbers on the peak. By 4:30, two and a half hours after the prearranged turn-around time, the last expedition members had begun to descend. Their intentions were good, but it was far too late to be high on the mountain. Time was quickly running out.

The majority of climbers soon found themselves in an exceptionally violent whiteout blizzard, far behind schedule and with no bottled oxygen left. Hours after nightfall, Hall, Fischer and an undetermined number of others had not made it back to camp. Separated, overcome by exhaustion and disoriented from the terrible storm, each collapsed in the snow and awaited death. Overnight temperatures of -70 degrees Fahrenheit (-57 Celsius) assured its arrival. A morning headcount revealed that a total of eight were dead. It was the worst disaster in Everest history—and it came just two months after the death of Andreas Munzer.

Although Munzer was from Austria, the ancestral homeland of Reinhold Messner, the world's all-time greatest mountaineer, he instead chose to pursue the pastime of fellow countryman Arnold Schwarzenegger—the all-time greatest bodybuilder. It was a fateful decision. Due to the timing of the tragedies, it's tempting to conclude that 1996 was simply a bad year for a few people with unusual and unrelated pastimes—and that comparing the two is more melodramatic than useful.

While on the surface the two activities bear little resemblance to each other, a closer look can suggest the opposite. Both ventures are accomplished through extreme physical exertion; both are individual activities that often attract fierce individualists; both attract risk-takers; both have extreme versions with the potential for huge risk; and critically, both have been infused with the element of competition.

The last factor made the May 11th Everest assault deadly. More than any single factor, it was the very concept of the commercial expedition, with its inevitable invitations of competition, that prompted Hall and Fischer to forsake good judgment at the most critical hour. It was likewise Andreas Munzer's desire to create the most muscular and defined build possible—and to showcase it, at its absolute peak, in competitions—that proved his undoing. If he had no competitions to enter, Munzer almost certainly would never have undertaken the extreme drug regimen that killed him. Nor would Mohammed Benaziza have dehydrated himself to death.

Especially in the case of Benaziza, it was the drugs bodybuilders were consuming in order to appear, on contest day, extremely lean, hard and "dry" that were causing the greatest mayhem. Due to the exceedingly high standards of modern bodybuilding's professional ranks, that same lean, hard and dry look is required to prevail or even do well.

Since the length of time such condition can be maintained is best expressed in hours, this became the purpose of the modern competitive bodybuilder: to achieve absolute top form and maintain it for one day. How a bodybuilder looked throughout the remainder of the year no longer mattered. Evidence of this is seen on scores of occasions each year, when top professionals guest-pose at amateur contests. Many are in deplorable condition, and while they're all rather large, some scarcely resemble bodybuilders.

This contrasts sharply with bodybuilding of the 1950s and before. During that era, it was the goal of competitive bodybuilders to be perpetually in top shape. Sometime around the beginning of the '60s, that began to change. It was the combination of competition and science that began pushing men from the days of Steve Reeves to those of Ronnie Coleman. Once the '60s were underway, suddenly bodybuilders were much larger and more defined than before. As the years went by, the bar was continually raised. By the end of bodybuilding's Golden Age, more radical strategies were sought, discovered and used. By the late 1980s, some were beginning to prove dangerous. By the 1990s, a few proved deadly.

Where there is competition, there is the will to win—and the will to win has historically impelled men to challenge anything that might limit personal triumph. When contests are staged by official and dignified-looking organizations, when they are held regularly, and when past winners become a roll call of bodybuilding's storied elite, the will to win is unbounded. Modern bodybuilders cannot become elite themselves without this will.

Nevertheless, statistics suggest that high-level competitive bodybuilding is far safer than elite mountaineering. Since the first time it was successfully summited in 1953, over 170 people have died trying to climb Everest alone—by freezing, falls or avalance. Nearby peak K2 claims one life for ever four climbers who reach the top. Another neighboring mountain, Annapurna, has a fatality rate of 41%. Bodybuilding on the other hand has had two famous fatalities directly related to competition. Out of the hundreds of competitors who might be considered "famous," there have also been a dozen or so notable early-age deaths that are thought to be the result of heavy long-term steroid use. (p. 203) Because the exact causes of these deaths are rarely conclusively known, it's impossible to determine bodybuilding's fatality rate. It might very well be under 5%.

Nevertheless, the fact remains that that the concept of the organized physique competition, brought to the world courtesy of none other than Eugen Sandow, has been as important to the evolution of bodybuilding as the emergence of appearance-enhancing drugs. It is after all the allure of titles and the perceived intoxication of victory that perpetually drives men to test the limits of muscularity. Long after retiring, Franco Columbu declared all of this to be very positive: "What makes the Mr. Olympia—the contest and the winner—so great is how the event forces physique standards to improve year by year." Though this statement was no doubt music to Joe Weider's ears, it doesn't take into account a significant problem with professional bodybuilding and that contest in particular: since the early 1990s there has been increasing disagreement over what exactly constitutes improvement.

* * * * *

It was a significant problem caused by a simple question: what should an ideal physique look like? The question had always existed, but for several decades it was subordinate to a more philosophical issue: what is the purpose of bodybuilding? By the reckoning of Eugen Sandow, the purpose of bodybuilding was to transform oneself into living sculpture. To Bernarr Macfadden, who spoke for early-20th century Physical Culturalists, bodybuilding was merely a necessary component of a healthy lifestyle. Macfadden's greatest discovery Charles Atlas unintentionally changed all that when he advertised bodybuilding as a means to assert dominance. Bob Hoffman disagreed. He saw athletic prowess as the means by which dominance ought to be asserted, and thought bodybuilding should only be seen as a side-effect of weight training. Hoffman's nemesis Joe Weider advocated the opposite: that pure bodybuilding was inherently good. His view prevailed.

Although Weider advertised his brand of bodybuilding to be something of which the Physical Culturalists would have approved, his end product was something quite distinct and far more simple. Bodybuilding's one true purpose had always been to build and display a muscular physique. Weider real-

Courtesy of Robert White

Courtesy of Robert White

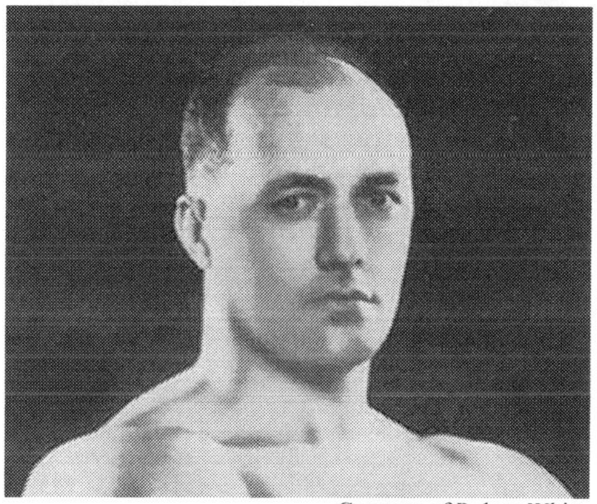

Courtesy of Robert White

Courtesy of Dan Hayes

The faces that shaped the evolution of bodybuilding:
right: Bernarr Macfadden; Charles Atlas;
Bob Hoffman; Joe Weider.
below: Eugen Sandow

Kevin Myles

Modern professional competitors,
2010 Mr. Olympia contest.
above: Branch Warren, Jay Cutler, and Phil Health.
below: Dexter Jackson.

Kevin Myles

ized this, exploited it, and rose to prominence because of it. By doing so he set bodybuilding upon the path that led it to its current state.

The Weider Empire took hold in the 1960s. The issue of bodybuilding's purpose largely vanished about that time, when it was replaced by the question of what constitutes an ideal physique. In the final decade of the 20th century, when ultra-massive competitors began winning bodybuilding's biggest titles, the problem became pertinent and serious. The ideal-physique debate reached its zenith in 2004, when the IFBB issued a directive aimed at abolishing distended abdomens. However, the matter quickly thereafter fell from favor. Things were not going to change, and everyone knew it.

Such was the state of affairs in professional bodybuilding when, in 2006, perennial runner-up Jay Cutler finally wrested the Olympia title from Ronnie Coleman. Cutler repeated the feat in '07 before losing to a lighter and more shapely Dexter

Jackson in '08. While Jackson's victory was imagined by some to mark the beginning of a return to the small-waist look of prior generations, additional victories by Cutler in the years that followed quashed any such ideas. The rise to prominence of men like Branch Warren suppressed them further still. In the eyes of bodybuilding's dominant governing body, and to fans throughout the world, there was now little doubt as to what constitutes an ideal physique.

In the late 19th century, some thought that Eugen Sandow possessed an ideal physique. His stage act was based on the idea of bringing, in the most literal sense possible, Classical sculpture to life. The audiences that gathered to see him found his displays to be captivating and enthralling. To those crowds, there was just something about seeing physical perfection, not hewn into stone, but present in the flesh. In the early 21st century, world-class bodybuilders looked nothing like sculptures from the Classical or Renaissance periods of art. They resembled art alright, though they were perhaps more like the caricatures of the heavy metal genre of illustration than anything Michelangelo or the Ancients would have conjured. Yet the same basic appeal remained. To bodybuilding fans, it wasn't enough to see illustrations depicting such men. Audiences clamored to see this new ideal, alive and in the flesh. The professionals who assembled before them were happy to oblige.

Like the ancient artists who gave bodybuilding its initial inspiration, top competitors of the current era sought to express themselves. Although both groups did so by presenting what each considered to be the ideal male form, their end-results were two very different things. It's true that each group used its own distinct medium and its own unique methods for shaping that form; but more importantly, each group sought to express wildly different sentiments. If bodybuilding did indeed take a torch that had been handed to it by artists of eons long since past, then it has to be realized that the glorification of balance and perfection had been replaced by a celebration of excess. And with that, after a meandering, tumultuous evolution, it could be said that *bodybuilding* more than lived up to its name.

Joe Weider with his champion, Jay Cutler. 2010 Mr. Olympia contest.

Kevin Myles

Bodybuilding: A Timeline

c. 4000 BCE Earliest known sporting competitions take place in China.

c. 520 BCE Greek wrestler Milo of Croton becomes the earliest known athlete to use resistance training.

480-490 BCE Greek City-States defeat the Persian Empire in the battles of Marathon and Salamis. Greek culture is preserved. The Classical tradition of artistic excellence is allowed to develop, as is the notion of physical perfection.

168 BCE Rome conquers Greece but absorbs its culture.

313 Roman Emperor Constantine converts to Christianity, precipitating the rapid expansion of that religion and signaling the death-knell of Classical paganism. Artistic masculine themes change from dynamic to static. The deft muscular warrior is eventually replaced by the solemn and reverent armored knight.

476 Rome falls. The Middle Ages begin. The Classical tradition of artistic mastery erodes. The enlightened thinking and artistic standards of the Classical Greeks lie dormant for more than 1000 years.

1475 Early Renaissance artist Antonio del Pollaiuolo completes the engraving *Battle of the Nudes*. Depiction of the muscular male form is revived.

1504 High Renaissance artist Michelangelo completes the colossal statue *David*. Depiction of the muscular male form exceeds Classical standards.

c. 1800 The Industrial Revolution begins. Daily life for a large part of the Western world changes.

c. 1820 The Physical Culture movement takes shape.

1860s Vaudeville strongman acts emerge.

1886 Famed Belgian strongman Louis Attila begins his tutelage of Eugen Sandow.

1893 Sandow executes a "muscle-display performance" at the Chicago World's Fair. Bodybuilding is born.

1899 Sandow invents the physique competition. A series of contests are organized in Great Britain.

1901 Sandow's "The Great Competition" attracts 15,000 spectators to London's Royal Albert Hall.

1905 Bernarr Macfadden's "Mammoth Physical Culture Exhibition" attracts 15,000 spectators to New York's Madison Square Garden. Macfadden is arrested on obscenity charges.

1922 Charles Atlas defeats a field of 750 competitors at Macfadden's "World's Most Perfectly Developed Man" contest. Atlas' Dynamic Tension course is made available, advertisements for which later become famous.

1930s "Muscle Beach" in Santa Monica becomes the center of US west coast bodybuilding. Jack LaLanne invents cable-pulley weight-training equipment. Harold Zinkin invents the multi-station weight-training machine.

1935 Croatian chemist Leopold Ruzicka completes the first synthesis of testosterone.

1939 The US Amateur Athletic Union (AAU) begins holding bodybuilding contests.

1940 The AAU stages the first Mr. America contest. Joe Weider publishes the first issue of *Your Physique* magazine.

1947 Weider and younger brother Ben create the International Federation of Bodybuilders (IFBB).

1948 The National Amateur Bodybuilding Association (NABBA) holds the first world-championship bodybuilding contest and names it Mr. Universe.

1951 Jack LaLanne begins a 35-year run as the host of a morning exercise TV program.

1954 Competitive weightlifters first use anabolic steroids. Before the end of the decade bodybuilders begin using them.

1958 Former Mr. America and Mr. Universe Steve Reeves plays the lead role in the Italian film *Hercules*. He achieves minor stardom. New attention is drawn toward bodybuilding. The oral steroid Dianabol first becomes available.

1959 IFBB Mr. Universe contest is first held.

1960s The size and muscularity of top bodybuilders increases dramatically.

1965 Gold's Gym opens in Venice, CA, and becomes the world's center of bodybuilding activity. IFBB Mr. Olympia contest is first held. Each year's winner is generally recognized to be the world's top bodybuilder.

1967 IFBB competitors are first allowed to pose to their own selections of recorded music. Sergio Oliva wins the first of three consecutive Mr. Olympia titles.

1970 Nautilus exercise machines are first sold. Arnold Schwarzenegger defeats Oliva to win the first of six consecutive Mr. Olympia titles. Chris Dickerson becomes the first black competitor to win the AAU Mr. America title.

1971 With the goal of securing a birth at the 1976 Olympics, the IFBB is restructured and new rules are enforced. Except for the Olympia, plans are made to eliminate all IFBB "mister" contest titles.

1972 In a controversial decision, Schwarzenegger defeats Oliva for a second and final time. Oliva quits the IFBB in protest. Judging practices are called into question.

1974 *Pumping Iron: The Art and Sport of Bodybuilding* is published, quickly becoming a New York Times bestseller.

1975 IFBB Mr. Universe and Mr. Olympia contests are documented by *Pumping Iron* authors Charles Gaines and George Butler for an upcoming film with the same name. Schwarzenegger retires from bodybuilding competition.

1976 The Whitney Museum in New York City hosts "Articulate Muscle: The Male Body in Art." Proceeds are used to fund the completion of *Pumping Iron.* IFBB efforts to get bodybuilding competition into the Montreal Olympic Games fail.

1977 *Pumping Iron* is released. Reigning Mr. Olympia Franco Columbu dislocates his lower leg competing in the inaugural World's Strongest Man contest. Frank Zane wins the first of three consecutive Mr. Olympia titles.

1978 Lou Ferrigno begins a five-year run playing the green monster in *The Incredible Hulk* television show. The first female bodybuilding contests are held.

1979 The fitness boom begins.

1980 The Weider publication *Muscle Builder* changes its name to *Muscle & Fitness.* Schwarzenegger suddenly comes out of retirement and in a highly controversial decision wins his seventh and final Mr. Olympia title. CBS refuses to televise the contest. 1979 Olympia heavyweight class winner Mike Mentzer, who placed fifth, quits bodybuilding competition permanently. Judging practices are called into question.

1981 Franco Columbu comes out of retirement and in an extremely controversial decision wins his second and final Mr. Olympia title. Zane, Boyer Coe and Dennis Tinerino boycott the event to protest the outcome of the 1980 contest.

1982 *Conan the Barbarian* is released. Schwarzenegger becomes the first bodybuilder to play a lead role in a big-budget, major-studio film.

1984 Schwarzenegger plays the title role in the highly successful film *The Terminator*. Lee Haney wins the first of eight consecutive Mr. Olympia titles. Charges are levied against Joe Weider by the Federal Trade Commission for making false advertising claims.

1985 Synthetic human growth hormone is first produced. Nautilus sells its 400,000th exercise machine. Weider is found liable for making false advertising claims, the third such judgment against him. Rich Gaspari sets new bodybuilding conditioning standards. (over)

1985 (continued) John Brown's posing routine at the Mr. Olympia contest expands the concept of physique presentation.

1986 Weider announces plans for drug-testing all IFBB competitors at an undisclosed date. Site-enhancement oil is invented. In the first edition of his book *Getting Stronger*, Bill Pearl admits to taking the anabolic steroid Nilevar in the early 1960s.

1988 After breaking the world record in the 100-meter dash, Ben Johnson is disqualified from the Olympics for the use of the anabolic steroid stanozolol. New light is cast on steroid use and its connection to bodybuilding. *Muscle & Fitness* distribution exceeds five million monthly readers.

1990 The IFBB drug-tests the Schwarzenegger Classic and Mr. Olympia contests. The World Bodybuilding Federation (WBF) is created.

1991 13 IFBB professionals defect to the WBF. The IFBB stops drug-testing professional events.

1992 The WBF disbands shortly after its second contest. Dorian Yates wins the first of six consecutive Mr. Olympia titles. Hours after winning the IFBB Dutch Grand Prix contest, Mohammed Benaziza dies from dehydration.

1993 The *Flex* magazine "Shocking" photo spread of Yates is published. A new standard for muscular mass is set.

1994 Yates suffers a complete tear of his left bicep but wins the Mr. Olympia "symmetry" judging round anyway. Judging practices are again called into question.

1996 Four days after his final contest, IFBB professional Andreas Munzer dies from undetermined causes. A biopsy reveals massive internal bleeding. His drug regimen is scrutinized. IFBB begins testing competitors for diuretics.

1998 Ronnie Coleman wins the first of eight consecutive Mr. Olympia titles.

1999 The AAU announces it will no longer hold bodybuilding contests.

2000s World's Strongest Man competitions largely replace bodybuilding shows on ESPN. The Arnold Schwarzenegger Classic Bodybuilding Championships changes its name to the Arnold Fitness Weekend, and later to the Arnold Sports Festival. The contest's original bodybuilding-only format is changed to include 45 separate sporting events.

2001 Greg Valentino's highly-publicized arrest brings the bodybuilding-steroid connection once more into public view. Awareness of site-enhancement oil is raised sharply.

2002 Weider Publications is sold to American Media, Inc. and Evercore Partners for $350 million.

2003 Five-foot-eleven Coleman wins his sixth Mr. Olympia title at a sharply-defined 287 pounds. In a special recall election, Arnold Schwarzenegger becomes governor of California.

2004 Coleman wins his seventh Olympia title at 295 pounds. The IFBB issues a directive aimed at eliminating distended abdomens. The directive is later widely believed to be ineffective.

Sources

Because this book is intended to be read as a popular account of bodybuilding rather than a scholarly work, I have largely forgone the use of footnotes. That being said, the following sources were used for research: the Weider brothers' co-autobiography *Brothers of Iron; Gorilla Suit: My Adventures in Bodybuilding* by Bob Paris; *Little Big Men: Bodybuilding Subculture and Gender Construction* by Alan M. Klein; *Mr. America: How Muscular Millionaire Bernarr Macfadden Transformed the Nation Through Sex, Salad, and the Ultimate Starvation Diet* by Mark Adams; *Muscle: Confessions of an Unlikely Bodybuilder* by Sam Fussell; *The Dan Lurie Story* by Dan Lurie with David Robson; *Getting Stronger* by Bill Pearl; *Muscle, Smoke and Mirrors* by Randy Roach; various bodybuilding magazines, including *Muscle & Fitness, Flex, Musclemag, Muscle Training Illustrated, Your Physique, Physical Culture, Muscular Development, Muscle Builder* and *Iron Man*; numerous internet sources such as bodybuilding.com and getbig.com; and of these, *The Definitive History of the WBF* from the Pro-Wrestling Chronicles website was particularly valuable.

Index

Author

Gordon LaVelle is an author of books and articles about bodybuilding and other fitness-related topics. His other books include *Training for Mass*; *Training for Mass, Second Edition*; and *How to Be Thin: An Instruction Manual for Getting Rid of Fat and Keeping it Off Forever*. He has a BA in Philosophy from the University of California at Santa Barbara.

His bodybuilding competition record is as follows: First runner-up finishes at the NPC California State Championships in 1995 and 1996; overall champion at the 1995 NPC Contra Costa; first place, heavyweight division at the 1995 NPC Orange County; and overall winner, 1987 AAU Mr. Western USA teenage division.

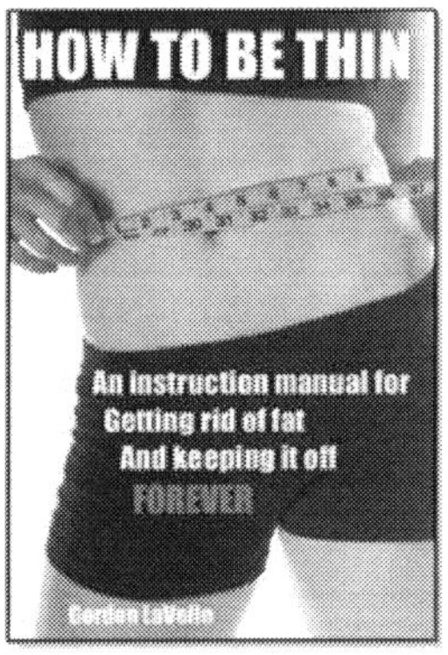

20689781R00128

Made in the USA
Lexington, KY
15 February 2013